About Island Press

Making Parks Work

Making Parks Work

Strategies for Preserving Tropical Nature

Edited by

JOHN TERBORGH

CAREL VAN SCHAIK

LISA DAVENPORT

MADHU RAO

ISLAND PRESS

Washington • Covelo • London

Copyright © 2002 Island Press

All rights reserved under International and Pan-American Copyright
Conventions. No part of this book may be reproduced in any form or by
any means without permission in writing from the publisher: Island Press,
1718 Connecticut Avenue, N.W., Suite 300, Washington, DC 20009.

ISLAND PRESS is a trademark of The Center for Resource Economics.

Library of Congress Cataloging-in-Publication Data
Making parks work : strategies for preserving tropical nature / edited
by John Terborgh . . . [et al.].
   p. cm.
Includes bibliographical references (p.).
  ISBN 1-55963-904-0 (cloth : alk. paper) — ISBN 1-55963-905-9 (paper :
alk. paper)
  1. National parks and reserves—Tropics—Management—Congresses.
2. Protected areas—Tropics—Management—Congresses. 3. Biological
diversity conservation—Tropics—Congresses. I. Terborgh, John, 1936–
  SB484.T73 M25 2002
  333.78'0913—dc21   2001006975

Printed on recycled, acid-free paper ♻

Manufactured in the United States of America

09 08 07 06 05 04 03 02 8 7 6 5 4 3 2 1

This book is dedicated to the memory of Rosa Marina Bolaños Riley. Conservation has lost a fighter, and we have lost a friend.

CONTENTS

Part III · Themes

Part IV · Conclusions

FIGURES

TABLES

PREFACE

In August 1999, thirty conservationists from field sites, universities, and conservation organizations throughout the world assembled at White Oak Plantation in northern Florida. The meeting, called Making Parks Work, was organized by the Center for Tropical Conservation at Duke University and the Wildlife Conservation Society, formerly known as the New York Zoological Society. The purpose was to share information from the front lines of conservation in the tropics—a region holding most of the world's biodiversity but where conservation is up against steep odds. Our mission was to focus on the "good news" and to examine the details of conservation success stories. Participants agreed that parks are essential for conservation and should therefore be made to work rather than abandoned. In lively plenary sessions the participants brainstormed on how experiences and information from all corners of the earth could be organized into a volume of principles for effective biodiversity protection. We now offer a brief guide to the book that emerged out of those deliberations.

Making Parks Work: Strategies for Preserving Tropical Nature is meant to be a reference guide for field workers, officers of funding agencies, government administrators, and nongovernmental organization (NGO) staffers who are involved with park management in the tropics.

The book is divided into four parts. Part I serves as a general introduction to the status of protected areas worldwide at the dawn of the twenty-first century. In Chapter 1, the editors address the fundamental issue of why the world needs parks—a self-evident issue to most readers of this book but one that must be raised to counter the contrary views that parks are either undesirable or ineffective as the principal strategy for conserving biodiversity. Leading from this discussion is a pragmatic and philosophical treatment of integrated conservation and development projects (ICDPs), the ascendant conservation paradigm of recent years. The authors argue that the philosophical underpinnings of ICDPs are irreconcilable with the active protection of parks that comprehensive conservation requires. Part I concludes by framing these important issues in a historical context. Experience shows that parks become cherished national treasures only after they have existed long enough to acquire popular constituencies. In the formative stages, nearly all parks are established against fierce local opposition.

Part II presents a series of case studies written by committed muddy-boots field researchers with long experience on the front lines of conservation in Africa, the New World, and Asia. Their rich personal accounts chronicle the ups and downs of carrying the banner of conservation into an extraordinary array of cultures and situations. Like so many leitmotifs in the largely anecdotal accounts of Part II, a series of cross-cutting themes collectively defines the mechanisms through which conservation is implemented, from the level of the isolated park guard to that of the large multinational donor organizations that provide much of the necessary financial support. Problems of underfunding, lack of enforcement, and political or social instability—to name but a few—appear and reappear with remarkable consistency in protected areas around the world.

Part III analyzes a wide range of problems that parks face at different hierarchical levels—from park-level practices to national policies on up to international considerations. We suggest policies and practices for overcoming these problems, and although there are few cures that can be applied universally, we offer a variety of suggestions. Most represent lessons from long experience, while some offer new ideas worthy of consideration. We hope that nearly all conservation practitioners, regardless of their own level of involvement and expertise, can consider at least some of these suggestions to good effect in their own situation.

Part IV returns to the broad philosophical questions of conservation and how protected areas can—and must—resist the mounting pressures of an overcrowded world. There are no easy answers, but there are promising new roads to be tried and proven. The choice ahead is clear: either parks are made to work or tropical nature is at risk. To be more effective in the future, we must profit from the past and be nimble in seizing new opportunities as they arise in a world that is changing faster than most of us realize.

Acknowledgments

Topping the list of those to whom we are indebted is the Howard T. Gilman Foundation, which hosted the August 1999 conference at the White Oak Plantation and covered the travel costs of the participants. Support from the Gilman Foundation also contributed enormously to the production of the book and is contributing to its dissemination by financing the distribution of free copies to conservationists and conservation organizations around the world. The Wildlife Conservation Society joined the Center for Tropical Conservation in organizing the conference and generously allowed time to Madhu Rao to participate in the editing of this volume. We are grateful to Marina Riley of the Center for Tropical Conservation for valuable assistance in organizing the conference and to Rebekah Hren for help in assembling the chapters into a coherent volume.

Peter Frykholm stepped in at a critical moment to assume the job of developmental editor, thereby keeping us from falling behind on the production schedule. We owe him deep gratitude for his unflappable spirit, single-minded focus, and astute editorial guidance.

All royalties generated by this book will go toward supporting the ParksWatch program of the Center for Tropical Conservation at Duke University (http://www.parkswatch.org). We are grateful to Chris Fagan for his dedication and perseverance in keeping the program growing and improving while we completed work on *Making Parks Work*.

John Terborgh and Lisa Davenport gratefully acknowledge the Foundation for Deep Ecology, which is supporting ParksWatch–Venezuela. Lisa Davenport wishes to thank Narendra Sharma and Walter Lusigi, who supported work at Tarangire National Park through a grant from the Africa Technical Department of the World Bank. Carel van Schaik wishes to thank the Wildlife Conservation Society for consistent funding of his fieldwork, which gave him the opportunity to observe first-hand many of the issues described in this book.

PART I

INTRODUCTION

1

Why the World Needs Parks

JOHN TERBORGH AND CAREL VAN SCHAIK

Experts estimate that extinctions are occurring at hundreds of times the rate recorded through normal times in fossil history, the so-called "background" extinction rate.[1] An accelerated extinction rate is but one symptom among many, reflecting what Aldo Leopold referred to as the "wounds" humans have inflicted on nature. The abnormally high extinction rates of the present will continue well on into the twenty-first century, but at some distant future date will inevitably return to the background rate. What will be the condition of the earth's biota when that date arrives? Will the humans of that time inhabit a world of weeds, or will they inhabit a healthy planet with intact ecosystems, clean air, clean water, and abundant natural resources? The question is not a facetious one, for if current trends continue for even another fifty years, we shall, like it or not, inhabit a world of weeds.

Those of us who strive to conserve the earth's biodiversity are thus engaged in a race against time. This is not to belittle the progress made to date. Formal protection has been accorded to roughly 5 percent of the earth's terrestrial realm.[2] Moreover, there is broad acceptance of the idea that humans have a moral obligation to share the earth with other forms of life. That moral obligation has been acknowledged by at least 80 percent of the governments on earth in the form of legally constituted protected areas.[3] (Many of the nations still lacking protected area systems are tiny island republics; very few major continental countries have not established parks.)

Certainly, these steps represent a good beginning, but the global conservation system now in place is far from attaining a good end. That is evident in the already high and still rising rate of extinction and is evident in many other ways as well. Five percent of the earth's terrestrial habitat is

3

not even close to being an adequate area in which to conserve the planet's biodiversity. Large numbers of future extinctions are foreordained if that number cannot be increased substantially. Even the 5 percent figure is partly an illusion, for much of the land now included in formally protected areas enshrines monumental scenery, in what is jocularly termed "the rocks and ice syndrome." Unfortunately, biodiversity tends to concentrate in fertile lowlands, lands that humans are reluctant to assign to other species, so protected areas in prime habitats tend to be small and few in number.

If rocks and ice occupy a disproportionate share of humanity's concession to nature (the world's largest park consists of the Greenland icecap), another large fraction of the total, no one knows precisely how large, is contained in so-called "paper parks." The term refers to parks that have not been implemented in any serious way and that enjoy only a virtual existence as lines drawn on official maps. Because they are not being actively protected, many paper parks are being degraded by illegal activities as documented in *Last Stand: Protected Areas and the Defense of Tropical Biodiversity*[4] and *Parks in Peril: People, Politics, and Protected Areas*[5] (see Figures 1-1a and 1-1b).

Efforts to conserve biodiversity thus face two major challenges. First, there needs to be more land dedicated to biodiversity—much more than is currently devoted to the purpose. And second, land that is dedicated to biodiversity conservation must be adequately protected from a whole host of erosive forces, many illegal but some legal. This book is directed primarily toward the second of these challenges, that of effectively implementing parks that already legally exist. *Continental Conservation: Scientific Foundations of Regional Reserve Networks*, recently published by Island Press, lays out the scientific principles that inform the design of comprehensive nature conservation systems.[6] In *Making Parks Work*, the emphasis is on strategies for managing (including financing) established protected areas, especially in the tropics where 75 percent or more of the earth's biodiversity resides.

Recent experience with protected areas in tropical countries has not been encouraging. A large majority of tropical parks have people living within them, sometimes legally as well as illegally.[7] Poaching of wildlife is a nearly universal problem. Blatantly illegal activities occur in many. The list is a familiar one and includes poaching, logging, agricultural encroachment, mining for gold, diamonds, and other precious materials, grazing, and extraction of natural products for the commercial market

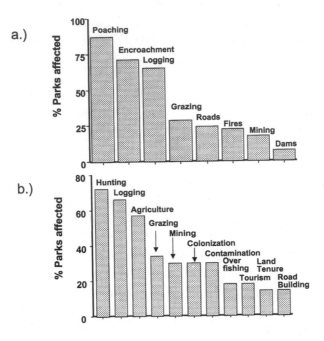

Figure 1-1. Results of surveys of significant degradation in tropical protected areas: (a) in a sample of 201 parks from sixteen tropical countries on three continents (van Schaik et al. 1997), and (b) in a sample of twenty-eight Latin American parks (Dugelby and Libby 1998).

(see Figures 1-1a and 1-1b).[8] In addition, many tropical protected areas have not been adequately demarcated, are inaccessible to tourists, are grossly underfinanced, and are staffed (if at all) by guards not empowered to carry arms or to make arrests. When parks are obliged to operate under so many handicaps, it is little wonder that institutional failure is more the norm than the exception.

Instead of abandoning the hundreds of parks that are currently foundering, ways of strengthening them must be found. In a growing number of countries, the parks are all that remain of the natural habitat, and are essentially the only places where any native large fauna survives. That can be said of Ghana and several other West African countries, but also of Cuba, the Dominican Republic, South Africa, Madagascar, India, Thailand, the Philippines, and several other Asian countries. A number of other countries—Mexico, Costa Rica, Kenya, Malaysia, and Nepal among

them—will not be far behind in arriving at this state. The survival of nature almost uniquely in parks is inevitable where there are no firm mechanisms in place to prevent unprotected wildlands from being converted to
human use.[9]

Sustainable Development

The exasperation felt by many field-based conservationists who have
been helpless witnesses to illegal activities in parks has led some to conclude that the whole concept of protecting nature in parks is viable only in
prosperous, industrialized countries. Elsewhere in the world, they assert,
parks simply don't work.[10] Efforts to conserve nature should therefore
take the form of encouraging sustainable development instead of delineating areas on the landscape and trying to curtail the exploitation of resources within them.[11]

The intellectual bandwagon generated by such thinking has gained so
much momentum, primarily among nonscientists, that some conservationists advocate the opening of parks to local populations for "sustainable use."[12] Permitting resource extraction to be conducted in parks flies in
the face of the very concepts of what a park is and the purpose it should
serve. No apology should be required for adhering to the accepted definition of a (national) park as a haven for nature where people, except for
visitors, staff, and concessionaires, are excluded. To advocate anything
else for developing countries, simply because they are poor (one hopes, a
temporary condition) is to advocate a double standard, something we
find deplorable.

Although the defeatist attitude that motivates many sustainable use advocates is understandable, there is great danger in yielding to it. Parks are
absolutely vital to the perpetuation of biodiversity in a human-dominated
world. And sustainable development, whatever the term may mean in
practice, cannot substitute for strictly protected areas.[13] Nature will survive best in the future as it has survived through millennia past in the absence of any artificial alteration or intervention. Inescapably, sustainable
use implies the intervention of humans on the landscape and the exploitation of natural resources.

Sustainable development other than ecotourism is incompatible with
nature conservation because, for one, humans and animals do not mix
well.[14] Humans tend to fear some animals, to eat others, and to regard still
others as nuisances. A recent study of humans and elephants in Africa, for
example, found that elephants persist until the human population of a re-

gion exceeds fifteen per square kilometer, which corresponds to a level of land transformation of approximately 40 to 50 percent.[15] Elephants are absent from more densely populated areas because they are killed or driven off by humans defending their crops. Large carnivores threaten livestock and are persecuted nearly universally. When persecution occurs around the boundaries of small- to medium-sized protected areas, their carnivore populations tend to disappear.[16] Thus, humans, even in low numbers, are incompatible with the persistence of megaherbivores and top carnivores, two groups of animals that are among the most crucial to maintaining normal ecosystem functioning. In the absence of large carnivores and herbivores, a "trophic cascade" ensues, resulting in a rush of extinctions, as the entire ecosystem collapses to a simpler, impoverished state.[17]

On a broader plain, our view is that "sustainable use" is more a utopian ideal than a reality, and that many positive assessments of sustainable use systems are either speculation or wishful thinking.[18] When so-called sustainable harvest systems have been examined critically, with appropriate measurements and statistical analysis, more often than not the results have shown that current harvest rates were in fact nonsustainable.[19] Other proposed benign uses of tropical forests, for example as repositories of future wonder drugs, remain in the realm of speculation.[20] As judged by the results to date of several large-scale bioprospecting efforts currently under way, these speculations appear greatly overtouted. It does a serious disservice to nature to overestimate the benefits to be realized through sustainable use, for it raises false expectations that can later turn to disillusionment.

By asserting that "sustainable development" other than ecotourism is not an acceptable management option, we are speaking only of strict nature preserves, such as national parks and other preserves with equivalent status. We fervently affirm that sustainable development outside parks is ultimately a necessity if the human economy is ever going to come to equilibrium with the limited supply of natural resources available on Earth. But let no one be seduced into thinking that efforts to promote sustainable development will result coincidentally in the preservation of nature, because there is no necessary link between the two.[21] Nature conservation must be pursued as a separate issue and according to scientifically validated principles.

Sustainable development will come about gradually over the course of many decades, perhaps centuries, as the human population stabilizes or (better) declines, and as new technologies and patterns of resource use replace the current unsustainable ones. Conserving nature cannot wait for this halcyon day; forests, coral reefs, and other vital habitats are disappearing now, so actions to prevent their complete loss must be taken straightaway. Given the urgency of the matter, preconditions cannot be countenanced.

Parks and Economic Development

Successful parks are not merely a concomitant of affluence. Some relatively poor countries have been able to maintain parks with little external help, and some relatively prosperous ones have conspicuously failed. Attitudes and the strength of indigenous institutions are major, perhaps crucial, components of success. Even in teeming India there are parks in which the condition of nature has improved measurably in recent decades (see chapter 14). On the other hand, Brazil, with the world's tenth-largest economy, has more "paper parks" than park guards in the Amazon.[22] Benefiting India's parks is a stable society in which children learn to respect the rights of others and the law. But a frontier mentality pervades Brazil and the "devil take the hindmost" attitude that goes with it (see also chapter 30).

One generalization that does cut across cultures is that parks are better supported by the public in countries with the affluence to experience them.[23] National parks in the United States, for example, cater to a public eager to enjoy scenery, wildlife, and recreational activities. U.S. parks are well staffed and provide facilities such as information centers, rest rooms, restaurants, and overnight accommodations as well as offering backcountry hiking and camping. Making parks user friendly requires only minimal compromises to their primary role as nature preserves. The fact that extinctions have occurred in many U.S. national parks is not so much a fault of management as it is a fault of design. Many are simply too small to retain area-demanding species, such as carnivores and other large mammals.[24]

The value of the national park system to U.S. citizens is suggested by the size of the annual budget that supports it—some $2.4 billion in 2001. When U.S. citizens are queried on their opinions of various domestic institutions, the National Park Service invariably comes out near the top, with more than 90 percent approval. Such high plaudits are not restricted to citizens, for millions of foreigners come to the United States every year for the primary purpose of visiting national parks.

Unfortunately, such high public appreciation of parks does not extend to much of the rest of the world. Outside of a few countries, parks are a relatively new phenomenon. The majority of the world's parkland was created in the decades of the 1960s, 1970s, and 1980s.[25] Many of these recently established parks are in developing countries burdened by poverty and massive external debts. In such countries there is a widespread view that parks largely benefit foreigners, so financially hard-pressed governments are understandably reluctant to allocate scarce resources to park protection. Even though the industrialized countries are increasingly reducing or canceling the debts of the poorest nations, the social needs of these countries continue to rise and, in some cases, appear almost insurmountable. It is thus unrealistic to imagine that parks will receive a larger share of the national budgets of countries in need. The conclusion seems inescapable that parks in the developing world will succeed only when there are substantial transfers of funds, practical experience, and commitment from the wealthy nations (see chapter 27).

Parks as Cultural Imperialism?

Some authors have argued that efforts to conserve biodiversity in developing nations through establishing parks represents a form of cultural imperialism, an attempt to force Western or Northern values on the unwitting citizens of poor countries at the cost of a diminished economic future.[26] The argument merits rebuttal, for it has a small but vocal following. There are two points to consider. First, one must ask whether it is "wrong" to export cultural values. Second, does the cost of creating protected areas to the individuals most affected exceed the benefit of having the protected areas once they exist?

As to the morality of exporting cultural values, the argument has no substance. The world is a free and open marketplace of cultural values. We in North America drink French wine, wear Italian shoes, and drive Japanese automobiles without giving a thought to being oppressed by other cultures. Indeed, we are eager for the trappings of cultural diversity, as are the citizens of developing countries, who aspire to learn Western languages, fly in jet aircraft, and surf the Net. There is nothing moral or immoral about this; it results from normal human desires and inquisitiveness.

Neither should North Americans have moral qualms about exporting a suite of more abstract cultural values to the citizens of developing countries. Literacy, science, medicine, democracy, equality, human rights, transparency, and public accountability are all virtues we hold dear. Why should we not export these values in the interest of making the world a better place? And should nature—the existence of beings other than ourselves—not hold a place among these values? The idea that it is somehow imperialistic or immoral to encourage the people of other cultures to value and conserve nature simply doesn't hold water.

The second point of the argument, namely that conserving nature entails costs, raises issues that are less black and white. Creating parks often does disrupt the lives of local people. Only in rare instances can a park be carved out of a completely uninhabited landscape. More commonly, there are people involved, either within the designated area or near enough to it that the park forecloses some opportunities. Should governments therefore be restrained on moral grounds from creating new parks?

Inconvenience to local people has seldom dissuaded governments from building roads and dams or installing military bases. The benefits to the commonweal are considered to outweigh the cost to the relatively small number of individuals whose lives are directly disrupted. Of course, in the best of worlds, the old English common law notion of "just and fair compensation" prevails, but poor people rarely have access to the legal means of ensuring that compensation is faithfully rendered.

A few widely publicized cases of institutional failure in the treatment of local people impacted by the creation of parks should not be taken as a reason for eliminating parks or forgoing new ones but, rather, as a reason for doing it better. Certainly, there are horror stories to be told about the forced relocation of people in conjunction with the construction of major dams, but few argue that these past mistakes constitute a compelling case against the construction of additional dams. The principles of just compensation, transparency, and public accountability, if freely applied, can go a long way toward preventing repetition of such mistakes.

After all, Americans do not rise up in wrath when the government condemns a home or even a whole neighborhood to make way for a new interstate highway, because there is a perception that we live in a society that practices fairness. If there were not that perception, reactions would be different. The answer is not to shy away from creating parks, but to strive for more fairness in the treatment of impacted populations.

On the benefit side of the equation is the value of the biodiversity conserved. This value is perpetual, which cannot be said of many alternatives, such as harvesting the area's game or timber resources. The benefits of conserving nature are both economic and intangible. The major economic benefits derive from tourism and ecosystem services—the gains to the region's population realized by having a clean and stable water supply, clean air, and natural geochemical cycling. Economists are learning how to calculate these benefits and are finding that they can be substantial, even when subjected to a discount rate.[27]

Who Benefits from Parks?

The most fundamental benefits to be derived from conserving nature are the intangible ones of recreation, psychic replenishment, and the intrinsic value of nature itself. These are the values that draw millions of visitors to U.S. parks every year. They are, we trust, permanent values of a high demeanor, notwithstanding their intangible quality. Yet these values are not so much intrinsic to a place as they are acquired tastes. It is the experience of visiting parks and seeing wildlife or spectacular scenery that creates constituencies. Therein lies a major irony—that popular support for a park can only develop after it exists, no matter how stunning the scenery or how abundant the wildlife (see chapter 3).

Lying behind nearly every major park in the United States is a history of opposition, stalling, minimalism, and political deal-making.[28] Park proposals were typically supported in Congress by Eastern and urban representatives whose constituencies lived far from the area in question and thus had only to gain from the new park. Locally, new parks were often viewed as limiting opportunities for future development and were vigorously opposed by coalitions of miners, loggers, real estate dealers, and others who failed to consider how the country as a whole might benefit. Naysayers who held key positions on congressional appropriations committees blocked several park bills on the grounds of cost (for instance, Everglades, Great Smoky Mountains, and Acadia), creating impasses that were resolved only when a philanthropist (John D. Rockefeller II) stepped up and donated the necessary funds to the nation.

Looking back at this history now, it evokes mixed emotions. One can feel pride and gratitude that the country was blessed with public-spirited philanthropists who came forward in the breach to give us some of our most cherished parks. But it is also painful to be reminded of the park proposals that died in Congress, victims of greed or small-minded expediency. Ensuing events have foreclosed these opportunities forever, and the American people are the losers.

So, let us learn from this history. Parks are now unquestionably popular in the United States, Canada, Australia, and other developed countries, where they enjoy enormous public support. Indeed, it is almost unimaginable that attitudes could take such a radical turn in the future that a majority of citizens of any developed country would favor the abolition of parks. In many developing countries, parks are something new, so we must recognize that attitudes toward them have not yet matured. When new parks are proposed, the governments of developing countries are every bit as susceptible to the kinds of negative political pressures that blocked, or attempted to block, park creation in the United States. Even today, proposals for new parks still confront many of the same negative attitudes in Congress.

It is important to realize this in thinking about parks in the developing world, where reluctance and outright opposition are bound to be stronger than they are in the United States. It is also important to realize that the attitudes of today will not be the attitudes of tomorrow. The world is changing at breathtaking speed, and no one can see the future clearly. Nevertheless, there is today an undeniable trend toward increasing park use worldwide, and in a number of middle-income countries, such as Thailand and Venezuela, the overwhelming majority of park visitors are nationals, not foreigners (see chapter 16). Parks become magnets for the citizenry when urban populations seek weekend recreational opportunities and relief from the crushing congestion of megacities. As other countries develop and become increasingly prosperous and urban, parks are going to enjoy ever-higher levels of public use and support, regardless of cultural background. That there will be growing pains at this early stage is inevitable and understandable. We conservationists should not despair at the challenges ahead but rather take heart in the confidence that nature will rank higher in the value systems of the future than it does today. The interim goal we must set ourselves is therefore that of making parks work.

Notes

1. R. M. May, J. H. Lawton, and N. E. Stork, "Assessing Extinction Rates," in *Extinction Rates*, ed. J. H. Lawton and R. M. May (Oxford: Oxford University Press, 1995), 1–24.

2. WCMC (World Conservation Monitoring Center), *Global Biodiversity: Status of the Earth's Living Resources* (London: Chapman and Hall, 1992).

3. WCMC, *Global Biodiversity*.

4. R. C. Kramer, C. van Schaik and J. Johnson, eds., *Last Stand: Protected Areas and the Defense of Tropical Biodiversity* (Oxford: Oxford University Press, 1997).

5. K. Brandon, K. H. Redford, and S. E. Anderson, eds., *Parks in Peril: People, Politics, and Protected Areas* (Washington, D.C.: Island Press, 1998).

6   M. E. Soulé and J. Terborgh, eds., *Continental Conservation: Scientific Foundations of Regional Reserve Networks* (Washington, D.C.: Island Press, 1999).

7. C. A. Peres and J. Terborgh, "Redesigning Amazonian Nature Reserves: An Analysis of the Defensibility Status of Existing Conservation Units," *Conservation Biology* 9 (1995): 34–36.

8. C. P. van Schaik, J. Terborgh, and B. Dugelby, "The Silent Crisis: The State of Rain Forest Nature Preserves," in R. Kramer et al., *Last Stand,* 64–89; B. Dugelby and M. Libby, "Analyzing the Social Context at Parks in Peril Sites," in K. Brandon et al., *Parks in Peril,* 63–75.

9. Van Schaik et al., "Silent Crisis"; J. Terborgh, *Requiem for Nature* (Washington, D.C.: Island Press, 1999).

10. K. B. Ghimire and M. P. Pimbert, eds., *Social Change and Conservation: Environmental Politics and Impacts of National Parks and Protected Areas* (London: Earthscan, 1997).

11. WCED (World Commission on Environment and Development), *Our Common Future* (Oxford: Oxford University Press, 1987); J. A. McNeeley, *Economics and Biological Diversity: Developing and Using Economic Incentives to Conserve Biological Resources* (Gland, Switzerland: IUCN [The World Conservation Union], 1988); IUCN/UNEP/WWF (The World Conservation Union/United Nations Environmental Programme/World Wildlife Fund), *Caring for the Earth: A Strategy for Sustainable Living* (Gland, Switzerland: IUCN/UNEP/WWF, 1991).

12. See, for example, J. F. Oates, *Myth and Reality in the Rain Forest: How Conservation Strategies Are Failing in West Africa* (Berkeley: University of California Press, 1999).

13. J. G. Robinson, "The Limits to Caring: Sustainable Living and the Loss of Biodiversity," *Conservation Biology* 7 (1993): 20–28.

14. K. H. Redford, "The Empty Forest," *Bioscience* 42 (1992): 412–422; (see also chapter 2).

15. R. E. Hoare and J. T. Du Toit, "Coexistence between People and Elephants in African Savannas," *Conservation Biology* 13 (1999): 633–639.

16. R. Woodroffe and J. Ginsberg, "Edge Effects and the Extinction of Populations inside Protected Areas," *Science* 280 (1998): 2126–2128.

17. J. Terborgh, J. A. Estes, P. Paquet, K. Ralls, D. Boyd-Heger, B. J. Miller, and R. F. Noss, "The Role of Top Carnivores in Regulating Terrestrial Ecosystems," in Soulé and Terborgh, *Continental Conservation,* 39–64.

18. C. M. Peters, A. H. Gentry, and R. O. Mendelsohn, "Valuation of an Amazonian Rainforest," *Nature* 339 (1989): 655–656; J. Terborgh, *Diversity and the Tropical Rain Forest* (New York: Freeman, 1992).

19. N. Salafsky, B. L. Dugelby, and J. W. Terborgh, "Can Extractive Reserves Save the Rain Forest? An Ecological and Socioeconomic Comparison of Nontimber

Forest Product Extraction Systems in Petén, Guatemala, and West Kalimantan, Indonesia," *Conservation Biology* 7 (1993): 39–52.

20. Myers, *The Primary Source*.

21. Robinson, "Limits to Caring"; Terborgh, *Requiem*.

22. Peres and Terborgh, *Nature Reserves*.

23. WCMC, *Global Biodiversity*.

24. W. D. Newmark, "Extinction of Mammal Populations in Western North American Parks," *Conservation Biology* 9 (30) (1995): 512–526.

25. WCMC, *Global Biodiversity*.

26. See, for example, J. Fairhead and M. Leach, "The Nature Lords: After Desolation, Conservation—and Eviction: The Future of the West African Forests and Their Peoples," *Times Literary Supplement*, 5 May 2000: 3–4.

27. G. C. Daily, ed., *Nature's Services* (Washington, D.C.: Island Press, 1997); G. C. Daily, T. Söderqvist, S. Aniyar, K. Arrow, P. Dasgupta, P. Ehrlich, C. Folke, A. Jansson, B-O. Jansson, N. Kautsky, S. Levin, J. Lubchenco, K-G. Mäler, D. Simpson, S. Starrett, D. Tilman, and B. Walker, "The Value of Nature and the Nature of Value," *Science* 289 (2000): 395–396.

28. S. L. Udall, *The Quiet Crisis and the Next Generation* (Salt Lake City: Peregrine Smith Books, 1988).

2

Integrated Conservation and Development Projects: Problems and Potential

CAREL VAN SCHAIK AND HERMAN D. RIJKSEN

This book builds on the premise that parks are the cornerstone of biodiversity conservation. In almost every country on Earth, unprotected land is rapidly being converted to human use. Already, in many countries, parks contain the only surviving remnants of natural habitat. Thus, without well-managed parks, there is no backstop against extinctions. Yet, as noted in the previous chapter, many of these parks are not adequately doing their job of protecting nature.

The international conservation community has responded to this problem (and to the opportunity to garner large sums of development funds) by creating *integrated conservation and development projects*, or ICDPs. Their stated objective is to reduce external threats to parks by promoting sustainable development in surrounding areas. Many ICDPs have failed, but it is important to identify both the weaknesses and the strengths of ICDPs in order to develop more effective ways of supporting park management from the outside. It is the aim of this chapter to do so. But to advance a proper understanding of the origins of the now predominant ICDP approach to managing tropical parks requires that we make a brief foray into history.

The History of ICDPs

The park movement started in the late nineteenth century in the industrialized nations and grew in importance during the twentieth century. It had a slower start in the tropics. Although parks were established piecemeal in the Old World tropics by the colonial powers, the park movement only gradually took hold after World War II, when many tropical countries gained independence and a handful of visionary conservationists from both North and South recognized the need for nature protection in developing countries.[1] At the time, most tropical forests comprised land-scapes with largely intact biological communities. Hence, these conservationists advocated the establishment of parks containing nature in its wild state, with no commercial exploitation other than tourism. A modest number of parks were established in the first few decades after World War II.[2]

Gradually, this approach ran into trouble. During the postwar decades, the developing world experienced population growth rates as high as 3–4 percent per year. Parks that had benefited from the passive protection afforded by remoteness when they were originally gazetted came under increasing pressure from the outside. By the late 1970s, it became clear in many countries that there was scant political will to defend them against these pressures—a reflection of the absence of a strong constituency for nature protection in the developing world itself. Not surprisingly, species preservation was low on the list of priorities of many poor countries because the benefits of preservation are long term and the immediate opportunity costs often appreciable.

Thus, the park concept itself came under attack.[3] First, critics pointed out that the wealth of the developed world was built in part on exploitation of erstwhile colonies and that it was unfair to deny tropical-forest countries the opportunity to exploit their own resources. At best, parks were a luxury maintained for the enjoyment of wealthy tourists and at worst, a Western conspiracy to keep the Third World from developing. A second line of criticism argued that excluding people from parks could not be justified as a condition for nature protection because people had lived in harmony with nature for centuries or millennia in these very same places. Excluding economically marginal people from access to traditional lands was unethical. The argument is erroneous (see boxed text at the end of the chapter) but was nonetheless very effective.

Partly in response to these criticisms, the professional conservation community changed course. New policies were announced in two publications of The World Conservation Union (IUCN), United Nations Environment Programme (UNEP), and World Wildlife Fund (WWF).[4] These documents considerably broadened the scope of conservation. The first, *World Conservation Strategy: Living Resource Conservation for Sustainable Development*, stressed the importance of conservation for sustainable economic development and advanced the concept of sustainable utilization of living resources as equivalent to conservation.[5] The second publication, *Caring for the Earth: A Strategy for Sustainable Living*, also promoted the concept of sustainable development as the guiding principle of conservation (although to this day there is no agreement on a workable definition). The new policies gave conservation a much broader political and societal basis and did lead to an acceleration of the establishment of parks in the 1980s and early 1990s.

However, these publications heralded a shift in the predominant conservation model. Conservation was no longer simply about protecting species from extinction but rather about keeping essential ecological processes going so that nature continued to provide economically vital services. Accordingly, the emphasis shifted from protection and exclusion to sustainable use and prevention of degradation and depletion, regardless of the legal status of the area. In short, the new conservation paradigm advocated a utilitarian, economic approach at the expense of scientific and aesthetic considerations. In this new climate, the earlier criticism of parks as elitist seemed to be embraced, and species protection became subordinate to socioeconomic development.

The new attitude is captured by the catchphrases "Use It or Lose It" and "Parks Are for People." Or, as put in a recent WWF leaflet, "Conservation goals can best be achieved by meeting human needs."[6] Hence, we should follow "strategies which help protect biological diversity by promoting sustainable use of fragile and threatened natural areas" and by "helping the poorest to conserve their natural capital."

Application of a utilitarian paradigm thus substituted for an earlier emphasis on enforcement as the preferred means for reducing pressures on parks. International assistance programs no longer supported a policy of excluding people from parks. Law enforcement became extremely unpopular because it represented the old colonial approach. Under the new concept, parks were to be integrated into the development process through sustainable use of their resources. Indeed, by some, parks were viewed as an instrument for achieving social equity because they could confer land rights on the poorest and most marginal forest-edge dwellers, thereby helping them to achieve sustainability. Who could reasonably disagree with such a win-win solution: erasing poverty while saving nature?

It may not be entirely coincidental that the new model allowed large conservation NGOs (nongovernmental organizations) to tap into funds for development assistance and to approach the government agencies responsible for development assistance (even though efforts of these agencies often produced unintended environmental problems).[7] For instance, the Netherlands allocates close to $100 million each year to conservation of tropical rainforests and their biodiversity, but virtually all the money goes toward rural development projects rather than biodiversity conservation.

Incidentally, in the process a double standard was created. ICDPs are run in developing countries, where public opinion does not favor conservation for species protection, but no one would seriously think of using the ICDP approach in the parks of the industrialized world, where rural poverty may also exist but the public broadly supports species protection. Does this suggest a permanent dichotomy, or is the ICDP approach a temporary one until economic development brings sufficient affluence?

Major Assumptions of Traditional ICDPs

The international conservation movement's embrace of sustainable development explains the birth and spectacular growth of ICDPs as well as many of their features. ICDPs have become the principal vehicle of foreign assistance with park management in tropical forest countries. A sufficient number of ICDPs have now been implemented that retrospective evaluations of their efficacy appear in the literature.[8] These reviews concur in characterizing ICDPs as rural development programs that confer only incidental benefits for nature conservation. Some have been successful in improving the lives of rural residents, but most have not been successful in reducing pressures on parks. Some have even been counterproductive.

ICDPs have failed to strengthen biodiversity conservation largely because they operate under mistaken assumptions, particularly the three listed below.

Mistaken assumption 1: Natural resources can be sustainably extracted from nature preserves by local residents (and hence no law enforcement is needed).[2] Most ICDPs have promoted dual objectives: the socioeconomic development of park-edge residents and conservation of biodiversity. The potential for conflict between these objectives is as serious as it is obvious, but it has been systematically underestimated. Project managers have frequently operated under two fallacies. One is to assume that biodiversity preservation is automatically achieved if ecological services are maintained. The other is to believe that park-edge residents would become conservationists, if only the ICDP could remove the obstacles for sustainable use.

Under the utilitarian paradigm, ICDPs should strive to maintain ecosystem functions and therefore ecological services that support socioeconomic development. Unfortunately, maintenance of ecological services and species conservation need not be tightly linked. Many ecological services can even be maintained by alien species. Hence, ICDP proponents would consider a particular project a conservation success if forest exploitation had not reached the point at which ecological services were visibly affected. On the other hand, if biodiversity criteria would be used to measure success, the same project may well have failed to reach its objective because most forest species do not respond well to exploitation, and even light forest use can affect biodiversity.

Light exploitation might not be a serious issue if humans were possessed of a natural conservation instinct that would guide our behavior and limit exploitation before irreversible damage is done. Unfortunately, our track record as a species is conspicuously poor: the Noble Savage never existed (see boxed text at the end of the chapter). Nonetheless, the myth dies hard. Traditionally, it was based on romantic notions of people living in harmony with nature, uncorrupted by Western notions of materialism. Today, the myth has resurfaced in a revised form, which argues that local communities, if given full control over their resources, will spontaneously practice sustainable use.[9] If local people were not using their natural resources in a sustainable way, proponents argue, it was because they were compelled to irrational behavior by poverty and lack of control over their resources. There is no question that poverty may lead to environmental degradation,[10] but the wealthy are also capable of environmental abuse, sometimes on very large scales. Control over resources is only one of several factors that create incentives to use resources sustainably.

Another fallacy promulgated by ICDP proponents is that local residents are interested in biodiversity preservation. A corollary of this assumption is that self-policing by the targeted communities makes law enforcement from the outside unnecessary. Failure of these presumptions to hold in practice has effectively destroyed any linkage at all between support for socioeconomic development and gains for biodiversity conservation. Moreover, acceptance of these fallacies has eroded support for law enforcement, even though it is demonstrably effective.[11] Worse, ICDPs often have adverse impacts. Stimulation of the local economy provides park-edge residents with more means to exploit park resources. When the ICDP attracts immigrants to the park's edge, this makes matters worse.[12] In some cases, the ICDP's support for illegal settlers encouraged others to invade as well.[13] These predictable human reactions to increased economic activity establish a perverse correlation between the socioeconomic success of the ICDP and stepped-up exploitation and land clearing.[14]

Some partners in the managing consortia of ICDPs have recognized these problems and voiced concerns. But the arguments of conservationists are less likely to be taken seriously by the funding agencies than the familiar and clearcut case for economic development. Moreover, the results of development are visible or tangible, whereas all that successful conservation can point to is the absence of destructive change. For these reasons, the incentive structure of ICDPs from the perspective of the contractors that carry them out works strongly against investment in conservation. As a result, despite the dual mandate inherent in the ICDP concept, biodiversity conservation is typically given the back seat to development. It is time that ICDPs return to their roots, or change their name.

Mistaken assumption 2: Small players do all the damage. ICDPs have generally concentrated on the threats to parks posed by local residents and ignored threats emanating from globalization, high-level corruption, and even the government itself. Locals may nibble at the edges of a park, poach timber and game, or gather nontimber forest products, but big players have the political backing and organizational resources to destroy nature on a large scale. Put simply: the big players take the real estate, whereas the locals take only the furniture.

Large-scale violations of protected areas are clearly illegal, but the individuals behind them are usually too powerful for local people, the ICDP, or the conservation agency to oppose. In the absence of any mechanism for combating high-level threats, the exclusion of local residents from parks becomes morally questionable. Governments operate through a hierarchical structure in which the several layers do not always act in harmony. A contract with the local government is easily overruled by a higher level of government, whereas national contracts are not always honored by local governments. Where corruption is rife, government guarantees at the start of the project may be worth little. Corruption can make law enforcement impossible, regardless of how well a project may be funded.[15]

Mistaken assumption 3: ICDPs are technical, fixed-term projects. Some ICDP problems arise from the structure of the projects themselves. Table 2-1 lists a variety of features that characterize many active or recent park pro-

Table 2-1.

Donor-imposed features of regular ICDP design and consequences for conservation.

Feature	Impact
Long technical preparation	Alerts resource pirates to step up exploitation
Short-term technical consultants	Neglect of policy component, and consequent lack of expertise
Ineligibility of group preparing plan to bid on next project phases	Loss of expertise of local social, political, and economic situation
Long delays between planning and implementation	Loss of flexibility, sometimes focus on wrong problems
Preparation of overly detailed and unrealistic workplans	Needless loss of resources, loss of flexibility in planning quid pro quo agreements
Unpredictable stagnations in funding	Loss of local credibility
Funding suspended during political instability	Lack of funds when pressures on park mounting
Lack of continuous monitoring and project adjustment	Inability to respond to changing threats
Short and finite project horizon, regardless of outcome	Usually ends before conservation can be achieved without external inputs
Large scale and inflexibility in size over time	Lack of proportionality between resources and needs (usually better to grow gradually)
Financing planned for entire project duration at inception	No flexibility to respond to new challenges
No provision for national-level activities	Inability to control policy decisions affecting park
Heavily centralized authority over spending	Slow and top-heavy administration; loss of flexibility in quid pro quo negotiations

jects and that have a negative impact on the effectiveness of conservation. Several of these features are the result of administrative procedures in the donor agencies that in themselves are understandable in that they prevent corruption or other forms of abuse but which have the perverse effect of undermining the projects' abilities to achieve their conservation objectives. This problem can be remedied by replacing the rigid emphasis on process with one that stresses outcomes while ensuring accountability through a system of audits.

Other design features of ICDPs reflect some of the main misunderstandings underlying traditional project design:

1. Project design reflects the assumption that the project is technical rather than political or managerial in nature. One important consequence of this assumption is that a definitive, detailed plan can be designed at the start for a finite period and yet will be valid for the duration. At present, many park projects are static solutions to a dynamic world; at best, they are the perfect solutions to yesterday's problems. In most cases, the projects are also too short to build a structure with secure funding that can take over at the end.

2. The project is assumed to be aid and thus to be desired and welcomed by a broad constituency. Instead, the recipients generally do not wait for it expectantly, and some of them are opposed to it. In effect, the rich countries wish to install a structure that is present legally but not implemented on the ground and is not (yet) wanted by many players (individuals and institutions) whose prerogatives may be curtailed. As a result, the project design allocates no resources to political-level actions that could prevent decisions that affect the park.

3. Projects are designed assuming that park management is about sustainable resource use rather than protection. Protection implies primary emphasis on prohibition whereas sustainable use implies stress on control and monitoring and prescriptions of use, or in other words prohibition beyond a certain exploitation level. Protection is technically very easy but requires a firm attitude of conviction and acceptance of the rule of law without exception, making it socially difficult. Projects generally do not allocate resources to those kinds of activities.

Regardless of the origin of these deficiencies, conservation effectiveness would be enhanced if these features could be modified. They should be the easiest to change, because they are largely under the control of the donor agencies themselves, which have their stated objectives.

Making Park Projects Work

We identified three major flaws in ICDPs: (1) the fallacy that local people are interested in sustainable use and biodiversity conservation; (2) the inherent lack of any means of counteracting high-level corruption and resource piracy; and (3) the inappropriateness of using an engineering model in designing conservation assistance projects. Many chapters in the book review ways of overcoming these as well as other obstacles to effective park management. Here we will only offer some suggestions on how to solve them. A more extensive discussion and synthesis will be provided in Part IV.

Sustainable Use Issues

A less naive approach to the sustainable use issue is desired. ICDPs have often encouraged sustainability of extensive agriculture and especially extractive uses, both directly and indirectly (e.g., buying the support of local communities by allowing some extractive activities). However, such uses have historically almost always been highly transient and obviously unsustainable (see boxed text at the end of this chapter, and also chapter 30). Appeals to "traditional" uses, when not based on a distortion of history, reflect a situation with far lower human densities and no commercial exploitation. Thus, traditional ICDPs will generally not provide stable solutions to problems facing protected areas and may even act to reverse existing trends toward more intensive and stable land use. We should not be surprised at this lack of interest in sustainable use: why hold park-edge residents to other standards than the rest of us?

There are situations in which attempts to reach local sustainability may be the only viable strategy, at least in the short run. First, some local communities do exercise restraint in the use of resources, but such communities are usually tightly knit socially and enjoy exclusive access to the resources. They are usually indigenous people in remote areas who are not integrated in the commercial economy, have no intention to do so, and wish to maintain their lifestyle of extraction and extensive agriculture. However, even here there is no guarantee that this is a stable situation (see chapter 22). Second, some 70 percent of tropical parks have people living within them. Where these are legal residents, either indigenous groups or prior residents that were grandfathered in when the park was established, the traditional approach of biosphere reserves with buffer zones may work. Katrina Brandon in chapter 31 provides a good overview of the kinds of measures most likely to lead to short-term sustainability in such cases.[16] However, we should recognize that these attempts at sustainable use are stopgap measures, not permanent solutions.

The lack of interest in sustainability is especially poignant where local communities are made up of recently arrived frontiersmen who have neither special affinity to nor special knowledge of the land they work, and who are primarily interested in maximizing economic benefits (see chapter 30). They view parks as an imposition of the government and as limiting options for the economic development of themselves and their children. Indeed, they may feel entitled to some form of compensation even if the park existed before they moved there. Where these attitudes prevail, law enforcement is deeply resented and consequently very difficult to implement. Weak law enforcement creates a situation where those who follow the rules are the losers.

Most park-edge residents in frontier zones feel entitled to compensation, whether legally justified or not. Consequently, ICDPs often run into the "ransom problem." The most serious exploiters tend to receive support first, leading to jealousy in neighboring communities that may then respond by threatening to increase exploitation. This is rational behavior on their part. Likewise, the original beneficiaries can come back after a period of time and ask for more support. New park support projects must successfully face this challenge and find ways to accommodate the desires of park-edge residents as well as find support for the park elsewhere.

Corruption

Conservation is impossible without law enforcement,[17] but that in turn requires fair and accountable governance. Even in ideal conditions, outside support for strengthening law enforcement is difficult and is partly beyond the reach of international assistance. It becomes impossible where the government agencies charged with law enforcement are not doing their job or are themselves involved in exploitation. Where corruption makes effective conservation management impossible, traditional approaches involving government-to-government or multilateral projects will not work. Where there is some freedom to challenge corruption, support for parks should be channeled through NGOs, which are more independent and in some cases can mount effective challenges to corruption.

Project Design

Designers of park projects face the challenge of finding ways to redesign projects so that they better reflect their goals and constraints. Park management is often less a technical and more a political task, and resources should be made available for awareness campaigns. Likewise, support requires a long time horizon with a gradual transition to self-supporting management, and a long-term commitment of broadly knowledgeable conservationists who continually monitor threats and adjust responses. Projects should be designed around outcomes rather than procedures, should be flexible enough to respond quickly to changes in the nature and location of threats, should train the next generation of park managers and staff, and should work toward financial sustainability of the park's management.

Conservation and Development

Many readers, conservationists or not, must by now have concluded that a focus on biodiversity implies that we abandon the rural poor. It is true that people living in or near parks, be they long-term residents or recent immigrants, are often poor and disadvantaged, neglected by corrupt or inept government, exploited by corporations. Frontier regions often act as sinks for marginalized and displaced populations. These people deserve development support, but not for behavior that destroys natural resources. The plight of the poor-near-parks needs to be addressed, but in novel ways that depart from those employed by many ICDPs so far. Parks are simply not the proper arena for resolving societal inequities.

The objective of parks is to preserve the biodiversity they contain. In the long run, it is hard to meet this objective when people are active in them. ICDPs have responded to this problem by striving to improve the economy at the park's edge. By and large, this has not reduced the pressures on biodiversity. This book therefore explores other solutions.

ON SUSTAINABLE USE AND THE NOBLE SAVAGE

Unsustainable use is one of the most perplexing problems in tropical conservation today. Uncontrolled exploitation has left many forests "empty" in many parts of the tropics, especially in tropical America and in West and central Africa, including numerous parks.[18] Commercial and subsistence hunting has left most accessible parks empty of wildlife large enough to be worth the price of a cartridge. The problem is not limited to bushmeat: illegal harvesting of species with commercial value has led to the local extinction of animals harvested for their fur, organs, or value as pets. Many valuable ornamental and medicinal plants have similarly been depleted.

Conservation through sustainable use has no evolutionary precedent. Our closest living relatives, the great apes, are extremely wasteful feeders, dropping fruits that are not yet ripe instead of leaving them on the tree to ripen. They can also be destructive in their feeding practices (as evidenced by the tattered appearance of fruit trees after their crop is exhausted) and in their nesting habits (we have seen orangutans destroy trees by making too many nests in them).

Our own species is not very different. Several detailed field studies on preindustrial hunters have demonstrated a lack of any conservation ethic.[19] Prey was harvested until it was locally extinct or too hard to find. When hunting yields dropped too far, the group moved on to a new locality. Archaeological evidence shows similar events during the late Pleistocene in the Mediterranean: seacoast dwellers first depleted slow-reproducing turtles and shellfish and subsequently had to turn to small mammals and birds.[20]

Massive prehistoric extinctions of scores of large birds and mammals (greater than 100 kilograms) followed in the wake of the spread of humans around the world. The so-called "overkill" was initially attributed to climate change, but abundant evidence now clearly indicts humans as the causal factor.[21] Increasingly detailed fossil evidence suggests that perhaps 20 percent of the world's bird species were exterminated by humans as they colonized the islands of the Pacific.[22]

Thus, like our great-ape cousins, humans do not possess any inherent predisposition to conserve resources for the future and so to guarantee sustainable use. The "Noble Savage" does not exist, except in the mind of romantic writers.

Conservation is strongly opposed by the two powerful phenomena that have left their imprint on the human psyche: the *collective action problem* (or, tragedy of the commons), and the *time preference problem* (or, the "discounting" problem). Garrett Hardin drew attention to the collective action problem under the banner of "Tragedy of the Commons."[23] In an open access system, an individual does better by exploiting resources now than by exercising restraint because restraint is penalized when others using the system do not practice it. The "discounting" problem shows that people prefer present consumption over future consumption. A resource is more valuable if consumed now rather than later: future consumption entails an opportunity cost, because either the actor or the resource may no longer be present.

Hence, to achieve conservation we must overcome powerful psychological and practical obstacles. Successful implementation of conservation requires two critical conditions to be met. First, there must be clear ownership so that particular individuals or groups have clear user rights over the resource. Second, enforcement must be strong enough to deter individuals from pressing their selfish advantages too far. We may not be intrinsically disposed toward conservation, but we are sufficiently flexible psychologically to adopt sustainable practices when this becomes the social norm. Most of us follow socially imposed restrictions on our behavior: we do not murder, steal, run red lights, and so forth, largely for fear of negative consequences if the transgressions are detected.

In many countries, forests are owned by the state and enforcement of forestry laws is weak, effectively making forestland an open-access resource. Local people respond to opportunity as rational economic actors and exploit the forest for profit (see chapter 20). Hence, the empty forest.

A conservation ethic and the practices to accompany it can arise spontaneously in small, highly cohesive social groups within which social constraints are effective. Scattered examples of such autochthonous sustainable use systems have been documented, and we should study them as models. A better understanding of how to motivate and structure such systems could lead to improved resource management. But the conservation biology literature is replete with studies showing that use is not sustainable even when the social conditions seem propitious. Hence, it defies the precautionary principle to bet too heavily on sustainable use when the price of failure can be the extinction of species. Moreover, as globalization takes hold in the developing world, sustainable use by small groups acting in their own self-interest is likely to go the way of the dodo.

These considerations leave only one rational conclusion: if the objective is to preserve tropical forest biodiversity, there must be areas in which no consumptive use of resources is permitted. Even though conservation has been achieved through sustainable use in some places some of the time, in parks, conservation needs to be practiced all the time.

Notes

1. J. F. Oates, *Myth and Reality in the Rain Forest: How Conservation Strategies Are Failing in West Africa* (Berkeley: University of California Press, 1999).

2. WCMC (World Conservation Monitoring Center), *Global Biodiversity: Status of the Earth's Living Resources* (London: Chapman & Hall, 1992).

3. See Oates, *Myth and Reality*.

4. IUCN, UNEP, and WWF (The World Conservation Union, United Nations Environment Programme, World Wildlife Fund), *World Conservation Strategy: Living Resource Conservation for Sustainable Development* (Gland, Switzerland: IUCN, UNEP, and WWF, 1980); IUCN, UNEP, and WWF, *Caring for the Earth: A Strategy for Sustainable Living* (Gland, Switzerland: IUCN, UNEP, and WWF, 1991).

5. H. D. Rijksen, "Conservation: Not by Skill Alone," *Environmentalist* 4 (1984): 52–60.

6. See H. D. Rijksen and E. Meijaard, *Our Vanishing Relative: The Status of Wild Orangutans at the Close of the Twentieth Century* (Wageningen: Tropenbos Publications, 1999), 335.

7. P. Alpert, "Integrated Conservation and Development Projects: Examples from Africa," *Bioscience* 46 (1996): 845–855.

8. M. Wells, K. Brandon, and L. Hannah, *People and Parks: Linking Protected Area Management with Local Communities* (Washington, D.C.: World Bank, World Wildlife Fund, and U.S. Agency for International Development, 1992); Alpert, "Integrated Conservation"; K. Brandon, "Policy and Practical Considerations in Land-use Strategies for Biodiversity Conservation," in *Last Stand: Protected Areas and the Defense of Tropical Biodiversity*, ed. Randall Kramer, Carel van Schaik, and Julie Johnson (New York: Oxford University Press, 1997), 90–114; Oates, *Myth and Reality*; John Terborgh, *Requiem for Nature* (Washington, D.C.: Island Press, 1999).

9. See, for example, S. Schwartzman, A. Moreira, and D. Nepstad, "Rethinking Tropical Forest Conservation: Peril in Parks," *Conservation Biology* 14 (2000): 1351–1357.

10. P. S. Dasgupta, "Population, Poverty, and the Local Environment," *Scientific American* 272, no. 2 (1995): 40–45.

11. A. G. Bruner, R. E. Gullison, R. E. Rice, and G. A. B. de Fonseca, "Effectiveness of Parks in Protecting Tropical Biodiversity," *Science* 291 (2001): 125–128.

12. Oates, *Myth and Reality*.

13. T. Soehartono and A. Mardiastuti, "Kutai National Park: Where to Go?" *Tropical Biodiversity* (in press).

14. R. Farris, "Deforestation and Land Use on the Evolving Frontier: An Empirical Assessment." Development Discussion Paper No. 678, Harvard Institute for International Development, 1999; C. Fagan, "Cultural and Economic Constraints to

Farming in a Core-Zone Community of the Maya Biosphere Reserve, Guatemala" (master's thesis, Duke University, 2000).

15. J. M. Y. Robertson and C. P. van Schaik, "Causal Factors Underlying the Dramatic Decline of the Sumatran Orangutan," *Oryx* 35 (2001): 26–38.

16. K. Brandon, "Perils to Parks: The Social Context of Threats," in *Parks in Peril: People, Politics, and Protected Areas*, ed. K. Brandon, K. H. Redford, and S. E. Sanderson, (Washington, D.C.: Island Press, 1998), 413–439.

17. Bruner et al., "Effectiveness of Parks."

18. K. H. Redford, "The Empty Forest," *BioScience* 42 (1992): 412–422; R. E. Bodmer, J. F. Eisenberg, and K. H. Redford, "Hunting and the Likelihood of Extinction of Amazonian Mammals," *Conservation Biology* 11 (1997): 460–466; Oates, *Myth and Reality*; J. G. Robinson, K. H. Redford, and E. L. Bennett, "Wildlife Harvest in Logged Tropical Forests," *Science* 284 (1999): 595–596; C. P. van Schaik, "Conservation and Development," in *Berjuang Mempertahankan Hutan (Kearifan Trandisional Masyarakat Aceh Melestarikan Ekosistem Leuser)*, ed. S. M. Ahmad (Medan, Indonesia: Leuser Development Programme, 2000), v–lxiii.

19. M. S. Alvard, "Evolutionary Ecology and Resource Conservation," *Evolutionary Anthropology* 7 (1998): 62–74.

20. M. Stiner, N. Munro, T. Surovell, E. Tchernov, and O. Bar-Yosef, "Paleolithic Population Growth Pulses Evidenced by Small Animal Exploitation," *Science* 283 (1999): 190–194.

21. E. O. Wilson, *The Diversity of Life* (Cambridge, Mass: Harvard University Press, Belknap Press, 1992); J. H. Brown and M. V. Lomolino, *Biogeography*, 2nd ed. (Sunderland, Mass: Sinauer Associates, 1998).

22. Wilson, *Diversity of Life;* J. H. Lawton and R. M. May, *Extinction Rates* (Oxford, Oxford University Press, 1995).

23. G. Hardin, "The Tragedy of the Commons," *Science* 162 (1968): 1243–1248.

3

The History of Protection: Paradoxes of the Past and Challenges for the Future

LISA DAVENPORT AND MADHU RAO

This book describes numerous recent efforts to protect the world's biological heritage within tropical parks, and analyzes successful patterns and lessons learned. And yet, to best plan for the future of biodiversity protection it is important to understand the changing nature of park creation and management through time. An historical perspective offers insight into both the lasting and the ephemeral effects of personalities, political events, and societal values.

In order to inform present park-creation efforts in tropical developing countries, this chapter looks to selected case histories of park creation in several industrialized countries. We do this *not* to set up park systems of the developed world as ideal models to be followed (in fact, due to new ecological findings and the evolving perceptions of why, where, and how to establish and manage parks, many systems of parks in developed countries now fail to encompass all desirable ecological functions), but rather to learn from their mistakes and successes. We need to understand the hurdles that must be overcome and recognize the biological and societal rewards that can follow.

Two central paradoxical themes that surface in the history of park creation in the industrialized world are that (1) societies tend to establish park systems only after experiencing painful losses of species or dramatic landscapes, and (2) popular support, especially by local residents of a proposed protected area, greatly lags behind the creation of protected areas. Park creation is often the conservation tool most sought after when other actions have been tried and failed, and when the threat of extinction becomes uncomfortably real. Although ultimately parks are almost universally popular, at the outset entrenched local interests repeatedly turn park creation events into sour political battles. Regardless of these obstacles, the optimal time to establish parks is certainly in advance of crisis situations. One hope underlying this chapter is that by studying park history, we can develop the will to bypass the stages leading to species extinctions and instead proactively plan for the future.

Geographical Focus

We begin with a review of what is known from world history about the earliest efforts to establish protected areas. We then focus on the recent histories of several developed nations, specifically, the United States, Australia, and South Africa. We chose these countries because they are industrialized nations that today maintain strong institutions of parks and protected areas. Clearly, though, the evolution of ideas on park creation in these countries was not entirely independent of one another, since they share common languages and a common Western European cultural heritage. To varying degrees, each was influenced by the ideas and actions of the others. Even so, sufficient cultural differences exist to make each case uniquely instructive.

The Earliest Protected Areas

Protected areas have deep historical roots: they have existed in myriad forms in diverse ancient cultures, dating back to early pre-agrarian societies in Asia and the Near East.[1] The first recorded measures for wildlife conservation were promulgated in India in the fourth century B.C., when all forms of use and extractive activity were totally prohibited in the sacred forest groves. In the Near East, early evidence for the protection of game goes back to 700 B.C. when Assyrian noblemen sharpened their hunting, riding, and combat techniques in designated hunting reserves. These were similar to the great royal hunting enclosures of the Persian Empire, which flourished throughout Asia Minor between 550 and 350 B.C. Laws to protect the wetlands of the Huang-Huai-Hai plain in northeastern China were established during the sixth century A.D.[2] The state of Venice established deer and wild boar reserves prior to the city's founding in 726,[3] and in Britain, the Forest Laws of King Canute were established early in the eleventh century.[4] In Russia, deep historical roots of protected areas were associated with the creation of sacred forests and groves, communal "forbidden places" and "holy places" in which hunting, fishing, tree cutting, and even human presence were prohibited.[5] Humankind has thus widely and repeatedly been challenged to find better ways of living with nature, with protected area institutions habitually being created in response.

Variation in the legal institutions for land ownership of course created vital distinctions between societies throughout history, with direct consequences for conservation systems. The Greeks were the first to democratize landscape aesthetics: their larger towns and cities, including Athens, provided citizens with a plaza for public assembly, relaxation, and refreshment. Thus began the early equivalents of the modern city park. Although urbanization throughout the Roman Empire led to similar experiments, medieval Europe, like Asia Minor, reverted to the maintenance of open spaces exclusively for the ruling classes. Hunting once more became a primary use of these lands; in fact, the word "park" stems from this usage. Originally, *parc* in Old French and Middle English designated "an enclosed piece of ground stocked with beasts of the chase, held by prescription or by the king's grant."[6] Trespassers were punished severely, especially poachers, who were often put to death.

Although reserves of various sorts have had a long history, the concept of a national park presupposes the existence of nations in the modern sense of sovereign nation-states. With the possible exception of the Greeks and Romans, therefore, the park idea as now defined is modern in origin; only recently has it come to mean both protection and public access.[7]

The rise of a "national parks movement" is believed by some to have occurred in response to the industrial revolution that set humankind upon a course that altered natural landscapes at a prodigious rate. The rapid and unprecedented transformation of the land provoked a call for the preservation of what was being so rapidly lost. Not surprisingly, the first such calls emanated from nations undergoing rapid industrialization where the effects were visible in less than one generation. The contemporary term "national park" was described as early as 1832 by the U.S. artist-explorer George Catlin. Arguing for the establishment of Yellowstone National Park in the United States, Catlin called for "A Nation's Park, containing man and beast, in all the wild and freshness of their nature's beauty!"[8]

The following section will concentrate on three modern attempts to set aside protected areas for scenic and wildlife preservation. Here, we can better appreciate the complexity of the settings, influences, and motivations that have led modern nations to develop strong park institutions.

Modern Protected Areas: Three Case Studies

In discussing the comparative histories of park creation in multiple countries, it becomes clear that similar motives drove the creation of protected area systems, although not all resulted in systems exactly akin to the national park system of the United States. For example, Australia's "national parks" are actually under the control of individual states, and many of Australia's environmental battles today center on the protection of "wilderness areas," often but not necessarily within true "parks." Therefore, the ideal way to discuss the issue is perhaps to compare systems of "protected areas." However, we choose to use the less-cumbersome "park" in this discussion, with the understanding that we are discussing the establishment of permanent institutions that serve to preserve biodiversity from consumptive use.

It is also important to note that in this short chapter we can hardly hope to treat even one country's park history thoroughly. Our strategy, therefore, is to emphasize particular events or periods most telling of the nature of each country's experience with park creation and wilderness issues. Similarities and differences between nations will be highlighted throughout in order to draw meaningful recommendations for other evolving park systems.

United States: The Duality of the National Park Mandate

It is appropriate to begin by examining park creation in the United States, where turn-of-the-century wilderness dialogues helped spark park creation in many other countries. Yet the U.S. experience itself was an ambiguous one. The National Park Service Act of August 1916, or the "Organic Act," gave the newly created National Park Service the dual mandate of managing national parks for public enjoyment while also leaving park resources unimpaired. This sometimes-contradictory mandate has generated much debate about how strong of a role preservation and conservation should each play in management of the nation's natural resources, and in particular of its national parks. By reviewing the history of naturalist John Muir's prolonged struggles, gains, and losses surrounding Yosemite, we can see how the dual mandate reflects the early clashes between local utilitarian interests and an emerging national identity that incorporated wilderness preservation values.

Muir first traveled to the Sierra Nevada and began exploring the Yosemite Valley in 1868. It had only recently (1864) been declared a public scenic reserve under California's control, created mainly to protect the watershed for downstream farming activities. Fifty-six years later, after unprecedented success in popularizing wilderness and national parks, Muir died one year after his greatest defeat—the drowning of the Hetch Hetchy Valley, which lay within the bounds of Yosemite National Park.

At about the same time as Muir's early Yosemite travels, the other great park achievement of the era—the discovery and struggle to create Yellowstone National Park—was being played out. Established in 1872, Yellowstone was the nation's first national park. As one scholar has noted, the creation of these parks filled a cultural void and came at a time when America was suffering from an inferiority complex with respect to noteworthy European landmarks, writing and art.[9] In addition, America had suffered humiliation at the hands of Europeans who resoundingly criticized the crass commercialization of Niagara Falls. The establishment of Yosemite and Yellowstone compensated for the harm done to U.S. pride and international standing resulting from the Niagara Falls debacle. Movements in art and writing flourished in concert with the park creation effort and directly fed into developing Romantic notions, enlivening debates between America and Europe about naturalism versus civilization.

In contrast to Yellowstone, whose remoteness made significant resource struggles less immediate, Yosemite soon faced considerable local opposition. Clashes ensued over redrawing the park's boundaries for commercial interests, and weak protection invited abuse by poachers. Early in his travels to the Sierra Nevada, Muir determined that the wilderness he loved was threatened by commercial overuse and local special interests—in the Sierras this was primarily from sheep herders and the timber industry. The solution, he decided, was national status and management for parks and forests: "All sorts of local laws and regulations have been tried and found wanting, and the costly lessons of our own experience, as well as that of every civilized nation, show conclusively that the fate of the remnant of our forests is in the hands of the federal government."[10]

His means of achieving national status for Yosemite were writing, talking, and reluctantly leaving his beloved mountains to become a political figure. For decades, Muir was Yosemite's most vocal and constant supporter, and he was greatly ahead of his time in recognizing the ecological importance of protecting lands surrounding the small reserve, which initially only included the most scenic mountain areas surrounding the valley. He inspired bills in the 1880s that saved the sequoia groves as federal parks, and he pushed for enlarging the Yosemite reserve to include a surrounding "forest reservation" of more than a million acres.

As founder of the Sierra Club, he organized the political will to defeat a coalition of lumbermen and stockmen who managed to get a bill through the House of Representatives that would have cut the park area in half, although smaller withdrawals were made for lumber, grazing, and mining interests. In addition, around 1895 he began a decade-long fight to improve the management of Yosemite Valley by including it in the surrounding national park. The state of California had allowed great damage to occur within Yosemite Valley itself, where concessionaires had been permitted to plow meadows, overgraze the forest floor, fell trees, and even dam Mirror Lake for irrigation.[11] Muir and the Sierra Club made allies out of President Theodore Roosevelt and railroad tycoon E. H. Harriman, among others, and in 1905 finally succeeded in returning Yosemite Valley to federal control and included as part of Yosemite National Park.

However, the victories were short-lived, with local interests quickly acting counter to the park initiatives. From 1901 on, San Francisco city fathers had openly coveted the Hetch Hetchy Valley as a site for a dam to provide water and power to the city. In a time when "ecology" did not exist as a science, and park boundaries were violable and routinely altered by local congressmen for local interests, utilitarianism played a dominant role in determining park boundaries. In Muir's original plan, the "Tuolumne Yosemite," as he called the Hetch Hetchy, would have been left wild and relatively untouched, with tourism concentrating in the Yosemite Valley itself. He was indignant and uncompromising against the very concept of the dam, famously saying: "Dam Hetch Hetchy! As well dam for watertanks the people's cathedrals and churches, for no holier temple has ever been consecrated by the heart of man."[12]

However, his idea of zoning for true wilderness was too advanced for the times, and the minimal tourist use of the Hetch Hetchy left it vulnerable in an era that essentially either demanded that parks be made from wholly "worthless lands" or that they offer a utilitarian value—in other words, tourism—in compensation for the loss of other utilitarian uses.[13] Even the initial creation of Yosemite had largely been noncontroversial because agriculturalists downstream had recognized the importance of protecting forested watersheds. However, no similar coalition of local interests could muster sufficient support for Hetch Hetchy, and in 1913, Congress authorized the Hetch Hetchy Dam.

Muir's failure in the Hetch Hetchy is partly indicative of his times, but it also reflects a grave problem that continues for parks today. Unfortunately, although park creation may offer the nation an undisputed treasure, parks frequently face powerful local opposition. For twenty years after Yellowstone's establishment, Montana's own congressional representatives offered bills to Congress that would have removed the protection granted Yellowstone. Similarly, Olympic National Park in Washington State (which harbors the country's only temperate rainforest), faced fierce opposition from local timber operators at its inception, resulting in one of the worst possible boundary delineations from the standpoint of biodiversity, and which exists to this day. In addition, in 1947, under the banner of supporting the war effort, a bill was introduced to Congress that would have reduced Olympic National Park by 56,000 acres to allow timber extraction. When this effort failed, the 1950s saw the implementation of regulations allowing windblown timber to be salvaged from within the park. Eventually, millions of board feet were extracted, including the cutting of mature trees that were perfectly healthy.[14] Even as recently as 1981, proposed national park additions in Alaska have faced opposition from Alaskan politicians, who, like their predecessors in California and Washington, side with industry against the protection of park resources. Yet, ultimately, all these parks have become hallowed grounds to the people of the United States, a fact which was actually predicted by Muir in 1914 shortly before his death, when he wrote, "They will see what I meant in time."[15]

In his final years, Muir came grudgingly to accept the political necessity of developing parks for tourism to bolster popular support. Tourism development was to become the primary focus of park management for nearly a half-century under the first park director, Steven Mather. Yet Mather also followed up on Muir's ideas regarding strict protection of park resources from poachers, and he enacted strong systems of enforcement, at first utilizing U.S. army troops, stationing them in several parks, but later developing the Park Service's own highly professional corps of park rangers.[16] Thus, the Organic Act's dual mandate was surely influenced by Muir's own complex desires, successes, and failures. Finding that proper balance of preservation and development called for in the Organic Act continues to be one of the major challenges for park managers today.[17]

Beyond the U.S. parks, Muir's persuasive prose in defense of wilderness drew many followers, even after his death. His writings nurtured dialogue about wilderness preservation, which not only aided the establishment of the National Park Service, but which also had great influence overseas. Since the creation of the National Park Service, 125 other nations have set aside parks and nature reserves.[18] The history of Australia is perhaps most closely connected in this regard, where much of the environmental consciousness of the country arose through issues centered on wilderness, with parks likewise becoming a major conservation tool for protecting what was viewed as national or even world-class natural heritage.

Australia: Wilderness and Heritage Battles

Many striking similarities can be drawn between the U.S. and Australian experiences with conservation and park creation—most notably, the dependence of the national psyches of both countries on their identification with the natural environment—but their approaches to establishing parks have been quite different. Although America's national park movement gained momentum early on, Australia lacked an organized nationwide parks movement until much later in its history. Instead, its park creation movement expanded from small local efforts to statewide efforts. It wasn't until the 1960s and 1970s that a conservation movement emerged which insisted on natural heritage protection through the designation of parks at the national, and even international, level.

Like the United States, Australia sought to distinguish itself from colonial Britain and Europe in the period coinciding with the Romantic movement in the early nineteenth century, and it did so by embracing its outback wilderness and rural lifestyles. In Australia, Romantic art and writing effectively created a national myth of paradise in the Australian bush. The Heidelberg School of painting combined French impressionism with uniquely Australian landscapes, and poets Henry Kendall and Adam Lindsay Gordon paralleled Muir in extolling both the beauty and the redemptive qualities of nature. Perhaps the most famous Australian cultural icon, A. B. "Banjo" Paterson (author of "Man from Snowy River" and "Waltzing Mathilda"), found a large following in his poems glorifying the rough life in the bush.

Park creation began during this period, just as it had in America. Emerging out of concern for widespread forest destruction, the first reserves were championed by the New South Wales Zoological Society. The first to be created was in the Fish River Caves district of the Blue Mountains in October 1866. Next came Jamieson Creek in 1870 and the Bungonia Lookdown in 1872.[19] Unlike Yellowstone, the Australian reserves of this period were small scenic viewpoints and were mostly located close to urban Sydney. The first genuine national park, National Park (later changed to Royal National Park), was the first truly extensive one, which grew to encompass 14,000 hectares by 1880.

Despite these early gains, the movement did not develop into a much larger park system, even within Australia's states, for some time, and no park service agency was created in any state until 1957. Instead, Australia next entered a period in which the Mountain Trails Club (established 1914) became a leading social phenomenon integrated with wilderness appreciation, "an association of those...who love the forests and the broad open life of the Bush...who have a definite regard for the welfare of wild life and the preservation of the natural beauties of the country."[20]

The bushwalking clubs, which at first were male-dominated "mateship" societies but later enlarged to public walking clubs, entered into park creation activism beginning in 1932, when the National Parks and Primitive Areas Council (NPPAC) was formed (with Myles Dunphy as secretary) specifically to advocate protection of tracks and paths in wilderness settings. However, their gains were modest and paralleled the U.S. trend in which parks were mainly sited on scenic but otherwise "worthless" lands. Usually, the acquisitions were inexpensive for the government by virtue of their small size and because they often already existed as Crown lands. Perhaps park history in Australia would have been quite different without the two World Wars,[21] but Australia's most significant park and wilderness fights, over dams on the wild rivers of Tasmania, rose only indirectly from the bushwalkers' efforts, and they had to await the prosperity of the 1960s and 1970s.

Lake Pedder: Australia's Hetch Hetchy

Throughout the 1960s and 1970s, Australia experienced a seminal conservation battle to save Lake Pedder National Park. The failed struggle is widely regarded as the wake-up call that spurred Australian environmentalism and formed a direct parallel to Muir's struggle to save the Hetch Hetchy.

Lake Pedder National Park was created by the Tasmanian Scenic Preservation Board in 1955 after receiving a request for its designation by the Hobart Walking Club. However, the Board was a weak institution, not a fully incorporated arm of the government. Also, Tasmanian politicians at the time were strongly counting on cheap hydroelectric energy to spur Tasmania's economic and industrial development. In 1967, the Tasmanian

Hydro-Electric Commission (HEC) publicly released a report stating its intent to flood Lake Pedder as part of the development of the Gordon River. Public outcry was strong and led to the Save Lake Pedder National Park Action Committee, which gathered 10,000 signatures (out of a population of about 350,000) to oppose the dam, and which organized events not only in Tasmania, but also in Melbourne and Sydney.[22] Even UNESCO entered the fray, writing, "The lake and surrounding area is of immense value....Its impending destruction to provide power production for about half a century must be regarded as the greatest ecological tragedy since the European settlement of Tasmania.[23] Never before had public outcry reached such a crescendo.

The debate became so intense that Tasmanian politicians who opposed preservation knew that they were fighting for more than just this one issue; if they lost to the environmentalists, they would also lose their political lives. Thus, in 1972 when the federal government offered financial compensation if a more expensive scheme that could help save Pedder was chosen, the offer was refused by Tasmania's Premier Eric Reece. Petty political egos lost the park for the nation and the world.[24]

Interestingly, the Pedder fight was not only about one utility (bushwalking) pitted against another (energy), but also about the question of the intrinsic value of wilderness separate from money and the inviolate nature that should accrue to parks. A Pedder activist, Dick Johnson, who was inspired by American wilderness thinking, stated: "The crucial spiritual components of wilderness have been ignored in that horror of emotional articulation which is the national gaucherie. In attempts to justify our stance we grope about for utilitarian explanations which simply don't exist. And for want of someone to say that Australians love their wild places, we stand about in embarrassed silence while our masters rip the living guts from the wilderness that is left."[25]

After the loss of Lake Pedder, the reluctance to support wilderness for its own sake changed dramatically in Australia. A second campaign arose with a 1976 proposal from the HEC regarding the "Gordon-below-Franklin." A fight again began between Tasmanian environmentalists and the HEC that centered on choosing between drowning a wild and scenic section of river or choosing an upper section of the Gordon River above the Franklin River juncture—an area already in use for hydroelectric power. The HEC and labor unions were pushing for flooding the Franklin.

This time, however, the environmental groups were better organized and spared the wilderness values of Franklin, although the fight was a dramatically close call. Again, the issue was about preserving wilderness for its own sake—and again the federal government and international considerations became heavily involved. "Before the Franklin River controversy was settled, national politicians had taken stands and the issue had twice come before the High Court, where the justices considered the Commonwealth's responsibilities and Australia's adherence to UNESCO's standards for World Heritage Sites."[26]

Beyond the battle for the Franklin itself, the movement had major repercussions for politics throughout Australia. During the fight for Lake Pedder, the world's first "Green" Party, the United Tasmania Group, had formed, and continued to gain strength. In 1980, when the battle for the Franklin River was at fever pitch, the first Green Party member was elected to the House of Assembly, followed by a second one in 1983, the year the Franklin was finally saved. Their success in the Franklin led to more Green wins; by 1989, they had won five seats, giving the Greens the balance of power in the Assembly.[27] Although today the Tasmania Green Party is diminished in power from its heyday, the Green Party movement has spread throughout Australia and is a strong minority voice in all the states and the Commonwealth government.

The example of Australia clearly shows the difficulties that parks and conservation can suffer in the face of the illogical forces of personality politics. However, it also is a unique case study showing how pressure at the international level can play a legitimate role in national conservation debates; indeed, today the Australian psyche seems particularly proud to be granted World Heritage designations in many of its parks, and conservationists successfully leverage this national pride when fighting for improved protected area regulations and legislation. These lessons are all germane to our final case study of South Africa. Here, we again see the disturbing effect of personality politics that so damaged the Lake Pedder campaign, particularly in the history of the Kruger National Park, which even today is still fighting to save itself from the excesses of the past.

South Africa: When Parks and Politics Mingle

When Europeans arrived in what is today South Africa, they found vast herds of wildlife. However, Europeans brought with them technology (especially firearms) and access to large markets that quickly spelled disaster for the region's fauna. Fertile lands led to agricultural clearing on a huge scale accompanied by widespread elimination of wildlife, which was believed to threaten agriculture. Extinctions ensued, most famously the quagga, a near relative of the zebra. Only the smallest tracts of land remained unaltered, and still today most of South Africa's parks are minute remnants of what once existed on a grand scale.

A notable exception, however, is Kruger National Park. A world-renowned park with extensive land, high animal diversity, and substantial tourist facilities, it is nevertheless a controversial subject within South Africa. For some South Africans, Kruger owes its existence to the repression of native peoples and as a national symbol is associated with the apartheid regime. Occasional calls to abolish it and redistribute land within it are heard today. Understanding how these views arose is critical to understanding Kruger National Park and the historical lessons one can draw from it.

Jane Carruthers, in her detailed history of the park, deals extensively with the interplay between national politics and Kruger National Park, from the political undertones that guided its naming to the park's controversial association with apartheid politicians. Yet, at the time of its establishment Kruger was not controversial but rather widely popular: people supported its creation because they urgently wanted to halt the near destruction of wildlife. Kruger's history thus begins well before its establishment in the late 1800s, during a time when policies were enacted to control the precipitous decline of wildlife but which were largely failing.[28] Although the real cause of the problem was probably multifaceted, including habitat fragmentation, disease, and poaching, the politically disenfranchised natives were a convenient scapegoat, and most politicians furthered the common belief that native poaching was the main culprit.

Two primary methods to halt wildlife decline were tried. The first focused on adding laws restricting both subsistence and commercial hunting, notably targeting Africans. In part, such restrictions were put forward to force Africans to enter into the exploitative labor market in the modernizing Transvaal.[29] Second, sportsmen helped gain support for the establishment of a number of heavily policed game reserves where no hunting was ever allowed. These reserves were established on a temporary basis (usually five-year periods), to be reconsidered for hunting use once populations of game had increased. The area that approximately comprises Kruger began as two such game reserves, the Sabi Game Reserve (proclaimed in 1898) constituting Kruger's southern section above the Crocodile River, and the Singwitsi Game Reserve (1903) reaching north to the Limpopo River. The native inhabitants of both areas were relocated.

Several such game reserves in the Transvaal failed to increase game populations and their protected status was eventually rescinded, notably the Dongola Game Reserve and the Rustenberg Game Reserve. The success of Kruger, however, was in large part due to the competent management of its second warden, an English gentlemen who had been an officer in the South African War. James Stevenson-Hamilton administered the Sabi and its reincarnation as Kruger National Park from 1902 until his retirement in 1946, overseeing the area's transition from a heavily armed backwater to South Africa's most popular tourist attraction. He was an avid naturalist, and for the period his views of wildlife protection were unusually preservationist. He wrote: "Man possesses no moral—even though he may hold the physical—right utterly to obliterate wonderful and beautiful types of creatures which Nature has placed on earth with him.... It is not as though destruction were invariably dictated by necessity... more often than not the pursuit to annihilation of the creatures of the wild is prompted by motives of sordid, temporary, and usually insignificant financial gain; sometimes by the mere lust for slaughter.... Since, therefore, the desire to exterminate still persists... modern efforts to preserve wild life have more and more centred [sic] round the creation of inviolable and suitably sited sanctuaries. Thus, protected from the fury of man, not only may the wild animals live, each according to its habits, but those persons who are interested in wild life for itself may have opportunities of viewing it under the very conditions in which it must have existed before man became a force upon earth."[30]

As in our other case studies, the Sabi soon came under political pressure to be reduced or excised altogether for transfer into departments of the central government that could administer more consumptive uses. Just after the Union of South Africa was established in 1910, the Department of Lands wanted to appropriate Sabi for the use of graziers in the southwestern part of the reserve, and the Department of Mines discussed exploiting the coal and copper in the reserve. Additionally, landowners who had signed temporary contracts allowing their lands to become part of the reserve lobbied to end the agreements when the contracts ended in 1913.

Stevenson-Hamilton was aware of the danger that the reserves faced and may have been the first person to suggest nationalization, writing to the Provincial Secretary in February 1913 about creating a "permanent game sanctuary." The matter became of interest to the central government. A commission was appointed to consider the idea, and the result was a strong endorsement for establishing a national park that would be managed for tourist enjoyment and scientific study. Discussions on finalizing the details dragged on for several years, however, in part because of protracted negotiations with landholders who were haggling over the price of land to be purchased from them.

Meanwhile, in 1924, the Smuts government lost a historical election to the Afrikaner National Party amidst a rising tide of Afrikaner nationalism. Initially, the significance of this event to Kruger National Park itself was probably minor, although it did help to conclude the protracted land negotiations because landowners feared the new government would not so easily give in to their demands. In addition, the new politics of the country was responsible for the decision to name the new park after the sentimental figure of former President Paul Kruger, an Afrikaner who had signed the proclamation establishing the original reserves. Other than signing the enabling documents, Kruger had little to do with establishing the reserves.

Carruthers explains that at the time, the Afrikaners and the Englishmen who were cautiously sharing power were seeking bridges between themselves. To the Afrikaners, Kruger National Park was to be a strong symbol of the Voortrekker past, with its history of strong ties to the land. Englishmen with their hunting and sporting heritage were also supportive of the park and were quite happy to enlist support for this shared interest by supporting the Kruger name.

Publicity for the park idea was widespread, due largely to a friendship between Stevenson-Hamilton and Stratford Caldecott, a landscape artist who had been trained in Paris. Since the park commission's recommendation appeared, the view that the park would be developed into a major tourism attraction had always been assumed. Politicians, catering to the votes of Transvaal farmers, promoted the view that the park would bring economic rewards to the lowveld.

Caldecott orchestrated a massive publicity campaign after visiting the park with Stevenson-Hamilton, creating posters depicting wildlife that would be viewable once the park became a reality. In 1926, The National Parks Act creating Kruger was passed by both houses of parliament with rare unanimity.

Like John Muir, Stevenson-Hamilton only grudgingly promoted the tourism that helped to bring this support, choosing "vulgarization" over abolition.[31] And, like National Park Service Director Steven Mather in the United States, Stevenson-Hamilton would oversee a massive tourism boom and a continuing investment in tourism infrastructure in the decades that followed, which evidently paid off in public support. He noted with satisfaction that history had abundantly proved that the seeming apathy of the public was due purely to understandable initial ignorance of the park's wonders.[32]

The history of Kruger National Park could end here but for the events that were to play a role in associating the park ever more deeply with the apartheid regime. The subsequent story of Kruger's administration offers a lesson well worth heeding. Recognizing the wild popularity of Kruger National Park, the Afrikaner administrators used it as a political tool, filling the park administration with National Party members and inventing a mythology that the park was an achievement of their own Paul Kruger and their political party.

Part of the fault for the subsequent abuse of Kruger came from the weak position initially given the park institution. The administration of the park was not governed by a national government department but was placed under the Minister of Lands and governed by a National Parks Board of Trustees. This board quickly came to be dominated by National Party politicians and its relationship with Stevenson-Hamilton was strained.

As South African politics became more extreme after World War II, the Board demanded and received support from Afrikaner politicians and in return singled out individual politicians for high public praise, including even white supremacist J. G. Strijdom, whose main impact on conservation was to force the closing of the Dongola Wildlife Sanctuary, in large part because it was a favorite project of the rival Smuts government, which wanted it to become "Smuts National Park." By 1954, all administrators within the National Parks Board were Afrikaners.

One of the known aims of National Party members was to concentrate power and influence into the hands of Afrikaaners. This was achieved in totality in Kruger shortly after Stevenson-Hamilton's retirement. His trained successor, English-speaking J. A. Sandenburgh, quickly became embroiled in an infamous corruption scandal, prompting a major government investigation known as the Hoek investigation. Sandenburgh refused to resign under the political pressure brought by the Hoek investigation, but he was nevertheless replaced in 1954 by an Afrikaner game ranger, Louis Steyn. By this point, all administrators within the National Parks Board were Afrikaners. Policies enacted after this point included restricting access to Africans, replacing all skilled labor in the park with whites, and creating a school of wildlife management for whites only at the University of Pretoria.

Clearly, Kruger's past is fraught with political shenanigans leaving a tar-nished legacy that remains today. However, we differ with Carruthers in her interpretation that parks must therefore be viewed as political entities and changeable social constructs. Instead, we suggest that in the process of planning parks to last in perpetuity, all efforts must be made to avoid similar political machinations and human rights abuses. Often, the con-ditions at park creation are critically important and should be carefully constructed to favor long-term park stability while also ensuring swift and just dealings with legitimate claimants for compensation.

Lessons Learned

• *Excessive politicization of park institutions can lead to parks holding an unstable place in society.* The case of South Africa and Kruger National Park is a worst-case example of the potential for abuse of power and politics within institutions responsible for park creation and admin-istration. Similarly, the loss of Lake Pedder National Park to the ego of a single Tasmanian politician is a reminder of the danger that extreme political polarization poses for parks. Although it is important to rec-ognize that potential flaws in the process exist, we maintain that park creation need not be inherently unjust, even to indigenous peoples (whose special needs are discussed elsewhere in this volume). Rather, the lessons we take away from the three case histories presented in this chapter lead us to propose that checks and balances must be established to minimize the petty political abuses that can indelibly blemish parks, socially and ecologically. In addition to legislative action, conservation groups in the developing world must seek to make best use of judicial systems, demanding legal standing where lacking. Additionally, groups working for human rights and land-use planning (including park estab-lishment) must work together more productively and reduce the polar-ization that often characterizes such relationships.

Parks must be established forever, or their existence is meaningless, particularly from the standpoint of biodiversity conservation. Ob-viously, the initial creation of parks will be dependent on political proc-esses. However, once established, parks should be administered as independently as possible from the political process. We urge that the developed world assist in ensuring that park establishment be pursued with just and legally binding forms of compensation, whether this in-volves transfer of funds, economic benefits from tourism, or land transfers. Much of this work will be required at the highest political levels if the solutions are to remain stable into perpetuity.

• *Although superficial differences exist among the motivations driving park creation, widespread public support for parks is evident across cultures and across time.* Protected areas have been sought by distinct societies in different ages. Practical considerations (e.g., watershed protection, income-generating tourism) are important for garnering political will for parks, but it is significant that arguments for park establishment throughout time and in all cultures have almost always contained aesthetic components as well. Quality of human life is diminished when all contact with nature is lost, and the quality of life for future generations is of near universal concern to noncorrupt governments.

For developing countries struggling to meet even basic human needs for their existing populations, the challenges to create parks will be great, and industrialized countries must be willing to step forward to assist. Chapter 23 specifically focuses on the issue of generating the political will to establish and maintain parks, and chapter 26 describes creative methods for financing new and existing parks.

• *External influences can play a useful and enabling role in the creation and management of parks.* In the process of setting up its park systems, America hoped also to improve its reputation in Europe; Australia was influenced by international World Heritage responsibilities; and by advancing Kruger National Park, South Africa eagerly hoped for international recognition and increased tourism revenue. International opinion can play a role in motivating concern for environment and park issues and in that regard should be seen as both a legitimate voice and a potentially constructive influence. All of humanity shares in the natural heritage of the earth, and constituencies for parks extend beyond a nation's borders. Currently, the power of international groups to work with national governments in implementing economic incentives and policy reforms friendly to parks and biodiversity is limited, but its potential should be more fully explored (see chapter 27 for more detailed discussion).

• *Democratic ideals and political realities point to a need to allow nonconsumptive use of parks in most situations.* As democracy gains strength around the world and an ever-expanding number of people participating in its benefits and influencing public policy, it seems likely that parks will need to include public access to maintain their popularity and social acceptability. In case studies presented in chapters that follow, it can be seen that visitor use in tropical parks varies widely, and some countries (e.g., Brazil) severely restrict tourism in their parks. Although the revenue brought in by expanded tourism may be important, not all park systems worthy of protection will be able to pay for themselves by tourism, nor should they be expected to. More important is the fact that public love and concern for an area is itself a real form of value, but to foster such a value the public must be able to access the area.

With this in mind, however, there exists a concern that opening parks to increased tourism will result in increased damage to park resources. Fortunately, a number of management techniques have been developed to address possible problems. Chapter 21 provides further details on strategies to optimize the benefits that tourism provides while proactively managing against problems that it may bring.

• *Local special interests may apply continual pressure for access to park resources.* In the three case histories presented in this chapter, we see repeatedly the difficulty of establishing parks and maintaining their boundaries and resources intact against would-be extractivists. That this problem is so prevalent, even in areas with low population densities, bodes ill for tropical developing countries whose population and resource problems are even more intractable. Unfortunately, parks will nearly always contain the world's last pristine natural environments, which promise the highest returns for the smallest investment. Even when it is demonstrable that a park is in the interest of a larger segment of society, it can be difficult to overcome influence pedaling (e.g., campaign-finance mechanisms or special-interest lobbying) even in minimally corrupted governments. This indicates that "top-down" mechanisms for setting aside land are desirable, such as those of the United States for establishing national monuments. When governments refuse to act in the public interest, private initiatives may be required, and can sometimes fill the void on a small scale. Such privatization can take a number of forms, many of which are discussed in Chapter 13.

However, legal provisions must be in place for these to function as well (see chapters 13 and 24). The means to better integrate large-scale land use planning in a way that satisfactorily accommodates both conservation and development is still lacking in developing and developed countries alike.

• *The establishment of protected areas does not assure immunity from violations, and active enforcement must be consistently maintained.* In both the United States and South Africa, protecting park resources required vigorous enforcement and often involved military intervention. Especially in the early stages, there will nearly always be cheaters, resentful locals, and special interests clamoring for access to natural resources. Political will, public activism, and willingness to train and use enforcers are critically important for ensuring the sanctity of parks and enforcing a country's resource laws.

• *The creation of a park and its ultimate constituency are often separated by place and time.* In all three case histories presented in this chapter, popular support for park creation lagged far behind the optimum time for creating parks that were biodiverse—that is, before wildlands came under the threat of development. However, the future-oriented vision that impels governments to set aside land for conservation is still not widespread in many political systems—a fact important for countries in the tropical developing world to recognize. History has shown that if urbanization and democratization are the future of tropical countries, the support base for parks within a country will grow—perhaps very quickly—in a rapidly urbanizing setting. It is of utmost urgency that more enabling work be aimed at this policy level, by enlightened politicians of tropical nations.

• *Publicity pays.* Of the three case studies, Kruger National Park stands out as the park most popular at its establishment, and it remains today the gem of the South African park system. This popularity can be attributed to the publicity campaign orchestrated by James Stevenson-Hamilton and Stratford Caldecott. National parks in the United States similarly benefited from publicity campaigns, including the "See America First" campaign, orchestrated by the railroad companies in association with Steven Mather. In developing countries where ecotourism has great potential, it may be appropriate for governments or tourism-related companies to actively promote domestic and international tourism to parks through aggressive publicity campaigns, and sponsorship of artistic and cultural events that highlight the parks.

• *Individuals matter.* Perhaps one of the most encouraging lessons from history is that a single individual can play a galvanizing role in conserving parkland. The chapters that follow will also strengthen this claim by portraying some of the most compelling conservation stories of our time. It is hoped that interested readers will heed the lessons of the past and present and consider how best their own combinations of talent, circumstance, and opportunities could change history.

Conclusions

In our modern consciousness, we tend to look toward the future rather than back at the past, believing that our current predicaments are new to humankind. But this chapter has shown that many of the problems that face supporters of wilderness and biodiversity preservation have long been with us. The views of ancient peoples, as well as John Muir, Miles Dunphy, the Australian Greens, and James Stevenson-Hamilton, can still guide us in our quest to retain remnants of our wild continents. Although this connection to the past may comfort us, we should still be alarmed by the pace at which the contemporary world is changing and about the accelerating loss of opportunities to protect what wildlands and biodiversity we do still harbor and can yet preserve for posterity. It would seem that the technological age requires a similarly accelerated application of wisdom to keep its powers in check, but we have yet to see if our current leaders and our own actions will meet this challenge.

Notes

1. C. W. Allin, *International Handbook of National Parks and Nature Reserves* (Greenwood, Conn.: Greenwood Press, 1990); A. Runte, *National Parks: The American Experience* (Lincoln, Neb.: University of Nebraska Press, 1997).

2. Zuo Dakang and Zhang Peiyan. "The Huang-Huai-Hai Plain" in *The Earth as Transformed by Human Action*, ed. B. L. Turner II, W. C. Clark, R. W. Kates, J. F. Richards, J. T. Mathews, and W. B. Meyer (New York: Cambridge University Press, 1990).

3. Allin, *International Handbook of National Parks and Nature Reserves*.

4. IUCN (The World Conservation Union), *Protected Areas of the World*, vol. 2, 345. (Gland, Switzerland: IUCN, 1992).

5. Y. Yazan, "Union of Soviet Socialist Republics," in Allin, *International Handbook*.

6. Runte, *National Parks*.

7. Runte, *National Parks*.

8. G. E. Machlis and D. L. Tichnell, *The State of the World's Parks: An International Assessment for Resource Management, Policy and Research* (Boulder, Colo.: Westview Press, 1985).

9. Runte, *National Parks*.

10. J. Muir, *Our National Parks* (San Francisco: Sierra Club Books, 1991).

11. S. L. Udall, *The Quiet Crisis and the Next Generation* (Salt Lake City: Peregrine Smith Books, 1988).

12. Runte, *National Parks*.

13. R. W. Sellars, *Preserving Nature in the National Parks: A History* (New Haven: Yale University Press, 1997); Runte, *National Parks*.

14. Sellars, *Preserving Nature in the National Parks*.

15. Udall, *Quiet Crisis*, 122.

16. H. M. Albright and M. A. Schenck, *Creating the National Park Service: The Missing Years* (Norman: University of Oklahoma Press, 1999).

17. Sellars, *Preserving Nature*.

18. D. F. Rettie, *Our National Park System: Caring for America's Greatest Natural and Historic Treasures* (Urbana, Ill.: University of Illinois Press, 1995).

19. C. M. Hall, *Wasteland to World Heritage: Preserving Australia's Wilderness* (Carlton, Victoria: Melbourne University Press, 1992), 91–92.

20. Dunphy quoted in T. R. Dunlap, *Nature and the English Diaspora: Environment and History in the United States, Canada, Australia, and New Zealand* (Cambridge, UK: Cambridge University Press, 1999), 195.

21. Hall, *Wasteland*, 111.

22. Dunlap, *Nature*, 290.

23. UNESCO quoted in K. Kiernan, "I Saw My Temple Ransacked," in *The Rest of the World Is Watching*, ed. C. Pybus and R. Flanagan (Sydney: Pan Macmillan Publishers, 1990), 26.

24. Kiernan, "Temple Ransacked," 31.

25. Johnson quoted in Dunlap, *Nature*, 292.

26. Dunlap, *Nature*, 293.

27. B. Brown, "Ecology, Economy, Equality, Eternity," in Pybus and Flanagan, *World Is Watching*.

28. Jane Carruthers, *The Kruger National Park: A Social and Political History* (Pietermaritzburg: University of Natal Press, 1995), 17.

29. Carruthers, *Kruger*, 31.

30. C. S. Stokes, *Sanctuary* (Cape Town: The Sanctuary Production Committee, Union of South Africa, 1942).

31. Carruthers, *Kruger*, 64.

32. Stokes, *Sanctuary*, 9.

PART II

CASE STUDIES

4

Scenes from the Front Lines of Conservation

PETER A. FRYKHOLM

The introductory chapters of this book paint an alternately sobering and hopeful picture of the future of conservation throughout the world. A litany of depressing statistics and historical examples amply demonstrates humankind's shortsighted misuse of resources and its propensity for destruction. Efforts at conservation, such as integrated conservation and development projects (ICDPs), often fall woefully short of baseline conservation needs even as the political and economic realities of development hasten degradation.

Yet, despite bleak forecasts and the arguably failed conservation paradigm of the ICDP, there are reasons for optimism. As development begets urbanization, and as globalization accelerates the transfer of technology and the transparency of government, protected areas may yet be saved by the gradual emergence of a worldwide conservation ethic. There is hope that enlightened and scientifically sound principles of development can be successfully implemented in areas of high population density and intensive land use, thus relieving extractive pressure on nearby protected areas and preserving a biological inheritance for future generations.

Although discussion of these overarching issues will be renewed in Parts III and IV of the book, it is now time to move from the general to the specific. Part II introduces the reader to issues of conservation as they are played out in individual protected areas and parks throughout the world. Although not exhaustive, the case studies that follow describe a compelling range of settings and circumstances. From montane to tropical forests, from anarchic to stable situations, from densely populated to remote regions, the reader will gain a broad perspective on the current state of conservation and conservation issues throughout the world. The first destination on this armchair tour is the continent of Africa.

Africa

Five chapters comprise the section on Africa. Chapter 5 offers a country-by-country panorama of West Africa, a region besieged by the ravaging effects of civil war and rapidly expanding populations. Acknowledging the grim realities of conservation in the region, the author argues that conservation efforts should be modest in scale and should focus on protection as fragments of natural forest may survive the crises and serve as a basis for expansion of forested land and biota in a brighter future. Discussion then turns southward to focus on the rich tropical forests of the Congo Basin of west equatorial Africa where the destruction is less but threats are nonetheless very real and mounting. Compounding the situation, reluctant policy makers remain to be convinced of the need for conservation. A case study of the Okapi Faunal Reserve in the Democratic Republic of Congo details the particularly tragic outcomes of that country's civil war of 1996–1997 but also draws attention to the fact that the Reserve's independent park project managed to maintain an effective presence on the ground. The next chapter provides a detailed account of Kibale National Park in Uganda, which shows how one person's persistence and dedication can make conservation a reality. The section on Africa concludes with a rich description of the activities leading up to the establishment of Ranomafana National Park in Madagascar. Here we find a showcase example of how development and conservation assistance can go hand in hand.

Latin America

The second section of Part II shifts attention to conservation issues in Latin America. Chapter 10 guides the reader into Brazilian Amazonia where powerful agents of disturbance are offset by the still-ample scope of land available for preservation. The author discusses ways to incorporate isolated protected areas into a wider network of conservation. The journey continues across the Andes into Pampas del Heath, Perú. This national sanctuary was a classic "paper park" from its inception until 1991, when a Peruvian nongovernmental organization (NGO) joined forces with The Nature Conservancy to take over management of the park. The author, who was manager of the park, describes an array of political and practical problems that beset this process of transition and ultimately led to the termination of the management agreement.

A more hopeful note is struck as attention turns to Costa Rica, a country readily associated with a thriving ecotourism industry and recognized for its record of conservation success. Chapter 12 describes the Monteverde Reserve Complex, an assemblage of six privately and publicly owned protected areas. Despite unfortunate design flaws, Monteverde nonetheless stands out as a laudable model for citizen initiatives in nature conservation. The private–public dichotomy of the Monteverde Reserve Complex receives fuller consideration in the subsequent chapter, as the issue of privately owned parks is discussed in depth. Although Costa Rica's private parks are a valuable element in that country's robust network of protected areas, the authors caution that little is actually known about how these parks are administered, and further research must be conducted before the practices of private park administration can be accurately gauged against more prevalent public models.

Asia

The third section of Part II focuses on Asia, beginning with the recent history of Nagarahole National Park in India, an area with an unusually dense and rich vertebrate fauna. Chapter 14 describes how rallying a broad coalition of supporters can rescue a park that is faced with seemingly insurmountable problems. Rich biodiversity characterizes the Leuser Ecosystem of northern Sumatra as well. Leuser's location at the forest frontier in a corrupt sociopolitical setting shares many of the same challenges that seem ubiquitous in the fight to preserve protected areas elsewhere. From Indonesia the focus shifts to Thailand. Chapter 16 delves into the status and prospects of two Thai protected areas. Although the lists of problems for these area run long, the authors are hopeful that a variety of approaches to protected-area management will secure a future for biodiversity in this part of Southeast Asia. The Asian tour concludes with a visit to Bhutan, whose many unique factors makes it an interesting conclusion to the case studies of Part II. Owing to its relatively small human population, its recent and gradual emergence from an archaic subsistence economy, and a prevailing Buddhist ethic of respect for nature, Bhutan poses unique conservation opportunities in a nation where already 26 percent of the land is devoted to national parks and wildlife sanctuaries.

Final Thoughts

The goals of Part II of this book are twofold. First, it is hoped that specialists interested in the particular regions covered in the chapters will benefit from the timely information, personal observations, and detailed analysis they contain. The contributing authors truly represent vanguard figures in the global battle to preserve tropical biodiversity. The second goal of Part II is to present a range of case studies that, when viewed as a whole, form an encompassing picture of the status of conservation world-wide. From Asia to Africa to Latin America, many struggles and obstacles to conservation are recurrent. It is our hope that by disseminating the information contained in these chapters and by encouraging comparative analysis of protected areas worldwide, conservation successes will one day become recurrent as well.

5

West Africa: Tropical Forest Parks on the Brink

JOHN F. OATES

In *Requiem for Nature*, John Terborgh describes the national parks in the tropical forest zone of West Africa as "a shambles" and argues that further money spent on conservation efforts in this area will be wasted due to the absence of appropriate social order and discipline.[1] He recommends maintaining in captivity the most spectacular endemic species of West Africa, such as the pygmy hippopotamus and Diana monkey.

Having been involved in research and conservation efforts in the West African forest zone for a span of over thirty years, I am also gloomy about the prospects for parks in this area, but I am not yet prepared to write the situation off as completely hopeless.[2] In this chapter, I provide a brief review of some of the conservation problems, but I also present evidence of conservation efforts that have had some degree of success.

I strongly agree with the view that we need effective protected areas (national parks or similar management units) in the tropical forest zone. In the face of growing pressures on natural ecosystems from humans all around the world, parks are surely our best hope of holding onto special pieces of nature, at least in the short term. The pressures in West Africa are particularly acute, but they are not unique. What is happening there today is not unlike what occurred in the temperate-forest zones of Europe and China in the past, and what is happening (or has happened) in the tropical-forest zones of India and Indochina, among other places. We should not stop seeking solutions to the conservation problems in the forests of West Africa; not only do they support unique plants and animals, but also the challenges they present today will surely arise elsewhere in the future.

Background

In this chapter I use "West Africa" in a standard geographical sense as referring to the area lying south of the Sahara and west of the boundary between Nigeria and Cameroon.[3]

The Nigeria–Cameroon border lies within a broad geographical region in which there is a complex pattern of faunal and floral change rather than an abrupt discontinuity. This region extends from the eastern edge of the main Upper Guinea forest block, in Ghana, to the western edge of the Central African forest block, which lies in southern Cameroon. Between those two forest blocks there are faunal disjunctions across the Dahomey Gap (a dry-forest area between southeastern Ghana and southwestern Nigeria), the lower Niger River, the Cross River, and the Sanaga River.[4]

In West Africa, tropical rain forest (lowland moist forest) is limited to parts of eight countries: Sierra Leone, Liberia, Guinea, Côte d'Ivoire, Ghana, Togo, Bénin, and Nigeria.[5] Most of these countries have a dense and still rapidly growing human population. In 1998, these eight countries were estimated to have contained 31.7 percent of the 567 million people inhabiting tropical Africa (excluding far northern and southern Africa, Madagascar, and offshore islands), and their average annual population growth rate during the 1990s was 2.8 percent.[6] A recent study projected that in 2000–2015 the average annual population growth rate of five of these countries would be 2.4 percent (compared with 2.6 percent in the absence of increased mortality from AIDS).[7]

Dense and growing populations put the rain forests of West Africa under tremendous pressure. The coastal regions to which the forest is restricted have had many centuries of contact with the outside world, and this contact has strongly influenced their societies and economies.[8] Today, the economy of large areas of the West African rain-forest zone is based on relatively intensive agriculture and/or the commercial exploitation of natural resources, including timber and "bushmeat" (the meat of wild animals). Most of the area that has a climate capable of supporting rain forest is not covered today by mature forest, and although Fairhead and Leach have challenged published estimates of recent West African deforestation rates, it is evident that the greater part of the forest that remains has been modified by centuries of human farming and tree cutting.[9] To quote Richards: "Forest which has never at any time been cultivated exists in West Africa on swampy sites . . . but elsewhere only on extremely limited areas, mostly on steep rocky slopes, etc."[10]

Much of the West African rain forest that remains occurs as a patch-work, with the scattered patches separated by areas of cultivation. Many of the patches have nominal status as "Forest Reserves," or "Forêts Clas-sées," indicating that a government forestry department exercises man-agement jurisdiction. Most of these managed forests have been logged to a greater or lesser extent, they have sometimes been severely damaged by farming and fire, and their wildlife is rarely given any serious protection against hunting. In a zone in which domestic stock do not thrive, bush-meat continues to be a major source of animal protein for many people, including those who have migrated to towns and cities. As a result, hunt-ing pressure is intense in almost all remaining forest areas, which is where most of the larger mammals and birds survive. Only a few areas of the re-maining rain forest theoretically have full protection, as national parks, for their full biotic community. These, and a few other areas of special protection, such as wildlife sanctuaries, will be described in the next section.

Country Overviews
Sierra Leone

Elsewhere I have described in detail how a wildlife sanctuary at Tiwai Is-land (12 square kilometers) grew out of a primate ecology research project that commenced in 1982.[11] Tiwai is home to seven species of rain-forest monkeys (including Diana monkeys) and to chimpanzees. Pygmy hippo-potamus use the Moa River around Tiwai and forage on the island as well as on neighboring islands and the mainland.

In the early days of the primate research project, researchers paid a small annual rent to nearby villages for use of the site in return for which the villagers agreed not to hunt on the island. After Tiwai became a formal sanctuary, this rent was replaced by a scheme under which local people obtained a share of fees paid by visitors. Local communities also obtained concrete benefits from the employment of their members in research and protection activities. Abiding by sanctuary regulations was made easier for local people by the facts that (a) the island was not a core farming area, and (b) they relied more on fishing than hunting for their animal protein.

In 1991, a rebel insurgency from Liberia terminated the research and conservation efforts at Tiwai. As this insurgency developed into a full-scale civil war, many towns and villages near the island were partially or totally evacuated for long periods. At the time of writing, rebel activity continues in Sierra Leone, but some southeastern parts of the country are reported to be relatively quiet and people have begun to return to their villages. In March 2000, T. Garnett of the Environmental Foundation for Africa (Monrovia, Liberia) visited Tiwai and reported that local people are "still very keen to protect the status of Tiwai. However, they regretted to inform us that extensive hunting had been going on and had significantly reduced the animal population in the sanctuary."[12]

If research or conservation efforts can be revived at Tiwai, they will have to be funded for a prolonged period from overseas, since the Sierra Leone economy is in ruins. The renewed presence of outside researchers would probably be the single most important positive influence on behalf of conservation. It is my perception that the key factor in protecting the island from 1982 through 1991 was the almost continual presence of outside researchers and/or Peace Corps volunteers.

Elsewhere in the Sierra Leone forest zone there have been long-standing proposals to establish a national park or strict nature reserve in at least part of the Gola Forest Reserves (748 square kilometers), which lie to the east of Tiwai and northward along the Liberian border.[13] The Golas are one of the largest remaining areas of moist lowland rain forest in Sierra Leone. Until the outbreak of the civil war, Britain's Royal Society for the Protection of Birds was involved in a Gola Rain-Forest Conservation Project with the Sierra Leone Forestry Division and the Conservation Society of Sierra Leone, and plans had been drawn up to assess ways of linking Tiwai with a larger Gola conservation area.

Liberia

Remote sensing surveys indicate that Liberia supports the largest area of lowland moist forest in West Africa.[14] This forest is in two main blocks, one in the west of the country (extending into Sierra Leone as the Gola Forest), and one in the east (extending into Côte d'Ivoire, where it connects tenuously with the Taï Forest). Planning for protected areas began in the 1970s, and by 1982 three forest national parks and four other protected areas had been proposed.[15] Only one of these, Sapo National Park (1,308 square kilometers), was ever formally decreed, in 1983.

Sapo contains populations of elephant, pygmy hippopotamus, giant forest hog, Jentink's and zebra duikers, seven species of rain-forest monkey, and the chimpanzee. The World Wildlife Fund (WWF) and the U.S. Peace Corps assisted the Liberian Wildlife and National Parks Department in demarcating park boundaries and drawing up a management plan for Sapo. Although a small protection force apparently prevented agricultural encroachment and logging in the park, hunting continued, since there is said to have been little rigorous policing.[16] After a brutal civil war started in Liberia in December 1989, organized conservation efforts ceased at Sapo. The war ended in 1996, leaving the country's "economy, infrastructure and institutions in shambles."[17] During the war it is reported that wildlife populations increased in the southeast of the country, because many people fled the area and "anyone carrying a gun would have been attacked."[18] Since the war ended, foreign and Liberian nongovernmental organizations have cooperated with Wildlife and National Parks staff on small-scale conservation actions in and around Sapo, but the overall condition of the park's vegetation and fauna is unclear.[19] Logging in the southeast of the country apparently continued during the war, and major logging operations are now in progress.[20]

Guinea

Much of Guinea's moist forest was lost or modified long ago by human activity, and a recent estimate suggests that only about 4,500 square kilometers of moist lowland forest and 210 square kilometers of montane forest remain, mostly in the southeast corner of the country near the borders of Liberia and Côte d'Ivoire.[21] Forest loss apparently continues at a high rate.[22] There are no national parks in the moist forest zone, the only strictly protected area being the Mt. Nimba Strict Nature Reserve (140 square kilometers), created in 1944 and designated a World Heritage Site in 1981. This reserve is said to be relatively well protected against hunting and farming encroachment.[23] Recently, two new national parks were created in the savanna zone of Guinea. The largest of these, Parc national du Haut-Niger, covers 12,700 square kilometers and includes dry forest that supports a population of chimpanzees.[24]

Côte d'Ivoire

During the 1970s and 1980s, Côte d'Ivoire was estimated to have suffered the highest deforestation rate of any country in the tropics.[25] Among several protected areas within the country's moist forest zone, by far the largest and best known is Taï National Park (3,400 square kilometers), which lies in the southwest of the country, close to the Liberian border. Adjacent to the northern part of Taï is the N'Zo Partial Faunal Reserve (950 square kilometers). Taï is the oldest rain-forest park in West Africa, having acquired national park status in 1972. A "parc refuge" was originally declared in the area in 1926, and it became a "réserve intégral pour la Faune et la Flore" in 1956. In 1982, it was declared a World Heritage Site. Taï supports populations of pygmy hippopotamus, Jentink's and zebra duikers, elephant, chimpanzee, and eight monkey species.

A UNESCO "Man and the Biosphere" project initiated at Taï in 1978 has evolved into the Autonomous Project for the Conservation of Taï National Park (PACPNT), which involves several foreign and multinational agencies. Among the efforts of this project have been agricultural research and development activities in the area around the park, an area that has experienced a large influx of migrant farmers.[26] In the period 1972–1980 alone, the population around Taï increased from 1.3/square kilometers to 7.7/square kilometers, due largely to immigration.[27] A contentious management issue at Taï has been the status of a 940-square-kilometer "protection" or "buffer" zone surrounding much of the park. Some have regarded this as a de facto extension of the park, while others have considered it as an area for sustainable human use.[28] The park itself has suffered from limited logging and mining, but the main current threat to its integrity is the poaching of wildlife. Animal populations on the eastern side of the park have been decimated by large-scale commercial hunting for the bushmeat trade (supplying urban restaurants), and on the west from smaller-scale poaching by village-based hunters.[29] The only areas of Taï National Park that suffer little poaching are two primate study sites near the town of Taï in the west, and an area being developed for ecotourism near Mont Niénokoué in the south.[30]

Ghana

By 1990 about 15,000 square kilometers of intact moist forest were estimated to remain in southern Ghana, down from perhaps 88,000 square kilometers in 1900. Almost all of this forest was in government-managed forest reserves and other protected areas; only about 1,000 square kilometers of forest were estimated to remain outside these areas.[31] The straight boundaries of the many small forest reserves, which are mostly surrounded by farmland, appear clearly on satellite imagery.

As logging and associated commercial hunting intensified in Ghana in the 1960s, calls were made for the establishment of nonhunting forest reserves.[32] This eventually led to the establishment of the national parks of Bia (in 1974) and Nini-Suhien (in 1976). Bia (78 square kilometers) and Nini-Suhien (166 square kilometers) are each attached to larger "resource reserves" (originally "game production reserves") within which the controlled exploitation of both timber and wildlife is supposedly permitted.

The resource reserve attached to Nini-Suhien is Ankasa (343 square kilometers). Bia and Ankasa/Nini-Suhien were neglected by outsiders from the late 1970s until 1990, when the European Commission funded a consultancy group to consider how management of the protected areas might be improved. The resulting management project did not begin until 1997, by which time there was little wildlife left in Bia National Park, and the Bia Resource Reserve was being heavily logged. Today, wildlife in Ankasa is said to be still under severe hunting pressure.[33] A visitor center is planned for Ankasa, however, as well as a research center at Bia.[34]

The third and most recently declared forest national park in Ghana is Kakum (210 square kilometers), in the Central Region. Kakum, created from an existing forest reserve in 1992, was established not so much because it had been identified as a high priority for biological conservation (although it does have a remnant elephant population), but rather as a component of an effort to develop tourism and thus the region's economy. With funding from USAID, Conservation International (CI) was brought in to advise on biological conservation issues.

T. Struhsaker and I visited Kakum in 1993 as part of the CI program. We found evidence of high levels of hunting on the Kakum primates. In subsequent surveys over a wider area of Ghana, including Bia and Ankasa, we failed to find any evidence of a surviving population of Miss Waldron's red colobus monkey (*Procolobus badius waldroni*), whose presence at Bia was one of the original reasons for choosing that forest as a national park. We concluded that this monkey, endemic to western Ghana and eastern Côte d'Ivoire, is probably extinct.[35] Kakum has been cited in a number of travel and natural history magazines as a success, but this assessment seems to be based largely on the experiences of casual visitors. Most of the outside funding going to Kakum has been devoted to constructing tourism infrastructure, to paying foreign consultants, and to purchasing vehicles and equipment. There is also a project to assist farmers in the growing and marketing of organic cocoa. Conservation-and-development efforts have been concentrated on the edges of the park, while its central areas appear to have been neglected. The park does not have a biological research station.

Togo and Bénin

There is a very small area of moist tropical forest on the western hills of southern Togo, on the border with Ghana. Chimpanzees are reported to have lived in this area in the past, but are probably now extinct. There is no protected area in these hills, and on a brief visit in 1995 I found the forest to be patchy and highly degraded.

Sandwiched between Togo and Nigeria is Bénin. A tiny area of southeast Bénin lies within the moist forest zone of White, but most of this area is now farmland, in which forest survives only as minute fragments, typically as sacred groves near villages.[36] A few of these sacred groves support groups of red-bellied guenons (*Cercopithecus erythrogaster erythrogaster*), as does the larger Lama Forest (163 square kilometers) further to the west.[37] Most of Lama, which is a dry forest, now consists of managed teak plantations and farmland, but a small area of natural forest (about 20 square kilometers) survives and is being protected as a "*noyau central*" by the Office National du Bois in collaboration with a German technical-assistance project. Although there is a small protection force, poaching is common in the *noyau*.[38]

Nigeria

Nigeria has the largest human population (estimated at 121 million in 1998 by the World Bank) of any country in Africa.[39] Many of these people live in the country's southern moist-forest zone, over much of which there is a density of more than 100 people per square kilometer. As a result, the remaining forest is highly fragmented. Almost all forest reserves (managed by numerous state governments) have been heavily logged, and many of them have had much of their natural forest replaced by plantations of exotic trees, by commercial oil-palm or rubber plantations, or by farmland. The largest intact expanses of forest are in Cross River State in the southeast of the country, along the Cameroon border. A substantial part of that southeastern forest is protected in the Cross River National Park. Just west of the northern sector of this park, the forests of Afi Mountain were gazetted in May 2000 as a wildlife sanctuary. In the southwest of the country, the Okomu Wildlife Sanctuary within the Okomu Forest Reserve was recently upgraded to a national park, and there is a small Biosphere Reserve within the Omo Forest Reserve.

Okomu National Park. Following a survey of southwestern Nigerian forests in 1982, Okomu Forest Reserve (1,240 square kilometers) was recommended as the site for a determined conservation effort, with a focus on the endangered white-throated guenon, *Cercopithecus erythrogaster*.[40] The state government did not formally create the sanctuary until 1986 and even then gave it an area of only 66 square kilometers, less than half the area we had recommended. In 1987, the Nigerian Conservation Foundation (NCF) took the lead in a project to manage the wildlife sanctuary at Okomu. Although the NCF project had some initial success in controlling poaching and tree cutting in the sanctuary, it came to devote a good deal of its energy to providing assistance with agricultural development to migrant farmers who were living on forest reserve land around the sanctuary.[41] Protection efforts flagged and in 1997 it was discovered that logging was occurring in the sanctuary itself; several of the NCF project staff were found to have been involved in this illegal activity.[42] Sanctuary management was handed over to Nigeria National Parks in May 1999, and the fully protected area extended to cover 181 square kilometers. When I visited Okomu in December 2000, I found that fifty-two staff had been assigned to the new park, and that protection efforts had improved.

Cross River National Park. The Cross River National Park (CRNP) is located in a hotspot of species richness and endemism, on the edge of the Cameroon Highlands between the Cross and Sanaga Rivers. Full documentation of this area's fauna and flora—and analysis of its similarities and differences to neighboring regions—has yet to be completed, but a number of statistics indicate its importance. For instance, sixteen primate species have been recorded from CRNP, and an additional species (*Cercocebus albigena*, the gray-cheeked mangabey) appears to have gone extinct in the area only recently. Four of these primate species are endemic to this region (including Bioko island), and seven of the other species are represented by endemic subspecies.[43] In 1995, Torben Larsen collected nearly 600 butterfly species in Oban (the southern part of the park, adjoining Cameroon's Korup National Park to the east). Based on this sampling, Larsen has estimated that Oban supports about 950 species and the whole of Cross River Park more than 1,000 species—the highest number for any similar area in Africa.[44]

The first formal proposal for a national park in the Cross River area was by G. A. Petrides in 1965.[45] It was not until 1988, however, that serious planning for a national park began.[46] The resulting "master plans," in which World Wide Fund for Nature–UK (WWF-UK) played a leading role, called for a park in two separate blocks, separated by the Cross River valley and cultivated land: Oban (approximately 3,000 square kilometers) in the south and Okwangwo (920 square kilometers) in the north.[47] The plans proposed a total budget of $49.9 million to be spent over a period of seven years. In addition to park buildings, vehicles, and staff, much of the money was to be spent on a variety of rural development projects and on the salaries of internationally recruited managers.

These CRNP master plans were never fully implemented. Although in 1991 the park was decreed by presidential order, the declaration covered only the existing forest reserve boundaries, rather than the boundaries recommended in the plans. Full European Community (EC) funding for the park development project was held up by the bureaucratic procedures of Brussels, by political events in Nigeria, and by wrangling among the various parties over who would control the very substantial funds. Apart from the foreign funding, limited support from the Nigerian federal government has provided for staff salaries and basic park operating costs. No research stations have been established, and tourist visits have been negligible.

Based on the master plans, many villages within 5–10 kilometers of the CRNP boundary were declared part of a "Support Zone" in which people would be involved in park activities and assisted with development projects. Only in the Okwangwo division has any actual funding been available for support zone development. Here, many villagers have come to view WWF as a development agency, and villages that were provided with some small assistance (with new crop plants, for instance, or school buildings), have come to expect more in the future. But, since little or no further assistance has materialized, people have become hostile to park officials, as they are already in the Oban area, where no significant development assistance was provided.[48] My own surveys have found very low densities of larger mammals in both the Oban and Okwangwo divisions of the park, and much evidence of poaching.

Afi Mountain. Afi River Forest Reserve is a 383-square-kilometer area immediately to the west of the Okwangwo Division of the Cross River National Park. The mountainous northwestern part of the reserve, covering about 90 square kilometers, contains a small population of a locally endemic gorilla subspecies (*Gorilla gorilla diehli,* the Cross River Gorilla). The presence of these gorillas and other endangered species led to a plan to create a wildlife sanctuary in this northwestern area of the reserve.

In 1996, a gorilla ecology research project began at Afi Mountain, led by Kelley McFarland of the City University of New York. McFarland and her trackers, who were recruited from several different local villages, patrolled the mountain and reduced levels of hunting.[49] In 1999, a small group of conservationists and scientists formed a consortium to work on the development of a sanctuary at Afi Mountain. A Liberian conservation-

ist took over supervision of McFarland's field team to monitor both gorilla movements and signs of hunting, farming, and logging. This field
work has been complemented by a series of community consultations
about the aims of the sanctuary.[50] The annual budget for this project in
1999–2000 was $20,500. This modest investment appeared to keep hunt-
ing at a low level, at least in the 30-square-kilometer area in which the
field staff concentrated their patrols. The project has tried to avoid suggesting to local people that the creation of the wildlife sanctuary will be
associated with economic or agricultural development projects.

In May 2000, the Cross River State government gazetted the Afi Mountain Wildlife Sanctuary, and we continue to work with them and local
communities to give this new protected area long-term effectiveness.

Discussion

The general picture I have presented of protected areas in the West African rain-forest zone is a somber one. The parks and other protected areas
that exist are few in number, often small, and generally heavily threatened. They are fragments in a landscape in which the numbers of people
continue to grow faster than in most other parts of the world and where
much of the forest outside protected areas has been removed or degraded
by farming and logging. In some areas, warfare and civil disorder make organized protection almost impossible. Terborgh's bleak view of conservation prospects in the region is, therefore, understandable.

And yet in other parts of the world, fragments of natural forest have
managed to survive similar past crises and, when times have changed, the
forest and its biota have expanded (eastern North America is an example).
Those observations, and the fact that there are people in West Africa and
abroad prepared to fight for the survival of the fragmented forest, lead me
to the view that we should not relinquish conservation efforts. The West
African forests contain a wealth of unique organisms, and therefore
unique ecosystems, which cannot be adequately maintained in zoos or botanical gardens.[51]

One encouraging sign is that there seems to be general, if grudging, acceptance of the boundaries of West Africa's protected forests. Most of the
national parks, strict nature reserves, and wildlife sanctuaries I have described have not been seriously damaged by farming and logging, at least
where the boundaries of these areas are clearly defined. When a state
completely fails, legal boundaries fall into jeopardy, but even after brutal

civil wars and anarchic situations in Liberia and Sierra Leone, somewhat organized states have endured, together with government departments responsible for forest and wildlife conservation.

In four important places, Sapo (1,308 square kilometers) in Liberia, Taï (3,400 square kilometers) in Côte d'Ivoire, Ankasa/Nini-Suhien (509 square kilometers) in Ghana, and Cross River (about 4,000 square kilometers) in Nigeria, the forest itself still appears to be relatively secure, and each, with the possible exception of Ankasa, still retains an almost intact fauna in terms of species composition. If well protected, the three larger parks could be viable ecological units in the long term. A review of some of the information published by R. F. W. Barnes suggests that one West African forest elephant may require a minimum of about 4 square kilometers of habitat, and that a population of at least two hundred is needed to have a high probability of persisting for one hundred years.[52] This indicates a minimum forest park size of 800 square kilometers for an intact fauna, although even in the absence of elephants an African forest can continue to support many other animal species, and possibly most of its original tree species.[53]

Hunting of larger animals, rather than habitat destruction, now appears to be the single biggest threat to the persistence of intact rain-forest ecosystems in West Africa's parks. Large-scale farming encroachment and logging are highly visible activities that can be stopped relatively easily by a small number of officials, if they have the will to do so, but illegal hunting is generally much harder to control. Forest hunters commonly operate on foot, alone, or in small groups, and sometimes at night. Although their access to the forest may be aided by roads, hunters can operate very well on narrow trails and footpaths, and their tools (shotguns and/or wire snares, and lamps) are readily portable. Meat butchered and smoked within the forest can be transported out of the forest without vehicles, and has a very high value per unit weight.

Control of such hunting requires a substantial, well-trained, well-equipped, highly motivated patrol force. In the West African cases I have reviewed, such law enforcement is generally inadequate. Most national and state governments have given a low priority to the protection of forest wildlife, and protection has also been de-emphasized by some of the foreign agencies involved in park conservation. From around 1980, when the "World Conservation Strategy" was published, international conservation organizations have encouraged agricultural and economic development projects focused on rural people as a means of protecting tropical parks.[54] In its most recent guise, "Caring for the Earth," this strategy has stressed the idea of devolving a significant component of management to local communities.[55] I have argued elsewhere that such policies have been adopted largely out of financial and political expediency rather than because rigorous protection efforts have been clearly shown not to work in a tropical context.[56]

These policies have led to tropical conservation being viewed as a form of business, in which money is extracted from large development agencies to be consumed through, among other things, purchasing vehicles, erecting buildings, obtaining salaries and consultancy fees, and undertaking a variety of socioeconomic development activities. Protecting wildlife for ethical or aesthetic reasons is given a low priority; indeed, rigorous policing by armed guards is often discouraged as being contrary to the ideals of community-based conservation. In the West African cases I have reviewed, a recurring theme is an emphasis by externally funded projects on agricultural extension activities and relatively weak protection efforts.

In this context of ineffective antipoaching activities, the forest primate populations that have been best protected are those at research sites such as Tiwai, Afi Mountain, and the primate study areas in Taï. This is the result of the long-term presence on the ground of people with a strong interest in studying and protecting wild animals. This suggests that research stations in forest national parks can play a significant role in conservation. In a large area such as Taï, however, such research efforts may only be effective over a limited area. If policy-makers can be persuaded to place greater emphasis on protection in West African parks, what scale of investment will be required for the effective protection of large areas, and how is this to be paid for?

My experiences at Afi and at Tiwai suggest that approximately one guard per 10 square kilometers is required to maintain basic monitoring of West African forest, although larger parks with relatively smaller perimeters may require a lower guard density. The actual force size depends on local factors, such as the density of the surrounding human population, and factors influencing potential hunting levels, including local demand for bushmeat. A complete cessation of hunting is probably not a realistic goal for a protection force. Instead, as with law enforcement in most places, the goal should be to keep illegal activity at a low level. If special attention is given to guarding the most vulnerable species, this should allow a viable animal community to persist.

Current annual expenditures to protect the 90-square-kilometer Afi

Mountain area are about $20,000; a more effective effort would probably require expenditures of at least $50,000 annually, or about $500 per square kilometer. This suggests a need for over $1 million annually for a large park like Taï, not including occasional large capital costs such as buildings and vehicles. Although such a sum is large by the budgetary standards of Third World countries, it is a relatively small amount from an international perspective. I have already noted that the WWF-sponsored plans for Cross River National Park assumed that it would be possible to raise nearly $50 million in Europe for a seven-year park development project, while a recent proposal from the Nigerian Federal Environmental Protection Agency to the Global Environment Facility (GEF) had a budget of $16 million for five years for three protected areas. Such budgets indicate that adequate sums of money are potentially available from rich countries to pay for the protection of West African forest parks. Money of this kind could best serve the purpose of long-term sustainable conservation if invested in trust funds.[57]

The argument that, even with better funding, the strict protection of tropical parks is impractical (and perhaps immoral) because it conflicts with the legitimate user rights of local people can be countered with the observation that, at least in the case of most of the major West African forest parks and nature reserves, these protected areas were, until recently, located in hinterlands far from human population centers. That is the reason their habitat has survived and why it was possible to establish them in the first place. Most of these forests had few people living in or near them and therefore had suffered relatively little exploitation pressure. Often, they had enjoyed some form of protection for several generations before they became parks, and this protection was understood locally. For instance, a forest reserve was first established in Nigeria's Oban Hills in 1912, and, as I have noted, the Taï Forest first gained a measure of official protection in 1926. Much of the recent pressure on these forests is from recent immigrants who have moved to frontier areas in search of economic opportunity and/or to escape conflicts. These migrants do not have long-term commitments to the areas they are moving to and are likely to be attracted to any economic development opportunities placed there.[58] This is a strong reason to encourage international agencies to place major development projects at a distance from parks—and preferably in or near towns and cities that already have a significant infrastructure—which would both draw people away from conservation areas and better assist national development.[59]

Although I have argued that conservation efforts for tropical parks must place greater emphasis on basic protection and less emphasis on community development projects, I acknowledge the need to involve local people in conservation efforts (the Tiwai project was based on this principle). Protection is much more difficult without the cooperation of people living near the park. However, measures to increase the compliance of local people with park regulations are more appropriately achieved by involving them in activities directly related to conservation efforts than by "bribing" them with inappropriate development schemes. For instance, it is appropriate to give priority to local residents in the hiring of staff for protection, research, and tourism efforts, and to arrange for revenue sharing where real income can be derived from tourism. Help can also appropriately be provided for schooling, particularly if conservation education is included in the curriculum. Some kinds of agricultural development may not be inappropriate if designed to complement ecosystem protection efforts; tree crops and organic production methods may be examples. Attempts to involve local people in conservation efforts must not, however, be seen as a substitute for strong law-enforcement actions to protect park ecosystems.

Finally, it remains true that, as Terborgh has pointed out, the pervasiveness of corruption and the general lack of enforcement of existing laws in West African countries will mitigate the effectiveness of stronger protection as a park conservation policy.[60] Conservationists therefore need to give their support, where practical, to those working to improve civil society in this region; already, the Nigerian branch of the Pro Natura organization has been able to combine conservation efforts with support to human rights organizations.[61] Fundamental sociocultural change will not come about quickly, however, and while we may hope for long-term improvements in the rule of law, in the short term nongovernmental organizations and scientists may be most effective in conservation if they concentrate their attention and resources on key parts of protected areas (or key species), and work with park authorities to hold the line in these places until such time as the overall climate for conservation improves.

Conclusions

Clear patterns emerge from the above analysis of conservation efforts in a sample of parks and protected areas in West Africa and are summarized as follows:

• Strategies emphasizing socioeconomic development activities as necessary to achieve conservation objectives have consistently failed. In this context, the disproportionate emphasis on development activities by conservation development projects has been routinely associated with increased intensity of threats, such as poaching and logging, due to the low priority afforded by such projects to the protection of wildlife.

• Locating major development projects away from parks and in existing urban areas will not only reduce conflicts in conservation areas but may also help achieve long-term development goals. Moreover, the direct involvement of local communities in conservation activities, by serving as research assistants, patrol guards, and the like, offers a more effective means of gaining local support for conservation compared to the false promises of prosperity associated with unsustainable development initiatives.

• Modestly funded research stations in parks and sanctuaries have played an important role in protecting limited areas from illegal activities. At larger scales, political backing is essential if priority is to be given to wildlife protection through law enforcement, but this is predictably lacking in war-torn countries. However, the investment necessary to protect West African parks through simple but effective protection measures such as patrolling and boundary demarcation is reasonable compared to the generous budgets of internationally funded conservation development projects.

Acknowledgments

I thank John Terborgh and Carel van Schaik for inviting me to the stimulating workshop at the White Oak Plantation that led to this contribution. Carel van Schaik, Madhu Rao, Thomas Struhsaker, and an anonymous reviewer made constructive comments on a draft of the chapter, and Johannes Refisch provided me with valuable information on Taï National Park.

Notes

1. J. Terborgh, *Requiem for Nature* (Washington, D.C.: Island Press, 1999).

2. J. F. Oates, *Myth and Reality in the Rain Forest: How Conservation Strategies Are Failing in West Africa* (Berkeley: University of California Press, 1999).

3. R. J. Harrison Church, *West Africa: A Study of the Environment and of Man's Use of It*, 8th ed. (London: Longman, 1980).

4. A. H. Booth, "The Zoogeography of West African Primates: A Review," *Bulletin de l'I.F.A.N.* 20, Sér. A (1958); J. F. Oates, "The Distribution of *Cercopithecus* Monkeys in West African Forests," in *A Primate Radiation: Evolutionary Biology of the African Guenons*, ed. A. Gautier-Hion, F. Bourlière, J.-P. Gautier, and J. Kingdon (Cambridge: Cambridge University Press, 1988).

5. F. White, *Vegetation Map of Africa* (Paris: UNESCO, 1981).

6. World Bank, *African Development Indicators 2000* (Washington, D.C.: World Bank, 2000).

7. United Nations Secretariat, *The World at Six Billion* (New York: Population Division, United Nations Department of Economic and Social Affairs, 1999).

8. C. Martin, *The Rainforests of West Africa: Ecology-Threats-Conservation* (Basel, Switzerland: Birkhäuser, 1991).

9. J. Fairhead and M. Leach, "Reconsidering the Extent of Deforestation in Twentieth Century West Africa," *Unasylva* 49 (1998).

10. P. W. Richards, *The Tropical Rain Forest: An Ecological Study* (Cambridge: Cambridge University Press, 1952), 29.

11. Oates, *Myth and Reality*.

12. T. Garnett in letter to M. Bakarr, personal communication.

13. A. G. Davies, *The Gola Forest Reserves, Sierra Leone: Wildlife Conservation and Forest Management* (Gland, Switzerland: IUCN [The World Conservation Union], 1987).

14. J. A. Sayer, C. S. Harcourt, and N. M. Collins, eds, *The Conservation Atlas of Tropical Forests: Africa* (Basingstoke: Macmillan, 1992), 12–13.

15. J. Verschuren, "Hope for Liberia," *Oryx* 16 (1982).

16. J. Mayers, "Liberia," in Sayer et al., *Conservation Atlas*.

17. Anonymous, "Liberia's Forests on the Block?" *Oryx* 34 (2000).

18. P. T. Robinson, "Update on Status of Sapo National Park, Liberia: Press Release from the Society for the Renewal of Nature Conservation in Liberia" (Temecula, Calif.: SRNCL, 1994).

19. Anonymous, "Liberia's Forests."

20. M. Appleton and J. Morris, "Conservation in a Conflict Area: Illegal Logging and the Re-emergence of the Conservation Movement in Liberia," *Oryx* 31 (1997); Anonymous, "Liberia's Forests."

21. R. Wilson, "Guinea," in Sayer et al., *Conservation Atlas*.

22. R. Ham, personal communication.

23. Wilson, "Guinea."

24. D. Brugière and E. Raballand, personal communications.

25. Gillis, 1998, quoted in Vooren, "Côte d'Ivoire," in J. A. Sayer, C. S. Harcourt, and N. M. Collins, eds., *The Conservation Atlas of Tropical Forests: Africa* (Basingstoke, England: MacMillan, 1992) 133–142.

26. Martin, *Rainforests*; E. P. Riezebos, A. P. Vooren, and J. L. Guillamet, eds., *Le Parc National de Taï, Côte d'Ivoire. Synthese des Connaissances* (Wageningen, Netherlands: Tropenbos Foundation, 1994).

27. Martin, *Rainforests*.

28. Sayer et al., *Conservation Atlas*; E. P. Riezebos, A. P. Vooren, and J. L. Guillamet, eds., *Le Parc National de Taï, Côte d'Ivoire. Synthese des Connaissances* (Wageningen, Netherlands: Tropenbos Foundation, 1994).

29. J. Refisch, personal communication.

30. J. Refisch and S. Shultz, personal communication.

31. D. Gordon, "Ghana," in Sayer et al., *Conservation Atlas*.

32. S. Jeffrey, "Ghana's Forest Wildlife in Danger," *Oryx* 10 (1970).

33. D. Kpelle and S. Moses, in letter to T. Struhsaker, personal communication.

34. M. Sam, personal communication.

35. J. F. Oates et al., "Extinction of a West African Red Colobus Monkey," *Conservation Biology* 14: 1526–1532 (2000).

36. White, *Vegetation Map*.

37. J. F. Oates, *African Primates: Status Survey and Conservation Action Plan* (Gland, Switzerland: IUCN, 1996); J. Kamstra, personal communication.

38. R. Matsuda, personal communication.

39. World Bank, *Development Indicators*.

40. P. A. Anadu and J. F. Oates, *The Status of Wildlife in Bendel State, Nigeria, with Recommendations for Its Conservation: Unpublished Report to the Bendel State Ministry of Agriculture and Natural Resources* (New York: Hunter College, 1982).

41. J. F. Oates, "The Dangers of Conservation by Rural Development: A Case Study from the Forests of Nigeria," *Oryx* 29 (1995).

42. Oates, *Myth and Reality*.

43. E. L. Gadsby, "The Status and Distribution of the Drill, *Mandrillus leucophaeus*, in Nigeria. Report to WCI and WWF," (1990); Oates, *African Primates*; Oates, "Distribution of *Cercopithecus* Monkeys."

44. T. B. Larsen, *Butterfly Research in the Oban Hills, Cross River National Park* (Calabar, Nigeria: WWF/CRNP Oban Hills Programme, 1995).

45. G. A. Petrides, *Advisory Report on Wildlife and National Parks in Nigeria, 1962.* Special Publication No. 18 (Bronx, N.Y.: American Committee for International Wildlife Protection, 1965).

46. Oates, *Myth and Reality*.

47. J. O. Caldecott, J. G. Bennett, and H. J. Ruitenbeek, *Cross River National Park (Oban Division): Plan for Developing the Park and Its Support Zone* (Godalming, England: World Wide Fund For Nature, United Kingdom, 1989); J. O. Caldecott, J. F. Oates, and H. J. Ruitenbeek, *Cross River National Park (Okwangwo Division): Plan for*

Developing the Park and Its Support Zone (Godalming, England: World Wide Fund For Nature, United Kingdom, 1990).

48. Oates, *Myth and Reality*.

49. K. McFarland, "Gorilla Killed in Cross River State, Nigeria," *Gorilla Journal* 17 (1998).

50. J. Suter and J. F. Oates, "Sanctuary in Nigeria for Possible Fourth Subspecies of Gorilla," *Oryx* 34 (2000).

51. R. A. Mittermeier, N. Myers, and C. G. Mittermeier, *Hotspots: Earth's Biologically Richest and Most Endangered Terrestrial Ecoregions* (Mexico City: Cemex, 1999).

52. R. F. W. Barnes, "Is There a Future for Elephants in West Africa?" *Mammal Review* 29 (1999).

53. W. Hawthorne and M. P. E. Parren, "How Important Are Forest Elephants to the Survival of Woody Plant Species in Upper Guinean Forests?" *Journal of Tropical Ecology* 16 (2000).

54. IUCN, UNEP, and WWF (The World Conservation Union, United Nations Environmental Programme, and World Wildlife Fund, *World Conservation Strategy: Living Resources for Sustainable Development* (Gland, Switzerland: IUCN, UNEP, and WWF, 1980).

55. IUCN, UNEP, and WWF, *Caring for the Earth: A Strategy for Sustainable Living* (Gland, Switzerland: IUCN, UNEP, and WWF, 1991).

56. Oates, *Myth and Reality*.

57. R. A. Kramer and N. Sharma, "Tropical Forest Biodiversity Protection: Who Pays and Why," in *Last Stand: Protected Areas and the Defense of Tropical Biodiversity* ed. R. A. Kramer, C. P. van Schaik, and J. Johnson (New York: Oxford University Press, 1997); M. Wells, *Trust Funds and Endowments as a Biodiversity Conservation Tool*, Divisional Working Paper No. 1991-26 (Washington, D.C.: Environmental Policy and Research Division, the World Bank, 1991).

58. A. J. Noss, "Challenges to Nature Conservation with Community Development in Central African Forests," *Oryx* 31 (1997); Oates, "Dangers of Conservation."

59. C. P. van Schaik and R. A. Kramer, "Toward a New Protection Paradigm," in Kramer et al., *Last Stand*; T. Trefon, personal communication.

60. Terborgh, *Requiem*.

61. Philip Hall, personal communication.

6

Parks in the Congo Basin: Can Conservation and Development Be Reconciled?

CAROLINE E. G. TUTIN

The Congo Basin of west equatorial Africa contains the world's second largest area of tropical forest: about 2 million square kilometers in the Democratic Republic of Congo (DRC), Congo, Gabon, Equatorial Guinea, Cameroon, and the Central African Republic (CAR). Tropical forest is the dominant vegetation in Congo, Equatorial Guinea, Gabon, and DRC, while in Cameroon and CAR evergreen forest occupies less space than drier habitats. These vast central African forests are among the least well-known habitats on Earth in terms of biological and ecological understanding. The multitude of endemic plant and animal species makes them a high priority for the preservation of biological diversity.[1] In addition, the forests play important roles in climate regulation and nutrient cycling at national, regional, and global levels.

Throughout the region, human population density is generally low, ethnic diversity high, and economies are based on the export of raw materials. Threats to biodiversity are increasing but remain low compared to most of the tropics. Major threats to the integrity of the Congo Basin forests come from hunting and logging. These two activities are often linked because logging activities create infrastructure that facilitates access for hunters and the export of meat toward urban centers.[2] Other threats are significant in some localities and include large-scale movements of people displaced by civil wars, invasions by exotic species, pollution of water by mining operations, and unsustainable harvesting of medicinal plants.

Protected areas (hereafter parks) are essential cornerstones for biodiversity protection. Analysis of their effectiveness provides an indication of the overall state of attitudes and activities in the broader domain of environmental policies. This chapter provides a brief overview of the status of parks in the forested parts of the Congo Basin region and identifies the obstacles they face within the socioeconomic context. Given that large areas of intact habitat remain and that threats and conflicts are not yet intense, it should be easier to establish and manage an effective network of parks here than in other parts of the tropics. Conditions certainly vary between countries and between localities within the region, but much of the analysis of the threats to parks and how to make them "work" is broadly applicable. However, eastern DRC (formerly Zaire) is an exception because it differs historically (its national parks have been in existence longer), biologically (it harbors many unique species and habitats), and politically (its civil wars have had a lasting impact; see chapter 7).

Parks exist in all six countries, covering from 4 to 12 percent of national territory. Ecological representation is not complete but it is possible to move toward this goal by creating new parks with unique biodiversity at well-chosen sites in each country.[3] Many of the existing parks are large (2,000–13,000 square kilometers) and sparsely populated, but a minority, notably in Cameroon, have concentrations of villages both inside and around the borders.

The arrival of large-scale funding for conservation activities in the Congo Basin is a recent phenomenon. In response to the increasing awareness of the global importance of tropical forests, "green" aid (i.e., donations and loans from the international donor community linked to environmental protection) began to flow into the region a little over a decade ago. The region's parks have benefited, and externally funded integrated conservation and development projects (ICDPs) are being implemented in most of them. The dawning of the era of "green aid" and the recognition of the global importance of the Congo Basin forests coincided with a period of economic recession in the region after a decade of "boom" years with high export earnings from oil and minerals. External economic factors influence profit margins in the field of natural resource development, and the logging sector has expanded significantly since the 1994 devaluation of the local currency (the CFA franc) shared by Cameroon, CAR, Congo, and Gabon. Timber differs from oil and minerals in that it is a renewable resource; the potential of the forests of the Congo Basin for sustainable economic and social development based on harvesting timber is enormous. Introducing ecologically sustainable forest management to production forests and effective management of parks are linked challenges that underline the need to reconcile exploitation and conservation.

Obstacles to Making Parks Work in the Congo Basin

Parks in the Congo Basin face many of the same hurdles as those in other tropical regions: insufficient funds and lack of trained management staff; scanty information about the flora and fauna; absence of functioning management plans; and conflictual relations with local populations. Direct threats such as large-scale poaching or encroachment within the region's parks do not yet exceed levels that can be controlled by conventional law enforcement strategies. Outside parks, notably in timber production forests, commercial bushmeat hunting and increasing traffic in ivory pose serious threats to the survival of large mammals. Conservation projects are under way in most of the region's parks and have adopted approaches that take into account the needs of local rural communities. The precise activities undertaken depend on local conditions, and major conflicts of interest are often resolved through zoning systems such that most parks include a strictly protected core area surrounded by or in juxtaposition to areas where controlled extractive use of resources by local populations is allowed.

On one level, parks seem to be working well. Despite the general absence of rigorous ecological monitoring systems (see chapter 28), the large size of many parks combined with generally low levels of hunting within them suggests that viable populations of most species will persist if direct threats do not increase. However, there are growing indications that serious indirect threats to parks exist. These threats emanate from a prevailing attitude that condones exploitation of forests. The unexpected perverse effects of attempts to reconcile conservation and development by integration at the local level have not helped to remedy this misunderstanding.

Within the region, there is no clear understanding of the role and importance of parks because the threats to biodiversity are not immediately visible. The sheer scale of the forests and the poor infrastructure mean that vast tracts of land have until recently been protected "naturally" due to their inaccessibility.[4] Deforestation rates are less than 1 percent per annum because demand for agricultural land is low given the generally low population density and the fact that export earnings have been used to pay for imported food.

Historical factors undoubtedly influence people's attitudes toward the forests. The Bantu, who make up the vast majority of present-day population, originated from savanna-dominated environments and moved into the Congo Basin starting about 5,000 years ago during periods of climate change that fragmented the major forest block.[5] The successive waves of Bantu migrations brought agriculture and iron technology to the region.[6] Exotic plants introduced long ago (e.g., bananas from Southeast Asia about 2,500 years ago), or more recently (manioc from the neotropics in the seventeenth century), are now staple foods. Few exclusive hunter-gatherer societies exist, as the Pygmy groups of the region have long-standing relationships with Bantu groups based on exchange of bushmeat for manioc and bananas. Since independence, cities in all of the countries have undergone rapid expansion. For example, 73 percent of the population of Gabon (1.1 million in 2,667,000 square kilometers) now live in towns, compared to 40 percent in 1960. Governments have been elected following democratic principles, but civil unrest and/or outright war have affected three countries (CAR, DRC, and Congo) in the past decade, bringing social and economic chaos that continues in parts of both of the Congos. Environmental problems are visible in the ever-expanding cities, and local environmental NGOs (nongovernmental organizations) are primarily concerned with pressing urban issues such as pollution, inadequate living conditions, health care, and nutrition.

However, all rural communities depend heavily on the forest for animal foods, for plants used as food and medicine, and for building material and cultural activities. Recently arrived city dwellers retain strong cultural links to their rural roots as witnessed by thriving commerce in wild plant and animal foods in urban markets. The belief that the forest will supply endless quantities of useful plants and animals is widespread and deep-rooted. Thus, there is no appreciation of a need for parks. Indeed, parks often have a negative image because they are perceived as depriving local communities of economic development and repressing traditional systems of free access.

This problem is exacerbated locally in some parts of the region by the migration of additional people to settlements within or adjacent to parks. As activities of ICDPs create opportunities for employment or improved livelihood, parks become poles of attraction to economic refugees. Much thought has been given about ways to integrate local populations into park management such that the park becomes a positive and lasting part of the local social and economic scene. Given the transitional nature of rural society in the region, it is difficult to find a working definition of "local." A system of fair sharing of benefits requires that there are sustainable benefits to share. This is not yet the case, since none of the region's parks are financially self-supporting. In addition, the prevailing social and cultural conditions favor maximizing short-term benefits rather than long-term investment in the arena of natural resource use.[7]

The immediate challenge is to make the concept of parks relevant to the citizens of the Congo Basin. Parks will not "work" unless the need for them is more widely understood by politicians and civil society. These are developing countries suffering from additional burdens of economic recession and wars. For their citizens, health, nutrition, employment, and education are immediate, pressing needs. At present, environmental concerns in general and parks in particular remain outsiders' business ("l'affaire des blancs"). This is a massive challenge, and a web of coordinated action is necessary, requiring years if not decades of sustained effort. Training and awareness campaigns are essential to promote understanding and support at all levels. There will be no "quick results," since existing curricula in schools and universities of the region are inadequate, leaving gaps that cannot be filled by crash courses or high-level studies. Institutional reforms and decentralization that will give the degree of autonomy and responsibility necessary for good stewardship of parks is another major and long-term challenge.

The other major indirect threat is a growing belief among politicians that sustainable management of forests reduces the need for parks, or even makes them redundant. Logging is highly selective with only one to three trees felled per hectare compared to twenty or more in other tropical regions,[8] but in the next decade logging will continue to spread. By 2010, it is likely that only 5 to 10 percent of the Congo Basin forests will not have been logged at least once.[9] Logging concessions exist in many of the region's parks and a recent law in Congo opened up a newly created national park to commercial logging. This literal application of the "use it or lose it" paradigm means that the area of forest in the region that is strictly protected is diminishing. More and more politicians and technicians argue that strict protection is an old-fashioned and outdated conservation tool. This new vision is apparent in policy documents such as national environmental action plans being produced by the countries with Global Environment Facility (GEF) funding. This is the biggest threat now facing forested parks in the region.

The timber industry is a key element of economic and social development, and the need to find sustainable ways to harvest timber is now recognized by governments, donor organizations, and the private sector. Considerable investment is being made in the field of sustainable forest management (SFM) by foreign aid agencies, forestry researchers, and some private companies. Recently, management goals in production forests have expanded to take account of the whole forest ecosystem and not just the valuable timber species. Media exposure of the direct and indirect links between logging and commercial bushmeat hunting has increased external pressure on the countries of the region to minimize this negative impact of logging operations. The will to achieve SFM exists but lack of knowledge and experience mean that methods to achieve ecological sustainability remain experimental.

Possible Solutions

The biological and cultural importance of parks appears esoteric in the eyes of both villagers and politicians, but arguments of more immediate relevance to the preoccupations of the Congo Basin countries do exist. There are two complementary ways to put the environment on the agenda. One is to argue that the global importance of the Congo Basin forests is so great that the international community must continue to pay the direct and indirect ("opportunity") costs of protecting them. The other is to construct clear arguments for the value of these ecosystems and the need to protect a representative sample within national parks, based on local social and economic realities.

These approaches can be promoted in complementary ways. Finding a mechanism for durable funding of parks is a goal that is being investigated by a number of people and institutions.[10] It is not feasible in the foreseeable future to aim at levels of on-site income generation that will be both sustainable and sufficient. Ecotourism can be a significant source of revenue, but there are costs as well as benefits and, as recent events in Rwanda and Uganda have shown, tourism is vulnerable. Few parks in the region can offer the combination of factors (reliable viewing of charismatic species, relatively easy access, and secure and comfortable living conditions) required to raise large revenues from tourism,[11] although small-scale ecotourism can make a significant impact locally. For parks in the Congo Basin, it is not realistic to expect national governments to bear all of the direct and indirect costs. The opportunity costs of maintaining forest parks, as opposed to logging them, are extremely high. For Cameroon, revenue lost to the government through not allowing logging in parks is estimated at \$15,000 per square kilometer per year.[12] Trust funds appear to be a promising solution for sustainable funding of the recurrent costs of protected area management, but who will produce the funds and who will manage them? The sums of money that have been invested in conservation and sustainable development are large, probably exceeding $200 million for the Congo Basin over the past decade, but much more will be needed to cover all direct and indirect costs. There are indications that some donors are increasingly willing to establish trust funds, and there is potential for significant funds from mechanisms such as the GEF. The private sector could become more directly involved through initiatives such as "carbon credits" and through biodiversity prospecting.

Within the region, efforts must be made to pass clear messages about why parks are important and how they fit into the broader scheme of social and economic development. For the foreseeable future, countries of the region will depend on the exploitation of natural resources as the mainstay of their economies. In the case of renewable natural resources, timber is the main product. Political will exists for the goal of sustainable forest management, but it is important to accept that the logging industry, local populations, and politicians all see biodiversity from an economic perspective. There is a pressing need to establish working partnerships between conservationists and the timber industry. Biodiversity issues have been marginalized and trivialized by the industry in the past, but this is beginning to change. Present understanding of the functioning of tropical forest ecosystems is incomplete, making it difficult for biologists to define sustainable harvesting methodologies. Research is a priority and should continue, but can we afford to wait for the results before defining recipes for SFM? Parks have not been integrated into SFM, but they have an integral role to play at a landscape level (i.e., countrywide or, better still, regionwide). Put simply, management of the region's forests for extractive use (timber in this case, but the same principles apply to hunting or use of nontimber forest products) is "experimental," and, as we do not yet have all the necessary data to feed into predictive models, we must insist on "controls." Parks are these controls.

Parks are the only proven way to protect ecosystems, but they have come under attack from the utilitarian philosophies of having to "pay their way" or "earn their living." This led to attempts to integrate conservation and development locally through ICDPs in parks. Ten years later, it is clear that attempts to integrate these two objectives at the same site are faltering. Retrospective analyses of the reasons for the failure underline the inherent conflicts between biological and economic perspectives on use of renewable natural resources. For local populations and the private sector, as well as the hard-pressed governments of the region, the economic perspective is paramount. If integration between conservation and development is to be achieved, it will not be at the level of single sites but at a higher level where different sites with different land-use designations (agriculture, timber production, or conservation of biodiversity) are linked in explicit partnerships. Parks will thus become useful and valued by all sectors of society. As reservoirs of species, populations, and genes, parks are equivalent to insurance policies. In addition, if they are sufficiently large and ecologically representative, the ecosystems within parks will continue to provide essential free services to local, national, and global communities. The trend in the Congo Basin countries to allow ever-increasing extractive use of resources within parks compromises their ability to fulfill these roles and weakens the region's potential to achieve sustainable social and economic development.

Conclusions

The large size of many parks in the Congo Basin of western equatorial Africa combined with generally low levels of direct threats such as hunting, agricultural encroachment, and the like indicate high potential for effective long-term biodiversity conservation. However, serious indirect threats exacerbated by the current socioeconomic status of the region and by unexpected perverse effects of attempts to reconcile conservation and development are of increasing concern.

The obstacles to making parks work and to potential solutions can be broadly classified into five categories:

1. The lack of appreciation of the need for strictly protected parks by politicians and civil society makes them a very low priority. Parks are largely perceived as depriving local communities of economic development and repressing traditional systems of free access. The immediate challenge therefore is to promote the concept of parks through training and awareness campaigns at all levels.

2. Parks in the Congo Basin face management problems similar to those faced by other tropical regions: lack of trained management staff, lack of functioning management plans, lack of relevant biological information, and insufficient financial resources. Long-term, sustainable financing mechanisms such as trust funds and carbon credits need to be carefully negotiated with international donor agencies and appropriately implemented.

3. The opportunity costs of maintaining forested parks are much too high for national governments with pressing economic concerns to bear on their own. It is therefore essential for the international conservation community to share the responsibility of maintaining parks in the region.

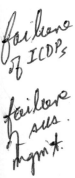

failure of ICDP's

4. Integrated conservation development projects create opportunities for employment and improved livelihoods, thereby serving as focal points for the migration of economic refugees. Inherent conflicts between biological and economic perspectives on use of renewable resources has consistently led to the failure of such projects.

failure sus. mgmt.

5. The growing belief among politicians that sustainable management of forests reduces the need for parks is by and large the most serious threat faced by parks in the region and is exemplified by an increasing number of timber concessions within parks. Although there is undoubtedly a pressing need to establish working partnerships between conservation and the timber industry, it is important to recognize the experimental nature of sustainable management and to consequently set aside large parks to serve as "controls."

Notes

1. R. A. Mittermeier, N. Myers, J. B. Thomsen, and G. A. B. de Fonseca, "Biodiversity Hotspots and Major Tropical Wilderness Areas: Approaches to Setting Conservation Priorities," *Conservation Biology* 12 (1998): 516–532; D. Olson and E. Dinerstein, "The Global 200: A Representation Approach to Conserving the Earth's Most Biologically Valuable Regions," *Conservation Biology* 12 (1998): 502–515.

2. E. Bowen-Jones and S. Pendry, "The Threats to Primates and Other Mammals from the Bushmeat Trade in Africa, and How This Could Be Diminished," *Oryx* 33 (1999): 233–246; D. S. Wilkie and J. F. Carpenter, "Bushmeat Hunting in the Congo Basin: An Assessment of Impact and Options for Mitigation," *Biodiversity and Conservation* 8 (1999): 927–955.

3. IUCN (The World Conservation Organization), *La Conservation des Ecosystèmes Forestiers d'Afrique Centrale* (Gland, Switzerland: IUCN, 1989).

4. T. O. McShane, "Conservation before the Crisis—An Opportunity in Gabon," *Oryx* 24 (1990): 9–14; C. E. G. Tutin and M. Fernandez, "Gabon: A Fragile Sanctuary," *Primate Conservation* 8 (1987): 160–161.

5. P. De Maret, "Pits, Pots, and the Far West Streams," in *The Growth of Farming Communities in Africa from the Equator Southwards*, ed. J. G. Sutton (London: The British Institute in Eastern Africa, 1996); J. Maley, "The Climatic and Vegetational History of Equatorial Regions of Africa during the Upper Quaternary," in *The Archaeology of Africa: Foods, Metals and Towns*, One World Archaeology, vol. 20, ed. T.

Shaw, P. Sinclair, B. Andah, and A. Okpoko (London: Routledge, 1993); J. Vansina, *Paths in the Rainforests: Towards a History of Political Tradition in Equatorial Africa* (London: James Currey, 1990).

6. Shaw et al., *Archaeology of Africa*.

7. S. Gartlan, "Every Man for Himself and God against All: History, Social Science, and the Conservation of Nature," in *Resource Use in the Trinational Sangha River Region of Equatorial Africa: Histories, Knowledge Forms and Institutions*, ed. H. E. Eves, R. Hardin, and S. Rupp, Bulletin Series of the Yale School of Forestry and Environmental Studies, no. 102 (New Haven: Yale University Press, 1998), 216–226; E. Ostrom, *Governing the Commons: The Evolution of Institutions for Collective Action* (Cambridge: Cambridge University Press, 1990).

8. L. J. T. White, "The Effects of Commercial Mechanised Logging on Forest Structure and Composition on a Transect in the Lopé Reserve, Gabon," *Journal of Tropical Ecology* 10 (1994): 309–318.

9. Global Forest Watch, *An Overview of Logging in Cameroon* (Washington, D.C.: World Resources Institute, 1999).

10. D. S. Wilkie and J. Carpenter, "Can Nature Tourism Help Finance Protected Areas in the Congo Basin?" *Oryx* 33 (1999): 332–338; D. S. Wilkie and J. Carpenter, "The Potential Role of Safari Hunting as a Source of Revenue for Protected Areas in the Congo Basin," *Oryx* 33 (1999): 339–345.

11. Wilkie and Carpenter, "Nature Tourism."

12. D. S. Wilkie, personal communication.

7

Conservation in Anarchy: Key Conditions for Successful Conservation of the Okapi Faunal Reserve

TERESE HART

This chapter provides an analysis of conservation activities in the war-torn eastern part of the Congo Basin in the Democratic Republic of Congo, formerly known as Zaire. I trace the plight of conservation before, during, and after the debilitating civil war that has ravaged this region of the Congo since 1996 in order to identify key factors influencing conservation during continuing war and anarchy. The region contains four national parks (Garamba, Maiko, Virunga, and Kahuzi-Biega) and a faunal reserve (Okapi Faunal Reserve). Four of these protected areas are World Heritage Sites and, at present, all five of them are within rebel-held territory.

The Prewar Situation
Conservation as a Low National Priority

Long before the war, during the long regime of Mobutu Sese Seko (1965 to 1997), Zaire's parks suffered from what resembled wartime rationing. During that period, as Zaire slid from poverty to destitution, the national parks institution suffered from two crippling deficiencies: lack of communication and lack of financial remuneration to its staff.

The central office of the Parks Authority was located in the capital, Kinshasa, in the far west of a country as large as the United States east of the Mississippi River. The meager infrastructure Zaire inherited from its colonial past slowly deteriorated, and with it communication between far-flung parks and the central administration also fell apart. There was no telephone service and no postal service to outlying areas. Even before the current war divided the country into eastern and western sectors, there

86

was no easy way to travel between Kinshasa in the west and the parks in the east. With no connecting roads or railroads, air travel offered the only option but was too expensive for personnel of the central Parks Authority (currently the Institut Congolais pour la Conservation de la Nature [ICCN]). Even from the nearest airstrip, reaching four of the five eastern protected areas required more than a hundred additional kilometers to be negotiated by land or private plane. Having negligible operating budgets, the core officials working out of the central office never visited most of the parks in their jurisdictions. To appraise the work of foreign conservation organizations (usually NGOs [nongovernmental organizations]) working in a park, the central office was dependent on the NGO itself to finance an evaluation trip. Even radio communication was lacking from a number of parks, including Okapi Faunal Reserve, when I first arrived in the early 1980s. The radio subsequently obtained for Okapi was purchased by an international NGO.

Lack of adequate or regular salary support compelled park personnel to live off the land. Even in times of peace, this practice led to steady declines of large mammals within African parks: scores of rhinos were poached in Garamba National Park for their horns; dozens of elephants from Okapi were lost to the ivory trade; truckloads of game meat were shipped to markets in larger towns. In effect, the parks served as the fiefdoms of the local park authorities and other government officials.

This large-scale poaching was carried out by high-level functionaries. The guards also used their positions to supplement salaries of only several dollars per month, which often came months late. In the past, Okapi guards set traps for game meat and levied a meat tax on the traditional BaMbuti (pygmy) hunters, leaving it unclear whether the BaMbuti's hunting was legal or illegal. A park guard's family relied on these and other similar income-generating activities. Even today, nearly every park guard depends on a family garden. In Okapi, where zones are still not clearly defined, the guards claim mature forest to clear for gardens.

International Conservation Aid Fills the Breach

Because park connections to the national government had been tenuous for years, the impact of their further isolation from the capital as a result of the outbreak of violence in late 1996 was minimal. Most of these protected areas had already long depended on outside aid donated by international conservation NGOs, although less fortunate parks, such as Maiko, received no aid and thus had almost no functional infrastructure;

its staff was obliged to wrest a living from the park. The protected areas that did have NGO support were those designated as World Heritage Sites. They adopted the priorities of their sponsors and accepted their infrastructure and training. By depending on an international conservation group's agenda, a park might primarily invest in improvement of a park's surveillance, develop a tourism industry, or concentrate on research and training.

Acknowledging its heavy reliance on outside sources of financing, the central park administration office in Kinshasa did little to regulate NGO inputs or to coordinate different groups. In turn, the lack of direction from a central authority left international donors free to determine park needs according to their own views and priorities. Some creative and potentially positive actions were taken locally. These included improving financial accountability, establishing internal park management committees, training guards and administrators, improving surveillance and monitoring techniques, and establishing a variety of community outreach programs. Together these small innovations resulted in higher work standards and a more professional staff. But innovations, like monetary inputs, remained local. Although they improved a given park at a given time, they did not improve the system as a whole.

In addition, conflicts between protected areas and nearby communities had to be resolved locally because the national government usually lacked the necessary information and financial resources to become involved. This too became the concern of international donors, and the actions they took to resolve conflicts usually varied from park to park. For instance, population pressure was most intense in the southern two protected areas (one with mountain gorillas and one with western lowland gorillas). International organizations active in these parks consequently promoted environmental education or attempted to improve living conditions for rural residents. In the northern two World Heritage Sites (one entirely forested with okapi, rain forest giraffe, the other largely savanna with northern white rhino), local human populations did not pose such immediate threats, so the NGOs operating in them invested less in community outreach.

Lack of direction from a central authority was especially detrimental to community outreach projects, although the more traditional conservation projects that focused on enhancing local park authority fared better. The relationship between community outreach and conservation was not always clear, with the result that proposed community projects were often evaluated on the basis of development feasibility with little or no thought to the possible consequences for conservation goals. For example, an NGO might build a school or a dispensary without considering whether the conservation impact would be positive or negative. Although there are examples of entire towns springing up from tiny forest villages where missionaries had established hospital/school complexes (for instance, Oicha and Mandima on the borders of the Okapi Faunal Reserve), such consequences are often not taken into account when community conservation projects are planned. In another example, visiting World Bank officials made casual promises to communities near the proposed Okapi Faunal Reserve regarding a possible community project that would benefit them. Unfortunately, the project was never funded, but the communities involved were convinced that the establishment of the Okapi Faunal Reserve was contingent on those promises and thus that the NGOs operating in the reserve must honor them. In this case, such miscommunications meant that local acceptance of the new reserve was seriously compromised.

Given the ineffectiveness of government authorities, international conservation organizations played a vital—though imperfect—role in the administration of the national park system. Although their financial and administrative contributions were imperative to the existence of the park system, these organizations still failed to foster a sense of unity between parks. Whereas the government had a patriotic basis for its goal setting and evaluations, foreign organizations set their goals in a kind of vacuum, without the benefit of local perspective and without the ability to factor in the contributions of other organizations.

A government agency operates with an assumption of permanence, whereas international aid organizations move from one temporary project to another. If local conditions made the execution of a project more difficult than anticipated, an organization might decide that it could meet its larger goals less expensively and less ambiguously by simply moving to another country. Without the backing of a national institution, support for a given park had no guarantee beyond the one- or two-year term of the current contract. These projects were often associated with NGO policies, such as development of tourism or involvement of local communities, which were not linked to a given protected area or country. Even a theme such as "rescue the gorillas" spanned several countries and emphasis could therefore be moved from one nation to another in accordance with central office priorities.

In summary, the international conservation organizations had the short-term advantages of not being crippled by government inertia, fat bureaucracies, and thin technical capacity. However, over a longer time horizon, they were severely limited by their concentration on "theme" projects and by a lack of site commitment. Their short-term outlook dispelled any incentive to integrate their efforts with those of similar organizations in neighboring sites. Nevertheless, imperfect as they were, the international aid organizations are what made conservation possible in a disintegrating Zaire.

The War
Development

For conservation, disintegration began well before the war of 1996. The political and economic situation declined precipitously in the early 1990s, and Zaire's ability to request aid diminished with the implication of the Mobutu government in a student massacre in the southeast. With the end of the Cold War, political support for aid dwindled in the West. Most bilateral organizations involved in conservation pulled out. The European Union completely withdrew a large conservation and development project from Virunga National Park. ECOFAC, the Union's environmental arm in central Africa, withdrew its support of the western park, Salonga. Many NGOs reduced their presence. The World Wildlife Fund, for example, withdrew from Okapi and reduced its activities in Virunga. As support dwindled, the challenges mounted. Refugee camps, harboring over a million Rwandan refugees needing firewood and craving game meat, perched on the very borders of Virunga and Kahuzi-Biega.

The deteriorating sociopolitical climate of Zaire in the mid-1990s severely compromised the ability of NGOs to work effectively. Many pulled out, but a few committed organizations remained. Those that stayed found it increasingly difficult to raise funds, but, nevertheless, as the war spread they provided the sole support to many parks, albeit in a fractured manner. Decisions to persevere in the face of adversity were mostly those of individuals within organizations rather than the organizations themselves. The key factor was the presence of one or more dedicated expatriates working in close collaboration with one or more dedicated Congolese. In short, it was individual commitment that led to NGO commitment.

Despite such adverse circumstances, a conservation ethic was nevertheless established in some parks before civil war broke out. Most commonly, it occurred in parks where the presence of international conservation groups ensured adequate funding for salaries, operating budgets, and training. Before the war, the official salary of park workers was supplemented through bonuses so that they did not have to live illegally off park resources. In addition, health conditions were improved, operating funds were provided, and the professionalism of park officials was encouraged through travel and conferences. In order to continue their professional behavior under the risks and challenges of war, the park staff had to believe that the international conservation organization would continue its aid.

The Immediate Impact

All four World Heritage Sites of eastern Democratic Republic of Congo: Garamba, Virunga, Okapi, and Kahuzi-Biega, were struck by the war at the end of 1996 or early 1997.

Open war broke out when the Walinda Amani swept through the refugee camps during the equinoctial rains of October 1996. The Maji-maji, the Walinda Amani, and the Allied Democratic Forces were separate groups united as an opposition force that eventually recognized Kabila as their leader. They fought north and west, pushing the Interahamwe, troops from the deposed Rwandan regime, and Mobutu's frazzled forces, ahead of them.

War brought a complete cessation of tourism to the parks. This was not particularly significant for Okapi; however, the effect was pronounced in Virunga and Kahuzi-Biega National Parks where tourism brought in large revenues.

Many expatriates representing a spectrum of NGOs fled. In all cases, the expatriates that fled tried to reestablish contact with their national collaborators at the first opportunity. Often, this was a number of months later. Many of the nationals associated with these NGOs and the park authority also had to flee or hide in the surrounding forest or nearby villages.

Massive looting accompanied the war. It was started by Mobutu's troops as they fled. Interahamwe sympathizers and fleeing Rwandan factions joined the melee. Later, looting was carried out by Maji-Maji and other purportedly liberating groups. Long after the major wave of violence had subsided, petty looting continued by a now unaligned but still armed military. Cars, motorcycles, computers, and radios were stolen from all sites in the first wave. In the anarchy that followed in late 1996 and early 1997, the local population in many areas declared the parks nonexistent and came in to scavenge anything that had been left by the armed looters. These further losses included lights, solar panels, furniture, bedding, kitchenware, and clothing. In Kahuzi-Biega, guardhouses were burned.

The Accumulating Impact

Eventually, an interim order was established, but the apparent peace did not permit the restoration of order to protected areas. Guards had been disarmed by military authorities and were ineffective in the midst of a heavily armed population. Poachers took advantage of the lack of authority to operate over much larger areas than they had previously. Artisanal mining of gold, diamonds, and niobium-tantalum (coltan) expanded and settlement moved into previously protected zones. The parks are now trying to reassert control over a seriously deteriorated situation.

In Kahuzi-Biega, guards were kept out of the park by Interahamwe and other armed groups. When the rebel military pushed these factions back, the population slipped across park borders, and poaching exceeded even the levels inflicted by the guerrilla groups. From interrogating apprehended poachers, park staff estimate that during the latter half of 1999, twenty gorillas were killed in what was the tourist sector and, in the same sector, three hundred elephants were poached. There is no information concerning conditions in the greater forested lowland sector of the park.

There is some hope for eventual improvement because conservation organizations (at least one in each of the four World Heritage Sites) continue to provide assistance. So far, the expatriates have made only brief on-site visits. These have been information gathering visits, too short to allow the resumption of substantial roles in administration, research, or technical training but long enough to maintain the interest and involvement of the international conservation organization.

Combating the setbacks brought by the war has given the beleaguered conservation groups a new sense of unity, as if they were all part of an underground movement. Because of continuing danger, nationals involved in conservation are compelled to meet with representatives of the conservation NGOs and with each other outside of the country, where they participate in training sessions and strategy meetings. In the absence of expatriates, in-country nationals have taken on greater responsibility and now collaborate between themselves, even if they work for separate foreign organizations. It is out of this new shared perspective that a vision of how the protected areas can be resurrected has grown.

A Congolese collaborator of mine is of the opinion that even if the war were resolved quickly and the country became one again, the problems these parks face would not be resolved by reestablishing connections to the agencies in the capital that oversee them. I share this view. Although the greatest desire of all Congolese I work with is to see the country reunited without loss of sovereignty, the war has not increased the national conservation organization's ability to provide leadership. The problems of inadequate communication and remuneration remain, while the challenges to conservation have increased. The population is poorer than ever but is now widely armed. Local strains of tribalism seethe below the surface in all corners of the country. An anarchistic "each for himself" attitude will not be quickly dispelled with national unity. The challenges to conservation growing out of these circumstances demand local solutions based on a profound understanding of local traditions, fears, and hopes.

Conservation during Continuing War and Anarchy

Although these challenges remain inescapably local, the national conservation organization, the ICCN, remains the identity of the park staff. Even those nationals who have only been employed by international conservation organizations want to be integrated into the ICCN. However, the ICCN cannot adequately carry out certain tasks for which it has been formally responsible.

One of these responsibilities is the dispersion of funds. It is not reasonable to provide the head office in Kinshasa with a grant expecting that the funds can reach the field. Under the current continuing strife, funds cannot be transferred to the east from Kinshasa without having to leave the country. Even within the western sector of the Democratic Republic of Congo the head office does not have the infrastructure to transfer funds. Furthermore, the Kinshasa office is acutely conscious of its own financial needs. Addressing these needs is important but it would not result in significant improvement to Congo's protected areas. It is unlikely that international NGOs will make the organization and running of a national parks institution their priority; rather, a higher priority would likely be that of maintaining individual protected areas.

Another major impediment arises out of the fragmented administrative structure within the country. Each of the five eastern protected areas has to deal with different state authorities. In some instances, ultimate power lies with Uganda, in others with Rwanda. None of the critical diplomatic relationships of the eastern parks could be facilitated by representatives of the Kinshasa government. In fact, quite the opposite was true. The protected areas must at least give the appearance of distancing themselves from Kinshasa.

In the absence of national unity, the international conservation organizations can only offer partial solutions. They serve as secure and reliable channels for funds, provide some medical security to protected area workers and their families, and facilitate education, research, and community action. However, like the ICCN, they are not the primary decision makers or diplomats.

Growing responsibility lies with the national on-site staff, which is reinventing itself in the face of the challenges presented by the current anarchy. In situations that can only be managed locally, they are the ones who must take action and set the tone: conciliatory, collaborative, or firm. They negotiate with local political authorities and the military. They develop relations with the surrounding communities and push ahead with surveillance in the protected areas. And, they not only apprehend those that commit infractions but also insist on a justice that will prosecute them.

Relationships established by the park staff with surrounding populations are critical. The confidence of local people is essential, and this can only develop through regular contact and rapid, appropriate actions. During the period of anarchy, there were no restraints, and local residents violated the parks at will. Now, much of the population is armed, so astute diplomacy is required. Decisions should reflect a thorough knowledge of local traditions and aspirations, and solutions should be long-term, not merely short-term, palliatives. One of the best ways to apprehend poachers is through close and collaborative relations with the local community. Locals also have the most current information regarding mineral exploitation. The process of reestablishing control over the protected areas will require the cooperation of local populations.

Financial support comes mainly from international conservation organizations, but there are other important sources of backing, including the fraternity of fellow national staff in other rebel-held areas, moral support from the ICCN, and intellectual exchanges with the larger African conservation community. Of paramount importance is continuity. Foreign conservation organizations have been indispensable in the crisis, but their impact is severely limited by their impermanence. When foreign organizations have demonstrated long-term commitment, it has usually been the result of the long-term commitment of key individuals within the organizations. Unfortunately, these individuals must eventually move on, leaving protected areas no closer to the goal of permanent solutions.

To ensure permanence and encourage professionalism in park staff, a secure source of support is necessary. Funds must be available to pay salaries commensurate with the level of skill and responsibility required of park employees. And funds are needed to support operations, training, and coordination among the many protected areas at both local and international levels. Even if peace were reestablished and a single national government took on responsibility for the parks, it would not have the financial ability to assure the level of excellence that is needed. A long-term international commitment to the parks and their staff is therefore required.

Conclusion

In eastern Congo, national staff working with the support of local villagers and backed financially by international conservation organizations have so far been able to weather several tumultuous waves of anarchy that have washed over the region since 1996. This experience provides essential lessons for guiding protected areas through a period of armed anarchy. Of course, it must be recognized that there can be no fail-safe formula for success, and that the fate of protected areas in eastern Congo remains in doubt as long as a political resolution of the civil war remains elusive. Nonetheless, it is possible to conclude that

- Individuals and international organizations that held firm saved the day; those that ran did not. Nothing counted more than committed individuals, whether nationals or expatriates. The greatest strength in the face of adversity derives from a clear sense of purpose. The greatest collective strength derives from an ability to unite around that purpose.
- Financial support is especially crucial in a crisis. Lost or damaged equipment should be replaced as soon as possible to restore operating capacity. Responding to unpredictably changing conditions requires great flexibility—including financial flexibility.
- A supportive and cooperative local population can contribute to park survival by exercising restraint when there is no authority present. A possible basis for such restraint is cooperative management in which there are clear advantages for local communities.
- Conservation organizations operating in politically unstable parts of

the world should develop contingency plans for keeping communication and supply lines open when armed anarchy persists.

• Support for conservation in Congo, as elsewhere in the poorer countries of the world, must continue to come from a committed international community that considers key tropical wild areas to be an international heritage worth protecting.

8

Strategies for Conserving Forest National Parks in Africa with a Case Study from Uganda

THOMAS T. STRUHSAKER

The need for effective conservation in Africa is urgent because of ever-increasing human pressures on Africa's forests and other ecosystems. These pressures are due to rapid population growth and aspirations for higher living standards modeled after those of developed nations. African parks have experienced mixed success, but detailed quantitative assessments of successes and failures are not available for most of these parks.[1] Consequently, we must rely heavily on qualitative impressions when evaluating problems and possible management solutions. Generally, it is easier to identify management failures than it is to demonstrate successes. Although the concept of integrating applied science with park management is not new, it is rarely practiced anywhere, even in parks containing scientific research stations.

This chapter outlines ideas for effective park management that I have developed over the past thirty-nine years of studying and working for conservation in Africa and elsewhere in the tropics. The great majority of my tropical experience has been in Africa (1962–2000). I developed and managed a biological research and conservation field station in the Kibale Forest of Uganda for nearly eighteen years (1970–1988) (Figure 8-1). Initially, the primary activity of the Kibale project was pure research on nonhuman primates. Within the first two years, however, we expanded the research to examine the effects of logging on forest regeneration, primate populations and other animal groups, and community ecology in general. We also assumed a far greater role in assisting the game and forest departments with protection of Kibale (at that time a government forest and game reserve) by providing logistical support and supervising two to three game guards to protect against poaching, timber theft, and illegal agricultural encroachment. I began lobbying for national park status for

Figure 8-1. Map of Uganda showing location of Kibale and all other significant forest parks and reserves remaining in Uganda.

Kibale in 1970, and it was eventually declared a park in 1993.[2] In addition, we trained graduate students (Ugandans and expatriates); gave educational field trips and lectures to school teachers and secondary school pupils; initiated tree planting activities with the local community; and publicized Kibale through the popular press and radio.

A First-Level Approach to Problem Solving: The Case of Kibale National Park

The ultimate measure of conservation success is the status of the flora and fauna in the area under consideration. This, in turn, is determined by at least four gross categories of variables: (1) surrounding landscape and land-use patterns; (2) human activities in the park; (3) park management policy and practice; and (4) biotic and abiotic parameters intrinsic to the park (Figure 8-2).

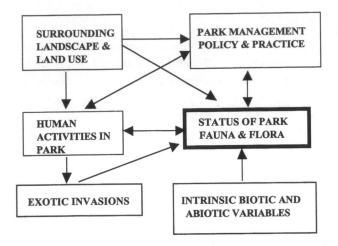

Figure 8-2. Categories of variables influencing the status of the flora and fauna in parks and other protected areas, and their interactions.

Surrounding Landscape and Land-use Patterns

The Kibale National Park is a 766-square-kilometer ecological island of forest, colonizing bush, grassland, and swamp surrounded by a sea of agriculture dominated by tea estates and subsistence farming. The southern end of Kibale is joined to the Queen Elizabeth National Park by a 6-kilometer-wide isthmus. Human population density around the park is relatively high. Kabarole (previously Toro) District, where Kibale is located, experienced an increase from 327,962 people in 1969 to 519,821 in 1980 and an annual growth rate of 4.6 percent.[3] Kabarole District covers 8,108 square kilometers of land (water area excluded), yielding a density of sixty-four humans per square kilometer in 1980. By 1991, the population in Kabarole had increased to 746,800 with an annual growth rate of 3.3 percent and was projected to reach 944,600 by the year 2000.[4] So, by the end of the year 2000, the human population density for Kabarole was at least 117 per square kilometer. However, in the twenty-seven administrative parishes adjacent to Kibale National Park, the human population density was even higher; probably greater than 300 humans per square kilometer in the year 2000.[5] Pressure from the surrounding human population is clearly a major issue facing the Kibale National Park.

Human Activities in the Park

During my studies in Kibale, human activities included poaching of duikers, bushpig, bushbuck, sitatunga, buffalo, and elephant; cutting of building poles and timber; production of charcoal; collection of firewood, weaving materials (reeds, palm leaves), lianas (bush rope for house construction), honey, and medicinal plants; exportation of drinking water; and harvesting of wild coffee. Monkeys and chimps were rarely hunted because the predominant tribes (Batoro and Bakiga) do not usually eat primates. Occasionally, I heard of Batoro killing monkeys to eat or to feed to their hunting dogs, but this was unusual. Until the early 1960s, there were some Bakonjo living adjacent to Kibale and they did hunt primates to eat. The Bakonjo were driven out of the area in 1964 during an intertribal dispute.[6] Now that Kibale is a national park, it appears that some illegal activities have greatly decreased, especially elephant poaching and timber theft.

Frequent human presence in the park may lead to the introduction of exotic plants, animals, and diseases that may adversely affect indigenous wildlife. Although there is little information on the degree to which this affects Kibale, it is known that three of the omnivorous cercopithecine monkey species in Kibale are infected with *Giardia* and *Entamoeba histolytica,* parasites indistinguishable from those found in the surrounding human community.[7] It is unclear whether the monkeys contracted these parasites from humans who were using the forest or vice versa. With regard to plants, there is evidence suggesting that plantations of exotic species of pines that were intentionally established within Kibale when it was a forest reserve may have led to a localized dieback of mature trees for three upper canopy tree species through the spread of a fungal pathogen.[8] There are as yet no major exotic plant invasions of Kibale. *Lantana* sp. is found along some parts of the forest perimeter and outside of the park. *Cyphomandra betacea* (a South American Solanaceae) occurs at low densities throughout much of the forest but nowhere does it appear to exclude indigenous species. *Senna* (*Cassia*) *spectabilis* (a tropical American Caesalpiniaceae) is also widespread along forest edges and in regenerating forest. Its competitive interaction with indigenous species needs to be studied because elsewhere (e.g., Mahali Mountains National Park, Tanzania) it is considered a problem. *Chromolaena* (*Eupatorium*) *odorata* (a South American Asteraceae) is currently invading most of the forests of West and West-central Africa and represents a very serious threat to forest regeneration because it excludes all other plant life, including tree seedlings and saplings. This species has apparently not yet reached East Africa, but seems to be spreading eastward and is now widespread in Gabon.

Management Policy and Practice

Kibale was originally created as a government forest and game reserve managed by the forestry department as a source of timber. Forestry agents regulated and monitored the harvest of trees and collected royalties from private timber companies that held the timber concessions and carried out the exploitation. The collection of firewood and drinking water by neighboring communities was legally permitted, but hunting and the cutting of building poles was officially prohibited. However, after the early 1970s there was little law enforcement by the forest department. To the contrary, many forest officers became involved in illegal activities (timber theft and allowing illegal agricultural encroachers into the reserve) within Kibale and all other forest reserves in the country.[9]

The Kibale project worked closely to assist the Uganda Game Department in protecting Kibale against hunting and the theft of timber. The department provided us with two to three armed game guards who had powers of arrest. Our role was to supervise the guards, assist with logistical support, and, on occasion, patrol with them. We paid these game guards bonuses for every poacher who was arrested and convicted, for every panga (machete), spear, net, snare, gun, crosscut saw, and piece of confiscated timber they brought to us. The bonus paid for each item was about 20 percent below the market value in order to discourage production or purchase of these items for profit by the guards themselves. The bonus system was a highly effective incentive that allowed the guards to increase their salaries by at least two- to threefold. The annual cost of this bonus system to our project in the 1980s was less than $500.

Occasionally we sought the support of the military, who would send in ten to twenty soldiers for a few days to patrol with the game guards. These activities were meant to deal with heavily armed elephant poachers who were more numerous and better equipped than the game guards. Based on information collected by informants, the military also made visits to households and villages alleged to be harboring poachers and thieves.

We also worked closely with the judicial system. This meant regular meetings with the Resident State Attorney and Chief Magistrate in the regional and district administrative center of Fort Portal. We discussed the importance of conservation with these individuals and explained the nature of the problems in Kibale. Each time the game guards arrested poachers in Kibale, we made an effort to inform the judiciary of these arrests and to inform the police imprisoning the poachers that higher authorities had been contacted. This seemed to reduce the frequency of bribes and pretrial releases.

With only two to three game guards, we were able to effectively protect about 80 to 90 square kilometers of Kibale against net and snare hunters who were after duikers, pigs, bushbuck, and sitatunga. Protection was most effective in those parts of the forest where we conducted our research. We were less successful in curtailing elephant poaching, but still managed to retain greater numbers of elephants in Kibale than any other forest reserve in Uganda and certainly did as well as any of the national parks. In the 1970s and 1980s all areas of East Africa lost, on average, about 90 percent of their elephants, regardless of the type of economy or government. Even the most heavily protected areas suffered. Much of this loss was probably due to corruption and participation by government officials all over Africa. What the Kibale study shows is that even with a very small team of dedicated and honest law enforcement officers, a great deal can be achieved in terms of wildlife protection.

Throughout the 1970s, we lobbied Forest Department officials and presented a strong case for research and conservation that resulted in the protection of 86 square kilometers of Kibale against logging. This area was declared a combined nature reserve and long-term research plot and was subsequently closed to logging. Eventually, in 1993 the entire reserve was gazetted as a national park. The economic collapse of Uganda in the mid-1970s also had a positive impact for forest conservation, because it essentially eliminated large-scale mechanized logging and forest refinement (treatment with arboricides to kill undesirable trees) that could not be maintained in the absence of foreign currency and imports of equipment, spare parts, and chemicals.

The problem of illegal agricultural encroachment in the southern part of Kibale was much more difficult for us as foreign researchers to address. This was because high-level government officials were involved in collecting bribes from the encroachers. Most of the encroachers were recent immigrants from Kabale (previously Kigezi) District known as Bakiga (descendants of the Hutu in Rwanda). Many of the encroachers admitted that they had paid bribes to the provincial forest officer, himself a Mukiga. The most blatant example of corruption involved this same forest officer who illegally appropriated a large piece of the forest reserve for himself and a close friend to convert to agriculture using Forest Department tractors.[10] Illegal encroachment into Kibale was further compounded by the political and social instability throughout Uganda during the 1970s and 1980s. It was not until 1992 that all illegal encroachers were removed from Kibale by President Museveni's government.

Intrinsic Variables

Although Kibale is relatively large compared to forest parks elsewhere in East Africa, it is small when considering species with intrinsically low population densities, such as chimpanzees and elephants. Even for species like the red colobus, which have very high population densities (300 per square kilometer) in some parts of Kibale, there is evidence to suggest that this species has suffered declines over a twenty-four-year period at one of the long-term study sites in spite of excellent protection against hunting and habitat degradation.[11]

The intrinsic variables influencing the flora and fauna of a park are difficult to evaluate because of the high degree of natural variation that makes scientifically rigid replications and controls virtually impossible. Intrinsic fluctuations in populations (e.g., due to reproductive failure, competitive or predator–prey imbalances, genetic drift due to small founder populations, etc.) are likely to have adverse effects on small populations, and the size of populations is expected to vary with the area of available habitat.

In addition to park size and population demography (density, age structure, natality, recruitment, etc.) for plants and animals, other intrinsic biological variables influencing the status of parks include the ecological integrity and successional state of the community. These, in turn, are often influenced by past human activities that are no longer in place but which have long-lasting effects. Examples of such activities include selective logging, shifting agriculture, and compression of large herbivore populations, such as elephants, resulting from habitat destruction and hunting pressures outside of the park. In other words, the ecological community of many, if not most, parks may not be in a state of equilibrium.

The role of abiotic factors is even less well understood. For example, long-term fluctuations in weather influence plant communities and eventually the entire ecological community. The increased frequency of El Niño events may prove to be an extremely important variable influencing parks, such as through its effect on fire, landslides, and plant phenology.[12]

Measures of Conservation Success: Duikers and Elephants in Kibale

The status of plants, animals, and the ecological community as a whole is the ultimate measure of successful conservation. This requires long-term ecological monitoring and detailed studies of ecological communities, in other words, environmental audits. Some would contend that such studies and audits are too difficult and expensive to be included in conservation projects, even though financial audits are routine, mandatory, costly, and do not measure conservation success. Furthermore, alternative indices of effective conservation, such as "threat reductions" or "degree of contentment of the neighboring human population" provide no information whatsoever about the flora and fauna being conserved nor are these indices necessarily less expensive to measure.

Primates are easily monitored, but, because they are not generally hunted in Kibale, they are not particularly useful in measuring the success of antipoaching activities. Chimpanzees, however, are often caught in wire snares and in some parts of the forest as many as 20 percent are maimed (missing digits, hands, feet, forearms, and lower legs).[13] It is not clear to what extent the chimps were caught in snares set in the forest or by those they encountered while raiding crops outside the forest.

The best indicators of conservation success at Kibale are the two most sought-after prey: elephants and duikers. Thirty years ago, I surveyed most of the forest reserves in western Uganda (Figure 8-1) and frequently encountered elephants and their spoor in all of them. In the intervening thirty years, Kibale retained a larger population than any other forest reserve in Uganda and did as well as any of the national parks.[14] Given the similarities in habitat between these areas, the only difference between Kibale and other reserves is that Kibale benefited from some degree of law enforcement. The presence of a research team also played a vital watchdog role in reducing elephant poaching. This was most evident following incidents of poaching when elephants would often move closer to our main research station and remain there for several days. In fact, this was sometimes our first clue that a poaching incident had occurred.

Two species of duikers (blue and red) were the main prey of meat hunters in Kibale. Our limited antipoaching activities and research presence effectively protected an area of about 80–90 square kilometers. The research sites of Kibale had higher indices of duiker abundance than any other forest reserve in western Uganda[15] and duiker populations in the protected areas of Kibale may have actually increased slightly over a 20-year period.[16] There is little doubt that even limited law enforcement was instrumental in protecting large and viable populations of duikers in Kibale.[17]

Other Measures of Conservation Success

It is less clear how our efforts at training and education influenced conservation in Kibale. These are both long-term approaches to conservation and, consequently, they do not yield immediate results. Furthermore, it is often difficult to separate the effects of one strategy from others. However, the training of qualified Ugandan conservation biologists in Kibale is important in several ways. First, having Ugandan professionals working in the park increases the probability of long-term effectiveness because of the continuity and permanency they bring to the project. Secondly, as nationals they are often in a better position and better qualified than foreigners to deal with conflict resolution involving residents living next to the park. Three of the Ugandans who earned doctorates during my tenure in Kibale have continued to work there for the past 17–27 years and now hold the positions of administrative and scientific directors of the Makerere University Biological Field Station at Kanyawara and project administrator for the research projects at the Ngogo camp in Kibale. This commitment by Ugandans represents an important step toward long-term conservation.

Educational field trips and discussions with secondary school teachers and their pupils probably converted some of them to conservation and certainly generated goodwill with the neighboring community. It represented an initial step toward developing attitudes more sympathetic to conservation. However, due to insufficient funds and personnel during my tenure in Kibale, not enough time and effort were invested in this strategy to yield tangible results, nor did we make any effort to evaluate the effectiveness of this approach.

Conservation Lessons: Aids to Effective Park Conservation

The conservation lessons I have learned from Kibale and elsewhere are summarized in Table 8-1. These are not listed according to any rank of importance. The relative importance of each of these lessons or strategies will likely vary between sites and even vary over time within a site. Most of these points are self-explanatory and obvious.

Table 8-1.

Requirements for successful conservation programs in national parks.

1. Effective law enforcement
2. Long-term commitment: longer than twenty years
3. Permanent collaborative association with overseas organizations
4. Training and participation of nationals
5. Scientific presence and monitoring
6. Flexible management plan: problems change with project ontogeny
7. Education and support at both local and national levels
8. Appropriate level of secure funding (e.g., trust funds)

• *Law enforcement* is imperative for effective conservation, just as it is in any form of governance. However, its effectiveness is usually contingent on appropriately trained, equipped, and salaried staff. Committed leadership is critical. A bonus system for effective antipoaching activities creates incentives for the park guards and informants. Guards must have powers of arrest. There must be an effective judicial system with checks and transparency to reduce corruption.

• *Long-term commitment* by donors and participants is essential for success. Therefore a secure source of funding, such as a trust fund, is crucial to sustaining commitment. In order to minimize misuse of these funds, it is recommended that the principal be managed by a board of trustees outside and independent of the recipient country. Annual interest payments, on the other hand, should be managed by a board within the recipient country working with the park management authority. Annual allotments should not be excessive as they can detract from conservation objectives and lead to individual and interagency rivalries. Furthermore, annual payments should be contingent on performance; that is, there must be accountability as determined by financial and environmental audits. Secure funding frees personnel to concentrate on conservation rather than fund raising.

Equally if not more important to financial security is the long-term dedication of qualified personnel. They form the foundation of any successful conservation program. Continuity of personnel requires the existence of a professional national conservation agency that is relatively independent of shifting political winds.

- One way of achieving long-term commitments is through establishing *permanent collaborative associations* with overseas research and funding organizations. Such linkages help ensure continuity of the project, as well as provide a continuing source of technical expertise.
- *Training and participation of nationals* are vital to building a core of committed personnel that is more likely to persist over the long-term than one consisting primarily of expatriates. Furthermore, nationals are more likely to remain effective during periods of political instability than are foreigners (also see chapter 7).
- *Scientific presence and ecological monitoring*, through permanent research stations, can provide scientific information and analysis relevant to the objective management of a park. Additionally, researchers can serve as conservation watchdogs and can provide the environmental audits that permit an evaluation of a park's conservation status. Without scientific studies and monitoring, evaluation of park effectiveness is largely subjective. Research stations should collaborate closely with park managers but retain a high degree of autonomy in order to preserve an independent judgment.
- *Conservation management plans must remain flexible* and sensitive to changing conditions. Long-term ecological monitoring is imperative for detecting change due to both extrinsic and intrinsic forces.
- *Education and public support* at local and national levels serves to win the support of the people living around the park. This not only reduces external threats, but also simplifies the task of law enforcement. It is important that local populations understand why a park exists, but it is even more important to instill an ethic of respect for other species and their right to exist. When such an ethic predominates, conserving the park becomes much easier. Teachers recruited from the local community can be extremely effective in this regard. Education at the national level often relies on several different strategies, including television, radio, newspapers, and lobbying politicians.

Buying the support of local populations with financial incentives is problematic at best because external market forces change, and growing populations with expanding aspirations lead to ever-increasing demands and expectations. Conservation can then be held hostage to the promise of escalating financial returns. If the benefits should decline for whatever reason, there is no reservoir of good will to inhibit people from making up the deficit by extracting resources from the park. Although certain economic activities such as tourism and revenue sharing can initially engage a local community in conservation, the benefits are usually too prone to the vagaries of politics and economics to have long-lasting consequences. Furthermore, in the case of Africa's forest parks, only a small proportion of the neighboring community derive financial benefits from these activities[18] and the realized income per capita is low. The majority of integrated conservation and development projects fall into this category. History demonstrates the tenuous nature of conservation efforts based solely on economic or other material benefits.[19]

A better way to relieve human pressure on a park is to develop alternative resources for neighboring residents. Privately owned wood lots are one such example. Great care must be taken to avoid development projects that attract immigration and thereby exacerbate conservation problems within the park that result from increased human populations.

The *population explosion* drives the increasing rates of consumption in the tropics and is the single-most important development hampering conservation in Africa. Consequently, *family planning* education and facilities should be considered critical components of any community conservation project. In the absence of human population stabilization, if not population reduction, we can expect a continued decline in both wildlife populations and human living standards. In those countries exporting natural resources to Western industrialized nations, high levels of per capita consumption in these more developed countries also plays an important role in resource depletion, especially so when these resources are grossly underpriced.[20]

Beyond the local context, official support for parks and conservation in general must be gained at the national level, where crucial political and financial decisions are made. The difficult question, for which there is no simple answer, is how to win political support without jeopardizing the park (compare chapter 23).

A General Framework for Analyzing and Solving Conservation Problems

The conservation problems facing parks and other protected areas are multifaceted, as are the potential solutions to these problems. Because each park has its own set of peculiarities and problems, we do not expect to find a set of solutions applicable to all. However, identifying the problems and their possible solutions is useful in developing realistic conser-

Table 8-2.

A general framework for analyzing and solving conservation problems.

Problem	Class of Problem	Solution	Time Frame
Violations of law	Proximate	Law enforcement	Short
Legislation	Proximate	Lobbying and financial incentives	Medium to long
Values/ethics	Proximate/ultimate	Education	Long
Population growth/ hyperconsumption	Ultimate	Education	Long
Management of parks and other natural resources	Proximate/ultimate	Research/monitoring	Medium to long

vation strategies (Table 8-2). In this coarse-grained system, five categories of problems are distinguished and classified according to whether they involve proximate or ultimate variables. Critical to this scheme is the emphasis on different time scales for different approaches to problem solving. For example, law enforcement can be very effective within a very short time period. But, for longer-term conservation effectiveness, other strategies must also be employed, such as education programs to change attitudes and behavior leading to greater empathy for other species and to reduce population growth and overconsumption. These approaches re-

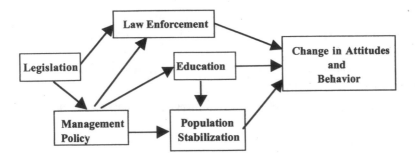

Figure 8-3. Dependency and interaction of conservation strategies: a hypothetical example.

quire much longer periods of time to have an effect than does law enforcement, but they are crucial to developing an ultimate solution to conservation problems everywhere. Other strategies, such as lobbying for effective legislation and conducting scientific research to improve management plans, often fall between medium- and long-term planning.

This framework acknowledges the temporal and strategic complexity of defining and dealing with conservation problems. The relative importance of any one of these classes of problems or solutions not only varies between parks, but also can vary over time within a park. Likewise, the way these variables and strategies interact and are interdependent will vary over time and between sites (e.g., Figure 8-3). Continued refinement of this kind of approach will increase the effectiveness and efficiency of our conservation efforts and resources.

Acknowledgments

I thank the organizers of and donors to the conference held at White Oak Plantation for the opportunity to attend this meeting. My paper was written in partial fulfillment of a contract with the Center for Applied Biodiversity Science of Conservation International.

Notes

1. T. T. Struhsaker, *Africa's Rain Forest Parks: Problems and Possible Solutions*. A report to the Center for Applied Biodiversity Science, Conservation International (2001).

2. For a detailed history of Kibale, see T. T. Struhsaker, *Ecology of an African Rain Forest: Logging in Kibale and the Conflict between Conservation and Exploitation* (Gainesville: University Press of Florida, 1997).

3. Uganda Census Office, *Uganda Census: Report on the 1980 Population Census, vol. 1: The Provisional Results by Administrative Areas* (P.O. Box 7086, Kampala, Uganda: Uganda Census Office, Ministry of Planning and Economic Development, 1982).

4. NEMA (National Environment Management Authority of Uganda), *Kabarole District Environment Profile* (P.O. Box 22255, Kampala, Uganda: NEMA, 1997).

5. Extrapolated from NEMA, *Kabarole District*.

6. T. T. Struhsaker, *The Red Colobus Monkey* (Chicago: University of Chicago Press, 1975).

7. W. J. Freeland, "Primate Social Groups as Biological Islands," *Ecology* 60, no. 4 (1979): 719–728.

8. T. T. Struhsaker, J. M. Kasenene, J. C. Gaither Jr., N. Larsen, S. Musango, and R. Bancroft, "Tree Mortality in the Kibale Forest, Uganda: A Case Study of Dieback

in Tropical Rain Forest Adjacent to Exotic Conifer Plantations," *Forest Ecology and Management* 29 (1989): 165–185; Struhsaker, *Ecology of an African Rain Forest.*

9. For details, see Struhsaker, *Ecology of an African Rain Forest.*

10. Struhsaker, *Ecology of an African Rain Forest.*

11. J. C. Mitani, T. T. Struhsaker, and J. S. Lwanga, "Primate Community Dynamics in Old Growth Forest over 23.5 Years at Ngogo, Kibale National Park, Uganda: Implications for Conservation and Census Methods," *International Journal of Primatology* 21 (2000): 269–286.

12. Struhsaker, *Ecology of an African Rain Forest.*

13. G. M. I. Basuta, *The Ecology and Conservation Status of the Chimpanzee* (Pan troglodytes Blumenbach) *in Kibale Forest, Uganda* (Ph.D. diss., Makerere University, Kampala, Uganda, 1987).

14. P. C. Howard, *Nature Conservation in Uganda's Tropical Forest Reserves* (Gland, Switzerland, and Cambridge, England: IUCN [The World Conservation Union], 1991).

15. Howard, *Nature Conservation,* and personal observation.

16. Struhsaker, *Ecology of an African Rain Forest.*

17. See also Howard, *Nature Conservation.*

18. Struhsaker, *Africa's Rain Forest Parks* .

19. R. Kramer, C. van Schaik, and J. Johnson, eds., *Last Stand: Protected Areas and the Defense of Tropical Biodiversity* (New York and Oxford: Oxford University Press, 1997); Struhsaker, *Ecology of an African Rain Forest*; T. T. Struhsaker, "A Biologist's Perspective on the Role of Sustainable Harvest in Conservation," *Conservation Biology* 12 (1998): 930–932; J. F. Oates, *Myth and Reality in the Rain Forest* (Berkeley and Los Angeles: University of California Press, 1999).

20. M. Gillis and R. Repetto, "Conclusion: Findings and Policy Implications," *Public Policies and the Misuse of Forest Resources* (Cambridge: Cambridge University Press, 1988).

9

Making a Rain Forest National Park Work in Madagascar: Ranomafana National Park and Its Long-term Research Commitment

PATRICIA C. WRIGHT AND BENJAMIN ANDRIAMIHAJA

Madagascar's Biodiversity

Madagascar, the fourth-largest island in the world, has been targeted as a conservation priority because it contains one of the richest assemblages of endemic flora and fauna on earth.[1] Isolated for 88 million years, Madagascar is a reservoir for relict groups from a Gondwanaland past, as well as a living evolutionary laboratory.[2] Madagascar harbors a unique flora and fauna, including six species of baobab trees, a whole endemic family of spiny desert flora, ten thousand rain-forest trees, thousands of orchids, all existing species of lemurs, two hundred species of frogs, over fifty species of chameleons, twenty-seven species of tenrec, nearly a hundred freshwater fish, and over 260 bird species. Eighty percent of over twelve thousand species of plants and 90 percent of the reptiles and amphibians are endemic. This diversity is particularly remarkable since 80 percent of the forest cover of Madagascar has already been destroyed[3] and all its megafauna, including seventeen species of giant lemurs, the giant tortoise, two species of hippopotamus, and the world's largest bird *Aepyornis* have become extinct within the last millennium.[4]

The loss of Malagasy biodiversity due to deforestation and fragile soils is a challenge for conservation.[5] Expanding human populations and their culture of burning habitat make biodiversity conservation urgent.[6] Satellite photos of forest cover show that forest destruction in Madagascar has been proceeding at the rate of 8 percent per year, and Malagasy forests and all the endemic biodiversity within them could disappear within a few decades.[7] Several initiatives have been launched to preserve the remaining biodiversity, and in this chapter we will describe a still-continuing conservation project, Ranomafana National Park.

Environmental Action Plan Phase (1989–1996)

In the 1980s, Madagascar reached an economic low, ranking among the world's ten poorest countries. Infrastructure such as roads, education, and health care had severely deteriorated and Madagascar was isolated from trade with much of the world. The gradual opening up of the country in the 1980s reignited the interest of the international community in Madagascar's unique biodiversity. In 1989, Madagascar drafted the first nationwide Environmental Action Plan (NEAP), a fifteen-year program to address environmental degradation in general, biodiversity loss in particular, and some of the systemic causes of those problems. International funding institutions put a high value on Madagascar's nature and committed over $160 million to the first five years of NEAP. Programs included establishing and strengthening national institutions concerned with the environment (primarily building the infrastructure and framework of a National Park Service), land titling, updating maps, and developing six integrated conservation and development projects (ICDPs) in areas critical to conservation.[8] The involvement of local people's needs was a strong component of this environmental plan.[9]

By the end of Phase 1, in 1996, a national park service, Association Nationale pour la Gestion des Aires Protegees (ANGAP), was in place and the ICDPs were incorporated into the national park system (Figure 9-1). ANGAP's parastatal nature, a private conservation agency with a public mandate yet with the Department of Water and Forests (DEF) strongly involved with early decisions, was modeled on the Kenya Wildlife Service and Wildlife Conservation Revolving Fund in Zambia.[10]

We will describe the evolution of one of the parks, Ranomafana, which was officially designated a national park in May 1991.[11] Both authors have been intimately involved with Ranomafana since before it was established as a park (1986–1991), during the large ICDP era (1991–1996), and now in the "clustered partners" era (1997–2002). With this long-term view, we will discuss the problems and solutions that have made Ranomafana one of the most successful parks in Madagascar according to the final evaluation by the donors.[12]

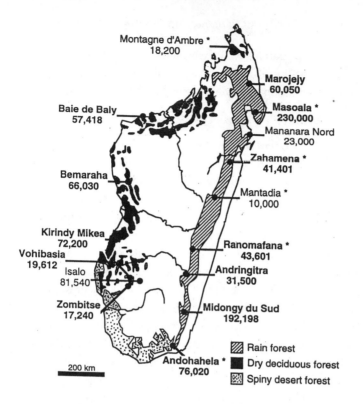

Figure 9-1. Map of the sixteen national parks in Madagascar gazetted by 2000. Park size in hectares is listed below each park name. Stars indicate parks that were Integrated Conservation and Development projects during the 1990s. Boldfaced park names indicate parks gazetted after 1990.

The Early History of Ranomafana Park (1986–1996)

The effort to protect Ranomafana was triggered by one major event: the discovery of the golden bamboo lemur in 1986.[13] In addition, a nationwide biological survey ranked the rain forests near Ranomafana as having a high level of biodiversity.[14] Ranomafana was a classified forest, and timber concessions totaling 5,600 hectares had been allotted in 1986–1988 by the Department of Water and Forests. The incentive for making this region a park was amplified by devastation of the forest where the new species had been discovered, and the timber exploiters abandoned the area by 1990.[15]

The Ranomafana classified forest was the watershed for twenty-seven rivers, including the Namorona, Faraony, and Ampasany. The hydroelectric power plant on the Namorona River in Ranomafana provided electricity for most of southeastern Madagascar. Protection of this forest was deemed to be essential to safeguarding regional sources of electricity as well as the integrity of this important watershed.[16]

Local Agreement on Boundaries

The first step toward gazetting the park was to explore its potential boundaries. A national road bisected the area, and rain forest lay both to the north and to the south. The ridge of mountains that runs north–south in Madagascar holds the last rain forests in Madagascar. Practically all the forests from mid-elevation to the coast have been cut and replaced with annually burned grasslands dominated by an invasive, intractable, non-endemic grass that is not very palatable even for cattle. The Ranomafana Park protects the narrow width of remaining forest from 400 meters up to the highlands at 1,534 meters, running north–south approximately 40 kilometers. With the input and agreement of each village and after compromises on both sides, the final park boundary encompassed 43,500 hectares. These lengthy negotiations ensured that the villagers felt they had important input into the decisions and that all the villagers knew where the park boundaries were located.

Strong Research Links

This protected forest at Ranomafana was appreciated by ornithologists, botanists, herpetologists, and primatologists for its high rain-forest biodiversity. A permanent facility ten minutes' walk from the park entrance was built in 1989 with improvements including a small research laboratory (1992) and electricity (1998). A strong research presence has been maintained twelve months a year by scientists who train Malagasy university students and local residents in addition to accomplishing their own research goals. Research usage has risen from thirty-eight to forty-two researchers per year in the early 1990s to over one hundred researchers a year by the end of the decade (Figure 9-2). Researchers come from about thirty-five international universities and museums, and many of the research projects are long term with research teams returning annually (Figure 9-3). Over 263 publications, 20 Ph.D. dissertations, and 79 master's theses have been produced.[17]

Thirty well-trained and highly skilled full-time research assistants from local villages are employed in addition to three Malagasy ANGAP staff and three Institute for Conservation Environments (ICTE)–Stony Brook scientific advisors. Salaries and prestige are two of the benefits gained by these local residents employed at the station. Many of these research

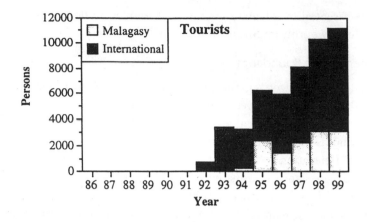

Figure 9-2. Number of researchers within Ranomafana National Park from 1986 to 1999. The increase of research in 1998 was caused by the International Society of Primatologists Meeting. Data from ICTE and ANGAP.

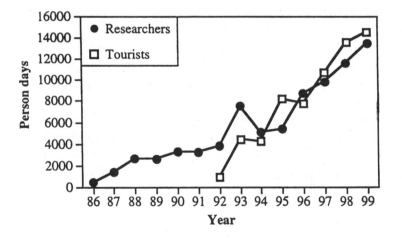

Figure 9-3. Contrasting number of person days spent in Ranomafana National Park by tourists and researchers. Average stay of a tourist in Ranomafana National Park is 1.3 days. Average stay for a researcher is around three months. Although researchers are less numerous than tourists (Figures 9-3 and 9-5), the longer tenure of researchers results in many contact hours with the local villagers, likely to be a major factor in conservation work.

assistants have worked in the park with researchers for over a decade and have accumulated vast knowledge of the flora and fauna from the researchers and from their own observations.[18] In 1995, a long-term ecological monitoring program was established at seven sites within the park and conducted year round with local residents who had trained for a decade as research assistants for international scientists.[19] Plant–animal interactions, such as pollination syndromes, predation, and seed dispersal, have been studied,[20] as well as the impact of selective logging on the biodiversity,[21] the impact of deforestation on watershed streams,[22] and the impact of villages on the health of the biodiversity.[23]

Health, Education, and Agricultural Development

Initial visits to thirty-five villages surrounding the park suggested that these rice agriculturists were some of the poorest in the world. In order to update demographic, economic, and lifestyle information, the first operator of the Ranomafana Project, Duke University, began with a research project funded by a Fulbright Fellowship and a U.S. Man and the Biosphere grant.[24]

Results of this study showed that both health and education were needed and valued by the village residents. Although 75 percent of the men and 51 percent of the women were literate, in 1990, because of lack of schools and schoolteachers, 70 percent of the children ages six to ten had no education, with 23 percent having one year and 6 percent having two years of schooling.[25] The education team assisted with literacy, rural libraries, small reforestation projects, and bringing conservation education materials to remote schools. Within five years, eight new schools were built and seven renovated. A conservation and cultural heritage exposition center was built in Ranomafana Town Center.

Poor health, especially of children, seemed to be linked with undernourishment. Child mortality was high (10 percent), with 13 percent of boys and 9 percent of girls below nine years of age emaciated according to World Health standards.[26] Intestinal parasite loads were some of the highest in the world, and over 50 percent of all people had malaria parasites in their blood.[27] Limited primary health care could only be found in the Ranomafana hospital, a walk of one to two days for most villagers.

Lon Kightlinger, a doctoral candidate from the University of North Carolina, Chapel Hill, organized the project health team of one Malagasy medical doctor (Marcel), a parasitologist (Kightlinger), a biological anthropologist (Hardenbergh), an ecological economist (Ferraro), and five

Malagasy nurses as part of his doctoral research. The popularity of the initial health care activities and the relationships established with the visiting health team led to the development of mutual trust between the local residents and the Ranomafana National Park (RNP) project from the beginning. This team continued to bring news, basic first aid and medical care, nutrition and sanitation education, and immunizations in monthly or bimonthly visits, beginning in 1990. When it came time to vote on endorsement of the park in 1991, the village residents voiced approval. The health team continued its village rotation throughout the ICDP years until 1997.

After the initial three years of research on soil quality,[28] agricultural production,[29] and forest product extraction,[30] RNP project ACDs (agents for conservation and development) were stationed in twenty-five peripheral zone villages to give technical advice in building microdams (to increase areas for paddy rice to replace slash and burn), improving beekeeping, beginning agroforestry, and improving rice yield. Between the years 1991 and 1999 the rate of tavy (swidden agriculture) was reduced inside the park compared to the rate outside the park.[31] However, the edges of the park suffered destruction from tavy.[32]

The Economics of Ecotourism

After researchers began their studies of behavior and ecology of lemurs, trail systems in the forest were developed and animals habituated for easy observation. With this new opportunity to view ten species of lemurs, ecotourism became a possibility. Almost no tourists visited the new national park in 1991. From the beginning it was decided to build up tourism infrastructure and link profits from entrance fees to the residents so that peripheral zone villages receive a direct financial benefit from the park.[33]

Early negotiations assured that entrance fees for protected areas (DEAP) would be shared with the local communities: half of this fee goes to ANGAP to run operations and half of the fee is returned to the villages for microdevelopment projects approved by ANGAP (Figure 9-4). The village elders present their village's project before the committee, which meets annually. Projects funded to date include seed grain for green beans or squash; beehives; fertilizers for rice farmers; a pig-raising initiative; a village granary; and a village tourist campground.[34]

An increase in tourism can be attributed to easier accessibility with improvement in main highways, easy visibility of the rain-forest lemurs because of the habituation by researchers (especially the bamboo lemurs),

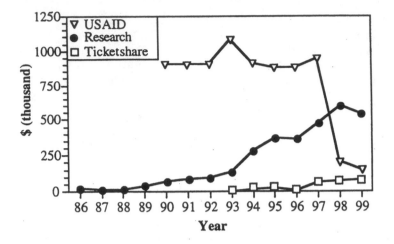

Figure 9-4. Funds allocated to Ranomafana National Park by USAID grants (ICDP and UDLP), by research foundations and institutions to individual researchers, and by the ticket share from half the tourist entrance fee, which is returned to villages. Not included are funds given to ANGAP by the World Bank to fund ANGAP-RNP staff salaries and operations, beginning in 1998. The increase in research funds is a result of the increasing numbers of researchers in the park (Figure 9-3).

the presence of the hot mineral springs, and better marketing through guide books and international press, most of the publicity based on the biodiversity research (Figure 9-5). In addition, tourist accommodations have improved with the new, locally run hotels (Domaine Nature [sixteen rooms] and Centrest [eight rooms],) which have electricity, hot water, and clean, comfortable rooms for less than $30 per night. Both have good restaurants.

Tourists had increased to twelve thousand per year by 1999, generating approximately $50,000 annually for DEAP projects (Figure 9-2). Additional income from tourism has made a major economic impact on the region, including sums from guide salaries, restaurants and hotels, local businesses (such as the park entrance snack bar), and handicraft-selling shops (both built with infrastructure and training money from the USAID grant). Tourists spend an average of $10 a day in addition to hotel and restaurant expenses and spend 1.3 days in the Ranomafana area.[35] Total tourism revenue generates approximately $350,000 annually to the region.

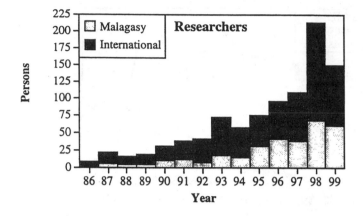

Figure 9-5. Number of Malagasy and international tourists visiting Ranomafana National Park, Madagascar, from 1991 to 1999. Data from ANGAP and Ministry of Tourism.

Training

The university teams (Duke, North Carolina State, State University of New York at Stony Brook, and Cornell) that operated the Ranomafana National Park Project focused on training throughout both the research and implementation phases of the project. From 1991 to 1997, the three international technical advisors (conservation, village economic development, and administrative management) had Malagasy counterparts who were trained in modern international methods of business, technology, and management. Madagascar previously had no experience in these park-related fields. In addition, thirteen of the park staff received short-term training abroad in GIS (geographic information systems), computer technology, and conservation principles (Figure 9-6).

Thirty people from the local villages were trained to identify plants, reptiles, amphibians, insects, birds, and mammals by working side by side with international scientists. They learned to speak and write in English and French and they became acquainted with Latin names for the species to facilitate communication with researchers. Local names were useful, especially in the absence of scientific identifications, since many of the taxa were rare or unknown to science.

An annual biodiversity training program was begun in 1993 with professors and students from five universities (three American and two Ma-

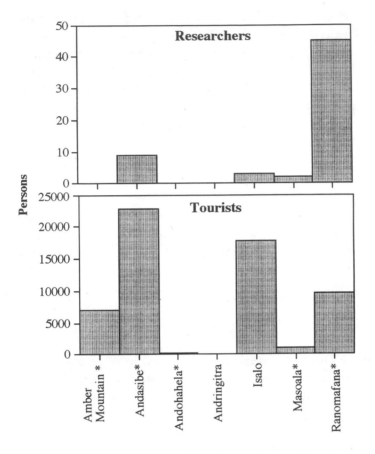

Figure 9-6. Comparisons in number of researchers and numbers of tourists among six parks in Madagascar. Asterisks indicate those parks that received international ICDP funding from 1990 to 1998. Data from ANGAP.

lagasy) learning biodiversity research techniques and conservation biology theory at the research station over three months. This five-year training grant was funded by the USAID University Development Linkage Program (UDLP) and included 131 students from 1994 through 1999 who graduated with certificates.

When the "Big Money" Ended

The ICDP approach set up a dual and equal focus on biological conservation and human development.[36] In Madagascar the conservation agencies assumed the ICDP projects would be funded by USAID for the full fifteen years of the Environmental Action Plan that began in 1989, but in 1996 the validity of ICDPs as an approach to conservation was being challenged by USAID, World Bank, ANGAP and ONE (L'Office National de l'Environnement). In most of the conservation/development projects in Africa, the integrated programs had limited success in their initial phases.[37] By 1997 the political pendulum was in full swing. ICDPs were described as "misguided efforts that fail to advance conservation, regardless of the success that can be achieved on the development side"[38] and the "bottom up" approach of working at the village level was deemed futile in the face of powerful economic forces such as inflation, fluctuations of trade barriers, global timber demand, warfare, and so forth. The high cost of ICDPs was criticized, and the disbursement of money to overhead and technical advisors was also faulted.[39] ICDPs were accused of putting money into assisting villagers but none into guarding the forest against trespassers, creating an "all carrot and no stick" situation.[40] Many experts challenged that the money from ICDPs should be put into a trust fund and the interest used in perpetuity for funding park operations.[41] Other conservationists suggested that the ecological foundations of biodiversity protection had been overlooked.[42]

Madagascar ICDPs were criticized as "too local in scope and too focused on the traditional concerns" of conservationists (protection of wildlife) and development experts (increasing agricultural production).[43] The runaway human population increases in Madagascar (3.1 percent) were not being adequately stabilized, and they dwarfed the positive advances of the ICDPs. Due to the success of the development projects, immigrants swelled the populations around the national parks, putting additional pressure on natural resources.[44] Although the Malagasy responded positively to the economic growth around the park, the necessary connection between the development projects and the conservation of the protected areas was not sound in the design phase and was even weaker in the implementation.[45] Expatriate advisors played an important role in training Malagasy counterparts and expediting programs that contained concepts new to the Malagasies. By Phase 2, Malagasies were active and vocal participants in conservation planning.

Because of the changing political climate in the United States, USAID decreased foreign aid, and Madagascar, which had grown to one of the largest USAID missions in sub-Saharan Africa, suffered a halving of its annual USAID budget from 1995 to 1997. This made it apparent there would be a reduction of funds available in Phase 2. The ICDP concept, a long-term approach, had only been in effect in Madagascar for three years out of the planned fifteen. But to address the criticisms and reduction of funds, USAID decided that its Phase 2 funds were not going to continue programs in and around protected areas but rather have a broader focus. The USAID funds would be spread over a whole region (landscape ecology approach), concentrating on partnering with other agencies and assessing socioeconomics and biological diversity in corridors between national parks.[46]

In 1997, the USAID-funded integrated conservation and development project Ranomafana National Park Project ended (see Figure 9-4). ANGAP took on direct responsibility for park management, conservation, and ecotourism in a limited number of protected areas. World Bank agreed to take over the funding previously provided by USAID to support the park operations for ANGAP, but the development funding was discontinued, and the international technical advisors were terminated. The jobs of 135 salaried local residents were in jeopardy.

For many ICDPs, the new policy meant the suspension of all health, education, and development operations. The transfer of responsibilities that was supposed to be taken by local Malagasy partner nongovernmental organizations (NGOs) to substitute for the USAID funding was occurring very slowly, because at the end of Phase 1, Madagascar had few Malagasy-run NGOs with proper infrastructure and training. A few "associations" had legal status but no ability to generate funds. Without continued agriculture, health, and education assistance, the agreements forged with village residents during 1987–1993 would be reneged with loss of trust and with repercussions that might include burning the park. Without international hard currency, there could be no computer upgrades, new equipment, or maintenance of already purchased equipment. Because of the need for maintenance caused by bad roads, all project vehicles were in jeopardy of becoming useless within three years. Protection of the park would have to be maintained, but there were neither policies nor funding to provide for effective law enforcement. How each of these problems was solved to accomplish sustainability is discussed below.

Management of Ranomafana National Park

Funding for the international "managers" (from Stony Brook and Cornell) and their technical advisors was terminated, and all Ranomafana National Park management responsibilities were turned over to ANGAP (National Park Service). At the same time that the management of RNP was given to

ANGAP, ANGAP was given direct management of twenty protected areas, with twenty-six more managed in collaboration with international NGOs and DEF.

The Ranomafana National Park's Malagasy staff was restructured and downsized. The infrastructure, salaries, and operations of the Ranomafana National Park were covered by a World Bank grant from GEF funds to the Republic of Madagascar for at least the five years of Phase 2. The three components retained from ANGAP personnel included conservation (border patrols, park infrastructure maintenance, and the ecological monitoring team), ecotourism (public awareness, entrance fee collection, tourist guides, and signage), and administration staff. The Malagasy park director maintained dynamic leadership of his well-trained and capable team.

Peripheral Zone Economic Development

When the ICDP was terminated, Cornell turned over all responsibilities for economic development of local communities to the Malagasy partner NGO, Tefy Saina, which lacks funding for operations in the peripheral zone of the park.

The agricultural assistance component is left to the return of half the revenue generated by the park entrance fees paid by tourists (Droit d'Entree Aires Protegees: DEAP). The amount generated annually by DEAP is divided into two parts, half for the communities and half for ANGAP to operate the park. The community share in 1998–1999 was approximately $50,000 (averaging $1,500 per village). There is a DEAP committee of twelve villagers from the peripheral zone (one voting member and one observer from each of the six *Firaisana* [counties]), which meet twice a year to discuss which villages will receive the funds. In the first few years, all DEAP funding was divided equally between the twenty-four *fokontany* (a cluster of two or three villages) which lie adjacent to the park boundary, dependent upon submission of accepted proposal by the DEAP committee.[47] Funded microdevelopment projects include building rice storehouses for the famine period, building small dams to expand paddy rice production in place of slash and burn, or buying seeds. It is possible that with expanding ecotourism, some villages will actually receive more financial assistance than they did under the ICDP.

Health, Education, and Research Components

With all salary and operational funds terminated for health, education, community development, and the Antananarivo RNP office, Stony Brook's

ICTE, the operators of the Ranomafana National Park Project sought to maintain personnel through this crisis.

The Ranomafana Park Project staff in charge of the health, education, and research facilitation component were reorganized into a Malagasy NGO called the Malagasy Institute for the Conservation of Tropical Ecosystems (MICET). This local NGO hired back the ICTE Malagasy staff trained in computers, finance, grant-writing, and conservation philosophy during the ICDP. Currently, funding for MICET and the health, education, and research assistant staff and programs is pieced together with small grants from Earthwatch Institute, a Stony Brook Fall Semester Abroad Program, small biodiversity research grants (written by international researchers), and small USAID development grants written by the MICET director and staff. The numbers of researchers and their financial contribution to maintaining the Ranomafana National Park Research Station staff and programs continues to increase (Figure 9-4). Researchers also contribute to the operation of MICET by paying a facilitation fee. The annual total generated by researchers for MICET is approximately $45,000, which pays for the fuel, repairs, and driver's salaries for six four-wheel-drive research vehicles, the salaries for thirty biodiversity research assistants based at RNP, and one administrative assistant's salary to translate proposals and reports and to obtain capture and export permits. The MICET NGO has recently expanded operations and, with the assistance of USAID funds, opened a regional office in Fianarantsoa for health and education.

Maintaining Research

Due to the unique biodiversity of Madagascar, Ranomafana has been a focus of numerous long-term research initiatives. Major studies include botanical plots, chameleon census areas, limnology monitoring, and lemur behavior. Stony Brook and other universities were committed to remaining in the Ranomafana Park, and yet there was a strong likelihood that research in the park would decrease.

When it took over management of the park, ANGAP invited ICTE to continue research within the park and its peripheral zone. The ecological monitoring team would remain under ANGAP but would be advised by ICTE. Research assistants would be salaried by ICTE, abiding by salary levels and regulations of ANGAP. ICTE agreed to share publications and data with ANGAP.

Overall research funding has made a lasting impact on the surrounding villages. Although individual research grants are small, when they are combined with fees paid by participants of programs such as Earthwatch and the Stony Brook Fall Semester Abroad Program in Madagascar, the sum adds up to over $500,000 a year (Figure 9-4). Much of the grant money is spent on the Malagasy local economy and salaries for local research assistants. The value of that research funding (versus large-donor funding) is higher to a Malagasy because research funds are not spent for either international administrative overhead or international salaries.

With an increasing demand for research, expansion of the research station facilities was necessary (Figure 9-3). Now researchers may stay continuously for two to eighteen months and come back annually over a research career (Figure 9-2). Not only does this generate money for the communities and the park, but also long-term social relationships develop between the scientists and the local residents. Through these long-term friendships, conservation ideas can have a wider impact through local families.

Finally, because of the high lemur diversity and accessibility in Ranomafana, many international educational film productions are shot in the park. This generates additional income for ANGAP through filming fees. The main value of films, books, and magazine articles is increasing international and national public awareness, which in turn generates untold numbers of tourists and donors.

Ecotourism

Although in Madagascar there were discussions of the possibility that parks could earn enough income to become self-sufficient, the truth is that even in wealthy countries like the United States or Costa Rica, parks must be subsidized.[48] It is clear that ecotourism may help the economic condition in roadside villages surrounding parks, but ecotourism is not the "silver bullet" that will provide funds to protect the remaining wilderness.[49]

Ranomafana, because of the unique opportunity to see six to eight species of lemur in a morning walk in the rain forest, is very popular with ecotourists. Although the revenue from tourism is welcome (Figure 9-4), management of tourists within the park is a problem. At present, high-end tourism, shown to offer the best economic return,[50] is not possible because of lack of infrastructure around the park, including the potholes in the narrow road. There are comfortable hotels, but no high-end luxury hotels.

Tourism has been increasing steadily (Figure 9-5), and restructuring tourist programming to limit tour groups on the trail system and to expand hours to include the afternoon or early morning is required in order to sustain or increase visits. Also, guidebooks have channeled all the tourists into one month (October), while Ranomafana is pleasant from September through December, and from late March through May. New ways to space tourist visits over many more months should be possible. But the fact remains that if both research and tourism increase in Ranomafana, careful planning must be done to avoid conflicts. Zoning is suggested in the management plan and should be fulfilled. ANGAP might consider hiring guides to habituate groups in other parts of the park and to spread out the impact.

Park Protection and Law Enforcement

Even though destruction and hunting are minimal, occasionally, village residents illegally collect crayfish for selling to restaurants, remove bamboo for housing, extract hardwoods for sale, and cut down large trees for honey within the park borders. At present the national park staff has no law enforcement authority. All enforcement in the park is delegated to the Department of Water and Forests (DEF), and if an infraction occurs, it is documented by the ANGAP staff and the appropriate DEF regional office is contacted. This creates a time lag between detection and enforcement that severely hinders enforcement. There are three parcels to Ranomafana National Park, and three separate regional offices of DEF are responsible for their protection. DEF is constrained by insufficient funds, lack of equipment, and no means of transportation. It is difficult to coordinate and successfully expedite enforcement between the two agencies.[51] Neither DEF nor ANGAP have authority to carry guns, but fortunately villagers do not own firearms in this region.

Ranomafana has a boundary of 251.13 kilometers (156 miles), which is patrolled by six to eight conservation agents employed by the park, totaling over 400 person days of patrolling boundaries annually. Patrols in the interior of the park are undertaken by an eight-person ecological monitoring team during scheduled surveys twice a year in four dispersed sites with a total of 504 annual person days of patrol in the interior.[52] People are caught encroaching, and the department of water and forests cites them, but the courts often let the timber exploiters off with a light fine. In 1991, a person was cited for timber exploitation but the case was not brought to court. In 1995, conservation agents discovered an area in the park where

125 hardwoods were cut and one timber exploiter received a suspension of his license.[53] None of the illegal exploitation was by people working for commercial companies.

The ANGAP Park Conservation agents patrol and document the exploitation of timber, bamboo, and crayfish, the setting of snares for lemurs and tenrecs, and tree cutting for honey collection. Although there have been responses by the park, such as public awareness campaigns, creation of bamboo plantations and crayfish ponds outside the park, and training in improved bee hive management, an enforcement presence is essential.[54] One solution is to increase the number of ANGAP conservation agents patrolling borders.

The new Code des Aires Protegees, approved by the National Assembly in 2000, gives ANGAP the power to conduct law enforcement inside protected areas. This law will increase the efficiency of enforcement.

The Ranomafana Research Station and Training Center

During the ten years of building up infrastructure within the parks of Madagascar, no long-term research stations with modern computer and scientific technology have been established. In a country with such high endemic diversity and high global biodiversity value, this lack of any central training center or modern biodiversity field stations is astounding. Research interest in biology, geography, anthropology, and conservation is increasing, but the infrastructural capacity to accomplish this research needs to be expanded.

Stony Brook/ICTE obtained initial funding from the National Science Foundation in the United States with matching funds from the University of Helsinki, Finland, for a research/training complex. The Ranomafana Biodiversity Research Station will have the capacity to train fifty people and to accommodate twenty-five short-term and ten long-term researchers. Air-conditioned laboratories will house a genetics laboratory (including a polymerase chain reaction machine and deep freezer), an entomology floor with voucher specimens and a database, an herbarium with voucher specimens, and will accommodate studies in limnology, aquatic studies, parasitology, and fecal hormone analysis. Audiovisual facilities will support international telecommunications and seminars.

This research station with international science standards opens up new research opportunities using modern technology for Madagascar scientists. It also offers a conservation education and training advantage to ANGAP, DEF, local schools, and universities of Madagascar. Plans to work closely with ANGAP to incorporate research results with park management will be useful to the park. The maintenance of a conservation library and a continually updated biodiversity and socioeconomic database for the park will be useful for tourists, teachers, scientists, and park managers.

Future Challenges in Malagasy Conservation

One of the major accomplishments of the conservation effort of the past eight years is the establishment of a functioning Madagascar national park system (ANGAP) with trained personnel, infrastructure, and sixteen parks (Figure 9-1).[55] ANGAP's network includes forty-six protected areas covering 17,103 square kilometers, but still less than 3 percent of Madagascar land is under the special protected status of national parks, special reserves, and strict natural reserves.[56] ANGAP's spatial analysis in and around protected areas demonstrates clearly that park or reserve status indeed has been a deterrent to serious loss of forest cover and biodiversity. But the small number of protected areas and the weak protection afforded them suggests that only with a large input of well-managed funding can we attain the goal of preserving Madagascar's unique biodiversity into the next decades. One of the major issues of the next five years is that of maintaining what remains of the natural corridors linking the protected areas of the country, especially down the east coast.[57] ANGAP addresses this protection of corridors in a systematic, positive, and concrete manner in its new five-year strategic plan, PLANGRAP, 2000.[58] Interest in Madagascar's biodiversity, spearheaded by publicity generated by researchers, has skyrocketed. Within the last decade, tourism has become the number one industry in Madagascar and 65 percent of the tourists that visit Madagascar visit protected areas (Madagascar Bureau of Tourism). In addition, most of the headwaters of Madagascar's river systems are sustained from the forested watersheds of national parks. If these disappear, irrigation for agriculture, hydroelectric power, and drinking water for humans and livestock will vanish. Malagasy, including the political leaders, are beginning to become aware that their own economic future depends upon successful conservation, continuing research, and appropriate tourism development in and around national parks.

But conservationists cannot rest on their laurels. No one has devised a reliable long-term solution to the problem of tavy, and without stopping the burning of forests, biodiversity destruction will continue. Madagascar is one of the world's "biodiversity hotspots,"[59] and more than any other geographic region may be struggling with the biggest risks following the loss of species.[60]

Conclusions

Ranomafana is a park that began as an ICDP, and in the long term is working. The ingredients that contributed to its success include the following:

• Parks in Madagascar can be relatively small, yet capable of containing and maintaining rich biodiversity making it relatively easier to generate adequate funding for neighboring communities and relatively easier to develop ecotourism that satisfies local needs. Ranomafana is easily accessible by road and is therefore able to take advantage of ecotourism potential.

• Madagascar's forests are not subject to large-scale commercial logging, compared to those of Southeast Asia and West Africa, making it relatively easier to defend the parks against large-scale commercial interests.

• The people living near the parks are relatively poor, making it easier for an ICDP to make important contributions to their basic needs and thus to have more influence on their decision making.

• The local people have strong traditions and respect for laws, unlike the frontier mentality prevailing in many unstable areas in the Americas, Asia, and Africa.

• Ranomafana National Park is an ongoing and dynamic process of identifying problems and designing solutions.

• From the very beginning, the park was closely linked to research scientists with long-term commitments to biodiversity and the human population. Research fees go directly for local salaries. Research knowledge, such as the long-term system of ecological and peripheral village monitoring, is used in park-management planning. Research news also attracts the international and national media, which in turn promotes public awareness, good public relations, and increased tourism to generate more funds for the park and its neighbors.

• Ranomafana's firm foundation began with good training of Malagasies in management skills, computer and technology skills, research skills, finance and/or administration; the end result is a committed and capable staff.

The ongoing trust of the villagers in the ICDP assisted in establishing good relations in the peripheral zone. Now, after the ICDP, village residents directly benefit from the park by receiving revenues generated by tourists. Ultimately, continued maintenance of this park in the future depends on a concerted effort to stop the "culture of burning" with new techniques to shade out the invasive nonendemic grasses and allow reforestation and agroforestry.

The long-term commitment by international and national research institutions with conservation priorities working in close cooperation with the Madagascar National Park Service (ANGAP) is a major part of the continued success of Ranomafana. The research station and training center promises to be a focus for the interchange among ANGAP, the researchers, and the residents. As environmental problems become more pressing around the world, the application of basic biological research to practical problems becomes more urgent, and close collaborations between universities and conservationists should be encouraged.[61]

Acknowledgments

Many thanks to the organizers of the conference, "Making Parks Work," held at the White Oak Plantation in Florida, Carel van Schaik, John Terborgh, Lisa Davenport, Madhu Rao, and the late Marina Riley. Jukka Jernvall, Rickie van Berkum, Sharon Pochron, Chris Chapple, Chia Tan, Peter Riley, Sarah Karpanty, and two anonymous reviewers added important ideas and advice regarding this manuscript. Figures are by J. Jernvall. Our special thanks to the funders, especially to the Liz Claiborne and Art Ortenburg Foundation, the John D. and Catherine T. MacArthur Foundation, Douroucouli Foundation, USAID, and UDLP. Our sincere gratitude to all the people who made the Ranomafana Park Project a productive, problem-solving endeavor.

Notes

1. N. Myers, R. A. Mittermeier, C. G. Mittermeier, G. A. B. da Fonseca, and J. Kent, "Biodiversity Hotspots for Conservation Priorities," *Nature* 403 (2000): 853–858.

2. R. A. Mittermeier, "Primate Diversity and the Tropical Forest: Case Studies from Brazil and Madagascar and the Importance of Megadiversity Countries," in *Biodiversity*, ed. E. O. Wilson and F. M. Peters (Washington, D.C.: National Academy Press, 1988), 145–154; P. C. Wright, "The Future of Biodiversity in Madagascar: A View from Ranomafana National Park," in *Natural Change and Human Impact in Madagascar*, ed. S. M. Goodman and B. D. Patterson (Chicago: University of Chicago Press, 1997), 406–418.

3. G. M. Green and R. W. Sussman, "Deforestation History of the Eastern Rainforests of Madagascar from Satellite Images" *Science* 248 (1990): 212–215.

4. R. E. Dewar, "Recent Extinctions in Madagascar: The Loss of the Subfossil Fauna," in *Quarternary Extinctions: A Prehistoric Revolution*, ed. P. S. Martin and R. G. Klein (Tucson: University of Arizona Press, 1984), 574–593; L. R. Godfrey, W.L. Jungers, K. E. Reed; E. L. Simons, and P. S. Chatrath, "Subfossil Lemurs: Inferences about Past and Present Primate Communities in Madagascar," in *Natural Change and Human Impact in Madagascar*, ed. S. M. Goodman and B. D. Patterson (Washington, D.C.: Smithsonian Institution Press, 1997), 218–257.

5. A. Jolly, "The Madagascar Challenge: Human Needs and Fragile Ecosystems," in *Environment and the Poor: Development Strategies for a Common Agenda*, ed. H. J. Leonard (New Brunswick, N.J.: Transaction Books, 1989), 189–211; J. U. Ganzhorn, P. C. Wright, and J. Ratsimbazafy, "Primate Communities: Madagascar," in *Primate Communities*, ed. J. G. Fleagle, C. H. Janson, and K. E. Reed (Cambridge: Cambridge University Press, 1999), 75–89.

6. D. W. Gade, "Deforestation and Its Effects in Highland Madagascar," *Mountain Research* 16 (1996): 101–116.

7. N. Myers, *Deforestation Rates in Tropical Forests and Their Climatic Implications* (London: Friends of the Earth Trust, 1989); Green and Sussman, "Deforestation History."

8. A. F. Richard and S. O'Conner, "Degradation, Transformation, and Conservation: The Past, Present and Possible Future of Madagascar's Environment," in Goodman and Patterson, *Natural Change*, 406–418.

9. A. F. Richard and R. H. Sussman, "Framework for Primate Conservation in Madagascar," in *Primate Conservation in the Tropical Forest*, ed. C. W. Marsh and R. A. Mittermeier (New York: Alan R. Liss, 1987), 329–341; Jolly, "Madagascar Challenge"; J. Durbin and J. Ralambo, "The Role of Local People in the Successful Maintenance of Protected Areas in Madagascar," *Environmental Conservation* 21, no.2 (1994): 115–120.

10. D. M. Lewis and P. Alpert, "International Trophy Hunting and Wildlife Conservation in Zambia," *Conservation Biology* 11 (1997): 59–68.

11. Wright, "Future of Biodiversity."

12. R. Swanson, *National Parks and Reserves, Madagascar's New Model for Biodiversity Conservation: Lessons Learned through Integrated Conservation and Development Projects (ICDP)* (s.l.: ANGAP/DIVB/SIG publication, 1996); R. Swanson, *Baseline Data: ICDP Protected Area Program (1994–1996) Vegetative Cover Evolution* (s.l.: ANGAP/DIVB/GIS publication, 1996).

13. B. Meier, Y. Rumpler, A. Peyriaras, R. Albignac, and P. C. Wright, "A New Species of *Hapalemur* in Southeastern Madagascar," *Folia Primatologica* 48 (1987): 211–215; P. C. Wright, "Primate Ecology, Rainforest Conservation and Economic

Development: Building a National Park in Madagascar," *Evolutionary Anthropology* 1 (1992): 25–33.

14. M. Nicoll and O. Langrand, *Les Aires Protegees de Madagascar* (Washington, D.C.: WWF and Conservation International, 1989).

15. Wright, "Future of Biodiversity."

16. J. P. Benstead, M. L. J. Stiassny, P. V. Loiselle, K. J. Riseng, and N. Raminosoa, "River Conservation in Madagascar," in *Global Perspectives on River Conservation: Policy and Practice*, ed. P. J. Boon, B. R. Davies, and G. E. Potts (New York: John Wiley & Sons, 2000), 203–229.

17. R. van Berkum and P. C. Wright, "The Publication List from Ranomafana National Park," ICTE, Stony Brook Report, 2000.

18. D. J. Overdorff, A. M. Merenlender, P. Talata, A. Telo, and Z. A. Forward, "Life History of *Eulemur fulvus rufus* from 1988–1998 in Southeastern Madagascar," *American Journal of Physical Anthropology* 108 (1999): 295–310; P. C. Wright, "Demography and Life History of Free-ranging *Propithecus diadema edwardsi* in Ranomafana National Park, Madagascar," *International Journal of Primatology* 16 (1995): 835–854; P. C. Wright, "Lemur Traits and Madagascar Ecology: Coping with an Island Environment," *Yearbook of Physical Anthropology* 42 (1999): 31–72.

19. C. Kremen, "Biological Inventory Using Target Taxa: A Case Study of the Butterflies of Madagascar," *Ecological Applications* 4 (1994): 407–422; Wright, "Future of Biodiversity."

20. D. J. Overdorff, "Differential Patterns in Flower Feeding by *Eulemur fulvus rufus* and *Eulemur rubriventer* in Madagascar," *American Journal of Physical Anthropology* 28 (1992): 191–203; D. J. Overdorff and S. G. Strait, "Seed Handling by Three Prosimian Primates in Southeastern Madagascar: Implications for Seed Dispersal," *American Journal of Primatology* 45 (1998): 69–82; C. Kremen, "Assessing the Indicator Species Assemblages for Natural Areas Monitoring: Guidelines from a Study of Rain Forest Butterflies in Madagascar," *Ecological Applications* 2 (1992): 203–217; Kremen, "Biological Inventory"; L. A. Nilsson, E. Rabakonandrianina, B. Pettersson, and R. Grunmeier, "Lemur Pollination in the Malagasy Rainforest Liana *Strongylodon craveniae* (Leguminosae)," *Evolutionary Trends in Plants* 7 (1993): 49–56; P. C. Wright and L. B. Martin, "Predation, Pollination and Torpor in Two Nocturnal Primates *Cheirogaleus major* and *Microcebus rufus* in the Rainforest of Madagascar," in *Creatures of the Dark*, ed. L. Alterman, G. Doyle, and M. K. Izard (New York: Plenum Press, 1995), 45–60; J. L. Dew and P. C. Wright, "Frugivory and Seed Dispersal by Four Species of Primates in Madagascar's Eastern Rainforest," *Biotropica* 30 (1998): 1–3; P. C. Wright, "Impact of Predation Risk on the Behavior of *Propithecus diadema edwardsi* in the Rain Forest of Madagascar," *Behaviour* 135 (1998): 1–30; Wright, "Lemur Traits."

21. F. J. White, D. J. Overdorff, E. A. Balko, and P. C. Wright, "Distribution of

Ruffed Lemurs (*Varecia variegata*) in Ranomafana National Park, Madagascar," *Folia primatologica* 64 (1995): 124–131; Benstead et al., "River Conservation"; E. A. Balko, "A Behaviorally Plastic Response to Forest Composition and Habitat Disturbance by *Varecia variegata* in Ranomafana National Park, Madagascar" (Ph.D. diss., SUNY, Syracuse, 1998).

22. P. N. Reinthal and M. L. J. Stiassny, "The Freshwater Fishes of Madagascar: A Study of an Endangered Fauna with Recommendations for a Conservation Strategy," *Conservation Biology* 5 (1991): 231–243; Benstead et al., "River Conservation."

23. J. Laakonen, J. Lehtonen, and H. Rakotovoany, "Incidence of Parasites in *Rattus rattus* in Peripheral Zone Villages and within Ranomafana National Park," *Conservation Biology* (in press).

24. P. Ferraro and B. Rakotondranjaona, *Preliminary Assessment of Local Population Forest Use, Forestry Initiatives, Agricultural Operations, Cultural Diversity, and the Potential for Rural Development in the Region of the Ranomafana National Park, 1990–1991. Report for MAB* (s.l.: U.S. State Department, 1991); L. Kightlinger, "Mechanisms of *Ascaris lumbricoides* Overdispersion in Human Communities in the Malagasy Rainforest" (Ph.D diss., University of North Carolina at Chapel Hill, 1993); S. P. Hardenbergh, "Undernutrition, Illness and Children's Work in an Agricultural Rainforest Community in Madagascar" (Ph.D. diss., University of Massachusetts at Amherst, 1993); S. P. Hardenbergh, "Behavioral Quality and Caloric Intake in Malagasy Children Related to International Growth References," *American Journal of Human Biology* 8 (1996): 207–223; S. P. Hardenbergh, "Why Are Boys So Small? Child Growth, Diet and Gender near Ranomafana, Madagascar," *Social Science and Medicine* 44 (1997): 1725–1738; L. Kightlinger, J. R. Seed, and M. B. Kightlinger, "The Epidemiology of *Ascaris lumbricoides*, *Trichuris trichura*, and Hookworm in Children in the Ranomafana Rainforest, Madagascar," *Journal of Parasitology* 81, no.2 (1995): 159–169.

25. Kightlinger, "Mechanisms."

26. Kightlinger, "Mechanisms"; Hardenbergh, "Behavioral Quality"; Hardenbergh, "Why Are Boys So Small?"

27. Kightlinger et al., "Epidemiology."

28. B. Johnson, "Soils of Ranomafana National Park," Report to Duke University, 1994.

29. D. Del Castillo, "Economic Development in Peripheral Zone Villages of Ranomafana National Park 1991–1993," Report to Duke University, 1993.

30. Ferraro and Razafimamonjy, *Preliminary Assessment*.

31. M. T. Irwin, T. M. Smith, and P. C. Wright, "Census of Three Eastern Rainforest Sites North of Ranomafana National Park: Preliminary Results and Implications for Lemur Conservation," *Lemur News* 5 (2000): 20–22; S. L. Lehman and P. C. Wright, "Preliminary Study of the Conservation Status of Lemur Communi-

ties in the Betsakafandrika Region of Eastern Madagascar," *Lemur News* 5 (2000): 23–25.

32. Maps in Swanson, *Baseline Data*.

33. S. Grenfell, "Management Plan for Ranomafana National Park," ICTE report, 1995; J. Peters, "Sharing National Park Entrance Fees: Forging New Partnerships in Madagascar," *Society and Natural Resources* 11, no.5 (1998): 517–530.

34. Swanson, *Baseline Data*.

35. Swanson, *National Parks*.

36. K. E. Brandon and M. Wells, "Planning for People and Parks: Design Dilemmas," *World Development* 20 (1992): 557–570; D. Western, M. Wright, and S. Strum, *Natural Connections: Perspectives on Community Based Conservation* (Washington D.C.: Island Press, 1994); P. Alpert, "USAID's Expanded Program to Conserve Biodiversity in Sub-Saharan Africa" *Ambio* 23 (1994): 167; P. Alpert, "Integrated Conservation and Development Projects: Examples from Africa," *Bioscience* 46 (1996): 845–855.

37. Alpert, "Integrated Conservation"; Swanson, *National Parks*.

38. J. Terborgh, *Requiem for Nature* (Washington, D.C.: Island Press, 1999).

39. T. T. Struhsaker, *Ecology of an African Rainforest: Logging in Kibale and the Conflict between Conservation and Exploitation* (Gainesville: University Press of Florida, 1997).

40. C. van Schaik and R. Kramer, "Toward a New Protection Paradigm," in *Last Stand: Protected Areas and the Defense of Tropical Biodiversity*, ed. R. Kramer, C. van Schaik, and J. Johnson (New York: Oxford University Press, 1997), 212–230; R. A. Kramer and N. Sharma, "Tropical Forest Biodiversity Protection: Who Pays and Why," in Kramer et al., *Last Stand*, 162–186.

41. M. Wells, "Social-Economic Strategies to Sustainably Use, Conserve and Share the Benefits of Biodiversity," in *Global Biodiversity Assessment*, ed. V. H. Heywood and R. T. Watson (Cambridge: Cambridge University Press, 1995), 1016–1033; J. Resor and B. Spergel, *Conservation Trust Funds: Examples from Guatemala, Bhutan and the Philippines* (Washington, D.C.: World Wildlife Fund–U.S., 1992); Struhsaker, "Ecology of an African Rainforest"; J. F. Oates, *Myth and Reality in the Rain Forest: How Conservation Strategies Are Failing in West Africa* (Berkeley: University of California Press, 1999).

42. K. MacKinnon, "The Ecological Foundations of Biodiversity Protection," in Kramer et al., *Last Stand*, 36–63.

43. Richard and O'Conner, "Degradation."

44. Swanson, *National Parks*.

45. Swanson, *National Parks*.

46. USAID report, 1998.

47. Grenfell, *Management Plan*.

48. M. A. Boza, "Conservation in Action: Past, Present and Future of the National Park System of Costa Rica" *Conservation Biology* 7 (1993): 239–247.

49. D. W. Yu, T. Hendrickson, and A. Castillo, "Ecotourism and Conservation in Amazonian Perú: Short Term and Long Term Challenges," *Environmental Conservation* 24 (1997): 130–138.

50. J. A. McNeely, "Critical Issues in the Implementation of the Convention on Biological Diversity," in *Widening Perspectives on Biodiversity*, ed. A. F. Krattiger, J. A. McNeeley, W. H. Lesser, K. R. Miller, Y. St. Hill, and R. Senanayake (Gland, Switzerland: IUCN [The World Conservation Union], 1994), 7–10.

51. Grenfell, *Management Plan*.

52. Grenfell, *Management Plan*.

53. Grenfell, *Management Plan*.

54. Grenfell, *Management Plan*.

55. Swanson, *National Parks*; Swanson, *Baseline Data*.

56. ANGAP, "PLANGRAP," report (ANGAP, 2000).

57. Irwin et al., "Census"; Lehman and Wright, "Preliminary Study."

58. ANGAP, "PLANGRAP."

59. Myers et al., "Biodiversity Hotspots."

60. J. Jernvall and P. C. Wright, "Diversity Components of Impending Primate Extinctions," *Proceedings of the National Academy of Sciences USA* 95 (1998): 11279–11283.

61. Alpert, "Integrated Conservation"; C. Kremen, J. O. Niles, M. G. Dalton, G. C. Daily, P. R. Ehrlich, J. P. Fay, D. Grewal, R. P. Guillery, "Economic Incentives for Rain Forest Conservation Across Scales," *Science* 288 (2000): 1828–1832; S. L. Pimm, "Conservation Connections" *Trends in Ecology and Evolution* 169 (2000): 262–263.

10

Expanding Conservation Area Networks in the Last Wilderness Frontiers: The Case of Brazilian Amazonia

CARLOS A. PERES

Tropical forest cover worldwide has been slashed by about half since the mid-1900s, and continues to shrink at an annual rate of about 0.8 percent.[1] Yet less than 5 percent of what remains is protected, even on paper.[2] To make matters worse, enforcement and adequate protection of tropical parks have typically failed to keep up with the growing assault of human activities around and inside them.[3]

The situation of parks is particularly acute in densely populated parts of mainland Africa, Madagascar, South Asia, Central America, and the Brazilian Atlantic forest where protected areas, whether or not shielded by a buffer zone, have become surrounded by a hostile matrix. Survival of plant and animal populations stranded in many of these isolates are likely to face the negative synergisms of habitat degradation, insularization, and resource exploitation. The fate of biodiversity in much of these regions will thus ultimately rest on the size and degree of de facto protection of existing nature reserves.[4]

In contrast, the last remaining tropical forest wildernesses, such as Amazonia, the Guyana shield, Gabon, the Congo Basin, and the island of New Guinea, remain comparatively intact. In these areas, opportunities are still available for expanding the existing system of reserves so long as financial, sociopolitical, and institutional constraints can be overcome. Before additional parks are established, however, thoughtful planning will be required because the financial and political costs of creating new reserves can detract from competing investments in the near-term implementation and management of existing reserves.

This chapter considers how conservation investments can be most efficiently allocated within regions where conservation planning still remains a realistic proposition. I explore the enormous disparity between nature reserve selection in theory and in practice, and focus on Brazilian Amazonia because this region presents one of the greatest opportunities for planning tropical biodiversity conservation on a near-continental scale. I also offer suggestions for a conservation agenda for "frontier forest" regions like Amazonia that remain chronically undersampled in terms of biodiversity distribution at varying spatial scales.

Selection of Conservation Areas

Reserve selection and design have become a major subdiscipline of conservation biology. The focus is on where, rather than how, to direct conservation action, and the challenge is to decide which are the most efficient combinations of available areas representing the best biodiversity value.[5] The issue of efficiency has been repeatedly flagged as crucial because the area of land or financial resources available for conservation is usually limited, and conservation often competes with incompatible land uses for managing unprotected areas.

Several optimization criteria for conserving biodiversity have been devised.[6] However, most priority-setting approaches require comprehensive biodiversity databases, which may be a reality in regions like Europe, Australia, southern Africa, and North America but are unavailable over most of the humid tropics. Even qualitative data on species distributions at coarse spatial scales lags behind habitat degradation brought about by widespread agricultural development. Identifying key biodiversity areas on the basis of optimality criteria is thus no longer an option where these could be informed by exhaustive biological inventories and the best conservation science. However, where large tracts of tropical wilderness still exist, real-world applications of reserve selection models are both feasible and desperately needed. Unfortunately, the available data on species distribution in such regions is sketchy at best. Consequently, optimization criteria for conserving biodiversity have not been successfully applied in countries that have already implemented a national reserve system or those that are yet to do so.[7] New approaches that build on data currently available, rather than on idealized comprehensive knowledge, are therefore needed.

Conservation in Brazilian Amazonia: Threats and Opportunities

Brazilian Amazonia is by far the largest tropical forest region under the jurisdiction of a single country and presents one of the last opportunities to design a robust system of nature reserves. Nowhere else is forest loss occurring faster than in the Amazon; deforestation rates between 1995 and 1999 averaged 1.9 million hectares per year, even if clearings of less than 6 hectares and areas extensively affected by logging and ground fires are excluded.[8] To make matters worse, in the one-third of Amazonia that repeatedly experiences strong seasonal droughts,[9] recurrent surface fires are likely to drive irreversible transitions in forest structure and composition that will rapidly erode the regional biota.[10] Time is thus rapidly running out for implementation of a comprehensive system of reserves to protect Amazonian biodiversity, particularly in areas threatened by forest fragmentation, selective logging, and surface fires.

The Brazilian Ministry of Environment recently commissioned one of the largest conservation priority workshops ever convened, finally honoring a commitment dating from the 1992 Earth Summit in Rio. The meeting, which took place in Macapá, Brazil (September 1999), was cosponsored at a cost of over US$350,000 by several multilateral and government agencies.[11] The meeting drew 168 specialists on the Amazon, including systematists, forest ecologists, social scientists, and land-use planners. The participants' collective knowledge of species richness, rarity, and endemism were coupled with socioeconomic and political criteria contributed by social scientists and development experts.

The Macapá meeting extended the approach used during a similar priority-setting gathering held in Manaus in 1990,[12] except that socioeconomic and political criteria were also considered given the demands of local communities, regional economic opportunities, and areas of greatest threats to biodiversity. However, deliberations within most biological working groups remained tied to species occurrence gradients perceived by the specialists who happened to be present. The final results of the workshop clearly recognized the huge geographical gaps in baseline knowledge for all taxonomic groups considered. This discomposing ignorance is primarily a function of the huge sampling bias toward accessible areas and forest types, the large variance in sampling effort across sites, and the very small proportion of the basin sampled at any intensity for even the best-known taxa. In fact, priority areas were delineated more often on the basis of the gut feeling and geographic experience of the specialists than by clear scientific rationale. Moreover, basin-wide distribution data even on the best-known groups, such as birds and mammals, when these eventually become available, will probably make poor predictors of the richest sites for endemic, rare, or threatened species in other taxa, as suggested by the poor cross-taxa congruence in hotspots in both temperate[13] and tropical regions.[14] The first two major Amazonian conservation priority workshops were thus almost equally limited by a similar set of problems, despite the ten-year research effort separating them.

Selecting Reserves at Broader Ecological Scales

In the absence of species distribution data, vegetation probably offers the best-available surrogate of species turnover for plant and animal assemblages.[15] This would be a "coarse filter" strategy for identifying conservation areas.[16] Natural vegetation types in tropical forest regions reflect environmental gradients that affect species distributions, including geomorphology, elevation, soils, seasonal variation in hydrology, and natural disturbance regime. The most refined classification of Amazonian vegetation was produced by Projeto RadamBrasil and identified a total of seventy natural plant communities, mostly on the basis of vegetation structure.

In lowland parts of the region, large rivers can form important geographic barriers.[17] A set of biogeographic units defined by the overlay of the most important river barriers and vegetation types could be used as a basis for evaluating the representation of existing conservation areas. The assumption here is that such a gap analysis would capture most of the region's biodiversity without the need to carry out detailed species inventories. This approach was used in a priority-setting analysis that defined twenty-three "ecoregions" on the basis of the IBGE (Brazilian Bureau of Geography and Statistics) vegetation map and thirteen major interfluvial regions.[18] The extent to which these ecoregions were included in existing nature and indigenous reserves was then evaluated. In this analysis, less than 4 percent of the area of sixteen (of the twenty-three) ecoregions comprised nature reserves, and four ecoregions remained entirely unrepresented. This is an improvement over a previous gap analysis considering the same vegetation types within the boundaries of nine Amazonian states (rather than interfluvial regions), which also concluded that only 37 of the 111 "vegetation zones" considered had any portion included in a conservation unit.[19]

The key to such coarse-grained approaches is maximization of complementarity in reserve representation across reasonably distinctive sub-
regional biotas. In the short term, this type of approach probably offers
the best hope of achieving a geographically balanced and robust pan-Ama-
zonian reserve network irrespective of ecoregional differences in species
richness, occurrence of rare and endemic species, ecosystem vulnerabil-
ity, and urgency to counteract threats. A limitation of such methods, however, is that they provide little guidance on the specifics of reserve design,
including size, shape, connectivity, position within watersheds, level of
protection of conservation units, and land use in the intervening habitat
matrix, all of which are crucial to the long-term biological integrity of future reserves.

Toward a Robust Reserve Network Embedded in a Benign Matrix

Ideally, one could imagine a regional mosaic of megareserves (greater
than 1 million hectares) interconnected by multiple-use forest areas under
different levels of protection. Offsetting such ideal visions is the harsh reality that state governments, their urban constituents, the rural population, and the private sector of regions like Amazonia all yearn for development. Conservationists are thus faced with a major challenge in
achieving a satisfactory balance between the growing economic aspirations of the populace and the long-term interests of biodiversity conservation. This will always be a difficult compromise, but any such balance
should go beyond the usual rhetoric of sustainable development and ensure the long-term maintenance of functional landscapes, large parts of
which must retain their full species assemblages. In Amazonia, this means
not simply retaining jaguars, small-eared dogs, woolly monkeys, Guianan
crested eagles, giant otters, kapok trees, and rosewoods, but also maintaining large-scale ecological phenomena such as fish migrations, and the
seasonal habitat shifts exhibited by a wide range of frugivores.[20] On a
smaller spatial scale, age-old *terra firma* forest salt licks, which are important to the nutritional ecology of many vertebrates, can only be maintained if fresh layers of clay continue to be exposed by large geophagous
mammals, such as tapirs.[21] The perpetuation of positive feedback between
species and ecological processes can only be ensured by an appropriate
degree of connectivity within an ecologically benign habitat matrix
around parks.

A promising way to promote the long-term retention of natural forest
cover outside parks would be to incorporate Indian areas, extractive

reserves, and national forests into a wider system of conservation areas under varying degrees of protection. Legally recognized Indian lands span tens of millions of hectares of undisturbed Amazonian forests, and account for 248 of all 459 officially designated conservation areas in all nine Amazonian countries or 52 percent of the entire area receiving some protection.[22] In terms of combined acreage, they currently represent over 100 million hectares, or 20.7 percent of Brazilian Amazonia.[23] Indian areas also tend to be larger, have low human population densities, remain relatively intact, and collectively provide better geographic representation than other reserve categories.[24] They therefore shelter a considerable fraction of the Amazonian biota that remains unprotected elsewhere and can serve as buffer zones for adjacent nature reserves. Similar conservation roles can be played by extractive reserves and national forests. This is offset by financial constraints in that recent macrostructural adjustments in Brazil have led to severe funding cuts to FUNAI (Fundação Nacional do Índio), the agency responsible for implementation of Indian areas. Clearly, this limits the ability of government conservation agencies to operate in Amazonia and means that fewer implementation targets, including reserve identification, demarcation, and aid programs, will actually be met. The vacuum left by the absence of government action further strengthens the significance of independent alliances between conservationists and native Amazonians.[25]

The expansion of Amazonian conservation areas finds political support in Brazil's 1998 constitution, which grants state governments considerable autonomy in land-use planning, which in turn has decentralized reserve creation and management initiatives. In fact, several Amazonian states are already engaged in a process of "economic and ecological zoning," each of which will include the establishment of a minimum number of reserves under varying levels of land-use restriction. These land-use plans must however ensure that they are coordinated across neighboring states.

How Much Is Enough?

Brazil is one of at least twenty-five nations that have ratified the IUCN/WWF proposal to protect at least 10 percent of their territories. Expansion to the 10 percent target would treble the acreage of Amazonian strictly protected areas (national parks, biological reserves, and ecological stations) that currently represent only 3.25 percent of the region.[26] The Brazilian Environment Ministry has vowed to create sixty new conservation units encompassing some 28.5 million hectares of forest by 2005.[27] Combined with the thirty existing federal reserves, these are expected to protect 41 million hectares or some 10 percent of the forest in Amazonia. Although these additional commitments to conservation are commendable, grave concerns could be expressed over the facile 10 percent target, which can give the false impression of being enough to avert mass extinction. Clearly, a flat figure is biologically inappropriate. Ecosystems differ greatly in their responses to habitat loss and fragmentation, and no predictions of extinction rates to be expected under different deforestation scenarios are currently available for Amazonia. However, the minimum area required to capture and preserve habitats for rare species, or to protect all plant species in different interfluvial regions, is likely to exceed 10 percent by a large margin. Estimates for the conserved area required to avert a mass extinction in most temperate regions range from 25 to 75 percent.[28]

Large reserves can also be justified by the needs of wide-ranging vertebrates that habitually move across two or more vegetation types on a seasonal basis. Although this entire phenomenon remains poorly documented, abundant anecdotal evidence suggests that forest types which typically fruit asynchronously can operate synergistically in supplying the year-round demands of a number of key bird and mammal species. Seasonal movements across adjacent forest types in Amazonia have been reported for several species of parrots, cotingas, fruitcrows, piping guans, primates, white-lipped peccaries, and a few bats.[29] To date, the need to accommodate short-distance migrations and lateral movements has barely entered discussions on reserve selection and design. Nevertheless, large reserves incorporating both terra firme and flooded forests will be more effective than equivalent areas of homogeneous habitat.

Consolidation of Land Titles

Private inholdings constitute a major threat to many officially designated protected areas in the Brazilian Amazon, and fewer than half of the federal parks in the region are wholly in the public domain. A 1992 estimate of the financial investments needed to consolidate land titles in all remaining preserves came to US$524 million.[30] Private landholdings and claims constituted 65 percent of the legal Brazilian Amazon by 1990,[31] and the percentage is undoubtedly much higher today given the relentless frontier expansion and land speculation.

To date the issue of private inholdings within protected areas is yet to be addressed, so the official statistics on total conservation acreage are largely illusory. In default of government leadership, the door remains open to private purchase of biologically important areas that fill in major regional gaps in the current distribution of protected areas. Opportunity knocks in the form of hundreds of large, defunct rubber estates that have been effectively on sale since the final collapse of the rubber boom. Land prices for primary forests in central Amazonia, which are often entirely undisturbed and nonhunted for several decades, can be as low as US$3–10 per hectare. For example, a small conservation NGO based in Manaus recently acquired 50,000 hectares of undisturbed forest at Lago Uauaçú, Amazonas for US$10 per hectare with funds granted by a private donor.[32] Despite its limited management capacity, this NGO was able to obtain a private reserve status (RPPN) from the Brazilian Environment Agency (IBAMA), which will formalize the conservation status of the area and reduce the reserve maintenance costs in the form of land taxes. Additional landholdings adjacent to this area could still be purchased to secure an ambitious expansion target of 500,000 hectares of permanently protected forests. This reserve is to be comanaged by a small *caboclo* community that has traditionally subsisted on small-scale harvest of Brazil nuts and will willingly help prevent commercial exploitation by outsiders. Given that affordable pristine forest landholdings are becoming available throughout several Amazonian states, this test case, which is already attracting considerable attention from large conservation NGOs, could become a successful model for the rapid expansion of the Amazonian conservation landscape.

Conclusions

A preventive rather than remedial approach to conservation action will always be far more cost effective in the last pre-frontier tropical forest regions. This includes the identification and creation of new reserves whether or not they can actually be implemented shortly thereafter. Forest disturbance and deforestation in Amazonia are more likely to occur in public lands of ambiguous or unofficial status than in conservation areas under any designation, even if protected "on paper" only. In the Brazilian state of Rondônia, for example, the proportion of forest cover cleared outside parks (47.1 percent) is far greater than that inside (3.1 percent) even within nominally protected preserves.[33]

This is all the more urgent given the sheer scale of deforestation and forest degradation predicted to occur in the aftermath of Avança Brasil, a massive infrastructural development program worth some US$40 billion.[34] A federally coordinated land-use plan for zoning the entire Amazon should be effectively implemented *before* powerful agents of disturbance are unleashed by new paved roads, pipelines, hydroelectric dams, powerlines, and river channelization projects. So far these efforts have been at best fragmentary, based on no particular ecologically rational criteria, and pursued by local governments under different spheres of political influence. Every measure and policy incentive to retain unlogged primary forest cover within private, communal, or public landholdings should be vigorously pursued. These may include financial compensation to local communities or municipal administrations for the opportunity costs of holding on to undisturbed forests, which may become a reality if Brazil reverses the current policy of rejecting carbon-offset funds from bilateral or multilateral agreements. Another cost-effective option that would complement the 10 percent expansion target for strictly protected areas would be the massive sequestration of newly accessible public lands into extractive reserves and sustainable forestry areas (national forests), thus reducing the supply of free-for-all forest resources and cheap landholdings,[35] that will continue to attract "cut and run" logging operations.

The Amazon urgently needs to reorganize its zoning regulations from a historically messy land titling system and include many more large forest reserves under varying degrees of protection ranging from people-free parks to areas under benign forms of exploitation. The private timber industry also needs to be severely restricted through steeper taxes and enforceable penalties, which could help fund field operations deployed by financially weakened environmental agencies. Although Brazilian legislators can pride themselves in having a highly sophisticated set of environmental laws, they tend to lack teeth in the vast Amazonian frontier. Haphazard frontier expansion without commensurate investments in government institutions to effectively enforce conservation legislation only perpetuates the boom-and-bust cycle that will continue to impoverish both the biota and the rural population of the largest tropical forest on Earth.

Notes

1. D. Bryant, D. Nielsen, and L. Tangley, *The Last Frontier Forests: Ecosystems and Economies on the Edge* (Washington, D.C.: World Resources Institute, 1997).

2. WCMC (World Conservation Monitoring Center), *Global Biodiversity: Status of the Earth's Living Resources* (London: Chapman and Hall, 1992).

3. C. A. Peres, "Exploring Solutions for the Tropical Biodiversity Crisis," *Trends in Ecology and Evolution* 9 (1994): 2–4.

4. R. Kramer, C. P. van Schaik, and J. Johnson, eds., *Last Stand: Protected Areas and the Defense of Tropical Biodiversity* (Oxford: Oxford University Press, 1997).

5. P. H. Williams, "Key Sites for Conservation: Area-selection Methods for Biodiversity," in *Conservation in a Changing World: Integrating Processes into Priorities for Action*, ed. G. M. Mace, A. Balmford, and J. R. Ginsberg (Cambridge: Cambridge University Press, 1998), 211–249.

6. See R. L. Pressey et al., "Effects of Data Characteristics on the Results of Reserve Selection Algorithms," *Journal of Biogeography* 26 (1999): 179–191; B. Csuti, S. Polasky, P. H. Williams, R. L. Pressey, J. D. Camm, M. Kershaw, A. R. Kiester, B. Downs, R. Hamilton, M. Huso, and K. Sahr, "A Comparison of Reserve Selection Algorithms Using Data on Terrestrial Vertebrates in Oregon," *Biological Conservation* 80 (1997): 83–97; S. L. Pimm and J. H. Lawton, "Planning for Biodiversity," *Science* 279 (1998): 2068–2069.

7. J. R. Prendergast, R. M. Quinn, and J. H. Lawton, "The Gaps between Theory and Practice in Selecting Nature Reserves," *Conservation Biology* 13 (1999): 484–492.

8. INPE (Instituto Nacional de Pesquisas Espaciais), *Deforestation Estimates for the Brazilian Amazon* (São José dos Campos, Brazil: Instituto Nacional de Pesquisas Espaciais, 2000).

9. D. C. Nepstad, A. Veríssimo, A. Alencar, C. Nobre, E. Lima, P. Lefebvre, P. Schlesinger, C. Potter, P. Moutinho, E. Mendoza, M. Cochrane, and V. Brooks, "Large-scale Impoverishment of Amazonian Forests by Logging and Fire," *Nature* 398 (1998): 505–508.

10. M. A. Cochrane, A. Alencar, M. D. Schulze, C. M. Souza, D. C. Nepstad, P. Lefebvre, and E. A. Davidson, "Positive Feedbacks in the Fire Dynamic of Closed Canopy Tropical Forests," *Science* 284 (1999): 1832–1835; C. A. Peres, "Ground Fires as Agents of Mortality in a Central Amazonian Forest," *Journal of Tropical Ecology* 15 (1999): 535–541.

11. ISA (Instituto Socio Ambiental), "Geographic Priority Actions for the Conservation and Use of Biodiversity in Brazilian Amazonia," Macapá, Brazil, 20–25 September 1999, Instituto Socio Ambiental (http://www.socioambiental.org/website/bio/).

12. A. B. Rylands, "Priority Areas for Conservation in the Amazon." *Trends in Ecology and Evolution* 5 (1990): 240–241.

13. J. R. Prendergast, R. M. Quinn, J. H. Lawton, B. C. Eversham, and D. W. Gibbons, "Rare Species, the Coincidence of Diversity Hotspots and Conservation Strategies," *Nature* 365 (1993): 335–337; A. S. van Jaarsveld, S. Freitag, S. L. Chown, C. Muller, S. Koch, H. Hull, C. Bellamy, M. Kruger, S. Endrody-Younga, M. W. Mansell, C. H. Scholtz, "Biodiversity Assessment and Conservation Strategies," *Science* 279 (1998): 2106–2108.

14. J. H. Lawton, D. E. Bignell, B. Bolton, G. F. Bloemers, P. Eggleton, P. M. Hammond, M. Hodda, R. D. Holt, T. B. Larsen, N. A. Mawdsley, and N. E. Stork, "Biodiversity Inventories, Indicator Taxa and Effects of Habitat Modification in Tropical Forest," *Nature* 391 (1998): 72–76; P. C. Howard, P. Viskanic, T. R. B. Davenport, F. W. Kigenyi, M. Baltzer, C. J. Dickinson, J. S. Lwanga, R. A. Matthews, and A. Balmford, "Complementarity and the Use of Indicator Groups for Reserve Selection in Uganda," *Nature* 394 (1998): 472–475.

15. J. M. Scott, F. Davis, B. Csuti, R. Noss, B. Butterfield, C. Groves, H. Anderson, S. Caicco, F. Derchia, T. C. Edwards, J. Ulliman, and R. G. Wright, "Gap Analysis: A Geographic Approach to Protection of Biological Diversity," *Journal of Wildlife Management* 123 (1993): 1–41.

16. R. F. Noss and A. Y. Cooperrider, *Saving Nature's Legacy: Protecting and Restoring Biodiversity* (Washington, D.C.: Island Press, 1994).

17. J. M. Ayres and T. H. Clutton-Brock, "River Boundaries and Species Range Size in Amazonian Primates," *American Naturalist* 140 (1992): 531–537.

18. L. V. Ferreira, R. L. Sá, R. Buschbacher, G. Batmanian, and J. M. C. Silva, "Identificação de areas prioritárias para a conservação da biodiversidade atraves da representatividade das unidades de conservação e tipos de vegetação nas ecorregiões da Amazonia Brasileira," report to PRONABIO (Programa Nacional de Diversidade Biológica), (Brasília, D.F., Brazil: PRONABIO, 1999).

19. P. M. Fearnside and J. Ferraz, "A Conservation Gap Analysis of Brazil's Amazonian Vegetation," *Conservation Biology* 9 (1995): 1134–1147.

20. T. Haugaasen and C. Peres, manuscript in preparation.

21. C. Peres and M. Eben, manuscript in preparation.

22. C. A. Peres, "Indigenous Reserves and Nature Conservation in Amazonian Forests," *Conservation Biology* 8 (1994): 586–588.

23. F. Ricardo, "Terras Indigenas na Amazônia legal," report to PRONABIO (Programa Nacional de Diversidade Biológica), (Brasília, D.F., Brazil: PRONABIO, 1999).

24. C. A. Peres and J. W. Terborgh, "Amazonian Nature Reserves: An Analysis of the Defensibility Status of Existing Conservation Units and Design Criteria for the Future," *Conservation Biology* 9 (1995): 34–46.

25. B. Zimmerman, C. A. Peres, J. Malcolm, and T. Turner, "Conservation and Development Alliances with the Kayapó, a Tropical Forest Indigenous Peoples," *Environmental Conservation* 28 (2001): 10–22.

26. Ferreira et al., *Identificação de areas prioritárias*.

27. MMA(Ministério do Meio Ambiente), *Amazônia sustentável: Agendas positivas* (Brasília, D.F.: Ministério do Meio Ambiente, 2000). Information available via the Internet at http://www.mma.gov.br.

28. Noss and Cooperrider, *Saving Nature's Legacy*; M. E. Soulé and M. A. Sanjayan, "Conservation Targets: Do They Help?" *Science* 279 (1998): 2060–2061.

29. C. Peres and T. Haugaasen, manuscript in preparation.

30. C. V. Espírito Santo and A. A. Faleiros, *Custos de implantação de unidades de conservação na Amazônia Legal* (Brasília, D.F.: Funatura, 1992).

31. INCRA (Instituto Nacional de Colonização e Reforma Agrária), *Cadastro rural e situação jurídica dos imóveis rurais* (Brasília, D.F.: Instituto Nacional de Colonização e Reforma Agrária, 1990).

32. M. van Roosmalen, personal communication.

33. L. Ferreira, personal communication.

34. W. F. Laurance, M. A. Cochrane, S. Bergen, P. M. Fearnside, P. Delamônica, C. Barber, S. D'Angelo, and T. Fernandes, "The Future of the Brazilian Amazon," *Science* 291 (2001): 438–439; C. A. Peres, "Paving the Way to the Future of Amazonia," *Trends in Ecology and Evolution* 16 (2001): 217–219.

35. G. Carvalho, A. C. Barros, P. Moutinho, and D. Nepstad, "Sensitive Development Could Protect Amazonia Instead of Destroying It," *Nature* 409 (2001): 131.

11

The National Sanctuary Pampas del Heath: Case Study of a Typical "Paper Park" under Management of an NGO

FERNANDO B. RUBIO DEL VALLE

In this chapter, I offer the reminiscences and reflections of an administrator charged with converting a "paper park" into a true protected area under the aegis of The Nature Conservancy's "Parks in Peril" program. The "paper park" in question was the 102,109-hectare National Sanctuary Pampas del Heath (SNPH) located at the foot of the Andes in the subtropical forest zone of southeastern Perú. The Rio Heath, which defines the sanctuary's eastern limit, also forms the international boundary with Bolivia. SNPH was established as a strict protected area in 1983 for the primary purpose of conserving the only example of humid tropical savanna found in Perú. A major impetus to the creation of the protected area was the discovery of two large mammals, the marsh deer and maned wolf, not known to occur anywhere else in the country.

SNPH is embedded in the southwestern Amazon, a region that has been internationally recognized as harboring extraordinary biodiversity and therefore accorded high priority for conservation. Together with Manu Biosphere Reserve to the west, Tambopata-Candamo reserved zone to the south, and Madidi National Park to the east in Bolivia, SNPH is part of one of the greatest concentrations of protected tropical forests in the world.

When the Pampas del Heath National Sanctuary was established as a reserve, there were no people living within its boundaries, although there were two communities nearby totaling about three hundred individuals. One of these was an Ese-eja indigenous settlement, and the other was made up of recent mestizo colonists from the Andes. In addition, about fifty licensed concessionaires from the departmental capital, Puerto Maldonado, collected Brazil nuts both inside and outside the borders on a seasonal basis. About a dozen concessions fell inside the reserve boundaries, but in practical terms the declaration of the protected area did not affect the collection of Brazil nuts.

Members of the indigenous community used the reserve for fishing, hunting, and gathering of forest products. The mestizo community depended more on the market system than did the Ese-eja, and in addition to hunting and fishing for their own consumption, they sold timber, Brazil nuts, game, and turtle eggs to generate income. There was also some commercial big game hunting organized by a local outfitter.

Management Philosophy

The planning process conducted prior to the establishment of the SNPH followed the centralized and vertical lines that characterized policy creation in the country as a whole. The process did not involve the local population or even the regional authorities in Puerto Maldonado. The setting of boundaries, definition of objectives, and designation of restrictions were all imposed from the national capital.

For eight years following the legal declaration of SNPH in 1983, the government took no steps to implement management. SNPH was truly a "paper park" that existed in an administrative vacuum and offered open access to resource users. Paper-park status persisted until 1991 when a Peruvian nongovernmental organization (NGO) (Fundación Peruana para la Conservación de la Naturaleza [FPCN], now Profauna) with the support of an international counterpart, The Nature Conservancy (TNC), obtained government authorization to manage the reserve under TNC's Parks in Peril program.

The sanctuary's management under the FPCN was relatively independent of the public sector within the framework of the agreement with the government. Independence was furthered by a lack of public-sector experience in protected-area management and the lack of any regional office of the government agency responsible for protected areas. Consequently, the administrative office for the sanctuary was established by FPCN in a private building.

Hands-on management of the sanctuary was a novelty for local public-sector officials, and for the population in general, and attracted great interest as to what was being done and not being done. At this time (early 1990s), the new ideas of ecology, protected areas, and conservation were becoming popular in Perú, spurred by the reporting of several influential print and television journalists. The popularity of the environmental movement in Puerto Maldonado could be traced to the influence of Manu National Park, the outreach activities of another NGO (Asociación para la Conservación de la Selva Sur) and the increasing prominence given to environmental issues by the media.

It is important to note that despite the tight link that existed between the management of SNPH and its NGO sponsor, I always had to keep in mind that I was representing a government institution. Consequently, every management action was undertaken explicitly in the name of the sanctuary and not that of the FPCN. This policy engendered greater public trust in the management and led to increased support from local stakeholder groups, but it also had its drawbacks (see below).

In 1990, occurring almost simultaneously with the signing of the agreement with FPCN to manage the SNPH, the government established a much larger classified area in adjacent lands to the south and east. This was the 1.5-million-hectare Zona Reservada Tambopata-Candamo (ZRTC). Under Peruvian law, a *zona reservada* (reserved zone) has only provisional status as a protected area, subject to later deliberations and legislation concerning its final status. The ZRTC completely surrounded the SNPH and included the Ese-eja and mestizo communities and Brazil nut concessions mentioned above.

Management Challenges

Management of the sanctuary by an NGO was a first for the National Administration of Protected Areas. At the official level, the agreement with the FPCN was not seen as a transfer of the sanctuary's management to private hands even though in practice that is what it was. Instead, the government viewed the agreement as a project to support the sanctuary. To government administrators, the agreement did not recognize the types of functions and responsibilities that FPCN was obliged to implement on the ground. Some in the government insisted that before FPCN assumed a management role the government should develop some form of management for the area. Of course, this didn't happen. Conflicting interpretations of the agreement then led to weak government support for the whole venture. This, in turn, worked against the FPCN, for lack of clarity with respect to its role and responsibilities weakened its hand in dealing with local communities as well as public officials in Puerto Maldonado.

Knowing something of the nature of the public sector, I believe the main reason why the office of the National Administration of Protected Areas did not openly endorse the management agreement was because of fear that FPCN could take actions or make public declarations that would go against policy interests of the government, including oil, roads, and other economic initiatives.

It proved difficult for both parties to discover a mutually agreeable legal and administrative structure that would support effective management of the sanctuary. Of course, there were no precedents to help define such a structure, and the situation was exacerbated by a mutual lack of trust between the NGO sector and the parks authority. In consequence, the language of the agreement lacked any specific declaration that the project involved a total transfer of management responsibilities to the FPCN. Again, lack of clarity in the agreement brought negative consequences that complicated management of the sanctuary.

The ambiguities just described translated into a delay of official recognition of the sanctuary's staff, even after it had become operational in the field. As director, I was obliged to wear two masks, one with local communities, who recognized me as the director of the sanctuary, the other with NGOs and government officials, who considered me merely the coordinator of the project. These contradictions were not lost on my staff, the park guards in the field.

At the level of the regional capital, Puerto Maldonado, government officials were fed misinformation and innuendo asserting that I was abusing my authority in interactions with local communities. Such rumors were never based in fact but were reflections of local resentment at the imposition of restrictions that are inherent in the management of any protected area. The behavior of regional authorities was not limited merely to the indifference shown in critical times when the sanctuary's management was in conflict with local communities but went further to include active opposition without seeking the facts from both sides. In a typical example, the sub-prefecto (lieutenant governor) sent a letter to the director of protected areas (in Lima), complaining that I had no authority to make decisions about the use of natural resources by local communities, nor to institute control measures. This was all a result of misinformation and a lack of direct consultation with me.

Unfortunately, the decision to act in the name of the sanctuary, rather than in the name of the FPCN, did not always have the intended consequences. The policy was insufficient to overcome adverse attitudes toward the FPCN administration and resentment at the independence of action that we enjoyed. This resentment translated into a low level of acceptance and support on the part of the public sector and the people in general. The local media stirred the pot by publishing biased information and even personal attacks on the director.

At the outset, the FPCN management team constituted the only institutional presence in and around the SNPH. It was natural then that the local communities interacted with our organization. The general perception was that the SNPH was limiting the economic options for the further development of these communities. Our strategy for mitigating the resentment caused by restrictions on resource use was to join with the communities in seeking development alternatives that did not depend on extracting resources from the sanctuary. Because of this policy, and also because we were the only institution with a constant presence in the area, it did not take long to instill a sense of respect for our authority.

Later, however, when other NGOs came to work directly with indigenous communities and also with government-sponsored development programs, the aura of importance SNPH enjoyed early on began to fade, engendering a new set of problems. Although it was never intended that SNPH be the only institution to work with communities, our plan was to direct activities and support through SNPH as the principal national institution having a permanent presence in the area. The intent was that the communities would perceive that the institution limiting their access to resources was also the one proposing new development alternatives.

Unfortunately, the desired perceptions failed to materialize either because the people resisted the idea or because the seeds of jealousy were sown by other organizations that began to work in the region. Competition between NGOs led to programs that tried to gain the sympathy of the communities through paternalistic practices. The communities, in turn, quickly realized their advantage and began to exploit the situation for short-term benefits.

Our first concern after installing the FPCN management team was how to curtail the open-access status of SNPH that had been the reality during its long existence as a paper park. The first activities developed by our administration consequently emphasized the importance of adhering to the law throughout the protected area. We attempted to inculcate respect for the law through the training of park guards, the construction of guard posts, and the dissemination of outreach programs among local communities and stakeholder groups. In communicating with these groups, we emphasized that achieving conservation objectives required limiting access to natural resources. We also used these opportunities to exchange concepts and to discuss expectations, hoping to encourage more local involvement in the management of the sanctuary.

The most difficult challenge we faced was prohibiting commercial logging and hunting, practices that were well engrained in the mestizo population. The Ese-eja were less affected because they did not engage in commercial activities and because they enjoyed legal rights to exploit resources for their own subsistence, even within the sanctuary boundaries. Our strategy toward the Brazil nut collectors was to wait until their concession contracts expired and then block their renewal.

Roughly concurrently, the Tambopata Candamo Reserved Zone was created, bringing more restrictions to the same communities. After the communities protested, the restrictions were modified to allow limited use of resources. To this day, however, commercial hunting and logging remain forbidden.

Conclusions

The vertical imposition of the SNPH without consultation of local interest groups and its subsequent neglect by the government as a "paper park" created a strongly negative background on which to implement management. The first real management of the sanctuary was made possible by an agreement between the government and the FPCN, a Peruvian NGO supported by The Nature Conservancy of the United States. Subsequent interactions between the FPCN management team and regional government officials were complicated by distrust and resentment at what was viewed as usurpation of authority by officials.

FPCN management succeeded initially in controlling threats to the sanctuary with the support of an excellent corps of park guards. However, a legalistic approach to management led to conflicts with local populations that had previously enjoyed unrestricted access to the area. Later, the management strategy was refined to focus on more limited conservation objectives while trying to harmonize these objectives with community interests.

This experiment, in which management responsibilities for a public conservation area were given over to a private organization, can be considered a partial success. The presence of an administration and a staff of dedicated guards resulted in a vast improvement over the prior "paper park" condition. However, attempts to impose full legal control over the area were frustrated by the resistance of local populations and a lack of institutional support from responsible government agencies. These more negative aspects of the experiment should not be interpreted as intrinsic to public–private partnerships but rather as complications arising from the introduction of new ideas and practices that appeared threatening to stakeholders.

Postscript

The SNPH ceased to exist in 1998 when it was absorbed into the newly created Bahuaja-Sonene National Park, whereupon the management agreement with FPCN was terminated.

12

Successes and Failings of the Monteverde Reserve Complex and Costa Rica's System of National Protected Areas

GEORGE V. N. POWELL, SUZANNE PALMINTERI,
BOB CARLSON, AND MARIO A. BOZA

Costa Rica's system of protected areas is one of the world's most impressive, an icon of successful conservation. All parks and biological reserves carry some level of on-site infrastructure that has, by and large, protected habitats and allowed most native biodiversity to survive. In this chapter, we analyze the reasons for the conservation success of a private reserve, the Monteverde Reserve Complex, and also scrutinize the Costa Rican park system as a whole.

In addition to government-sponsored protected areas, Costa Rica contains a number of private nature preserves. The Monteverde Reserve Complex is certainly the largest and most renowned of these. It comprises a 27,000-hectare cluster of privately and nationally owned preserves situated astride the Tilaran mountain range in north central Costa Rica. The reserve complex is unequivocally a short-term conservation success because it has prevented the primary forest from being converted to cattle pasture, the fate of most unprotected forests in the vicinity. In addition to preserving most regional biodiversity, the reserve has earned local acceptance through its outreach programs and by creating a demand for visitor services. Nationally, the reserve contributes to fostering understanding of and support for conservation by annually drawing some fifty thousand tourists to experience the exquisite beauty of a tropical cloud forest. Globally, Monteverde is known to millions through television specials and exquisite photos that grace the pages of calendars and coffee table books.

These indicators of success are partly illusory if one takes a long-term perspective, because the reserve suffers from design flaws at both local and regional levels. At the local scale, the protected area is too small to sustain area-sensitive species and to fully represent all available habitats. On a larger scale, major gaps in habitat representation and a lack of critical linkages between protected areas will likely lead to biodiversity losses over time. On a temporal scale, global climate change can be expected to drive some habitats to extinction while redistributing others.

The Monteverde Reserve Complex

The Monteverde Reserve Complex (MRC) is a complex of six privately and publicly owned protected areas that were established over the last fifty years through a range of largely private initiatives. The reserve complex consists of a number of separate units that share common borders (Figure 12-1).

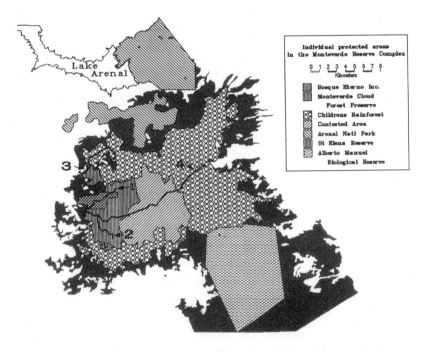

Figure 12-1. Individual protected areas that constitute the Monteverde Reserve Complex. The four trails, which existed prior to the establishment of the reserves, allowed access for deforestation. Purchasing the surrounding development rights allowed the trails to be closed to all but ecotourists.

1. Bosque Eterno Monteverde (550 hectares), the first element of the reserve complex, came into being when a group of dairy farmers who had immigrated to Costa Rica in 1950 set aside part of their holdings as a watershed protection area. The block officially became a protected area in 1976 when the owners incorporated themselves as Bosque Eterno SA (Eternal Forest Inc.). They then leased the land symbolically, for $1 per year, to the Tropical Science Center (owners of another private reserve in the area) for management as a protected area. To date, the owners of Bosque Eterno have played no active role in the management of their property but have deferred to the Tropical Science Center.

2. The Monteverde Cloud Forest Preserve (2,600 hectares) is owned and operated by the Tropical Science Center. It was created in 1972 by a U.S. graduate student and his wife in collaboration with one of Monteverde's dairy farmers. The three purchased rights to the land with personal funds and small donations raised from individuals and U.S. conservation organizations. The property was then turned over to the Tropical Science Center about a year later.

In 1976, the initiators of the Monteverde Cloud Forest Preserve obtained what at that time was considered a very large donation ($75,000) from the World Wildlife Fund. This enabled the Tropical Science Center (TSC) to enlarge the initial holdings and hire the first paid staff to manage the area. TSC has continued to expand its holdings between 1973 and the present through donations from a variety of foreign sources.

An additional 4,500 ha of protected forest was purchased through fundraising efforts of the Monteverde Conservation League, a local conservation group, on behalf of the Monteverde Cloud Forest Preserve. However, ownership has never been transferred to TSC and there is currently a legal battle between TSC and the Monteverde Conservation League over control of that land.

3. The Children's Eternal Rainforest (17,000 hectares), the third unit to be established, is owned and operated by a local nonprofit conservation organization, the Monteverde Conservation League (MCL), which was founded in 1986 through the efforts of expatriate biologists and the same local farmer who cofounded the Bosque Eterno. The MCL and its collaborating international funding organizations, The International Children's Rainforest Campaign, World Wildlife Fund (WWF)–Canada, and others, initially focused on eliminating the Penas Blancas development corridor, a swath of private land that traversed the continental divide and threatened to isolate major components of the reserve.

With the proceeds of a fundraising campaign that eventually reached around the world and attracted more than 100,000 donors, MCL purchased the holdings of at least one hundred individuals within the Penas Blancas corridor. Then MCL, in collaboration with TSC, successfully solicited the Costa Rican government to decommission a public road into the area.

Many individuals who sold land to the MCL had their primary properties, usually small dairy farms, in communities near the growing reserve complex. By investing the monies they received from the Penas Blancas land sales in their primary holdings they were able to increase their overall productivity, a fact that earned important local support for the MCL land purchase campaign.

4. The Santa Elena Cloud Forest Reserve (341 hectares) was established as a protected area in 1992 through the activity of a small group of residents of the nearby community of Santa Elena. The property is owned by a Costa Rican bank and leased and operated for ecotourism by a local public high school. The property was acquired by the bank upon default of a loan and left unattended for about fifteen years. This

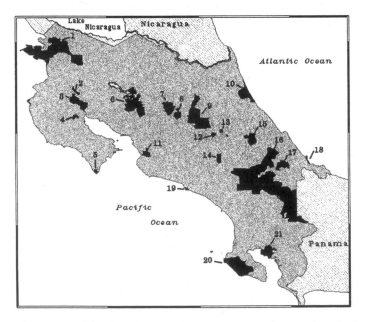

Figure 12-2. The distribution of protected areas (national parks, biological reserves, and private reserves) in Costa Rica. See Table 12-1 for attribute data.

allowed the forest to mature and become a tourist attraction.

    5. The Costa Rican Interior Ministry (MINAE), with support from the Canadian government, established Arenal National Park in the early 1990s on the northern side of the Tilaran mountains, adjacent to the Children's Rainforest. The national park has added another 2,700

Table 12-1.

Attributes of absolute protected areas in Costa Rica.

Identity Number	Conservation Area	Terrestrial Size (ha)
1	Guanacaste (NP)*	91,000
2	Lomas Barbudal (BR)	400
3	Palo Verde (NP)	16,800
4	Barra Honda (NP)	2,295
5	Cabo Blanco (NR)	1,235
6	Monteverde Reserve (Private and NP)	27,000
7	Juan Castro Blanco (NP)	14,312
8	Volcan Poas (NP)	6,506
9	Braulio Carrillo (Private and NP)	49,200
10	Tortuguero (PN)	23,903
11	Carara (BR)	4,838
12	Volcan Irazu (NP)	2,310
13	Volcan Turrialba (NP)	1,577
14	Tapanti (NP)	5,113
15	Barbilla (RB)	12,830
16	La Amistad (PN)	244,279
17	Hitoy Cerere (BR)	9,154
18	Cahuita (PN)	1,068
19	Manuel Antonio (PN)	682
20	Corcovado (PN)	41,789
21	Piedras Blancas (PN)	14,100

NP = national park; BR = biological reserve; NR = national reserve, which are all publicly owned; Private = privately owned reserves

*Guanacaste is an aggregate of three NP units.

hectares of forest to the reserve complex.

6. An additional national protected area, the Alberto Manuel Brenes Biological Reserve (8,300 hectares), which exists largely as a "paper park," is situated on the southwestern border of the Monteverde Reserve Complex. Although the area is still largely forested, it is only nominally protected.

In addition to this core of larger protected areas, a number of smaller holdings scattered around the complex receive varying degrees of protection from individual private owners. The Monteverde Institute, another local nongovernmental organization, has an outreach program that is implementing formal conservation easements with landowners in the area. We estimate these holdings amount to another 500 hectares. Although the area is small, the biological value is great because the habitats are otherwise poorly represented in the reserve complex.

The resulting complex of private and publicly owned protected areas totals about 27,000 hectares of middle elevation forest (1,000–1,800 meters). These holdings comprise about 10 percent of the Cordillera de Tilaran and 45 percent of the remaining forest in the region.

The birth and growth of the Monteverde Reserve Complex have been paralleled by the development of Costa Rica's national system of protected areas. Like Monteverde, the national park system was founded in the early 1970s when a single historic site, the Santa Rosa battlefield, was declared a national park. From this humble beginning, the national system of parks and biological reserves has grown into one of the most famous and admired in the world, now consisting of over twenty-four units covering 13 percent of the national territory (Figure 12-2, Table 12-1).[1] Erstwhile private lands have been purchased by the government, generally through international funding. Another 12 percent of the country receives less-strict protection as wildlife reserves, forest reserves, national wetlands, and similarly designated areas. Costa Rica's national parks are described in detail later in this chapter

Measuring Success

The success or failure of a protected area ultimately depends on the extent to which ecological processes that maintain biological diversity can be sustained over the long run. To meet this goal, a protected area must be well designed and adequately implemented. Successful design requires adequate representation of habitats and the ecological processes that maintain them (e.g., fire, floods), viable populations of all native species (including top carnivores), and connections to other protected habitat.[2] Successful implementation entails defining boundaries, removing squatters, controlling poachers, and motivating area residents and other stakeholders to respect the reserve and its conservation goals.

In the context of its brief three decades of existence, the MRC is unequivocally a conservation success that transcends its biological role of protecting local biodiversity. It has prevented the higher elevations of the Tilaran mountain range from being converted into cattle pasture, as has occurred in surrounding areas, and has permitted habitat recovery along the development corridors that were targeted in the land acquisition campaign. Currently, almost half of the remaining forest habitat in the Tilaran Mountains lies within the reserve. Most biodiversity known for the area is still extant, with the exception of some thirty amphibian species (see below).

Not all problems have been solved, however. A few sites within the reserve are under legal challenge by squatters who claim they were never appropriately compensated. As well, poaching remains a nuisance, but its incidence is declining.

The grassroots effort to create Monteverde has received widespread acclaim and contributed to global awareness of the need to conserve tropical rain forests. Benefiting from spectacular documentary films and by its location in Costa Rica, widely renowned as a "peace country," Monteverde has become a mecca for ecotourism. By 1990, annual visitation topped fifty thousand, about 80 percent of which was international. With tourism came magazine articles, photographs, and other media exposure.

A burgeoning ecotourism business has helped fuel economic growth in the communities adjacent to the reserve, creating a level of affluence that is atypical for such an isolated area. An unpublished 1991 study by Carmen Hildalgo revealed that tourism had produced at least four hundred full-time jobs in the area and was contributing on the order of US$3 million to the local economy, the exact figure depending on the multiplier used to account for local recycling of incomes. The positive economic impact of the reserve has yielded major dividends with respect to its acceptance by the surrounding communities.

Key Factors for Success

The successful implementation of the MRC must be ascribed to the dedication of a small number of individuals who have worked tirelessly on behalf of the reserve, even in the face of seemingly insurmountable odds. Without special training and guided only by a dream, these inspired individuals have raised funds, conducted legal work, negotiated land purchases, established a physical presence, enforced laws, and built local and national support for the reserve. We now elaborate on some of these steps.

Land Acquisition

Everyone with a justifiable land claim or use rights in an area within the Monteverde Reserve Complex identified as a conservation priority was bought out at a mutually agreeable price. All owners thus surrendered their rights voluntarily, which ensured that the acquisition process did not engender resentment. Many of those who sold holdings invested the proceeds locally, which fostered positive sentiment toward the reserve in the community. Had the land acquisition process not been so scrupulously executed, disgruntled claimants might have created a backlash that could have jeopardized the conservation effort.

Maintaining a Presence

It was clear from the outset that the local community would respect the conservation project only if community members maintained a physical presence in the area. The concept of conserving forest was initially alien and understood by few local residents. But because some of those involved in the effort were respected members of the community, for the most part residents were willing to accept the effort as something that would benefit, or at worst have a neutral effect on, their personal well being.

Although most community members were indifferent to establishment of the reserve, a small minority resisted. The hostile element of the community consisted mainly of poachers and squatters who hacked clearings in the forest in the hope of selling them as "improved" property. Active patrolling has been extremely important in minimizing the impacts of these two groups.

Law Enforcement

A need to protect the reserve while simultaneously maintaining good relations with the community required tact and sensitivity. Whenever possible, those caught hunting on the reserve were turned over to legal authorities. In the worst cases, repeat offenders had their dogs and arms confiscated. Evenhanded enforcement coupled with sensitivity to local values has engendered community support of the reserve and helped cast hunting in a negative light.

Defending the reserve against squatters presented a special challenge. The threat of invasions was especially serious at the beginning because Costa Rican law considered standing forest to be "unused," and provided protective legal mechanisms for poor people who appropriated forestland for their own use.

The reserve's managers were thus challenged to find a mechanism that would confer legal recognition of intact forest. This was achieved by registering all holdings under a forest-management law and filing a corresponding management plan that called for selective logging in the distant future. This action shifted the status of the land from unused to managed and made the government responsible for enforcing the management criteria, both with respect to actions taken by the landowner (the reserve) and by anyone attempting to appropriate land within the reserve.

Resolving the squatter challenge eventually required involvement of the Department of Forestry, the Colonization Institute, and the judicial system. Eventually, it emerged that the group of squatters that had been most persistent had been encouraged and financed by local "troublemakers" who were opposed to the existence of the reserve. Again, widespread community support for the reserve helped to deflect the challenge.

Building Local and National Support

The MCL maintains a local orientation and is made up exclusively of local residents at least half of whom are active farmers. At one time, the MCL engaged more than one hundred farmers in programs that focused on sustainable land use, watershed protection, and, indirectly, biodiversity conservation. Better understanding of the importance of forest protection for maintaining stream flow through the dry season has been crucial to consolidating local support for the protected area. One program, Bosques en Fincas, emphasized the creation of corridors on community farms as a means for maintaining populations of charismatic species such as the resplendent quetzal. Farmers subsequently fenced dozens of small forest fragments and planted small plots between them with native tree species to create corridors.

Through the efforts of the Tropical Science Center, Monteverde Cloud Forest Preserve has become a major destination for both national and international tourists. A visitor center, self-guided nature trails, a hummingbird feeding station, and other attractions have helped thousands of Costa Ricans to appreciate the value of biodiversity conservation. A modest environmental education program caters to local students. Economic benefits brought by hundreds of tourism-related jobs have fostered acceptance of the reserve, although the attitude of local merchants is less enthusiastic than one might wish.

Costa Rica's National Parks

The development of the national park system in Costa Rica has paralleled that of the private Monteverde Reserve Complex, though obviously at a much larger scale. National parks have been implemented through many of the same steps employed in Monteverde, including purchase of property rights, installation of a physical presence, law enforcement, and building local and national support.

However, the national park system operates under a large politically influenced bureaucracy that, in general, is less efficient than the small, nongovernmental organizations that were responsible for developing Monteverde. Substantial funds, generally from foreign sources, have been expended to purchase parklands (although inholdings still remain in many parks). All national parks now employ guards and benefit from secure boundaries.

To date, the task of building local and national constituencies has been a low priority of the national park system. With a few notable exceptions, such as the highly visible programs of Guanacaste National Park, little effort has been expended in outreach. Fortunately, the unforeseen rise of ecotourism as a major industry in Costa Rica has bolstered the political will that is necessary to defend a national commitment to protected areas. For example, when illegal gold miners invaded Corcovado National Park, little action was taken until the park service threatened to close the area to tourists. Only then did the government move to expel the miners.

Measuring the Success of Costa Rica's National Parks

Like Monteverde, Costa Rica's national parks have largely succeeded in protecting biodiversity. With a few exceptions, such as Corcovado National Park on the Osa Peninsula (which gold miners periodically invade), parks are largely stable entities with defined, respected boundaries. In most cases, the government has acquired full legal title to the land and actively protects boundaries through patrolling and legal actions. Poaching

Table 12-2.

Current and proposed coverage of life zones in Costa Rica's system of protected natural areas and distribution of remaining unprotected forest with respect to underrepresented life zones.

Life Zone	Zone Number	Adequacy of Representation[1]	Total in Costa Rica	Currently Protected (km²)	%	Total (km²)	Protected in Monteverde (km²)
(km²%)							
Tropical dry forest	1	*	943	51	5	29	0
Tropical dry–moist transition	2	**	291	2	1	0	0
Tropical moist forest	3	*	7,235	64	1	484	0
Tropical moist–dry transition	4	**	1,143	43	4	166	0
Tropical moist–wet transition	5	**	1,564	10	1	105	0
Tropical moist–premontane transition	6	**	761	17	2	100	0
Tropical wet forest	7	+	8,435	786	9	18	0
Tropical wet–premontane transition	8	+	2,601	372	14	108	9
Premontane moist forest	9	**	870	0	0	54	0
Premontane moist–basal transition	10	+	4,688	686	15	238	0
Premontane wet forest	11	*	4,364	98	2	340	6
Premontane wet–basal transition	12	+	6,984	139	2	239	0
Premontane wet–rain transition	13	**	759	35	5	162	4
Premontane rain forest	14	+	4,372	1371	31	500	173
Premontane rain–basal transition	15	**	76	0	0	0	0
Lower montane moist forest	16	**	238	0	0	0	0

Lower montane wet forest	17	**	1,125	42	4	45	3
Lower montane wet–moist transition	18	**	14	0	0	0	0
Lower montane rain forest	19	+	3,520	1764	50	134	57
Montane wet forest	20	**	16	2	13	0	0
Montane rain forest	21	+	1,170	624	53	0	0
Montane rain–L. montane transition	22	100%	10	10	100	0	0
Paramo	23	100%	43	43	100	0	0

Note: Underrepresented zones 1–6 are northwest seasonally dry habitats, zones 9, 11, 13, 16–18, and 20 are Pacific slope habitats between 500 and 1,500 meters.

[1]Adequacy levels:

+   minimum goal of 100 square kilometers, or at least 50 percent of life zones less than 10 kilometers in size, protected

*   50 to 100 square kilometers protected

**   less than 50 square kilometers protected

Figure 12-3. Breeding area and nonbreeding migratory sites of the resplendent quetzal (*Pharomacurs mocinno*) in the Monteverde area. Each point represents the centroid of the home range of a radio-colored individual during the non-breeding season. Individuals remained on their home ranges, which were mostly outside the protected area, for two to four months.

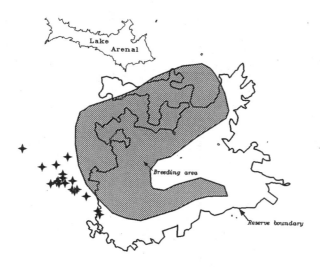

Figure 12-4. Breeding area and nonbreeding migratory sites of the three-wattled bellbird (*Procnius tricarunculata*) in the Monteverde area. Each point represents the centroid of the home range of a radio-collared individual during its initial migration in the nonbreeding season. Individuals remained in this area outside the protection of the reserve complex for about three months.

remains a problem at many locations, but overall the level is not serious enough to threaten species with extinction.

Prospects for Long-term Success

The prospects for long-term success of a protected area are best judged by applying the principles of conservation biology. These include the presence of all naturally occurring species within an area large enough to sustain top carnivores as well as natural ecological processes (e.g., floods), and connections via habitat corridors to other protected habitats.

Long-term Success of the Monteverde Reserve Complex

On the basis of the above criteria, the long-term prognosis for the Monteverde Reserve Complex is strongly negative. An area of 35,000 hectares of tropical forest will inevitably be too small to support the most area-demanding species if there is no connectivity between it and other large habitat blocks. A recent analysis of minimum area requirements for large predatory species, such as jaguar and harpy eagle, suggested that all such species are likely to be lost from protected areas smaller than 1,000 square kilometers.[3]

Already, Monteverde has lost its harpy eagles, and the local jaguar population is thought to consist of just a few individuals.[4] Unless continuing habitat loss in the greater Monteverde area is somehow checked, the reserve complex will continue to lose connectivity to the jeopardy of its remaining populations of large raptors and other predators.

Much of the biodiversity of the Tilaran Mountains is contained within its abundant and varied habitats, a wide elevational band of territory encompassing both the wet Caribbean slope and the relatively dry Pacific slope.[5] Adequate representation of all these habitats is crucial to ensuring the long-term success of the reserve. However, the Monteverde Reserve Complex includes only six of fifteen major habitat types that exist in the greater Monteverde area (Table 12-2).[6]

The importance of including the remaining major habitat types in the Monteverde Reserve has been demonstrated by several studies.[7] Bird distributions in the Tilaran Mountains, for example, are closely associated with life zones.[8] Up to one-third of mountain-dwelling bird species may engage in altitudinal migrations.[9] These depend seasonally on habitat types that are poorly represented in the reserve complex (Figures 12-3 and 12-4).[10] In addition, up to half of more than five hundred native species of butterflies migrate altitudinally in apparent response to precipitation cycles.

Considering these migratory patterns in relation to the habitats adequately protected by the reserve suggests that many species are at risk over the long term. These species have persisted to date because they are able to survive portions of their migratory cycles in unprotected forest fragments outside the reserve. Ironically, some of these areas have recently come under development pressure because new settlers are being drawn to Monteverde by the ecotourism boom.

Other elements of Monteverde's biodiversity are threatened by global climate change. For example, as many as thirty species of amphibians have disappeared from the reserve within the last two decades. The loss of so many species from a protected area can hardly be an accident. Recent research has attributed it to increasingly severe dry seasons accompanied by higher cloud cover and unprecedented periods without recorded precipitation. These trends, in turn, appear to be related to higher sea surface temperatures in the nearby Pacific Ocean.[11] As global warming intensifies, further losses of biodiversity from the Monteverde Reserve Complex appear inevitable.

Long-term Success of Costa Rica's National Parks

Costa Rica's national parks are similarly vulnerable to long-term losses of biodiversity, because quite generally they are of insufficient size to sustain viable populations of key species, lack connectivity, and seldom represent the full range of local habitat types. Only nine life zones out of the twenty-three found in the country are represented within Costa Rica's national park system by more than 100 square kilometers.[12] Another three are represented by 50–100 square kilometers. An additional eleven life zones, comprising 35 percent of the country, are scarcely represented at all, accounting for only 2 percent of the area protected (Table 12-2).[13]

Apart from the issue of representation, most protected areas in Costa Rica are too small to support viable populations of large predatory species.[14] Of the twenty-one national park system complexes (parks and biological reserves), only four are larger than 40,000 hectares. To compensate for their small size, connectivity among Costa Rica's protected areas becomes critical, a fact recognized by the government. But while plans are being made, progressive isolation of protected areas by agricultural lands continues.

Notes

1. M. A. Boza, *Parques nacionales Costa Rica* (Santo Domingo de Heredia, Costa Rica: Incafo, 1992).

2. R. Noss and A. Y. Cooperrider, *Saving Nature's Legacy: Protecting and Restoring Biodiversity* (Washington, D.C.: Island Press, 1994).

3. M. E. Soulé, "Where Do We Go from Here?" in *Viable Populations for Conservation*. ed. M. E. Soulé (New York: Cambridge University Press, 1987), 175–184; S. Palminteri, G. V. N. Powell, A. Fernandez, and D. Tovar, *Talamanca Montane-Isthmian Pacific Ecoregion-Based Conservation Plan: Preliminary Reconnaissance Phase*, report (Washington, D.C.: World Wildlife Fund, 1999).

4. Wilford Guindon, personal communication.

5. B. Young, D. DeRosier, and G. V. N. Powell, "The Diversity and Conservation of Understory Birds in the Tilarán Mountains, Costa Rica," *AUK* 115 (1998): 998–1016.

6. L. R. Holdridge, *Life Zone Ecology* (San Jose, Costa Rica: Tropical Science Center, 1967); R. A. Bolaños and V. Watson, *Mapa ecologica de Costa Rica segun el sistema de clasificacion de zonas de vida del mundo de L. R. Holdridge* (San Jose, Costa Rica: Centro Cientifico Tropical, 1993).

7. M. P. L. Fogden, *A Check List to the Birds of Monteverde and Penas Blancas* (San Jose, Costa Rica: Michael Fogden, 1994); Young et al., "Understory Birds."

8. Young et al., "Understory Birds."

9. D. J. Levey and F. G. Stiles, "Evolutionary Precursors of Long-distance Migration: Resource Availability and Movement Patterns in Neotropical Landbirds," *American Naturalist* 140 (1992): 447–476; B. A. Loiselle and J. G. Blake, "Population Variation in a Tropical Bird Community: Implications for Conservation," *Bioscience* 42 (1992): 838–845.

10. G. V. N. Powell and R. D. Bjork, "Implications of Altitudinal Migration for Conservation Strategies to Protect Tropical Biodiversity: A Case Study of the Quetzal *Pharomachrus mocinno* at Monteverde, Costa Rica," *Bird Conservation International* 4 (1994): 243–255.

11. A. Pounds, M. P. L. Fogden, and J. Campbell, "Biological Response to Climate Change on a Tropical Mountain," *Nature* 398 (1999): 611–615.

12. After E. Dinerstein, D. M. Olson, D. J. Graham, A. L. Webster, S. A. Primm, M. P. Bookbinder, and G. Ledec, *A Conservation Assessment of the Terrestrial Ecoregions of Latin America and the Caribbean* (Washington, D.C.: World Bank, 1995).

13. G. V. N. Powell, J. Barborak, and M. Rodrigez, "Assessing Representativeness of Protected Natural Areas in Costa Rica for Conserving Biodiversity: A Preliminary Gap Analysis," *Biological Conservation* 93, no.1 (1999): 35–41.

14. Palminteri et al., *Conservation Plan*.

13

Privately Owned Parks

JEFF LANGHOLZ

Establishment of protected natural areas has long been considered a task for governments. The quality of governmental protection, however, has often proven inadequate, with many parks existing only on paper.[1] Even if publicly owned parks were well protected, more than 93 percent of the world's land area and most of its biodiversity would still remain unprotected.[2] Given ongoing habitat destruction, especially in the tropics, it is imperative that the conservation community develop new and innovative approaches for in situ biodiversity protection.

Privately owned protected areas have emerged as one option. Private parks are proliferating throughout the world, yet little is known about them. Research has begun to address private parks, but only indirectly.[3] A few case studies highlighting various aspects of specific preserves have been completed,[4] and three researchers have conducted international mail surveys revealing private parks' activities, problems, economics, and other attributes.[5] Additional studies have verified the private sector's increasingly large role in biodiversity conservation.[6] In effect, what Dixon and Sherman called "a small but important development in protected area management" only a decade ago has evolved into a major new direction in conservation.[7]

Despite the sudden proliferation of private parks, and studies of them, they remain a mystery. Even experienced conservationists are hard-pressed to name more than a few of the world's privately owned parks let alone place them into a larger context. Given the limited public resources available for conservation and the growing interest in private sector initiatives, it is important that a systematic examination of this conservation phenomenon begin. This chapter takes a step in that direction. It reviews the current state of knowledge regarding privately owned parks and provides a country-level example from Costa Rica.

Overview of Privately Owned Parks

Contrary to popular belief, privately owned protected areas have existed in various forms for centuries.[8] The first scholarly reference to them occurred in 1962, when the First World Congress on National Parks acknowledged that many nature reserves throughout the world are "owned by private individuals, but are nevertheless dedicated in perpetuity to the conservation of wild life and of natural resources."[9] Since then, the private park niche has undergone rapid expansion. Unfortunately, this expansion remains largely undocumented, with virtually no information available on the number of privately owned parks in existence or their locations. The most recent United Nations list of the world's protected areas, for example, did not include privately owned parks. It did, however, briefly discuss them, noting that they are important because of the quality of the management and the protection afforded to them, and that they may become increasingly important, particularly in tropical countries, where state resources are very limited.[10] Similarly, the World Conservation Monitoring Center (WCMC) has only recently initiated an effort to collect data on private parks.

Anecdotal evidence suggests that private parks number in the thousands and that their numbers are growing rapidly. The amount of land they protect could be substantial. Alderman, for example, estimated that the sixty-three private reserves in her study were protecting roughly one million hectares.[11]

Private parks continue to thrive and proliferate both in industrialized countries and in the developing world. In Africa, for example, a huge nature tourism potential and long history of game ranches have prompted creation of private reserves. Private parks are also expanding in Latin America. Colombia, in particular, has a well-organized network of more than one hundred private reserve owners. Commenting on this network, the World Wildlife Fund notes, "the expansion of private reserves in Colombia provides an alternative to the government's insufficient management of natural lands and resources. The private approach to conservation increases the total area of protected lands, and, more importantly, directly involves citizens as stewards of their country's own natural resources for the future."[12] Likewise, Brazil has more than a hundred private reserves and a government incentive program to support them. Chile has a policy to promote private parks and is home to 270,000-hectare Pumalin, the world's largest private park.[13] The private-reserve phenomenon has been so strong that private reserves appeared on the agenda at a recent international conference on Latin American protected areas. They were also the topic of a special conference in late 1999 devoted exclusively to private parks' rapidly expanding role in Latin America.

Among industrialized countries, the United Kingdom has a long history of conservation on private lands. Examples include the National Trust and the Royal Society for the Protection of Birds, both of which have extensive networks of small protected areas.[14] Likewise, Australia has a growing private reserve niche filled by organizations such as the Australian Bush Heritage Fund and The Australian Koala Fund.[15] In the United States, The Nature Conservancy has a system of more than 1,300 reserves protecting well over half a million hectares. Safeguarding 1,725 rare species and communities, the parks range in size from 1.3 to 130,000 hectares and constitute "the largest private nature reserve system in the world."[16] Nonprofit land trusts also protect vast amounts of land, often through conservation easements if not by outright purchase.[17] In the western United States, a tradition of hunting reserves thrives, which is currently diversifying to include reserves devoted to wildlife viewing.[18]

If documentation of the private nature reserve niche has been lacking, an assessment of the motivating forces behind it has been nonexistent. Three closely related factors are likely driving the private-reserve phenomenon. The first factor—government failure—stems from the public sector's unwillingness or inability to meet society's demand for nature conservation. As noted earlier, government parks have proven inadequate in terms of quantity and quality of protection, especially in the tropics. Worse, many developing countries are deeply in debt and are decreasing rather than increasing funding for parks. The second factor—rising societal interest in biodiversity conservation—culminated in Brazil with the 1992 Convention on Biological Diversity.[19] Supplementing this international treaty is extensive documentation of biodiversity's ecological, genetic, social, economic, scientific, educational, cultural, recreational, aesthetic, and other values to humanity.[20] The final factor behind private-park proliferation is the explosion of ecotourism. Ecotourism has emerged as the fastest-growing segment of the larger tourism sector, which is generally regarded to be the world's largest industry.[21] Various authors have discussed its uneasy alliance with biodiversity conserva-

Table 13-1.

Strengths and weaknesses of the private-reserve model.

Strengths	Weaknesses
ECOLOGY	
• Protect biodiversity, especially compared to likely alternative land uses.	• Often small in size, which limits its ability to support biodiversity, especially of megafauna.
• Provide many of same values as public parks (e.g., purification of air and water, climate regulation, water production, and recreation).	• Informal status may lead to temporary or tenuous protection for some reserves.
• Can serve as temporary "way station," protecting valuable habitat until it can be declared a park by the government.	• Little, if any, monitoring and evaluation by higher authorities (i.e., governments).
ECONOMICS	
• Often profitable, allowing owner to earn a livelihood while protecting resources.	• Dependency on ecotourism revenues may be a vulnerability for some.
• Represent a substantial savings for governments that would otherwise have to purchase land and pay for its protection as a park.	• The need for financial self-sufficiency can lead to activities that place economics over ecology.
SOCIAL	
• Can be example of "devolution" of control over natural resources.	• Can sometimes be islands of elites, owned and visited only by the wealthy.
• Can be example of "participation" in resource decision making.	• Can cause social displacement and support land concentration by wealthy elites.
	• Foreign ownership may be viewed as new form of neocolonialism, causing considerable resentment.

tion,[22] including its role as impetus for private conservation efforts.[23]

Like the biological diversity they protect, privately owned protected areas vary dramatically. They have evolved into variations capable of filling a wide variety of conservation niches. Langholz and Lassoie have proposed a category system for private parks that supplements The World Conservation Union's (IUCN) existing typology for publicly protected areas.[24] Specific categories range from extremely formal natural areas gazetted as units in a nation's park system, such as those described in Langholz, Lassoie, and Schelhas,[25] to informally protected areas owned by farmers, community groups, corporations, and others.

Like every new conservation tool or trend, private parks offer advantages and disadvantages. Given their broad diversity, any sweeping generalizations about private parks are highly suspect. Langholz and Lassoie also peer beyond various manifestations of the private-park model to explore generally applicable strengths and weaknesses.[26] A brief synopsis appears in Table 13-1.

The Case of Costa Rica

Thus far, the nascent private reserve literature has relied primarily on case studies and international surveys. The former have been too specific, and the latter too broad, to provide a detailed assessment of private reserves' role in a national conservation strategy. What has been missing is a country-level assessment that analyzes their overall conservation niche—a study that combines both breadth and depth, at the national scale.

This section begins to fill that knowledge gap. It attempts to characterize the conservation role played by private nature reserves in Costa Rica, answering several key questions. For example, how many private reserves exist in Costa Rica? How much land are they protecting? What types of habitats do they include? What types of private reserves exist? Who owns them? What kinds of activities occur within the reserves? To what extent do they serve as corridors and buffer zones for public parks? Answers to these questions will increase our understanding of private reserves and their potential contribution to national conservation strategies.

This section is based on fieldwork conducted in Costa Rica from 1996 to 1997. The fieldwork included face-to-face interviews with sixty-eight private reserve owners (Table 13-2), as well as key government officials, community members, NGO (nongovernmental organization) representatives, and owners of seven reserves that formed a pilot test. Readers are referred to Langholz for detailed description of methods[27] and for the complete analysis and findings.[28] For data and analysis on additional topics such as reserve owners' diverse motivations, please consult Langholz, Lassoie, and Geisler.[29] For the purposes of this chapter, private reserves were defined as areas of at least 20 hectares that were intentionally maintained in a natural condition and were not owned by a government entity at any level.

Number and Types of Reserves

The first finding that the study revealed was that 211 private reserves exist in Costa Rica, of varying types and sizes. The total number of private reserves is estimated to be in the vicinity of 250 based primarily on additional reserves that surfaced after the study's completion. Although the final number will depend on the definition used (e.g., minimum-size requirement), these figures suggest a sizable private nature reserve niche in Costa Rica.

Private reserves fell into eight of the categories described in Langholz and Lassoie.[30] These included formal parks, program participants, ecotourism reserves, biological stations, hybrid reserves, farmer-owned forest patches, personal-retreat reserves, and NGO-owned reserves. This diversity suggests that like publicly protected natural areas, private nature reserves comprise several types. Policy-makers in other countries can choose to encourage or discourage certain types, given their country-specific circumstances.

Amount and Type of Land Protected

Likewise, it was found that sixty-eight reserves in the study were protecting a total of 34,688 hectares. According to figures contained in Boza and Ceva, the median size of national parks in Costa Rica was 14,258 hectares.[31] Thus, in purely geographical terms, private reserves in the sample added the equivalent of 2.4 national parks to the protected-area system. A more appropriate comparison, however, would be not with national parks but with the closest public equivalents of reserves—national wildlife refuges. In strictly geographical terms, reserves in the study group were adding the equivalent of 36.4 national wildlife refuges to the protected area system based on the median size (953 hectares) of Costa Rica's twelve publicly owned terrestrial national wildlife refuges.

Like public parks in Costa Rica, private reserve sizes varied dramatically. They ranged from 20 to 22,000 hectares, with a median of 101 hectares. Using the sample group as a base and the formula contained in

Table 13-2.

Private nature reserves in sample group.

Name of Reserve	Region	Size (hectares)
1. *Agua Buena*	Southern Zone (Palmar N.)	252
2. Aguila de Osa	Osa Peninsula (Drake Bay)	90
3. Albergue Buena Vista	Guanacaste (Liberia)	500
4. Albergue Cerro Alto	Talamanca Mountains (Cartago)	29
5. Albergue Monte Amuo	Talamanca Mountains (Buenos Aires)	147
6. Albergue Rio Savegre	Talamanca Mountains (San Isidro)	400
7. Arbofilia*	Central Pacific (Orotina)	80
8. *Aviarios del Caribe*	Atlantic Coast (Cahuita)	39
9. Bahia Esmerelda	Osa Peninsula (Matapalo)	20
10. Bosque del Cabo	Osa Peninsula (Matapalo)	96
11. Cabanas Escondidas	Central Pacific (Dominical)	32
12. *Cacyra*	Central Pacific (Orotina)	41
13. Carate Jungle Camp	Osa Peninsula (Carate)	100
14. Casa Orquideas	Golfo Dulce (Golfito)	22
15. Cebios	Osa Peninsula (Drake Bay)	100
16. The Children's Rainforest*	Tilaran Mountains (Monteverde)	22,000
17. *Cobano*	Osa Peninsula (Puerto Jimenez)	839
18. Corcovado Lodge Tent Camp*	Osa Peninsula (Carate)	80
19. *Costa Esmerelda*	Guanacaste (Sardinal)	60
20. *Curu*	Nicoya Peninsula (Paquera)	84
21. Dolphin Quest	Golfo Dulce (Golfito)	300
22. Drake Bay Wilderness Camp	Osa Peninsula (Drake Bay)	48
23. Durika Biological Reserve*	Talamanca Mountains (Buenos Aires)	792
24. EARTH*	Atlantic Slope (Guapiles)	600
25. Ecolodge San Luis	Tilaran Mountains (Monteverde)	40
26. El Barantes / La Garita	Guanacaste (Abangares)	84
27. El Mirador de San Gerardo	Tilaran Mountains (Monteverde)	35
28. Escuela Centroamericana de Ganaderia*	Central Valley (Atenas)	200
29. *Finantica*	Central Valley (Santa Ana)	35
30. Finca El Cedral	Puntarenas (Playa Cocal)	535
31. Ganaderia San Lorencito	Tilaran Mountains (San Ramon)	540

Name of Reserve	Region	Size (hectares)
32. *Genesis II Cloudforest Reserve*	Talamanca Mountains (Cartago)	47
33. Reserva Guapil	Central Pacific (Dominical)	100
34. *Hacienda Baru*	Central Pacific (Dominical)	227
35. Hacienda La Pacifica	Guanacaste (Las Canas)	650
36. *Hara Heinrik*	Nicoya Peninsula (Paquera)	42
37. Heliconia	Tilaran Mountains (Monteverde)	240
38. *Ingalls Family*	Nicoya Peninsula (Montezuma)	130
39. JadeMar	Osa Peninsula (Drake Bay)	21
40. Kiri Forest Reserve	Central Valley (Orosi)	65
41. Reserva Tangara	Sarapiqui (La Virgin)	238
42. *La Avellana*	Central Pacific (Orotina)	200
43. *La Ceiba*	Nicoya Peninsula (Paquera)	284
44. *La Ensenada*	Guanacaste (Chomes)	390
45. *La Marta*	Atlantic Slope (Turrialba)	1500
46. Laguna de Lagarto Lodge	Northeast (Pital)	250
47. Las Cusingas	Atlantic Slope (Guapiles)	17
48. Los Laureles	Central Pacific (Uvita)	45
49. Mapache Wilderness Camp	Southwest (Palmar Norte)	40
50. *Marenco Biological Reserve*	Osa Peninsula (Drake Bay)	800
51. Pacuare/Mondoquillo*	Atlantic Coast (Limon)	749
52. *Platanares*	Osa Peninsula (Puerto Jimenez)	249
53. Poas Volcano Ldge*	Central Mountains (Alajuela)	30
54. *Portalon*	Central Pacific (Quepos)	420
55. Punta Achiote	Central Pacific (Dominical)	78
56. *Punta Leona*	Central Pacific (Jaco)	20
57. Rainbow Adventures Lodge*	Golfo Dulce (Golfito)	543
58. *Rancho la Merced*	Central Pacific (Uvita)	150
59. Rancho Naturalista	Atlantic Slope (Turrialba)	36
60. *RHR Bancas*	Osa Peninsula (Golfito)	242
61. Rincon de la Vieja Lodge	Guanacaste (Liberia)	296
62. Samasati	Talamanca (BriBri)	95
63. Reserva Santa Elena	Tilaran Mountains (Monteverde)	310

(continues)

Table 13-2. *(continued)*

Name of Reserve	Region	Size (hectares)
64. Tropical America Tree Farms	Central Pacific (Silencio)	1650
65. Tiskita Jungle Lodge	Golfo Dulce (Pavones)	101
66. Vereh-Tayyutic	Atlantic Slope (Turrialba)	400
67. Vitacura	Atlantic Slope (Tortuguero)	68
68. *Werner Sauter*	Nicoya Peninsula (Samara)	100

Notes: The following seven reserves participated in a pilot test: La Garita, Casa Turire, Pacuare Lodge, Rara Avis, Las Quebradas Biological Reserve, Volcan Turrialba Lodge, and Campanario Proyecto. Although Las Cusingas did not meet the 20-hectare minimum size requirement, its owner has founded a local conservation organization that is protecting 1,800 additional hectares in the vicinity. An asterisk (*) signifies that the person interviewed was a designated reserve manager but not an owner (for example, cases in which the reserve was owned by an absentee foreigner or by a nonprofit organization). The twenty-two italicized reserves were officially gazetted formal units in the government's Private Wildlife Refuge Program.

Langholz,[32] the total amount of land being protected by all private reserves is estimated to be 63,832 hectares. Again, relying on the authoritative source on Costa Rican protected areas,[33] this amount would be equivalent to 1.2 percent of the national territory, 4.5 additional national parks of median size, or sixty-seven additional median-sized national wildlife refuges.

Table 13-3 shows the amount of land, according to habitat type, that reserves in the study group were protecting. With more than half of their land in primary forest, it is clear that these reserves contain ecologically valuable habitat. Policy-makers may wish to protect even more valuable habitat by targeting incentive programs to ecologically important or vulnerable areas. The "Other" category consisted primarily of recently reforested lands. Despite the biologically rich habitat contained in private nature reserves, this study did not attempt to determine the quality of the protection. An important topic for future research would be to assess actual levels of habitat protection offered by private reserves—in effect, to see if they suffer similar "paper park" problems as national parks and

Table 13-3.
Amount and type of habitat protected by reserve owners.

Habitat Type	Percentage of Reserves with This Habitat	Total Hectares by Habitat	Percentage of Total Area, by Habitat
Primary forest	83.8 (57)	20,963	60.4
Secondary forest	77.9 (53)	10,508	30.3
Reforested areas	35.3 (24)	782	2.3
Wetlands	42.7 (29)	897	2.6
Other	41.2 (28)	1,538	4.4
Total	(na)	34,688	100

Note: for purposes of this analysis, each kilometer of coastline counts as 5 hectares of wetland.

other government protected areas. In the meantime, the current data suggest the presence of a thriving private nature reserve sector in Costa Rica that is providing a substantial supplement to a government's national conservation strategy.

Ownership Patterns

Who owns private reserves in Costa Rica? From an organizational viewpoint, it was found that the most common form of ownership was the individual or family-based corporation. Forty-four percent of all reserves ($n = 30$) were owned in this way, with the corporation's board of directors composed exclusively of family members and close friends. An additional 23.5 percent ($n = 16$) were owned at the individual or family level but had not yet been legally incorporated as businesses. Thus, over two-thirds of the reserves studied ($n = 46$) were owned at the individual or family level. These reserves were usually working ranches that included natural areas and small-scale ecotourism lodges.

An additional 20.6 percent ($n = 14$) of reserves were owned by corporations not on the individual or family level. These typically included larger lodges and resorts. An example would be Punta Leona, which maintains 30 hectares of primary forest in a strip on either side of the 300-hectare resort's entrance road, as well as other small natural areas along the seashore. The remaining 11.8 percent ($n = 8$) of reserves were owned by nonprofit organizations as well as by universities such as EARTH and the Escuela Centroamericana de Ganaderia.

Of the sixty-eight reserves in the study group, 52 percent ($n = 35$) were owned exclusively by Costa Ricans. Another 27 percent ($n = 18$) were owned exclusively by foreigners. The remaining 22 percent ($n = 15$) were owned by partnerships of foreigners and Costa Ricans. In calculating these percentages, three owners who maintained dual citizenship and three who had become naturalized citizens of Costa Rica were counted as Costa Rican citizens. Partnerships occurred in the form of marriage (e.g., Aviarios del Caribe) and through nonprofit conservation organizations with international roots (e.g., The Children's Rainforest and the Pacuare/Mondoquillo). Results for Costa Rica were consistent with those documented by Alderman for Latin America in general.[34]

Land Uses within Reserves

The study found that owners use their reserves for a wide variety of activities (Table 13-4). The most common use was for "personal enjoyment," which included activities such as relaxing, hiking, swimming, and birdwatching. Eighty-four percent of owners reported using the reserve for this purpose either "sometimes" or "often." Ecotourism was also an extremely common activity, with more than half of all reserves engaging in it on some level. Especially interesting was the finding that 40 percent of reserves conducted ecotourism "rarely" or "never." This surprisingly high percentage refutes a common perception that all private reserves are involved in the ecotourism industry. It is a signal to policy-makers that private reserves can thrive independent of a well-established tourism industry.[35]

Reserves contribute to our understanding of biodiversity through numerous research projects. Examples of topics include amphibian and reptile inventories (Aviarios del Caribe), primate reintroductions (Curu), medicinal plants (La Marta), ecotourism management (La Ensenada), vampire bats (Cebios), forest dynamics (EARTH), green macaws (Laguna de Lagarto Lodge), and quetzals (Albergue Rio Savegre). Marenco Biological Reserve, in fact, has five biologists on permanent staff and has conducted numerous studies on topics including amphibians, plants, fish, and bats.

Spatial Implications

The study also found that when assessing private reserves' overall contribution to biodiversity conservation, data on the amount of land and types

Table 13-4.

Land uses within private nature reserves in Costa Rica.

Type of Activity	Percentage and Number of Reserves Used "Sometimes" or "Often"
1. Personal enjoyment	83.8 (57)
2. Ecotourism (with overnight visitors)	60.3 (41)
3. Ecotourism (with daytime visitors)	45.6 (31)
4. Conducting research projects	44.2 (30)
5. Harvesting logs for construction or artisanal products	25.0 (17)
6. Collecting firewood for home use	23.5 (16)
7. Harvesting decorative plants	23.5 (16)
8. Harvesting medicinal plants	22.1 (15)
9. Grazing cattle or horses	19.1 (13)
10. Harvesting wild food plants for nursery or home use	19.1 (13)
11. Mining rocks or sand (for sale or construction)	16.2 (11)
12. Harvesting wild food plants for sale	10.3 (7)
13. Harvesting logs, standing or fallen, to take to a sawmill	3.0 (2)
14. Collecting firewood for sale	1.5 (1)
15. Harvesting wildlife for home use or for sale	1.5 (1)

Note: In citing the frequency with which they engaged in an activity, respondents chose between "never," "rarely," "sometimes," and "often." Mean scores for items were used to break ties in percentages.

of habitats being protected provide only part of the picture. Equally important are the locations of private reserves in relation to other parks. Island biogeography theory suggests that the number of extinctions in a given area will be inversely correlated to the amount of contiguous land being protected.[36] Newmark, for example, showed mammalian species richness to be positively correlated with amount of area protected by twenty-four North American national parks.[37] It is clear, therefore, that all but the largest protected areas need to consider their proximity to other parks if they hope to sustain current biodiversity levels over the long term. The theory is especially relevant to private reserves, because of their small size.

Roughly half (51 percent, $n = 35$) of the reserves in the study group are located next to, or within, a national park or other government protected area. Their proximity enhances government parks by adding to the amount of contiguous land under protection. Reserves' presence in key buffer zones and corridor areas also lends support to a nation's overall effort to protect biodiversity. The connectivity cuts both ways, with private reserve owners benefiting from having large public parks as neighbors. These benefits include less encroachment by poachers and agriculture, the park's ability to attract tourists to the area, and the ability to support an increased number of species (especially megafauna that require large ranges).

Finally, at an average distance of 13 kilometers, those reserves in the study group that were neither next to nor within a government park were still located close to government parks. Also, many of those not adjoining a government park were adjacent to one or more privately owned parks, which likely mitigates adverse effects of their isolation. Policy-makers should carefully weigh the advantages and disadvantages of having private nature reserves in close proximity to public parks.[38]

Conclusion

This chapter has provided a broad overview of privately owned protected areas and a country-level example from Costa Rica. As private reserves continue their quiet proliferation, the conservation community would benefit from exploring their promise and pitfalls. Given current threats to biodiversity and reductions in public investment in protected areas, we desperately need to characterize this growing phenomenon and ascertain its potential contribution to biodiversity conservation. Additional country-level analyses should help enhance our understanding of this little-known conservation tool. The number of private parks continues to grow regardless of what the conservation community thinks or does. The challenge for academia and practitioners is to engage this trend and help channel its growth in a way that safeguards both biological integrity and human dignity over the long term.

Although much uncertainty remains about the role of private parks, one thing is quite clear: private parks are not a "silver bullet" for the world's biodiversity woes. Like community-based natural resource management (CBNRM), integrated conservation and development projects

(ICDPs), and other recent conservation themes, they represent but another option in the toolbox. Like all tools, they are best used in situations that maximize their particular strengths while minimizing their weaknesses. In chapter 24, Randall Kramer, Jeff Langholz, and Nick Salafsky make a much-needed attempt at defining how to go about this crucial task.

Notes

1. See, for example, G. Machlis and D. Tichnell, *The State of the World's Parks: An International Assessment for Resource Management, Policy, and Research* (Boulder, Col.: Westview Press, 1985); S. Amend and T. Amend, "Human Occupation in the National Parks of South America: A Fundamental Problem," *Parks* 3 (1992): 4–8; C. van Schaik, J. Terborgh, and B. Dugelby, "The Silent Crisis: The State of Rain Forest Nature Reserves," in *Last Stand: Protected Areas and the Defense of Tropical Biodiversity*, ed. R. Kramer, C. van Schaik, and J. Johnson (New York: Oxford University Press, 1997); *Parks in Peril: People, Politics, and Protected Areas*, ed. K. Brandon, K. Redford, and S. Sanderson (Washington, D.C.: Island Press, 1998); IUCN, *Threats to Protected Areas: A Survey of Ten Countries Carried Out in Association with the World Commission on Protected Areas* (Gland, Switzerland: IUCN, World Bank, World Wide Fund for Nature, 1999).

2. World Resources Institute, The United Nations Environment Programme, The United Nations Development Programme, and the World Bank, *World Resources 1998–99* (New York: Oxford University Press, 1998).

3. See, for example, J. Sayer, *Rainforest Buffer Zones: Guidelines for Protected Area Managers* (Gland, Switzerland: IUCN's Forest Conservation Program, 1991); J. Schelhas and R. Greenberg, *Forest Patches in Tropical Landscapes* (Washington, D.C.: Island Press, 1996); J. Barborak, "Institutional Options for Managing Protected Areas," in *Expanding Partnerships in Conservation*, ed. J. A. McNeely (Washington, D.C.: Island Press, 1995).

4. R. H. Horwich, "How to Develop a Community Sanctuary—An Experimental Approach to the Conservation of Private Lands," *Oryx* 24 (1990): 95–102; S. Wearing and L. Larsen, "Assessing and Managing the Sociocultural Impacts of Ecotourism: Revisiting the Santa Elena Rainforest Project," *Environmentalist* 16 (1996): 117–133; B. Alyward, K. Allen, J. Echeverria, and J. Tosi, "Sustainable Ecotourism in Costa Rica: The Monteverde Cloud Forest Preserve," *Biology and Conservation* 5 (1996): 315–343.

5. C. Alderman, "The Economics and the Role of Privately Owned Lands Used for Nature Tourism, Education, and Conservation," in *Protected Area Economics and Policy: Linking Conservation and Sustainable Development*, ed. M. Munasinghe and J. McNeely (Washington, D.C.: IUCN/World Bank, 1994); J. Langholz, "Economics, Objectives, and Success of Private Nature Reserves in Sub-Saharan Africa and

Latin America," *Conservation Biology* 10 (1996): 271–280; C. A. Mesquita, "Private Nature Reserves and Ecotourism in Latin America: A Strategy for Environmental Conservation and Socio-Economic Development" (master's thesis, Turrialba, Costa Rica, Centro Agronomico Tropical de Investigacion y Ensenanza, 1999).

6. V. Edwards, *Dealing in Diversity: America's Market for Nature Conservation* (Cambridge: Cambridge University Press, 1995); J. Merrifield, "A Market Approach to Conserving Biodiversity," *Ecological Economics* 16 (1996): 217–226.

7. J. A. Dixon and P. B. Sherman, Economics of Protected Areas: A New Look at Benefits and Costs (Washington, D.C.: Island Press, 1990).

8. A. Runte, *National Parks: The American Experience* (Lincoln: University of Nebraska Press, 1976); Alderman, *Privately Owned Lands*.

9. A. Adams, ed., *First World Conference on Parks* (Washington, D.C.: National Park Service, 1962), 379.

10. IUCN, *United Nations List of National Parks and Protected Areas* (Gland, Switzerland: IUCN, 1994).

11. Alderman, *Privately Owned Lands*.

12. World Wildlife Fund, *The Network of Private Nature Reserves: Strengthening Private Efforts in Conservation and Management of Natural Lands and Resources (Project Profile)* (Washington, D.C.: World Wildlife Fund: 1997).

13. Jon Bowermaster, "Take This Park and Love It," *New York Times Magazine*, 3 September 1995, 23–27; Ana Rodriguez and S. Garcia, "La Batalla de Palena," *Que Pasa* (Chile), 25 March 1995, 18–19.

14. See, for example, K. N. Alexander, "Historic Parks and Pasture-Woodlands: The National Trust Resource and Its Conservation," *Biological Journal of the Linnean Society* 56A (1995): 155–175; R. Hawes, "Finding Nature's Way: National Trust Woodland Management One Hundred Years On," *Quarterly Journal of Forestry* 89, no. 4 (1995): 300–307; V. Templeton, "Buying Back the Bush,"*Search* 24, no. 4 (1993): 112–113.

15. J. Bennett, "Private Sector Initiatives in Nature Conservation,"*Review of Marketing and Agricultural Economics* 63 (1995): 426–434.

16. W. Murray, "Lessons from Thirty-five Years of Private Preserve Management in the USA: The Preserve System of The Nature Conservancy," in *Expanding Partnerships in Conservation*, ed. Jeffrey McNeely (Washington, D.C: Island Press, 1995).

17. See, for example, Susan Roakes, *The Land Trust as a Conservation Tool* (Chicago: Council of Planning Librarians, 1995); Janet Dwyer, *Countryside in Trust: Land Management by Conservation, Recreation, and Amenity Organisations* (New York: Wiley, 1996).

18. Edwards, *Dealing in Diversity*.

19. T. Swanson, *Global Action for Biodiversity: An International Framework for Implementing the Convention on Biological Diversity* (London: Earthscan, 1997).

20. See, for example, E. Wilson, *The Diversity of Life* (Cambridge, Mass: Harvard University Press, Belknap Press, 1992); *Global Biodiversity Assessment*, ed. V. H. Heywood and R. T. Watson (Cambridge: Cambridge University Press, 1995); S. R. Kellert, *The Value of Life: Biological Diversity and Human Society* (Washington, D.C.: Island Press, 1996).

21. WTTC (World Travel and Tourism Council), *Travel and Tourism's Economic Perspective* (London: WTTC, 1995).

22. See, for example, E. Boo, *Ecotourism: The Potentials and Pitfalls*, Vols. 1 and 2 (Washington, D.C.: World Wildlife Fund, 1990); T. Whelan, *Nature Tourism: Managing for the Environment* (Washington, D.C.: Island Press, 1991); M. Wells, *Economic Perspectives on Nature Tourism, Conservation, and Development, Environmental Economics Series*, No. 55 (Washington, D.C.: World Bank, 1997).

23. K. Brandon, *Ecotourism and Conservation: A Review of Key Issues*, Global Environment Division, Biodiversity Series, paper no. 033 (Washington, D.C.: World Bank, 1996); J. Langholz and K. Brandon, "Ecotourism and Privately Owned Protected Areas," in *The Encyclopedia of Ecotourism*, ed. D. Weaver (Wallingford, UK: CAB International, 2001), 303–314.

24. J. Langholz and J. Lassoie, *Perils and Promise of Privately Owned Protected Areas* (in press).

25. J. Langholz, J. Lassoie, and J. Schelhas, "Incentives for Biodiversity Conservation: Costa Rica's Private Wildlife Refuge Program," *Conservation Biology* 14, no. 6 (2000): 1735–1743.

26. Langholz and Lassoie, *Perils and Promise*.

27. J. Langholz, "Conservation Cowboys: Privately Owned Parks and the Protection of Tropical Biodiversity" (Ph.D. diss., Cornell University, 1999).

28. J. Langholz and J. Lassoie, *Combining Conservation and Development on Private Lands: Lessons from Costa Rica* (under review).

29. J. Langholz, J. Lassoie, and C. Geisler, *Motivations for Land Stewardship in Costa Rica* (under development).

30. Langholz and Lassoie, *Perils and Promise*.

31. M. Boza and J. H. Ceva, *Costa Rica National Parks and Other Protected Areas* (San Jose: Incafo Costa Rica, S.A., 1998).

32. Langholz, *Land Stewardship*.

33. Boza and Ceva, *National Parks*.

34. Alderman, *Privately Owned Lands*.

35. Readers interested in additional analysis of ecotourism at private reserves, including its relationship to reserve profitability, are referred to J. Langholz, "Ecotourism Impact at Independently Owned Nature Reserves in Latin America and Sub-Saharan Africa," in *The Ecotourism Equation: Measuring the Impacts*, ed. J. Miller

and E. Malek-Zadeh, Yale School of Forestry and Environmental Studies Bulletin Series, no. 99 (New Haven, Conn: Yale University Press, 1996).

36. See, for example, R. H. MacArthur and E. O. Wilson, *The Theory of Island Biogeography* (New York: Princeton University Press, 1967); J. M. Diamond, "Island Biogeography and Conservation: Strategy and Limitations," *Science* 193 (1975): 1027– 1029; D. S. Simberloff and L. G. Abele, "Island Biogeography Theory and Conservation Practice," *Science* 191 (1976): 285–286.

37. W. D. Newmark, "Mammalian Richness, Colonization, and Extinction in Western North American National Parks (Ph.D. diss., University of Michigan, 1986).

38. For a detailed analysis of mutual advantages of public and private parks adjoining one another, the reader is referred to J. Langholz, J. Lassoie, D. Lee, and D. Chapman, "Economic Considerations of Private Protected Areas," *Ecological Economics* 33, no. 2 (2000): 173–183.

14

Nagarahole: Limits and Opportunities in Wildlife Conservation

K. ULLAS KARANTH

India possesses a rich vertebrate fauna because of its unique geological, evolutionary, and ecological histories.[1] However, over several centuries India's wildlands have been under tremendous pressures from the growth of human and livestock populations.[2] Effects of widespread poverty, land hunger, predominance of agriculture and animal husbandry as occupations, and use of plant biomass as a source of energy and shelter, impinge heavily on Indian parks. Pursuit of rapid economic growth through large developmental projects further compounds these pressures. However, the traditionally more tolerant attitude of most Indian people toward animals has made it relatively easier to establish wildlife parks.[3]

The present distribution of most terrestrial, extinction-prone vertebrate species[4] is virtually restricted to parks that occupy less than 4 percent of the land. Given the magnitude of the pressures during the last century, it is quite extraordinary that these parks have survived at all, let alone "worked." The case of Nagarahole National Park in Karnataka State of southern India is fairly representative of parks in most parts of India, except the hill states of the northeast. (Because of major differences in culture, religion, land ownership patterns, and local political power structures, the conservation context in the parks of the northeastern hills of India is closer to that of tribal areas in Southeast Asia.)

Given the above background, I have defined an Indian park as "working" if larger vertebrate species exist at relatively high densities[5] and in viable populations[6] that are fulfilling their functional roles in an ecological community.[7] I use this definition because some academics argue that the idea of "conservation" is a mere social construct that can be defined from different perspectives.[8] I concede the point that alternative "social constructs" may consider Nagarahole to be "working" even if its entire large vertebrate fauna is extirpated. However, such an alternative construct would not define a "working park" for our purposes.

I have been involved with conservation issues in Nagarahole since 1967 and have studied the population ecology of its large mammals since 1986. In this chapter, I summarize critical quantitative ecological data on Nagarahole, relying on qualitative observations to describe the tactics that worked—or did not work—in this long-term, landscape-scale, conservation experiment.

Nagarahole: Ecology and Ecological History
Landscape, Vegetation, and Animal Ecology

The Nagarahole National Park covers an area of 644 square kilometers. Many streams and two rivers drain the tract. The natural vegetation consists of tropical moist-deciduous forests in the western moist zone (rainfall is more than 1,200 millimeters per year) and tropical dry deciduous forests in the eastern dry zone. Plantations of teak cover about 14 percent of the park. Low-lying areas in the moist zone contain productive grassy swamps called *hadlu*. The park is part of a larger landscape matrix comprising other government-owned forest reserves as well as private lands under coffee and rice cultivation on the west and a variety of dry crops on the east (Figure 14-1).[9]

Nagarahole supports a rich, intact large-mammal assemblage.[10] Some species such as tiger, leopard, dhole, Asian elephant, and gaur—considered threatened over most of their range—are fairly abundant in Nagarahole. The better protected parts of Nagarahole (about 75 percent of the area) support high mammalian densities per square kilometer: 0.8–3.3 elephants; 4.5–9.6 gaur; 3.9–5.5 sambar; 38.1–66.2 chital; 3.3–6.6 muntjac; 3.3–6.6 wild pigs, 23.8–32.6 hanuman langurs; 0.6–15.3 bonnet macaques, 8.1 giant squirrels; and a total ungulate biomass density of 14,508 kilograms per square kilometer.[11] Consequently, the density of tigers is also high (11.5 tigers per 100 square kilometers) in such areas.[12] However, in the remaining areas of Nagarahole that are impacted by illegal hunting, densities of species preferred by poachers are depressed by as much as 92 percent for wild pig, 86 percent for chital, and 88 percent for langur.[13]

Ecological History

In the precolonial period, Nagarahole harbored tribal hunter-gatherers and agricultural settlements. The British colonial administration established political hegemony over the area in A.D 1800. The present park area

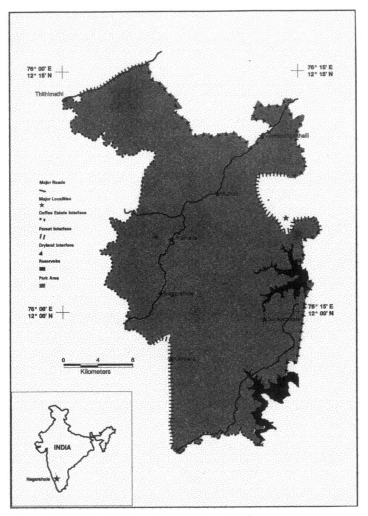

Figure 14-1. Map of Nagarahole National Park.

was declared a government timber reserve and administered by the Forest Department after 1870. The department was empowered to prohibit swidden agriculture by tribal people and encroachment by settled farmers, and to "scientifically harvest" valuable timber species for the expanding regional markets. The ultimate management goal was to replace all mixed natural forests with more profitable teak plantations.[14]

The colonial foresters—and, after 1948, their Indian counterparts—pursued this goal energetically. Simultaneously, the postcolonial Indian gov-ernment's "grow more food" campaign encouraged immigration of local people from the surrounding areas to cultivate rice in productive *hadlu* in the interior areas and to provide cheap logging labor. The advent of the insecticide DDT eradicated endemic malaria from the tract, helping such colonization. Until 1955, there were no wildlife protection laws, and hunting of large carnivores was encouraged with bounties. The ready availability of guns, flashlights, and motor vehicles in the postwar period further intensified the hunting pressure earlier exerted by local people using an array of ingenious native hunting techniques. This hunting supplemented the consumption of meat from domestic animals and was for local trade. It was not true subsistence hunting.[15]

In 1955, the northern half of Nagarahole was declared a game sanctuary where legal hunting was forbidden. A wildlife protection wing was established within the Forest Department. However, the antihunting laws were weak and poorly enforced. Following stricter laws enacted in 1974, antipoaching measures became more effective. Nagarahole was expanded to cover a 572-square kilometer area. Stock grazing was curbed and many squatters (more than one thousand people) were moved out of the park into resettlement colonies between 1974 and 1980. However, poor planning and human concerns hindered the process of enforcing the new laws.[16]

After 1974, largely in response to pressure from conservationists, forest exploitation was successively reduced. Clearcutting to plant teak, collection of nontimber forest products, wood collection on head-loads or ox-carts, and livestock grazing were gradually curtailed from 1974 to 1982. Subsequently, selective cutting of timber and extraction of dead and windfelled timber were stopped in 1994. Meanwhile, the antipoaching operations were intensified, and in the resulting encounters armed poachers as well as forest staff were occasionally killed.

However, the efficiency and commitment of individual Forest Department staff members engaged in protective duties, rather than any general systemic feature, largely determined the effectiveness of on-ground protection. As a result, intensity of protection in different parts of the park varied over time in correlation to the turnover of individual staff. Despite such fluctuations, overall the animal populations increased in response to these preservationist measures.[17] For example, the parkwide density of tigers is estimated to have increased from 2.3 to 8.0 tigers per 100 square kilometers between 1970 and 1986.[18] However, these protective measures engendered deep resentment among local communities living in and around the park, leading to occasional conflicts with the park authorities.

Emergence of Current Conflicts

After the mid-1980s, increased fragmentation of the Indian polity and greater devolution of political power to local governments led to increased interference of local politicians in the positioning of individual park officials. This in turn led to a steady deterioration in administrative efficiency. Meanwhile, advancing social empowerment and democratization in Indian society set the stage for more-severe confrontations between park staff and local communities over the issue of regulating illegal activities such as poaching, cattle grazing, forest-products collection, and encroachment of forest land. As a result of these social and political factors, the ability of park managers to enforce the law steadily declined after the mid-1980s, even as commercial demands on Nagarahole's rich resources mounted.

The local communities in the coffee plantation areas (Figure 14-1) do not depend on the park for their biomass needs. In this zone, poaching and, to a lesser extent, smuggling of nontimber forest products and timber by local miscreants are major pressures. However, because of the high density of guns in this area, sometimes there were lethal encounters between park patrols and armed poachers. Such incidents were often used by local leaders to whip up resentment against the park staff. In March 1992, rumors about a poacher being shot led to rioting by a mob of local landowners that assaulted park staff and burned a 20-square-kilometer forest area.

In the dry farming zone that interfaces the park on the eastern side, there is widespread pressure from cattle grazing and organized timber theft. Smuggling of hardwoods and the sale of cowdung as manure to distant markets have emerged as important cash income sources for villagers in this area, exacerbating pressures on the park. As a result, local people frequently defy the law, sometimes in large uncontrollable mobs.

In addition to such outside pressures, Nagarahole harbors about 1,550 families of tribal people living inside its boundaries: 650 families on its fringe and the rest in interior settlements (a density of about ten humans per square kilometer within the designated park boundaries). Earlier, these tribal people were hunter-gatherers, swidden farmers, or collectors of nontimber forest products for sale in markets. They are usually poor, landless, and socially dominated by other caste groups and live primarily off wage labor. However, some tribal men are skilled hunters and, because of their familiarity with the terrain and legal access to the park interiors, are preferred as guides by outside poachers.[19]

Under the wildlife laws enacted in 1974, Nagarahole's tribal people virtually became illegal squatters. Their rice cultivation in *hadlu* became impossible because of increased crop damage from elephants, and their livestock were often killed by predators. Furthermore, their chief "traditional" sources of cash income—logging and nontimber forest products collection—were curtailed under the new wildlife laws. However, a parallel boom in the coffee plantation economy outside provided alternative employment for tribal people. This multicrop economy also depended on other profitable subsidiary crops, such as ginger, pepper, and citrus, that buffer the impact of fluctuations in coffee price. Consequent to these economic changes, during the 1970s and 1980s many tribal families moved out of the park to work in the coffee plantations.

In 1991, some tribal leaders presented a memorandum to the state government indicating their willingness to resettle outside the park if agricultural land and other forms of support were provided. In response, the state government initiated a voluntary resettlement project that required complex federal approval and funding. However, the on-ground implementation of the project began only in 1999. This delay, resulting from bureaucratic inefficiencies and concerns of the World Bank, caused frustration among the project's potential beneficiaries.[20] At the same time, another group, supported by social activists from outside, insisted on being given agricultural land, social amenities, and hunting rights within the park, under a "people's plan" that essentially demanded the dismantling of existing wildlife laws and park administration.

Conservation Interventions: What Has Worked and Why
Official Law Enforcement

A comparison of animal densities between areas in Nagarahole that differ in terms of effective law enforcement clearly shows that enforcement has been the most critical conservation factor that has worked. A comparison of animal abundance in Nagarahole with ecologically similar forests outside highlights the importance of consistent, long-term application of enforcement in making Nagarahole work.[21]

However, many among the park staff perceive law enforcement as a tough, unrewarding task. Therefore, as individual officials are changed following the normal three-year tenure, the effectiveness of enforcement fluctuates greatly. Moreover, due to larger problems with civil service policy, staff vacancies of 20 to 30 percent have existed since the early 1990s in Nagarahole and other Indian parks.[22]

After 1974, Karnataka (and other state governments in India) lost huge amounts of logging revenues as parks were created under federally mandated conservation measures. The loss of revenue from logging in Nagarahole is estimated at 100 million rupees (US$2.5 million) *per year*, dampening the enthusiasm of the state government for wildlife parks. Consequently, timber production and community forestry, both of which involve handling large amounts of money, are considered higher-priority jobs compared to wildlife protection by the state government. As a result, incompetent, unmotivated, or physically unfit staff are often posted to wildlife parks.

Since the early 1990s, the state government appears to be gradually abdicating its role as an effective protector of Nagarahole. Similar trends are evident in other parts of India.[23] The global shift in emphasis from preservation toward more user-friendly conservation models actively promoted by international donors and conservation agencies[24] contributed significantly to the undermining of protection in Indian parks, including Nagarahole.[25]

However, in the foreseeable future, strict law enforcement and preemptive use of force against illegal exploiters of forest and wildlife resources (although they may be a small fraction of the local community) will continue to be a key factor in making Nagarahole and other parks in India work. Whether such enforcement is best carried out by the present Forest Department, by a new wildlife service, or by other local authorities is an issue that must be debated and addressed.

Community-based Conservation: GEF-World Bank Interventions

In 1995, the federal government initiated moves for implementing the India Ecodevelopment Project (IEP) in Nagarahole and six other Indian parks, with support from the World Bank and Global Environmental Fund (GEF). "Ecodevelopment" plans, prepared by "expert Indian consultants" (most with no formal training in wildlife ecology), made out an attractive case for reducing biomass pressures inside the park through community-based conservation activities. The plans also attempted to improve park protection, monitoring, and research capabilities.[26] IEP envisaged a massive five-year outlay of 387 million rupees (US$9 million), or eight times the normal park budget for Nagarahole. These funds were to be spent largely by park officials or consultants (mostly retired officials). Barely 20 percent of this investment was earmarked to improve protection infrastructure.

Not surprisingly, IEP was strongly backed by state and federal officials. On the other hand, most nongovernment conservationists were critical of IEP. Specifically, I predicted in 1996 that the following consequences were likely to ensue in Nagarahole if the IEP was implemented:[27]

1. The massive infusion of funds into the hands of local officials, with abundant scope for "leakage," would attract officials of dubious integrity and poor conservation track records to key positions in Nagarahole.

2. The existing park protection staff (already depleted by 20 to 30 percent vacancies) would be diverted to implement community-based activities and numerous reporting functions envisaged under IEP. Such diversions would seriously undermine patrolling and law enforcement activities inside the park.

3. The ongoing federally funded *voluntary* resettlement project for tribal people would be hamstrung and delayed because of the World Bank's concerns over *forced* displacement. Such concerns would also seriously retard the routine activity necessary to stop *illegal encroachments,* making the park vulnerable to fresh encroachments.

4. The consultancy structure of IEP precipitated hiring technically unqualified project consultants and, as a result, no scientifically credible management planning, research, or monitoring would be undertaken.

5. "Income-generating economic activities" in the form of ecologically unjustified logging and other vegetation manipulations could be taken up under IEP and would have adverse impacts on wildlife habitats.

6. The micro-level socioeconomic interventions carried out under IEP outside the park and delivered through the bureaucratic apparatus would not make any real impact on the levels of illegal biomass extraction from the park, nor would such interventions change the basic attitudes of the local people toward the park.

Currently, as the IEP reaches its end, the above predictions have generally come true, contributing further to the erosion of park protection and conservation values. Even more unfortunate, the adverse impacts of IEP on Nagarahole are not being documented accurately, because the project does not have a credible research or monitoring component in place despite claims to the contrary.[28] The overall lesson from the IEP experience in Nagarahole and other Indian parks appears to be that large, bureaucratically administered "community-based" conservation projects hinder rather than help in making parks work better.

Ecotourism

About fifty thousand tourists annually, most of them from the surrounding region, pay a small fee to visit the park headquarters at Nagarahole. Although this low-budget tourism does not generate a net income for the park, and sometimes causes disturbance to wildlife, it does appear to have increased the park's public profile and support among local people. A more exclusive tourism facility on the edge of Kabini Reservoir (Figure 14-1) that caters to affluent Indian and Western tourists has an annual turnover of twelve million rupees (US$580,000). However, fees paid by this facility to the park do not even cover the maintenance cost of tourism roads and other infrastructure. Overall this facility constitutes a net drain of about US$25,000 per year from the park's financial resources. Although the Kabini facility has made Nagarahole National Park well known outside the region, it is viewed negatively by some local people who feel that their access to the park is being curtailed for the benefit of rich tourists. Such local resentments recently led to protests, legal challenges, and closure of another proposed luxury facility at Murkal.

At present, tourism helps to generate broader public support for Nagarahole, but its revenues do not support park protection or the local economy to any significant extent. Although Nagarahole's charismatic fauna can potentially generate higher tourist revenues, innovative schemes that channel tourism revenues to meet local community needs and benefit conservation do not exist now in Nagarahole. Recent work on such innovative ecotourism schemes in Chitwan Park, Nepal, suggests that this option can be explored further in Nagarahole.[29]

Nongovernmental Conservation Interventions

Since the early 1980s, and, later in association with K. M. Chinnappa (a retired park ranger with an outstanding conservation record), I have tried to build a network of local conservationists. The volunteers for the network were carefully selected based on their interest in wildlife, field skills, and conservation commitment. After 1989, this network was strengthened through the participation of such volunteers in research data collection. Drawn from a variety of social backgrounds, these "Wildlife First" volunteers brought new skills and resources to campaign in support of preservation of Nagarahole.

Since 1989, the Wildlife Conservation Society (WCS) has supported the above initiatives in partnership with several local nonprofit organizations led by the Centre for Wildlife Studies. The efforts to influence the conservation process in Nagarahole have included my research projects on tiger and prey ecology since 1986, and the Nagarahole Wildlife Conservation Education Project (NAWICOED) led by Chinnappa since 1994.

These initiatives were followed by a more comprehensive intervention in 1998, called the "Karnataka Tiger Conservation Project" (KTCP[30]), to improve park protection through provision of vehicles, wireless communication, field kits, and innovative incentive schemes for the park protection staff. KTCP was supported by a "Save the Tiger Fund" jointly managed by the National Fish and Wildlife Foundation of the United States and Exxon-Mobil Corporation. The community interface work by volunteers tried to facilitate the ongoing government project for voluntary resettlement through an initiative called Living Inspiration for Tribals (LIFT). This agency has the explicit goal of assisting tribal people in Nagarahole to resettle outside the park boundaries voluntarily.

It is perhaps too early to evaluate the efficacy of these conservation initiatives. However, the following broad trends seem to be emerging. Since 1994, the community education project NAWICOED has tried to reach out to over fifteen thousand local youth around the northwestern boundary of Nagarahole and appears to have brought down local support to lawbreakers. As a result, people do not commonly rally in support of poachers in confrontations with park staff as they did earlier in this area. The effort to educate tribal people to meet their genuine needs for land and social amenities through voluntary resettlement has also progressed, with about 200 families opting to resettle during 1999–2001, and a majority of the rest indicating their willingness to do so. Official lethargy and World Bank–related concerns, however, continue to retard the project's progress. The LIFT initiative does suggest that there is scope for implementing such voluntary resettlement schemes in many Indian parks through partnerships between conservation and development agencies.

Conclusions

Nagarahole appears to work, albeit imperfectly, because the productive landscape outside of the park can potentially meet the subsistence needs of the people. Development plans that incorporate productive use of land outside the park boundaries to humanely and adequately accommodate a few hundred families currently living in the park interiors offer the only realistic, long-term framework for conserving the park's biological integrity without compromising on basic human rights concerns. I argue that such voluntary resettlement projects should form the core of models for integrated conservation and development projects (ICDP) for the future in India. Apart from bringing benefits to parks, such projects significantly prevent deleterious human–wildlife conflicts (see chapter 19).

Because Nagarahole and many Indian parks harbor valuable forest products and several conflict-prone species, implementing a conservation model with strong protection at its core appears to be the only practical option to make these parks work.[31] However, the kinds of social mechanisms that can best protect the park in the future still need to be identified.

Any utilitarian scheme for "sustainably" harvesting forest or wildlife products or for sharing among "local" beneficiaries is unlikely to work in Nagarahole, because the number of potential beneficiaries is too large (greater than 100,000) compared to the park's size and resource base.[32] Consequently, raising unrealistic expectations of benefit-sharing among local people will undermine the park's chances of long-term survival.

Although difficult to implement, a more honest alternative conservation model that educates local community leaders about the noneconomic values of Nagarahole appears to hold some promise. This approach has worked largely because of a combination of specific factors: a degree of social tolerance of the rights of wildlife to survive (at least in abstract terms), strong antihunting laws, curtailment of forest product and wildlife utilization, a growing regional economy, high literacy rates, and sustained efforts of a motivated cadre of local conservation leaders.

Identifying and supporting local conservation leaders who combine care for wildlife with a rational understanding of how parks can be made to work in their specific local contexts will be the central challenge of this century.

Acknowledgments

I would like to acknowledge the funding support I received from the Wildlife Conservation Society, New York; United States Fish and Wildlife Service (Division of International Conservation), Washington D.C.; Global Tiger Patrol, UK; Save the Tiger Fund of the National Fish and Wildlife Foundation; and ExxonMobil Corporation for some of the activities reported here. I also acknowledge the facilitation of my work in Nagarahole by the Karnataka Forest Department and the Government of India, Ministry of Environment and Forests. I am indebted to K. M. Chinnappa, Thamoo Poovaiah, M. K. Appachu, T. S. Gopal, Praveen Bhargav, and M. D. Madhusudan for sharing their insights about the conservation issues examined here. Useful comments made on the earlier version of this manuscript by the editors and two reviewers are gratefully acknowledged.

Notes

1. V. M. Meher-Homji, "Vegetation Types of India in Relation to Environmental Conditions," in *Conservation in Developing Countries: Problems and Prospects*, ed. J. C. Daniel and J. S. Serrao (Bombay: Oxford University Press and Bombay Natural History Society, 1989), 95–110; W. A. Rodgers and H. S. Panwar, *"Planning a Wildlife Protected Area Network for India"* (Dehradun: Wildlife Institute of India, report, 1988).

2. M. Rangarajan, *Fencing the Forest: Conservation and Ecological Change in India's Central Provinces 1860–1914* (New Delhi: Oxford University Press, 1996).

3. M. Gadgil and R. Guha, *This Fissured Land: An Ecological History of India* (New Delhi: Oxford University Press, 1992).

4. Rodgers and Panwar, *Planning*; J. Terborgh, "Preservation of Natural Diversity: The Problem of Extinction-Prone Species," *Bioscience* 24 (1974): 715–722.

5. J. F. Eisenberg, "The Density and Biomass of Tropical Mammals," in *Conservation Biology*, ed. M. Soulé and B. A. Wilcox (Sunderland, Mass.: Sinauer Associates, 1980), 36–66.

6. M. A. Burgman, S. Ferson, and H. R. Akcakaya, *Risk Assessment in Conservation Biology* (New York: Chapman and Hall, 1993); G. Caughley, "Directions in Conservation Biology," *Journal of Animal Ecology* 63 (1994): 215–244.

7. J. Berger, *Anthropogenic Extinction of Top Carnivores and Interspecific Animal Behaviour: Implications of the Rapid Decoupling of a Web Involving Wolves, Bears, Moose, and Ravens*, Proceedings of the Royal Society, London B 266 (1999); Terborgh, "Preservation of Natural Diversity."

8. M. E. Soulé, "The Social Siege of Nature," in *Reinventing Nature? Responses to Post-Modern Deconstruction*, ed. M. E. Soulé and G. Lease (Washington, D.C.: Island Press, 1995), 137–170.

9. K. U. Karanth and M. E. Sunquist, "Population Structure, Density and Biomass of Large Herbivores in the Tropical Forests of Nagarahole, India," *Journal of Tropical Ecology* 8 (1992): 21–35; V. M. Meher-Homji, "Vegetation Types."

10. Karanth and Sunquist, "Population Structure"; K. U. Karanth and M. E. Sunquist, "Prey Selection by Tiger, Leopard and Dhole in Tropical Forests," *Journal of Animal Ecology* 64 (1995): 439–450.

11. Karanth and Sunquist, "Population Structure"; Karanth and Sunquist, "Prey Selection"; K. U. Karanth, M. E. Sunquist, and K. M. Chinnappa, "Long Term Monitoring of Tigers: Lessons from Nagarahole," in *Riding the Tiger: Tiger Conservation in Human-dominated Landscapes*, edited by J. Seidensticker, S. Christie, and P. Jackson (Cambridge: Cambridge University Press, 1999), 114–122; M. D. Madhusudan and K. U. Karanth, "Hunting for an Answer: Local Hunting and Large Mammal Conservation in India," in *Hunting for Sustainability in Tropical Forests*, ed. J. G. Robinson and E. L. Bennett (New York: Columbia University Press, 2000), 339–355.

12. K. U. Karanth and J. D. Nichols, "Estimating Tiger Densities in India from Camera Trap Data Using Photographic Captures and Recaptures," *Ecology* 79, no. 8 (1998): 2852–2862.

13. Madhusudan and Karanth, "Hunting for an Answer."

14. K. K. Somaiah, "*Working Plan for the Eastern Deciduous Forests of Coorg*" (Madikeri, India: Coorg Forest Department, report, 1953); E. P. Stebbing, *The Forests of India*, Vol. 1 (London: The Bodley Head Ltd., 1929).

15. Madhusudan and Karanth, "Hunting for an Answer."

16. Karanth et al., "Long Term Monitoring."

17. Karanth et al., "Long Term Monitoring"; Madhusudan and Karanth, "Hunting for an Answer."

18. Karanth et al., "Long Term Monitoring."

19. Madhusudan and Karanth, "Hunting for an Answer."

20. Anonymous, *India Ecodevelopment Project*, Report No. 14914-IN (Washington, D.C.: Environment Department, World Bank, 1996).

21. K. U. Karanth, "Sacred Groves for the Twenty-first Century," *Seminar* 66 (1998): 25–31; Karanth et al., "Long Term Monitoring"; Madhusudan and Karanth, "Hunting for an Answer."

22. V. Thapar, "Tragedy of the Indian Tiger: Starting from the Scratch," in Seidensticker et al., *Riding the Tiger*.

23. V. Thapar, "Tragedy of the Indian Tiger."

24. IUCN, UNEP, and WWF (The World Conservation Union, United Nations Environmental Programme, and World Wildlife Fund), *Caring for the Earth: A Strategy for Sustainable Living* (Gland, Switzerland: IUCN, UNEP, and WWF, 1991); R. A. Kramer and C. P. van Schaik, "Preservation Paradigms and Tropical Rain Forests," in *Last Stand: Protected Areas and the Defense of Tropical Biodiversity*, ed. R. A. Kramer, C. P. van Schaik, and J. Johnson (New York: Oxford University Press, 1997), 3–14; J. G. Robinson, "Limits to Caring: Sustainable Living and the Loss of Biodiversity," *Conservation Biology* 7 (1993): 20–28; J. Terborgh and C. P. van Schaik, "Minimizing Species Loss: The Imperative of Protection," in Kramer et al., *Last Stand*, 15–33.

25. Karanth, "Sacred Groves."

26. Anonymous, *India Ecodevelopment Project*; K. Mackinnon, H. Mishra, and J. Mott, "Reconciling the Needs of Conservation and Local Communities: Global Environment Facility Support for Tiger Conservation in India," in Seidensticker et al., *Riding the Tiger*.

27. Anonymous, *India Ecodevelopment Project*.

28. Anonymous, *India Ecodevelopment Project*; Mackinnon et al., "Reconciling the Needs."

29. E. Dinerstein et al., "Tigers as Neighbours: Efforts to Promote Local Guardianship of Endangered Species in Lowland Nepal," in Seidensticker et al., *Riding the Tiger*.

30. K. U. Karanth, P. Bhargav, and S. Kumar, "Karnataka Tiger Conservation Project" (New York: Wildlife Conservation Society, report, 2001).

31. Madhusudan and Karanth, "Hunting for an Answer"; Terborgh and van Schaik, "Minimizing Species Loss."

32. Madhusudan and Karanth, "Hunting for an Answer."

15

Conserving the Leuser Ecosystem: Politics, Policies, and People

MICHAEL GRIFFITHS, CAREL VAN SCHAIK,
AND HERMAN D. RIJKSEN

The Leuser region in northern Sumatra (Indonesia) is one of the premier centers of biodiversity in Southeast Asia. Spanning an altitudinal range of 3,400 meters, it encompasses all major habitats found on the island except mangrove forests and mudflats, and contains potentially viable populations of the Sumatran subspecies of the major large land mammals: elephant, rhino, tiger, and orangutan.

It is possible that this high biodiversity, including the intact large-mammal community, can be attributed to the historic scarcity of human settlement in the region. The best available evidence indicates that forest-dwelling people did not settle the interior of Leuser until the eighteenth century. Indeed, about 90 percent of the population of the province of Aceh until very recently lived in the narrow coastal plain, within some ten miles of the sea, with the remainder scattered among the larger river valleys farther inland. The various people living in the region were predominantly farmers, fishermen, and traders.

The region's importance for conservation has been recognized since the 1920s. Although, beginning in 1934, many parts have been declared protected areas, the region has in fact received inadequate protection.[1] Improving an ineffective conservation situation requires an analysis of the causes. We classify these causes into three categories (ecological, social, and institutional), each requiring a different response.

Ecological Analysis

The technical basis for effective conservation is knowledge of the distribution of biodiversity and of the ecological and space requirements of key species. Knowledge of biodiversity distribution is always imperfect, especially in large and inaccessible rain-forest regions. Leuser, however, was fortunate in that various kinds of field research had been conducted for some twenty years.[2] Using information from these studies, responsible decisions could be made.

An essential assumption was that setting aside sufficiently large areas to contain viable populations of the species with the largest range requirements would automatically conserve the great majority of species and guarantee stable and functioning ecological communities. The animals with the largest range requirements in Leuser are Sumatran rhinos, orangutans, elephants, and tigers. These also play crucial ecological roles.

The historical and current distribution and equilibrium densities in various habitats of these species were approximately known,[3] allowing us to calculate minimum requirements for them. To create viable populations, we delineated contiguous areas allowing migration between the separate concentration areas of elephants and orangutans (tigers cover the whole habitat matrix and, due to relentless poaching, Sumatran rhinos were artificially confined to a few small remote areas).

This exercise combined all remaining contiguous parts of habitats for these key species, as well as the intervening forest matrix in the mountains, into one area, called the Leuser Ecosystem.[4] We used four additional ecological criteria to assess whether minor adjustments to the outlines of this area were needed. First, earlier research had shown that the highest mountains have high numbers of endemic plants and animals. Thus, the montane elements needed to be represented. Second, it is well known, and confirmed for Leuser, that biodiversity is especially high in the lowlands. Because orangutans and elephants, in particular, need lowland forests, the requirement of representing lowland forests was already met. Third, complete representation of distinct habitat types was needed. Virtually all terrestrial and freshwater habitats, altitudinal zones, and land systems (characteristic combinations of soil type, topography, and parent material[5]) occurring in the region were represented in the area delineated based on the above criteria. Finally, we checked for coverage of special elements, such as lakes, caves, and mineral licks.

As a result, the approximately 2.5 million hectares of the Leuser Ecosystem actually cover the major landscapes or habitats of Sumatra, going from coastal beaches and peat swamps through lowland rain forests to montane forests and alpine meadows (Figure 15-1). Importantly, all remaining primary forest in the region is included in this ecosystem. Although not strictly a single ecosystem, it is a natural unit with mostly nat-

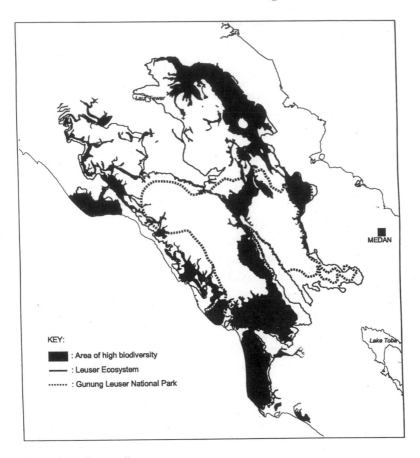

Figure 15-1. Leuser Ecosystem.

ural boundaries such as watersheds, major rivers, coastlines, and lower portions of mountain ranges.

However, by calling it an ecosystem, which at the time had an undefined legal status, it was possible to choose a new management model. The Leuser Ecosystem provided the opportunity for establishing a multiuse area that would include a large protected core surrounded by a forested buffer zone. The protected core will become a new conservation area, probably a national park. This new park will differ dramatically from the existing (designated) national park, which was found to actually exclude most of the prime ecological areas. The buffer zones, while allowing a variety of forestry/plantation-based economic activities, will ideally be free of permanent human habitation. Thus the Leuser Ecosystem, if properly managed, should be able to maintain viable populations of the great majority of the species of the region.

Social Analysis

We recognized three major social obstacles to effective conservation. First, an exploitationist (or *resourcist*) mentality existed throughout the government and most of the populace. Second, government land is widely regarded as being freely available for colonization. Third, there is a widespread cultural perception that forests are untamed and threatening and therefore should be cleared. This perception supports the official dogma that development can only be achieved through the eradication of forest.

The obstacles were addressed as follows: in light of the prevailing resourcist mentality, law enforcement was considered a high priority for any future conservation efforts. The perception of forest as open land was addressed by establishing a management body run by local leaders whose authority over the area would be clearly recognized.

Although the idea that forest conservation is an obstacle to development is now common to all levels of society in the region, there have always been people living around the Leuser Ecosystem that have traditionally espoused conservation. In fact, as far back as 1928 the leaders of southern Aceh lobbied the colonial government to protect the forests of much of what is now called the Leuser Ecosystem. Their requests were only partially met, but the program has built on this latent support to develop a strong commitment for the conservation of the Leuser Ecosystem through the involvement of informal, religious, and cultural leaders in Aceh. These commitments have been expressed in several Leuser Declarations, signed by over 350 leaders of the region (Figure 15-2).

Institutional Analysis

Defense of legally protected areas has been ineffective in most of Indonesia, and Leuser was no exception for the following reasons:

- *A corrupt bureaucracy.* This resulted from a culture of political patronage, low salaries for bureaucrats, and low morale. Such a situation has provided a fertile environment for logging concessionaires and plantation concerns to offer influential bureaucrats money, shares, or positions on company boards in return for licenses and permits.[6] This has resulted in conservation areas being relegated to logging concessions, and these concessions in turn being converted to plantations.

DEKLARASI LEUSER

بسم الله الرحمن الرحيم

هُوَ الَّذِي خَلَقَ لَكُم مَّا فِي الأَرْضِ جَمِيعًا ...

"Allah yang Maha Kuasa telah menciptakan bumi dengan segala isinya untuk kepentingan hidupmu . . . .
(QS Al-Baqarah,29)

Bahwa sesungguhnya lingkungan alam dengan ekosistemnya adalah ciptaan Allah Swt. untuk dimanfaatkan bagi keselamatan dan kesejahteraan umat manusia. Oleh karena itu lingkungan alam dengan ekosistemnya serta sumber daya hayati dan non-hayati yang terkandung di dalamnya harus dijaga, dilindungi dan diupayakan kelestariannya.

Ekosistem Leuser dengan segala sumber daya hayati dan non-hayati, plasma nutfah, flora, fauna serta fungsi ekologisnya adalah milik Allah yang dititipkan pada tangan manusia dan merupakan salah satu khazanah bangsa Indonesia yang sangat tinggi nilainya, perlu dipertahankan keutuhan dan kelestariannya.

Majelis Ulama Indonesia Propinsi Daerah Istimewa Aceh, Lembaga Adat dan Kebudayaan Aceh, Majelis Pendidikan Daerah Propinsi Daerah Istimewa Aceh sebagai institusi masyarakat Daerah Istimewa Aceh, setelah melakukan Muzakarah tentang Pelestarian Sumberdaya Alam dan Pengelolaan Ekosistem Leuser bagi Kesejahteraan Manusia tanggal 12 - 13 Agustus 1997 di Banda Aceh merumuskan "Deklarasi Leuser" sebagai berikut :

1. *Ekosistem Leuser dengan segala sumber daya alam hayati yang terkandung di dalam dan di lingkungannya adalah milik Bangsa Indonesia yang harus dijaga dan dipertahankan sebagai amanah Allah Swt. dan titipan untuk generasi mendatang secara turun temurun.*

2. *Seluruh Ulama, Pemuka Adat, Pemimpin Masyarakat, dan masyarakat pada umumnya wajib dan bertanggung jawab untuk melakukan segala upaya mempertahankan, menyelamatkan, melindungi dan melestarikan Ekosistem Leuser secara utuh.*

3. *Kebijaksanaan dan tindakan pemanfaatan sumber daya alam yang terdapat dan terkandung di kawasan Ekosistem Leuser haruslah berdasarkan kaidah-kaidah agama dan ketentuan hukum yang berlaku, serta berdasarkan kaidah ilmu pengetahuan dan nilai - nilai adat serta budaya masyarakat di sekitarnya.*

Kami para Ulama, Pemuka Adat dan Pemimpin Masyarakat Propinsi Daerah Istimewa Aceh :

PROF. TGK. ALI HASJMY   PROF. DR. SYAMSUDDIN MAHMUD   H. BUSTANIL ARIFIN

H. TEUKU DJOHAN   H. A. R. RAMLY   TGK. H. SOFYAN HAMZAH

PROF. TEUKU SYAMSUDDIN   PROF. DR. DAYAN DAWOOD, MA   DR. SAFWAN IDRIS, MA

TGK. H. IBRAHIM KAOY   PROF. DR. M. ALI BASYAH AMIN, MA   H. SAYED MUDHAHAR AHMAD

PROF. DR. IBRAHIM HASAN

Figure 15-2. Leuser Declaration.

• *A bureaucratic system ill equipped to react to rapid changes.* Until recently, Indonesia's Ministry of Forestry and Plantations (formerly, the Forestry Department) controlled some 70 percent of the country's landmass making it difficult to envision the likelihood that a relatively small bureaucracy in the capital could manage this vast estate. Furthermore, the bureaucratic nature of the government system makes it incapable of reacting with appropriate speed to the ever-increasing pressures threatening the region, especially because the nature of these threats changes from year to year.

• *A widespread resourcist/exploitationist mentality pervading government and the business sector.* Like most government agencies, the Forestry Department has, at least until recently, given priority to resourcist policies. This situation was made worse when the Forestry Department was subsequently given authority over the conservation service, PKA, the effect of which was to deprive PKA of sufficient funding and personnel to function effectively. It also meant that low priority was given to conservation issues in forest policy decisions.

• *Lack of recognition of the designated national park by local government.* Some local governments whose regencies are partly inside the designated national park refused to acknowledge its existence or resisted the implications that this park would have for their own development priorities.

Such problems could be addressed by putting management in the hands of a nongovernmental organization (NGO) that meets four basic qualifications. First, the organization must display integrity, not tolerate conflicts of interest, and show flexibility in dealing with new challenges. Second, it should have the support of the local people and their leaders. Third, this body should have political influence in order to be respected by other government agencies and departments. Fourth, since an organization's power in a bureaucracy depends largely on its financial strength, it should have adequate funding[7]

A Solution: The Leuser Development Programme

This analysis forms the basis of the Leuser Development Programme (LDP) described in the LDP master plan.[8] Its objective is to create the conditions for effective long-term conservation of the Leuser Ecosystem. Its design reflects the need for Leuser to be managed by a private organization meeting the criteria described in the previous section.

The conservation strategy followed by the LDP arose from consultation in participatory sessions with stakeholders and from earlier involvement in the same area by its designers,[9] who worked for an integrated conservation and development program (ICDP) funded by the European Union in the southern part of Leuser. The lessons learned during the three-year period of this ICDP were incorporated into the design of the LDP, including the need to conserve a much larger area. The ICDP also provided a platform for the lobbying of both Indonesian and European Union governmental officials. In particular, the ICDP staff worked to reach a consensus on the concept of the Leuser Ecosystem and on the need for privatized management for a conservation concession, with direct funding by the host government. The structure to support these activities was formalized in 1995 in a Financing Memorandum between the European Commission and the government of Indonesia.

The Minister of Forestry selected a private organization, the Leuser International Foundation (LIF), to manage the Leuser Ecosystem. This foundation had recently been formed with the full intent of conserving Leuser, was of local origin, had considerable political influence, and had the potential to raise funds. Because it lacked technical experience, a body of experts was to support its task during an initial period. Thus, the management of the Leuser Development Programme has been delegated to the Leuser Management Unit (LMU), led by a consortium of European and Indonesian experts.

The LMU's mandate goes beyond the conservation of the Leuser Ecosystem and includes regional spatial planning, socioeconomic research, and development initiatives. The LMU supports locally desired developments provided that they are linked to verifiable conservation commitments by the local communities and their representatives. To avoid overlapping roles and to provide sufficient time to build up the LIF's capability, all parties agreed that the implementation of conservation management in the Leuser Ecosystem would be delegated to the LMU for the duration of the Leuser Development Programme (seven years). In spite of token consent, the bureaucracy of the Ministry of Forestry as well as the authority of one of the eight districts that covered the Leuser Ecosystem have consistently attempted to sabotage and frustrate the project.

However, establishing such a program was essential if the many conservation problems in the Leuser region were to be remedied. The program was established through lobbying, contacting influential people, and working with government officials. Perhaps most important is the fact that the work to establish such a program was carried out in the capital city, far from the area that needed protection. In retrospect, there were three critical elements for its effective functioning: (1) knowledge of the workings of the government bureaucracy (often learned the hard way) made possible by long-term experience with the country, its culture, and its political system; (2) a top-down approach in order to create the right conditions for establishing effective conservation (including sustainable development and community involvement); and (3) sufficient funding.

Achievements

By 1999, the program had achieved the following goals:

1. Tripling the original conservation area, as delineated in the designated national park, to form a more viable and natural unit. Some 3,000 kilometers of boundaries (approximately 80 percent) have been demarcated.

2. Canceling four transmigration projects, six logging concessions, two roads and various swamp-forest drainage projects; designating one swamp area as a protected area; and preventing the establishment of five large oil palm plantations. Many of these developments had a questionable legal basis, but were nonetheless strongly supported by some local authorities.

3. Seeking and receiving a commitment by the government allowing private management of the Leuser Ecosystem by the Leuser International Foundation (LIF). This commitment was formalized in a Presidential Decree in 1998 mandating that the Leuser Ecosystem be managed by the LIF for a period of at least thirty years, although the decree requires ongoing negotiations to achieve full consent.

4. Mobilizing a large support network, including NGOs, religious and cultural leaders, and students. This initiative has helped generate a counter movement against exploitationist tendencies, particularly against unsustainable logging concessions and inappropriate plantation development.

5. Encouraging a shift in the attitudes of some provincial government agencies from exploitation toward sustainable development planning. For example, the Leuser Management Unit is now a member of the regional planning team for Aceh. This team determines land-use policy in the province.

Subsequent Developments

Indonesia has undergone rapid political and social change since 1998. The rocky transition from the authoritarian New Order regime to a more democratic society, precipitated by the Asian financial crisis, has led to a considerable weakening of state power and to near-anarchy in its forests.[10] In the short run, this has created many problems, such as a wave of illegal logging in all forests, regardless of their legal status.[11] At the legislative level, it has led to decentralization of many government functions, including forestry, and in many parts of the country this appears to be detrimental to the ecological and productive integrity of the forests. Although conservation land is officially not included in this decentralization, many cases throughout Indonesia show that parts of parks are now successfully being excised for agriculture by local politicians.[12] Finding effective answers to the conservation threats posed by decentralization is arguably the major challenge for Indonesia's conservationists in the next few years.

Most of the Leuser Ecosystem is in the province of Aceh. Since the fall of the Suharto government the long conflict over Aceh's independence has flared up again and has spread farther south than ever before. The result was not only more dead, including those affiliated with the program, but also a further erosion of the authority of the police and army, which were critical elements of law enforcement in conservation areas.

The LDP is responding to these developments by infusing itself more into local and regional government and communities, and working on agreements at this level. In fact, the political change came at a time when the program, having established the right macroenvironment in which it could become effective locally, was about to switch its emphasis toward local government and communities.

Keys to Success

The following essential elements for the success of the program can be recognized after its nearly four years of operation:

• The imagination to propose a major enlargement of a conservation area that was already considered too large by many officials.
• The adoption of a clear objective—namely to conserve the Leuser Ecosystem—and having this limited objective recognized by the government and the donor community.

- The creation of privatized management by a locally based NGO to manage the conservation area in order to provide an alternative to a government management and law enforcement system that was corrupt and ineffective. While privatized management has yet to be fully acknowledged, the recognition of this foundation's role by the people of Aceh and North Sumatra had an effect of slowing down the encroachment and destruction of the ecosystem.
- The ability to effect policy changes by lobbying. New legislation favorable to conservation in Leuser was achieved by lobbying at the central-government level in explicit recognition of the fact that many processes affecting protected areas emanate from here. This persistent lobbying involved personal contacts and working with high-level bureaucrats, mainly in the capital city. The strongly centralized decision making at the time actually simplified this process once access was obtained to the top levels of government.
- The mobilization of sufficient funds to implement projects that create political support or can be directly linked to conservation objectives.
- The creation of strategic alliances that effectively influence the existing power structure to produce decisions favorable to the conservation of Leuser. Like all alliances, these are built on overlapping interests and may therefore change over time. For example, at the outset of the program, it was important to make strong linkages at the highest level of government. Now, the changing political climate in Indonesia favors a more diversified approach, which includes building alliances at all levels, from grassroots communities, local, national, and international NGOs, and the three levels of government.
- Access to ecological knowledge of the regional ecology. Because most of the available fundamental long-term information tends to be unpublished, this had to be based largely on personal contacts and discussions with ecologists.

Comparisons with Other Indonesian Parks

Most national parks in Indonesia, as elsewhere, have faced a variety of serious threats for years.[13] Recently, these pressures have mounted due to the political instability following the fall of the Suharto government. Although Leuser has also been affected by this wave of illegal activities,[14] other parks have fared worse. For instance, Kerinci Seblat National Park in central Sumatra suffered from wide-scale encroachment, with over

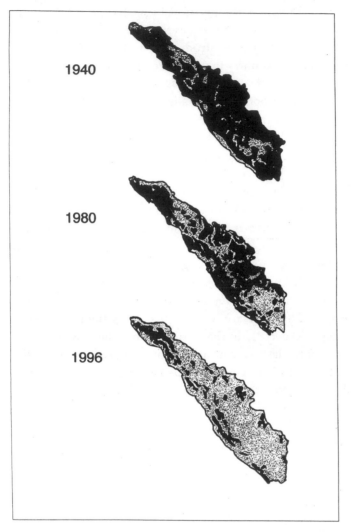

Figure 15-3. Deforestation and degradation of old-growth forests from 1940 to 1996 has led to a rapid loss of old-growth forest in Sumatra.

300,000 people now living inside the original park boundaries, and has now lost most of its lowland area to logging concessions, forest fires, and conversion into oil-palm plantations. Likewise, all conservation areas in Kalimantan are suffering serious encroachment and demolition.[15] The Kutai National Park in East Kalimantan, initially about 350,000 hectares, and a stronghold of the eastern Bornean orangutan, has now lost all of its old-growth forest due to mining, illegal logging, forest fires, and agricultural encroachment. Also, Tanjung Puting National Park has been overrun by miners and has lost three-quarters of its forest to illegal logging and fires. Thus, the inadequacies noted in the introduction for Leuser apply to most other national parks in the country in much stronger quality.

However, two national parks, Way Kambas and Ujung Kulon, have had some degree of success. In both cases, many people had settled in these areas before they were declared parks. Only in these two parks did the authorities resolve the conflict between humans and large fauna, which was accomplished by moving the settlers to alternative sites. In the time since these initiatives were undertaken, the wildlife have showed a dramatic recovery, and the parks now represent major refuges for large mammals. Ujung Kulon National Park contains the most important remaining habitat for Javan rhinoceros, whereas Way Kambas contains one of the most important populations of the Sumatran rhinoceros and elephant, as well as important populations of Sumatra's large cats.

Deforestation and degradation of old-growth forests has led to a rapid loss of quality wildlife habitat in Sumatra (Figure 15-3). Most remaining undisturbed forests of Sumatra are concentrated along the mountainous Bukit Barisan range—especially in the north—within the Leuser Ecosystem. Leuser is one of the last remaining areas of sufficient size to save intact natural communities, but maintaining its biological richness requires restoring its old-growth forests as much as possible.

Remaining Challenges

Challenges for the future include strengthening law-enforcement activities, developing NGO capacity, achieving privatized management, answering the criticism of disenfranchised stake holders, reversing recent encroachment by local people and plantation concerns, broadening the constituency of public support for the Leuser Ecosystem, and securing sufficient financial resources to keep the momentum of protection and develop economic sustainability through controlled use of buffer areas.

The most serious remaining challenge is to bring about effective law enforcement within a privatized management structure. Law enforcement has been stymied by the fact that officials in the law enforcement agencies have themselves benefited from illegal logging and other violations.[16]

Another major challenge is to fully develop the capacity of local organizations (including organizations based on customary law, local NGOs, student groups, village heads, etc.) to participate actively in the protection of the Leuser Ecosystem. Likewise, the LIF needs to be strengthened. In particular, for it to be able to carry out its mandate after the expiration of the LDP, a sufficiently large endowment fund needs to be developed.

After four years of the LDP, some resistance remains to the concept of privatized management, which has arisen from fear of losing the driving power of corruption and collusion and from additional confusion over the respective roles of the government and the foundation. Such confusion has affected the efficiency of management implementation and delayed the achievement of some conservation goals. The challenge remains to seek full acknowledgment of the concept of privatized conservation management on state forest land so that revenues of sustainable use can be acquired and fed back for effective management of the area.

In the increasingly politicized climate in Indonesia, the program will have to address criticism organized by disenfranchised stakeholders (e.g., logging companies and plantation owners) who use various channels to voice their opposition. This kind of criticism is expected to increase as more logging permits are revoked and plantation applications are rejected.

Recent encroachment into the conservation area will have to be reversed in order to secure sufficient habitat for viable populations of large mammals. This issue is less politically sensitive than it may seem, because many local people have traditionally been accustomed to moving over a wide area and will usually agree to relocate if sufficient financial incentives are provided to offset the disincentives (e.g., the lack of public services of living in remote areas).

To continue to broaden the constituency of public support for the Leuser Ecosystem, an even greater emphasis on awareness building is needed. The new political environment in Indonesia will provide a good infrastructure for this aim. The increased freedom of the press, the increased ability of NGOs to flourish, and increased transparency in the judicial system will all enable effort in this field to be more fruitful.

In sum, since the inception of the program, the political climate in Indonesia has changed enormously, and fortunately the project has been dynamic and flexible enough to make timely adjustments. Some areas around Leuser experienced widespread civil unrest and localized anarchy. This presents a whole new range of challenges. By keeping the objectives of the program clearly in sight and by maintaining an adaptive approach in responding to the changing political landscape, there is good reason to be optimistic that the rain forests of Leuser can remain one of the prime conservation areas in Southeast Asia.

Acknowledgments

We acknowledge the support of the government of Indonesia and the European Commission. We would also like to thank the senior management staff of the Leuser Management Unit for their valuable input. Carel van Schaik's work in Leuser has received consistent support from the Wildlife Conservation Society. The work of Herman Rijksen was made possible by the support of the Institute for Forestry and Nature Research (IBN) and the Golden Ark Foundation in the Netherlands.

Notes

1. H. D. Rijksen, "A Fieldstudy on Sumatran Orang Utans; Ecology, Behaviour and Conservation," *Meded. Landbouwhogeschool Wageningen* 78, no. 2 (1978); J. Wind, "Gunung Leuser National Park: History, Threats and Options," in *Leuser: A Sumatran Sanctuary*, ed. C. van Schaik and J. Supriatna (Depok, Indonesia: YAB-SHI, 1996), 4–27.

2. Van Schaik and Supriatna, *Sumatran Sanctuary*.

3. S. Poniran, "Elephants in Aceh, Sumatra," *Oryx* 12 (1974): 576–580; Rijksen, "Fieldstudy"; N. J. Van Strien, "The Sumatran Rhinoceros in the Gunung Leuser National Park, Sumatra, Indonesia: Its Distribution, Ecology and Conservation" (Ph.D. diss., Wageningen University, 1985); van Schaik and Supriatna, *Sumatran Sanctuary*.

4. H. D. Rijksen and M. Griffiths, *Leuser Development Programme Master Plan* (Wageningen, Netherlands: AIDE Environment/ IBN-DLO, 1995).

5. See RePPProT (Regional Physical Planning Programme for Transmigration) Vol. 1: main report; Vol. 2: annexes 1–5 (London: Land Resources Department; and Jakarta: Direktorat Bina Program, Department of Transmigration, 1988).

6. Confer J. M. Y. Robertson and C. P. van Schaik, "Preventing the Extinction of the Sumatran Orangutan," *Oryx* 35: 26–38.

7. The placement of PKA in the Ministry of Forestry cannot be addressed directly and solely by the Leuser Development Programme, but it has played a role in influencing the proposals by the European Commission and the World Bank, who have invited the LDP to participate in the review of Indonesia's forestry structure and policies.

8. Rijksen and Griffiths, *Master Plan*.

9. Rijksen and Griffiths, *Master Plan*.

10. Confer Robertson and van Schaik, "Preventing the Extinction."

11. C. P. van Schaik, K. Monk, and J. M. Y. Robertson, "Dramatic Decline in Orangutan Numbers in the Leuser Ecosystem. *Oryx* 35 (2001): 14–25.

12. Robertson and van Schaik, "Preventing the Extinction"; T. Soehartono and A. Mardiastuti, "Kutai National Park: Where to Go?" *Tropical Biodiversity* (in press).

13. C. P. van Schaik, J. Terborgh, and B. Dugelby "The Silent Crisis: The State of Rain Forest Nature Preserves," in *Last Stand: Protected Areas and the Defense of Tropical Biodiversity*, ed. R. Kramer, C. van Schaik, and J. Johnson (New York: Oxford University Press, 1997), 64–89.

14. Van Schaik et al., "Dramatic Decline."

15. H. D. Rijksen and E. Meyaard, *Our Vanishing Relative: The Status of Wild Orangutans at the Close of the Twentieth Century* (Kluwer Academic Publishers, 1990).

16. Robertson and van Schaik, "Preventing the Extinction"; Rijksen and Meyaard, *Our Vanishing Relative*.

16

Conservation of Protected Areas in Thailand: A Diversity of Problems, a Diversity of Solutions

SOMPOAD SRIKOSAMATARA AND
WARREN Y. BROCKELMAN

Thai protected areas face serious problems. Perhaps most intractable are intrinsic limitations that threaten the long-term survival of biodiversity, such as the fact that most protected areas in Thailand are too small, poorly configured, or encompass incomplete or unsustainable ecosystems.[1] We acknowledge the reality of such intrinsic limitations in many Thai protected areas but shall not discuss them further. Instead, we shall focus on the extrinsic problems faced by managers, such as illegal incursions and the regulation of visitors. Much progress has been made in protected-area management in Thailand since the first national park, Khao Yai, was established in 1962, providing grounds for optimism that much of the country's biodiversity could be preserved.

The problems facing Thailand's protected areas (hereafter PAs) are similar to those encountered elsewhere, but their relative severity varies from one area to another. In protected coral reefs, bombing and illegal trawling by fishermen are serious problems. In central Thailand, overuse by visitors is a central concern. In the North, hunting and forest clearance by tribal peoples represents a longstanding struggle. Commercial-scale logging still occurs in a few PAs near the Burmese border, and the last few wild riverine ecosystems in Thailand are threatened by proposed dams.

Thailand's culture, laws, history, and stage of development are distinct from those of other countries, so lessons learned in Thailand are not necessarily applicable everywhere. Nevertheless, some of the principles that emerge from our analysis may have broad application. From the outset, however, we state our opinion that there is no single recipe for solving the diverse problems facing PAs.

We begin by briefly summarizing the culture of Thailand and the legal context of conservation management. We then comment on how these factors have affected the solutions to conservation problems. In the final section of the chapter, we report on some of our experiences in two Thai PAs as they relate to solving problems of conservation.

Culture

Thailand is a predominantly Buddhist country (except for the far south-ern provinces, which are strongly Muslim), and Buddhist temples, or "wats," dot the landscape everywhere. One of Lord Buddha's teachings is not to kill living things, but in real life this principle is observed only in ritualistic ways, and hence does little to protect biodiversity. The precept that living things are to be cherished applies in practice only to monks. To ordinary citizens it applies only within temple compounds or within small sanctuaries that sometimes surround them. Some of these sanctu-aries provide protection for colonies of nesting waterbirds, fruit bats, and monkeys. Some authors have attempted to use the Lord Buddha's teach-ings as a pretext for conservation, but the effort does not seem to have much chance of succeeding beyond the temple gate.[2]

History of Protected Areas

The legal basis of park conservation in Thailand is strong and dates to 1960 and 1961 when laws defining national parks and wildlife sanctuaries were passed. Thailand's PA system has grown rapidly since then, and at present there are seventy-five terrestrial national parks and forty-four wildlife sanctuaries, which cover approximately 16 percent of the land area of the kingdom (513,115 square kilometers). This is a commendable achievement.

Most Thai PAs are in forested upland areas and include important watersheds. Wetland areas are protected mostly by a category called "non-hunting area," which permits some use of the environment, such as fishing. There are laws protecting a long list of threatened species both in-side and outside of the PA system, but these laws are seldom applied because (1) there are few threatened species surviving outside the PA system anywhere, and (2) no manpower is devoted to protection of wild-life outside the system. Only the Asian elephant and (more rarely) gaur habitually wander outside of PAs, and only in a few local areas. Hence, protection of wildlife outside of PAs is only occasionally an issue.

One might suppose that the allocation of 16 percent of the area of a well-populated country such as Thailand to biodiversity conservation would have involved a comprehensive accounting of economic benefits and costs to the nation and projected effects on future development. Nothing could be further from the truth—to our knowledge no such analysis was ever even suggested.

The relatively large size of the conservation estate in Thailand is attributable to a number of serendipitous factors. First, all forested areas of the kingdom are managed by the Royal Forest Department, and private ownership of forestland is not allowed. Hence, protected areas could easily be carved out of forest reserves at no expense to the government. Second, the Forest Department realized that its system of logging concessions—widely known to be riddled with corruption—was not achieving the goal of sustainable harvest. Instead, forest lands were unintentionally being degraded into scrub or converted to agriculture. Millions of landless farmers, hired by loggers to cut and haul logs, had moved into recently harvested areas and finished the destruction with shifting agriculture.[3] Hence, commercial logging in Thailand completely collapsed, and in 1989, all commercial logging concessions were revoked by the government. Most of the last remaining upland forest reserves were added to the PA system, with watershed protection being an important consideration. Since national parks and wildlife sanctuaries are the only forest management categories with resident armed guards for protection, it is only these PA categories that can forestall further destruction of the forest estate.

There is a relatively strong and growing constituency for conservation in Thailand, and members of the expanding middle class increasingly visit national parks for recreation. Roughly 90 percent of the several million yearly visitors to national parks are Thai. To date, government agencies have not effectively promoted international ecotourism.

Threats to Thailand's Protected Areas

Thai PAs are faced with a number of generic problems that confront parks the world over. Here, we briefly describe ways in which these problems have been dealt with locally under the constraints that operate within the Thai culture and administrative system.

Resident Indigenous People

About half of a million tribal peoples of diverse ethnic backgrounds inhabit the highlands of north and northwest Thailand. Indigenous inhabitants were thus included in many of the PAs established in these parts of the country. By Thai law, any type of use of PA resources is prohibited, so the Forest Department's policy has always been to evict and resettle tribal occupants outside the PA system and other important watershed areas. By now, nearly all tribal peoples have been resettled, but some villages still exist in a few areas such as Karen in Thung Yai Naresuan Wildlife Sanctuary in west Thailand. In its commitment to relocate these last villages, the Forest Department is opposed by many nongovernment organizations, academics, and some other Thai government departments, who argue that these Karen, who are mainly upland rice farmers, have a sustainable and nondestructive lifestyle and have mostly given up hunting.

Despite the fact that many tribal agricultural practices are sustainable, given sufficient area, it is almost universally agreed in Thailand that wildlife conservation and tribal peoples are generally incompatible. The decimation of large and even medium-sized wildlife, and their forest habitats, throughout the northern mountains is largely due to the presence of migrant tribal peoples.[4] In the lowlands, agricultural expansion by landless Thai farmers and commercial logging are major factors in the disappearance of wildlife. It has been the policy of the Forestry Department not to declare protected areas in the lowlands.

Poaching and Illegal Harvest of Minor Forest Products

Harvest of forest products in national parks and wildlife sanctuaries is strictly prohibited by law, but illegal extraction nevertheless occurs in all PAs. In some, the taking of subsistence resources such as bamboo shoots, wood for tool handles, wild fruits and vegetables, and so forth, is not actively suppressed by officials, provided the products are not sold in the market. Unfortunately, however, many animals and minor forest products are harvested on a rather large scale for illicit markets. Some species such as deer, wild cattle, elephants, and rhinoceroses have been heavily impacted by commercial trade in horns, antlers, skins, and ivory.[5] In fact, virtually every kind of wildlife has its uses and illegal markets—primarily for meat, trophies, medicinal products, and the pet trade.

The important role of commercial trade in the decline of Thailand's wildlife is due in large measure to the traditional openness of the Thai economy and the growth of capitalist markets. This has been true for the last several centuries during which Thailand became a major exporter of lumber and rice. In the 1960s and 1970s, Thailand's business and trade boomed and opened further to the demands of the outside world, often with disastrous consequences.[6]

Dams and Other Large Development Projects

Large reservoirs exist in several PAs, and plans exist to dam all remaining free-flowing rivers in upland areas. Opposition to economically unjustifiable "water resource development" must come from outside the Forest Department, and public opposition has succeeded in squelching several large dam projects. The requirement for carrying out detailed environmental impact analyses has been a powerful tool of conservationists in a relatively open political climate. Environmental issues, such as large dams, can be debated by opposition political leaders and a relatively free press, which tends to be pro-environment and supportive of local residents.

Some Notes from the Field

Here we report on our personal experiences in protected areas that have shaped our opinions.

Terrorism in Khao Yai Park

In 1979, a villager near Khao Yai reported to the press a tragic incident in which he and five of his comrades were apprehended for poaching a valuable wood called *mai hom*. His five friends were "executed" in the forest by park guards, but the one villager managed to escape.[7] Forestry officials deny the execution ever occurred; the truth will never be known. What is true is that it is almost impossible to bring poachers to justice, as the police and courts seldom cooperate by locking them up. Guards thus experience frustration at seeing violators go free after they have invested effort and taken risks to arrest them.

A number of years later, another fatal incident occurred in which two park guards were killed and two others seriously wounded when about forty "insurgents" ambushed and shot up a border post one night. Since Khao Yai was created, several dozen park guards have been killed or seriously wounded by poachers.

We have encountered armed people in the forest that look more like insurgents than village poachers, some wearing military fatigues, rubber sandals, and carrying AK-47s. Fortunately, such people have become rare since real insurgency has declined in Thailand. Nevertheless, in 1989, long after insurgency around Khao Yai was thought to have disappeared, a group of these people came out of the forest and robbed thirty cars that were passing through the park. They were never caught by the Forest Department or the police. Khao Yai appears safe now, as there has not been another such incident since then. However, if PA conservation were to escalate to a war between poachers and forestry personnel, we have no doubt who would win.

A Village Help Project

In 1981, one of the authors (Brockelman) asked the chief of Khao Yai Park if he could provide a few park rangers to accompany some biologists who wanted to survey the northwest corner of the park for primates and other wildlife. To our astonishment, the chief replied that that part of the park was too unsafe for forestry personnel and that he could not provide protection. But if we were willing to accept the risks, we could go in ourselves and ask the nearest village headman for guides.

The author went into a village on the northwest border of the park, accompanied by a couple of students, and met the headman. He was friendly, but refused to provide us with any guides or to help us go up the steep mountain into the park. "It is not safe," he said, "and if you meet any park rangers, they may shoot the villagers."

Disappointed but not yet discouraged, we decided to try one more village, this one in a picturesque location nestled in the foothills of the steep escarpment that forms the northern side of the park. The headman of this village was more friendly, and agreed to supply us with some young villagers to accompany us on a trek. Later, we made a successful five-day trek over the mountains.

We reported our experiences to government officials in Bangkok, who responded by collaborating in the launching of a village help program. Villagers benefited by being hired as guides, cooks, and truck drivers, for researchers and trekkers.[8] The scope of the effort was later expanded when several nongovernmental organizations (NGOs) brought new projects into the village.[9] These projects were then extended by Wildlife Fund Thailand to villages adjacent to other problem areas of the park. The projects have included establishing cooperative low-interest loan funds, agricultural extension services, assistance with marketing, and so forth.

Villagers were eligible for loans if they pledged not to hunt wildlife in the park.

These programs were demonstrably successful, because it soon became safe for forestry personnel to patrol in problem areas. The Forest Department has supported NGO involvement in village development activities, although the department is legally restrained from carrying out such projects itself. Forestry personnel do, however, conduct education and extension sessions around parks to try to convince villagers of the need to save wildlife and forest resources from destruction.

Aromatic Wood

Mai hom in Thai means aromatic or sweet-smelling wood. The term refers to the resin-impregnated wood (caused by fungal infection) often found in the core of several species of trees of the genus *Aquilaria* (Thymelaceae). *Mai hom* poaching is one of the most serious PA management problems of South and Southeast Asia, as the product has been harvested throughout the region for centuries.[10] Aromatic compounds are distilled from resin-stained parts of the wood, processed, and marketed for a large number of medicinal, cosmetic, and culinary uses. The largest markets for the wood or its distillate have traditionally been China and several Middle Eastern countries, but in recent years cities such as Bangkok have developed processing centers and a vigorous retail trade. The distillate is worth much more than its weight in gold, and high-grade resin-stained wood from the forest may sell to dealers for several hundred U.S. dollars per kilogram.

Poaching of *Aquilaria* trees occurs in nearly every Thai PA, and *mai hom* collectors are by far the most numerous poachers in Khao Yai. Since the financial crisis hit Thailand in 1997, with its destructive effects on banks, businesses, employment, and income levels in nearly all sectors of the economy, we have noticed a sudden increase in the amount of *mai hom* poaching. Groups of collectors wander about every day near roads, in research areas, and even near park headquarters. Poachers are occasionally caught, but the great majority continue their work unimpeded, as they can usually flee or hide from rangers.

Aquilaria trees are not rare and occur at densities of several per hectare throughout most of the park. Most large *Aquilaria* trees have been hacked open at the base to determine if any darkened wood is present, and many trees are felled. But the most serious problem caused by *mai hom* collectors may not be the decimation of the tree itself, which appears to sustain itself under moderate poaching, but the shooting and trapping of birds, mammals, and other game to sustain gangs of collectors while they work in the forest.

In the past, most *mai hom* poachers were experienced professionals who came from faraway villages and penetrated deep into remote areas of the park. Villagers will nearly always tell you that the poachers around their village come from other villages. However, a recent survey by the NGO Wild Aid found that hundreds of inexperienced people from villages around the park are now involved in poaching.

The poachers are supported by a Mafia-like network of buyers and processing factories, which are located in towns near the park. Much of the highest-quality *mai hom* is sold to dealers in Bangkok, who have their own distilleries and produce many attractive (and expensive) retail products, including soaps, body oil, shampoos, perfumes, medicines, and the like. The main market appears to be well-heeled Middle Eastern tourists.

The chief of Khao Yai Park admits that he does not have the resources to combat the problem at the park level. Concurrently, the Wildlife Conservation Society in Thailand and Wild Aid have taken steps to reduce the problem, including offering a ranger training course (in collaboration with the U.S. Fish and Wildlife Service and the Global Survival Network), and funding a special suppression operation. The NGOs have also hired some ex-poachers to help in patrolling. It remains to be seen how effective these measures will be, because poachers continue to be so numerous that they interfere with forest research projects. What has been lacking is a concerted effort to reduce demand for the product itself.

Mobs of Tourists

The headquarters of Khao Yai is situated near the center of an elevated plateau that makes up most of the park. The headquarters complex includes a reception hall, an exhibition pavilion, a roofed lecture amphitheater, short-order food stalls, restrooms, numerous bungalows, a campground, hiking trailheads, and other facilities. The concentration of human activity in the middle of the forest disturbs some of the larger species of wildlife, such as elephant and gaur, which stay away. On weekends, traffic is heavy and noisy. Large numbers of visitors come to walk along the roadside, visit the waterfalls and picnic, or hear lectures and presentations by park staff. Most visitors come in large organized tours, but some come in small groups to watch birds and observe other wildlife. More than 1.2 million visitors now pass through the gates each year, approximately 90 percent of which are Thai. The benefits of receiving weekend mobs year after year have become apparent: Khao Yai has acquired a mass constituency that has probably helped save it from some major threats.

The park lies astride four watersheds. One northern stream feeds the Mekong River drainage in the northeast, and three other major streams feed rivers entering the central plain and the Gulf of Thailand. Dams and reservoirs have been designed by the Royal Irrigation Department for at least three of these streams. So far, all these projects have been cancelled or shelved, except for one that may be built at the southern edge of the park outside major wildlife areas.

Conservationists in Thailand have been effective at fighting against large dams in the PA system. The success is attributable to a relatively open political system (in which conservation issues often become part of political debates), growing support for the environment in the civil service and the educated public, and a rather free press (especially on environmental issues).

It seems that most people in Bangkok have been to Khao Yai at some time, if only for a day's visit to a waterfall or the visitor center. The fond memories visitors take home have helped to tip the balance in favor of protecting the parks of Thailand from questionable development projects. Nevertheless, some politicians and government agencies doggedly pursue environmentally destructive projects such as large dams, but public outcry, the media, and pro-environment officials can often squelch these initiatives. It is ironic, however, that the outcome is seldom determined by informed reason and analysis—it is almost invariably emotional argument and political struggle that win out.

Ungulate Populations in Huai Kha Khaeng Wildlife Sanctuary

One of the authors (Srikosamatara) has carried out extensive surveys of wild cattle throughout the country.[11] Huai Kha Khaeng Wildlife Sanctuary (HKK) is part of a large forest complex in western Thailand containing eight contiguous administrative units totaling over 12,000 square kilometers.[12] It is the largest and most species-rich PA complex in the country.

Several areas known to support gaur and banteng were surveyed in the late 1980s and through the 1990s. Wildlife in these areas was heavily poached during the mid-1980s.[13] Most poachers active in Huai Kha Khaeng were seeking trophies, as the distances to their villages were so great as to discourage carrying out meat.

In 1991, a strong antipoaching effort was implemented by PA personnel and, according to Forest Department personnel and researchers there at the time, poaching declined. Dung counts increased during the 1990s in areas of reduced poaching near the sanctuary boundary, indicating that the cattle had returned and that the population had increased significantly.[14] The wild cattle population is estimated at close to six hundred and is concentrated around salt licks where protection efforts can be focused. At the same time, the number of tigers using the area increased from approximately one during 1988–1989[15] to six to eight during 1994–1996.[16]

In Khao Yai Park, gaur can survive in dense forests on mountains that are remote and difficult for poachers. Improved protection and village-help projects carried out by Wildlife Fund Thailand have also led to an increase in their numbers during the 1990s.[17]

How can the wild cattle of Thailand be protected? There is no simple formula. Success depends on a combination of fortuitous factors: motivating protection personnel with encouragement and collaboration from NGOs, researchers, and the press; protection of critical salt licks and meadows; and maintaining good relations with villagers living near critical habitats.

Conclusions

Our experiences indicate that a variety of approaches to protected-area management are essential in Thailand. Some of the approaches currently being suggested by conservationists often do not work, or cannot readily be applied in Thailand. There is no magic bullet. Rather, a diverse portfolio of solutions must be selectively applied in accord with local customs, economic factors, and public opinion.[18] PAs affect the human populations around them in many different ways, so few management actions will benefit or please everybody.

However, we do wish to make some generalizations about what seems to work and what seems not to work in the PAs we know. Most solutions fall into two general categories: first, convincing people that protected areas are needed and valuable, and second, enforcing laws to prevent the inevitable raids on the resources within them.

• *Community-based conservation does not persuade villagers to conserve PAs.* Although community-based conservation (CBC) has been widely practiced, particularly in Africa,[19] the approach is ineffective in most

Thai PAs. The main reasons are (1) Thai law strictly prohibits use of PA resources, (2) there are no significant forest areas or wildlife outside of PAs, and (3) many poachers do not live in nearby villages, and many people who do are transients or recent immigrants who lack roots in the area. In some cases, however, buffer zone projects have been initiated to provide benefits to locals so that they will not encroach or hunt in the PA.[20]

• *Armed enforcement is most effective when it is perceived as fair.* Law enforcement is most likely to be accepted when it is applied evenly. Eventually, lawful behavior becomes habitual, although the first reaction is likely to be one of resentment. Attitudes can change quickly when *some* villagers gain benefits from a PA (e.g., through employment or tourism). Greater tolerance for the PA may then spread through the village. Education and extension activities also help convince villagers that forest protection brings indirect benefits. We have seen resentment change to tolerance in villages where the Forest Department has supported village help projects. Guards can be effective so long as they do not have to oppose strong outside market forces.

• *Research and monitoring can be important activities.* Researchers can be an asset to managers by providing information about violations and the effectiveness of protection measures. They can also help to motivate PA personnel. For example, many of our expeditions have uncovered evidence that resulted in increased patrolling of remote areas. Ideally, Forest Department staff should institute and direct regular monitoring activities, but they seldom have the necessary time or resources and often lack needed training. Academic researchers can fill some of these gaps, but the presence of academics is haphazard and does not support a sustained activity. A better solution is long-term projects that involve PA staff, as well as volunteers and/or villagers. Such projects generate interest and demonstrate to the rangers that their often-boring jobs are important and appreciated.

• *Commercially driven poaching is nearly impossible to control and demands an expanded approach to conservation.* The most intractable enforcement problems in PAs involve poaching or harvesting for commercial markets. Commercialization can quickly drive populations to extinction, because the exploitation involves large numbers of poachers harvesting what, in effect, are common property resources distributed over very large areas.

Neither poachers nor the merchants who buy their bounty would find a sustainable harvest plan attractive, even if it were possible to implement one, because sustainable harvest rates are typically many times lower than the rates achieved by poachers. And when legal trade operates alongside illegal exploitation, as in the case of *mai hom* (where wood from neighboring countries can be legally processed and sold), the trade will continue even after the local product becomes very rare.

The Royal Forest Department has little legal capacity and no trained police investigators. To combat something as complex and far ranging as trade in *mai hom*, rhino horns, elephant ivory, illegal orchids, and so forth, conservation agencies must staff themselves with competent investigative and legal personnel. They must also coordinate better with existing international regulatory agencies such as CITES (Convention on International Trade in Endangered Species) and the U.S. Fish and Wildlife Service, as well as the Thai Police Department. Conservation is not something that can be achieved within protected areas alone.

Building Constituencies

Conservation is not only the job of conservation agencies. In Thailand, it has already become the concern of the general public, as well as politicians and government officials in numerous agencies. Most of these constituencies have something to gain, or something to lose, from conservation. Their attitudes and actions also influence whether conservation succeeds or fails. The various constituencies, or "stakeholders," to use a trendier term, must be informed, educated, awarded benefits, or arrested at gunpoint, as appropriate. In most countries, the number and diversity of stakeholder groups is growing. In Thailand, the policy of allowing large numbers of weekend visitors to disturb wildlife in certain limited areas seems to be paying off by generating widespread public support for Khao Yai Park and other protected areas.

Acknowledgments

Our field research has been supported by the New York Zoological Society (now the Wildlife Conservation Society), the Biodiversity Research and Training Program (BRT 239001), the Thailand Research Fund, and the National Science and Technology Development Agency. We are grateful to Thattaya Bidayabha, Nikhom Putta, and Saksit Simcharoen for kindly supplying observations on wild cattle.

Notes

1. W. V. Reid and K. R. Miller, *Keeping Options Alive: The Scientific Basis for Conserving Biodiversity* (Washington, D.C.: World Resources Institute, 1989); T. C. Whitmore and J. A. Sayer, eds., *Tropical Deforestation and Species Extinction* (London: Chapman & Hall, 1992); M. E. Soulé and M. A. Sanjayan, "Conservation Targets: Do They Help?" *Science* 279 (1998): 2060–2061.

2. C. Kabilsingh, *Buddhism and Nature Conservation* (Bangkok: Thammasat University, 1998); L. E. Sponsel and P. Natadecha-Sponsel, "The Role of Buddhism in Creating a More Sustainable Society in Thailand," in *Counting the Costs: Economic Growth and Environmental Change in Thailand,* ed. J. Rigg (Singapore: Institute of Southeast Asian Studies, 1995), 27–46.

3. A. Arbhabhirama et al., *Thailand Natural Resources Profile: Is the Resource Base for Thailand's Development Sustainable?* (Bangkok: Thailand Development Research Institute, 1987).

4. Arbhabhirama et al., *Thailand Natural Resources Profile*; P. Dearden, "Development, the Environment and Social Differentiation in Northern Thailand," in *Counting the Costs: Economic Growth and Environmental Change in Thailand,* ed. J. Rigg (Singapore: Institute of Southeast Asian Studies, 1995), 111–130; P. D. Round, "The Status and Conservation of the Bird Community in Doi Suthep-Pui National Park, North-West Thailand," *Natural History Bulletin of the Siam Society* 32 (1984): 21–46.

5. S. Srikosamatara, B. Siripholdej, and V. Suteethorn, "Wildlife Trade in Lao P.D.R. and between Lao P.D.R. and Thailand," *Natural History Bulletin of the Siam Society* 40 (1992): 1–47; S. Srikosamatara and V. Suteethorn, "Wildlife Conservation along the Thai-Lao Border," *Natural History Bulletin of the Siam Society* 42 (1994): 3–21.

6. P. Phongpaichit and C. Baker, *Thailand: Economy and Politics* (New York: Oxford University Press/Asia Books, 1997).

7. Anonymous, "5 Persons 'Executed' in Khao Yai—Villagers," *The Nation Review* (Bangkok), 22 July 1979, p.1.

8. W. Y. Brockelman and P. Dearden, "The Role of Nature Trekking in Conservation: A Case Study in Thailand," *Environmental Conservation* 17 (1990): 141–148.

9. J. Gradwohl and R. Greenberg, *Saving the Tropical Forests* (London: Earthscan Publications, 1988), 91–94.

10. K. Chakrabarty, A. Kumar, and V. Menon, *Trade in Agarwood* (New Delhi: WWF-India/TRAFFIC-India, 1994).

11. S. Srikosamatara, "Density and Biomass of Large Herbivores and Other Large Mammals in a Dry Tropical Forest, Western Thailand," *Journal of Tropical Ecology* 9 (1993): 33–43; S. Srikosamatara and V. Suteethorn, "Populations of Gaur and Banteng and Their Management in Thailand," *Natural History Bulletin of the Siam*

Society 43 (1995): 45–83; S. Srikosamatara and V. Suteethorn, "Factors Reversing Population Decline of Gaur and Banteng in Thailand," (manuscript).

12. W. Y. Brockelman and V. Baimai, *Conservation of Biodiversity and Protected Area Management in Thailand: World Bank/GEF/Pre-investment Study on Conservation Area Protection, Management, and Development Project* (Bangkok: MIDAS Agronomics, 1993).

13. S. Nakhasathien and B. Stewart-Cox, *Nomination of the Thung Yai-Huai Kha Khaeng Wildlife Sanctuary to Be a UNESCO World Heritage Site* (n.p.: Wildlife Conservation Division, Royal Thai Forest Department, 1990).

14. T. Prayurasiddhi, *The Ecological Separation of Gaur (Bos gaurus) and Banteng (Bos javanicus) in Huai Kha Khaeng Wildlife Sanctuary, Thailand* (Ph.D. diss., University of Minnesota, 1997).

15. A. Rabinowitz, "The Density and Behavior of Large Cats in a Dry Tropical Forest Mosaic in Huai Kha Khaeng Wildlife Sanctuary, Thailand," *Natural History Bulletin of the Siam Society* 37 (1989): 235–251.

16. N. Bhumpakpan, *Ecological Characteristics and Habitat Utilization of Gaur (Bos gaurus H. Smith, 1927) in Different Climatic Sites,* (Ph.D. diss., Kasetsart University, 1997); T. Prayurasiddhi, "Ecological Separation"; S. Simcharoen, personal communication.

17. S. Srikosamatara and V. Suteethorn, *Gaur and Banteng*; Y. Trisurat, A. Eiumnoh, S. Murat, and M. Z. Hussain, "Improvement of Tropical Vegetation Mapping Using a Remote Sensing and GIS Technique: A Case of Khao Yai National Park, Thailand," *International Journal of Remote Sensing* 21 (2000): 2031–2042.

18. A. Inamdar et al., "Capitalizing on Nature: Protected Area Management," *Science* 283 (1999): 1856–1857.

19. W. M. Getz et al., "Sustaining natural and human capital: villagers and scientists," *Science* 283 (1999): 1855–1856.

20. C. McQuistan, ed., "Buffer Zone: A Strategy Towards Sustainable Forest Management." Proceedings of a Workshop, 28–30 Jan. 1997, Khon Kaen, Thailand (Bangkok: Thailand Environment Institute, 1997).

17

Biodiversity Conservation in the Kingdom of Bhutan

HERMAN D. RIJKSEN

The Kingdom of Bhutan is a landlocked country, covering almost 47,000 square kilometers. It borders the Tibetan plateau (China) in the north and the Indian states of Sikkim, Assam, and Arunachal Pradesh in the west, south, and east, respectively. The Kingdom is estimated to have fewer than 800,000 inhabitants comprising a number of ethnic groups. The official language is Dzongkha, but virtually all officials and the educated younger generation can communicate in English. The Tantric, or Mahayana, form of Buddhism is Bhutan's major religion. Respect for all forms of life is held to be a basic principle of this religion.

The country comprises the southern slopes, or Siwalik foothills, of the Himalayan range, including peaks over 7,500 meters along its northern boundary and sloping down to an altitude of around 300 meters along its southern boundary, which is formed by the northern valley fringe of the Brahmaputra River. The northern portion of the country is highly mountainous. An alpine zone extends above 3,500 meters and contains meadows, tundra vegetation, snow-clad peaks, and glaciers. This zone occupies almost 17 percent of the country and is only seasonally utilized by yak and cattle herders. The steeper slopes of the geologically young and unstable landscape in the south are subject to considerable natural erosion, which is further exacerbated by human (slash-and-burn) activities and heavy grazing. Although forest still covers some 64 percent of Bhutan's land area, some 28 percent of the country is inhospitable, consisting of steep mountains, marshes, bodies of water, snowfields, and barren alpine pastures. Over 60 percent of Bhutan's human population live in the relatively warm southern climatic zones (some 35 percent of the country's area).

Demographically, Bhutan is very much a rural society in the early stages of modernization. The estimated annual population increase is 3.1 percent, and the average fertility rate is 5.6. Having the example of overpopulated Nepal next door, the government realizes that population growth threatens Bhutan's current aspirations for sustainable development. Nevertheless, the effect of an official policy espousing two surviving children per woman has so far been limited.

Most of the population follows a traditional subsistence lifestyle that combines slash-and-burn cultivation, permanent agriculture, horticulture, and animal husbandry—all supplemented by barter. The growing demographic pressure in the period 1966–1983 led to an increase of 18 percent in land converted for agriculture.[1] All parts of the country that are suitable for cultivation and extensive use are now occupied, and the potential for further agricultural expansion is limited.[2]

Owing to its steep geomorphological profile, Bhutan is endowed with considerable hydroelectric power–generation potential. The twenty major hydroelectric power stations in operation in 1996 generated 25 percent of all government revenue. However, lighting, heating, and cooking in virtually all rural (and many urban) households is still dependent on fuelwood harvested from the wildland forests in the surroundings.

Conservation History

Bhutan's geographical position at the fringe of the tropics and dramatic topography create broad climatic gradients from tropical in the southern lowlands to alpine in the north. Tropical and subtropical conditions are interspersed between the lower foothills along the Indo-Bhutan border and the mid-montane ranges up to an altitude of 1,800 meters. Subtropical conditions extend at places up to the base of the higher Himalayan ranges.

It is not surprising, therefore, that Bhutan harbors an extraordinary biodiversity drawn from Eurasia, Malaysia, the Indian subcontinent, and Eastern Asia. More than 145 species of mammals live in Bhutan, while 774 species of birds have been identified. Over 60 percent of the endemic plant species of the eastern Himalayas are believed to occur in the country—including fifty-two species of rhododendron. More than five thousand vascular plant species have been registered to date, including at least forty-seven endemics and some 168 species introduced as ornamentals to European markets.

Organized nature conservation was introduced to Bhutan in 1977 by the World Wildlife Fund (WWF), in collaboration with FAO (the United Nations Food and Agriculture Organization).[3] International influence has played a major role in the establishment of conservation organizations, including the government agency for nature conservation, the Royal Society for the Protection of Nature, and Bhutan's Trust Fund. The WWF identified, designed, and sponsored nearly all conservation projects until the early 1990s. In 1992, it established a country program and since then has maintained an office in the capital, Thimpu.[4]

Since 1993, nature conservation has been the responsibility of the Nature Conservation Section (NCS) of the Forestry Services Division of the Ministry of Agriculture. Under the Forest and Nature Conservation Act of Bhutan (1995), NCS is charged with protecting and managing conservation areas. The mission of NCS is "to conserve the biological diversity of the Kingdom, in line with the government's policy of sustainable development and environmental conservation." However, the institutional capacities of the NCS are extremely limited, and its mandate is restricted by conceptual constraints and contradictory political policies. Moreover, the training of the staff in resource management has instilled an outlook that often conflicts with the conservation function of the agency. As a consequence, the development of basic conservation policies, as well as the planning and management of some major parks, have largely been left to experts affiliated with WWF. Thus, a national conservation plan for Bhutan[5], the first biological diversity inventories,[6] and at least two "management plans" for major national parks were produced largely by outsiders. In the field, government organization—if present at all—has often been subordinate to international influence, fulfilling no more than a bureaucratic liaison role.

Since the establishment of NCS, the Dutch government has collaborated in a three-phase project. The first phase will deal with development of protective conservation management of the conservation areas, the second with integration of conservation in the district government system, and the third with development of central authority for conservation in the national government.

In 1989, a National Environmental Commission (NEC) was established. The NEC, along with WWF, was instrumental in the establishment of the Bhutan Trust Fund for Environmental Conservation under a collaborative agreement between the government and the United Nations Development Programme (UNDP). International donors have already contributed over US$20 million to the fund. A condition for the establishment of the fund was that the former wildlife division would be upgraded to NCS. Additional provisions were that the curriculum of the Bhutan Forestry Institute had to provide greater emphasis on wildlife conservation, that a biodiversity information system would be established, that the national conservation area structure would be revised, and that four new conservation areas would be gazetted. Several of these conditions have been met, but the required disbursements from the fund have so far been behind schedule.

Bhutan's sole private conservation NGO, the Royal Society for the Protection of Nature (RSPN), came into being in 1986 under patronage of the king. The principal objective of RSPN is "to raise the level of awareness on conservation issues both within the government and among the general public, so as to enable the wise management of the rich natural heritage of the Kingdom." From its inception, the Society has maintained strong ties to the World Wide Fund for Nature.

Table 17-1.

Current and revoked conservation areas in Bhutan.

Name of Conservation Area	Extent in km²	Year of Establishment
Currently Established Reserves		
Royal Manas National Park	1,023	1966
Jigme Dorji National Park	7,813	1974
Black Mountains National Park	1,400	1993
Trumshing-la National Park	768	1993
Kulong Chhu Wildlife Sanctuary	1,300	1974
Khaling-Neoli Wildlife Sanctuary	273	1984
Phipsoo Wildlife Sanctuary	278	1993
Torsa Strict Nature Reserve	644	1993
Sakteng Wildlife Sanctuary	650	1993
Bumdeling Wildlife Sanctuary	?	1998
Earlier, Revoked Reserves (1993)		
Sumar Wildlife Reserve	160	1984
Mochu Wildlife Reserve	175	1974
Pochu Wildlife Reserve	140	1974
Namgyel Wangchuk Reserve	195	1974

Conservation Areas

Twenty-six percent of the country is included in wildlife sanctuaries or national parks representing all major climatic and altitudinal zones. In early 1999, the Royal Society for the Protection of Nature presented a proposal for an ecological structure that would link national parks through existing forest corridors. The new structure was formally approved by the king in November 1999, in the context of the WWF's Gift to the Earth campaign.

The government's eighth Five Year Plan (1998) lists four national parks and five major nature reserves. Earlier sources mention some eleven to thirteen conservation areas.[7] The inconsistencies result from a revision of the conservation area structure that took place in 1993. Table 17-1 provides information currently available regarding existing conservation areas.

The 1993 revisions reveal that it was comparatively easy to revoke and reallocate conservation land in the country, indicating that nature conservation so far has been mainly a paper exercise. Even now, it is obvious that the organization, planning, and management of protected areas are still at an incipient stage of development, despite almost a decade of international intervention.

Management Problems

The tropical Royal Manas National Park is contiguous with the Manas Tiger Reserve in Assam (India) but cannot at present be controlled properly due to the presence of at least three different factions of Assamese insurgents. The insurgents seek independence from India and use the conservation area on the Bhutanese side as their hideout.

All protected areas in Bhutan have significant human habitation and are subject to unrestrained use, notably in the form of widespread grazing, harvesting of firewood, and agricultural production. The distinction between a formal protected area and its surroundings is that official timber exploitation is curtailed. Given the nonprotection of the conservation area network, voracious international markets are exerting a growing (albeit largely unnoticed) pressure on Bhutanese biodiversity by inciting massive poaching and illicit trade in many wildlife products.

High-altitude parks such as Jigme Dorji National Park suffer from extensive harvesting of medicinal plants for the Chinese market and from other forms of poaching—euphemistically called "traditional harvesting of nonforest produce." The other conservation areas have similar problems of "resource use" (e.g., the widespread poaching of musk deer, bears, and tiger). They also suffer the massive impact of grazing of feral livestock herds that are owned largely by the country's upper classes. The harvesting of natural products for the "traditional" market, grazing of livestock, and collecting of dung for traditional fertilizer all contribute to habitat degradation.

Another problem is firewood collection, an activity so massive in scope it exerts a tremendously degrading impact on the forest cover. Although reforestation of bare slopes for erosion control is common policy of the forestry service, special firewood plantations are extremely rare, if established at all. As in many developing countries, harvesting of dead wood for fuel is freely allowed, while cutting of live trees for firewood is regulated by permit issued by a local forest ranger. It is hardly necessary to note that this quasi-regulation is wide open to massive abuse, even if it *were* subject to serious control.

Control is difficult for at least three reasons. First, grazing is based on an elaborate system of traditional rights. Second, the government policy of Gross National Happiness teaches that conflicts must be avoided. And third, there exists a reluctance to contradict the national mystique that Bhutanese people have unconditional respect for life. Together, these factors instill a powerful ambiguity among authorities toward enforcement of legal provisions covering matters of land and resource use. Under the prevailing mindset, protection becomes virtually impossible. In practice, it means that nature conservation is not yet taken seriously in Bhutan. Grasping the nettle of law enforcement is particularly difficult in the face of phoney alternatives, such as the illusion of "sustainable use" and the creation of benign goodwill through official exhortation. As for the future, it is obvious that the accelerating transition from a small, archaic subsistence society to a modern state will unleash a flood of environmental degradation.

Analysis of the Problems

The government of Bhutan asserts that resource management and conservation are key requirements for sustainable development and long-term economic growth. Unfortunately, however, it has done very little so far to transform such assertions into reality, or even to contemplate their implications for government. Thus, Bhutan's biodiversity has so far been conserved largely by default rather than by design. First, population pressure is still localized. Second, there is little pressure for commercial exploitation of the country's forests because of the high revenues generated by the export of hydroelectric energy and generous foreign aid. And third, powerful religious and ideological influences tend to keep the rural economy mainly one of subsistence.

Except for a line on a map, there is scarcely anything that distinguishes a Bhutanese conservation area from its surroundings. So far, conservation management has consisted of little more than antipoaching patrols. Public relations have focused on interventions in support of rural development for park residents. Such interventions are falsely designated as integrated conservation and development projects on the authority of the WWF and other international aid agencies.

To be effective, there is no doubt that nature conservation must be integrated with district development. In other words, conservation must become a guiding concept of government, allowing for better planning, control of demographic movements, and more efficient land use around conservation areas. The park manager cannot simply act as a reactive law enforcement agent but should be part of an overall government structure in the region, fulfilling a proactive role in rural development. However, no matter what the values of integration may be, the real conservation of a wildland estate will be fully dependent on effective law enforcement.

Despite public statements suggesting the contrary, nature conservation is not a major political issue but rather is left to a small, subordinate service laboring under a largely illusionary self-image. It is therefore hardly surprising that the management displays a tendency to manage by proxy—through "technical assistance" proffered by foreign "experts," or, worse, by the peasant residents who, since the early 1990s, find themselves within the boundaries of a park. The top management of NCS, although very well educated, is told by the international conservation agencies that nature conservation is essentially identical to "resource management," that it requires protection and establishment of constraints on resource utilization, while land use is consistently ignored, if not outright denied. Perhaps due to the abundant presence of people with vested (consumptive) interests inside the protected areas, "collaborative management" by local people in the area has eagerly been adopted as a most appropriate way of conservation in the Bhutanese context. There will be no resettlement of the people already residing in areas recently designated as conservation areas unless they want to move or it is absolutely necessary to move them. The policy includes the principle that there should be only minimal disruption to the residents in the existing enclaves of protected areas. It is clear that this form of management is not conducive to conservation of biodiversity.

The official thrust of wildlife policy is the protection of endangered species from poaching and the study of their habitats and population dynamics.[8] Nonetheless, some animals have become rare or are on the verge of extinction (e.g., the dhole, the *farra* or Tibetan wild dog, the wolf, the snow leopard, the tiger, at least two species of bear, the gaur, and the elephant) due to direct human impact in the form of hunting, poaching, and indiscriminate poisoning. This is a consequence of the laissez-faire conservation area management. For in the real world of Bhutan's rugged terrain, it is incongruous that an organization of a handful of academic bureaucrats would aspire to protect dwindling populations of endangered species under "the principle that there should be only minimal disruption to the residents in . . . protected areas." Indeed, it is scarcely acknowledged that poaching exists at all in Buddhist society. Thus, it appears that the corruption of nature conservation as sustainable utilization of natural resources through collaborative management by local people has already gained a foothold in Bhutan even before its conservation structure is consolidated.[9]

Before the 1980s, Bhutan was hardly of interest in the international arena. Although it cannot match the superlative mountains of Nepal, Bhutan has subsequently managed to become a prime exotic destination for exclusive tourism. Hence, the small kingdom is persistently lauded as a *Shangri-La* by outsiders, and its government is showered with international offers for much more financial and technical support than its authorities can handle. Remarkably, Bhutan may well be the only country whose authority is still so honest and sincere as to refuse aid or to ask for a considerable reduction of the offered support commensurate with its own planned pace of development.

It will be hard to organize effective nature protection in Bhutan, for who would ask to change a nonconfrontational desk job for a quintessentially confrontational enforcement role out in the rugged terrain curtailing the most cherished basic freedom of a rural majority to exploit nature's bounty? The prospect is all the more incongruous when one considers that authoritative, international organizations appear to advocate the comfortable laissez-faire position.

The Bhutanese situation is unique. On one hand, the country can boast the lowest human population and highest forest cover of any nation in

Eurasia. On paper, it has the highest percentage of its national territory conserved. On the other hand, the country is showered with "aid" that promotes use of protected areas. Its government is possessed of opportunistic self-deceit with respect to nature. Yet the greatest opportunity for development in Bhutan is the sincere honesty and wish for self-reflection instilled by its cultural and religious tradition.

Notes

1. J. H. Blower, *Nature Conservation in Bhutan: Project Findings and Recommendations*. Report prepared for the Royal Government of Bhutan by FAO, FO: DP/BHU/83/022, Rome 1986.

2. K. P. Upadhyay, *Shifting Cultivation in Bhutan: A Gradual Approach to Modifying Land Use Patterns* (Rome: FAO, 1995).

3. Blower, *Nature Conservation*.

4. J. R. MacKinnon, *National Conservation Plan for Bhutan: Annexe 1, Forestry Master Plan for Bhutan* (Thimpu: Asian Development Bank/Royal Government of Bhutan, 1992).

5. MacKinnon, *Plan*.

6. P. B. Yonzon, *Strategies of Wildlife Inventory in Conserving Bhutan's Biodiversity* (Thimpu: WWF, 1992, unpublished).

7. F. Pommaret, *Bhutan* (Kent: Hodder and Stoughton, 1994).

8. S. Wangchuk, "Local Perceptions and Indigenous Institutions as Forms of Social Performance for Sustainable Forest Management in Bhutan" (Ph.D. diss., Swiss Federal Institute of Technology, Zurich, 1998).

9. J. A. McNeely, "Protected Areas and Human Ecology: How National Parks Can Contribute to Sustaining Societies into the Twenty-first Century," in *Conservation for the Twenty-first Century*, ed. D. Western and M. Pearl (New York: Oxford University Press, 1989), 150–157.

PART III

THEMES

18

Overcoming Impediments to Conservation

JOHN TERBORGH

The case studies presented in the first half of this book have emphatically demonstrated that many parks in the developing world are threatened by the three *D*s of degradation, downsizing, and degazetting. The diversity of problems that confront parks is daunting. Impediments to improved management vary in severity from the mundane—budgetary woes—to the exotic—warfare and the collapse of social institutions. Just as extinction is forever, if parks are to serve the primary function of averting extinctions, then they must be structured to last, if not forever, then for that very long time referred to in legal documents as "in perpetuity." If not, why bother? Parks must therefore be nurtured in an institutional structure that makes them resilient to the full gamut of contretemps that can arise over an unforeseeable future.

Often, when beleaguered tropical parks hold their own or even work well, it is attributable to the long-term commitment of a dedicated and charismatic champion who tirelessly organizes supporters and fends off challenges. The human element is often key to success or failure, but most integrated conservation and development projects (ICDPs) or other attempts to support parks are not designed to make full use of this human element. We will return to this issue in Part IV. Institutional factors are more easily identified and quantified. Therefore, the emphasis in the second half of the book will be on institutional matters related to making parks work.

Here in Part III, we explore a series of crosscutting themes that bear on the success of any park. Many new ideas are being tested in different parts of the world. Our goal is to bring some of these ideas together under one cover so that an interested manager or administrator can sort through them to see which could apply to a particular case.

We begin at the most proximate level, that of the individual park, with chapters on such everyday topics as enforcement, ecotourism, human–wildlife conflicts, and the issue of people in parks. The next set of chapters focuses on the national level, addressing such questions as how to increase political will for creating and supporting parks, what role the private sector can play in conserving biodiversity, and how to respond to periods of political instability. The third section turns to issues of international scope with chapters on biodiversity protection as a global responsibility, and how to create financing mechanisms needed to meet this responsibility. The section concludes with chapters on various models for monitoring parks, guiding principles for implementing protected area conservation strategies, and discussion of the frontier model of development and its implications for the future of conservation.

Institutional Needs

The institutional needs of parks fall into many categories. Ideally, all parks should have an adequate budget, a professional staff, a solid institutional foundation, popular support, independence from political excess, and so forth. Because there are so many factors that bear on the well-being of parks, the aphorism of the weakest link applies. Excellent people on the ground can be hamstrung if they are not supported by the political appointees above them. Conversely, a skilled and dedicated administrator can only do so much without an adequate budget and trained personnel.

Enforcement

Lack of institutional capacity to enforce regulations is a nearly ubiquitous problem faced by tropical parks. Improved enforcement must go hand in hand with strengthened management, or the pernicious effects of illegal activities will continue to degrade the quality of nominally protected lands. Enforcement is unpopular but absolutely necessary. It is especially difficult in frontier regions, where an attitude of lawlessness prevails. Those who view enforcement as distasteful might take heart in the memory of the painful imposition of game laws in the United States about a century ago. Rural citizens, still imbued with a frontier mentality, resisted vehemently, even to the point of assassinating game wardens. It was an uphill battle in the early decades of the twentieth century, but now no one questions the need for game laws and their enforcement any more than we question the need for traffic laws. The frontier mentality dies hard, but die it must in a world that will soon lack frontiers.

Secure Land Title

Even when the basic requirements of money, personnel, and the authority to carry out enforcement are more or less met, more obscure obstacles can tie the hands of managers. A little-known but disturbing fact is that title to many formally recognized parks lies partly or entirely in private hands. This patently contradictory situation arises because in many countries the formal declaration of a park and acquisition of the land are legislatively uncoupled. The consequent legal ambiguities have only rarely been resolved. Lack of clear land title endangers hundreds of parks in dozens of countries and represents a vast hidden obstacle to conserving biodiversity.

The matter of land tenure is fundamental to gaining the necessary absolute legal and administrative control over parkland but is enormously complex because traditions and accepted practices vary so widely in different parts of the world. In some countries much or most land is communally owned (Mexico, Mongolia, Papua New Guinea), whereas in others, it is nearly all privately held. Conservation can be implemented much more easily where wildlands are held in the public sector. The conservation status of even state-owned land can be compromised if above-ground and below-ground rights are legally assigned to different ministries. The mixed system of public, private, and communal (indigenous) land that has evolved in the United States, Canada, and Australia is unusual globally but is highly favorable to conservation and could be emulated to good effect by other countries.

People in Parks

Many parks are the homes of indigenous peoples whose traditional use of the land enjoys no legal recognition and whose relationship to the park is undefined. Because of these ambiguities, managers are left without explicit policy directives or clear legal jurisdiction, and so the overwhelming tendency is simply to ignore the problem. Many tropical parks also contain residents who are not "indigenous people," strictly speaking, but mobile land seekers who have colonized the region within historical memory. When such residents established homesteads prior to the gazetting of a park, administrators can be presented with a quandary. Even when the presence of nonindigenous residents is directly contradictory to the statutes governing a park, the legal status of such residents can remain ambiguous because they can claim prior occupancy. One solution to this dilemma has been to create so-called "zones of special use" within parks to confer quasi-legal status on a nonconforming human presence. We view this and similar expedients as extremely prejudicial to the integrity of any park. Nevertheless, practical solutions to the people-in-parks problem are all too commonly beyond the grasp of managers whose efforts to remove or relocate internal residents are often not supported by politicians, the police, or courts. Such a lack of institutional backup and cooperation can stymie efforts to remove even the most blatantly illegal invaders. The people in parks issue remains an extremely difficult and complex one that admits of no easy solution.

Private Initiatives

The longest sustained bull market in history has generated trillions of dollars in the U.S. economy alone. There are unprecedented opportunities for private philanthropy to engage in international conservation. Concurrently, laws and attitudes toward private, even foreign, ownership of conservation lands are becoming more favorable, especially in the Americas. Changes in the legal environment in developing countries are opening the door to implementing nontraditional conservation mechanisms, such as conservation concessions, easements, mitigation swaps, and lands dedicated to carbon sequestration. To accompany these new opportunities, creative financing mechanisms are needed that will facilitate land acquisition as well as encourage private–public collaborations of the kind so successfully employed by The Nature Conservancy in the United States.

Ecotourism

Ecotourism can help to counteract some threats by drawing attention to a park and by giving the local business community a stake in its continued well-being. Ecotourism is also indispensable for building loyal constituencies at the local, national, and international levels. The long-term security and stability of any park ultimately depend on the support of such constituencies.

Political Instability

Parks are often anomalous islands of order in freewheeling frontier zones, exposing them to legions of rapacious opportunists. And, when worst-case scenarios arise, parks need to be like hospitals equipped with auxiliary generators—able to withstand periods of social disorder or even the complete absence of a functioning government. At least a dozen countries have suffered lapses in social order over the last decade alone, and more are certain to follow. Flexibility in decision making, especially at the local level, is extremely important to weathering such crises.

Financing Mechanisms

Successful implementation of parks in the developing world will require money—money that will not be forthcoming from endogenous sources, at least in the near-term future. Hundreds of millions of U.S. dollars are spent annually in the name of international conservation by U.N. agencies, multilateral banks, bilateral aid agencies, and private organizations. Far too much of this is currently being siphoned off into short-term ICDPs that do little to ensure the permanence of conservation, so a redirection of these moneys toward direct support of protected areas is urgently needed. The challenge here will be in reorienting the bureaucracies and vested interests that have built up to support the ICDP industry.

On the management side, the short-term project approach utilized by so many international organizations has proven inadequate to meeting the needs of strengthening parks for the long haul. Such vital functions as planning and hiring of qualified staff require a predictable and sufficient income stream. National budgets in developing countries are notoriously unstable and remain unreliable sources for sustaining the permanent effort that conservation requires. A promising new mechanism for putting a solid foundation under park budgets is the Trust Fund for Nature pioneered by the World Wildlife Fund. More than thirty of these endowments have been put in place in countries all over the world and are beginning to vitalize park management programs.

Internationalization

Social and political instability coupled with inadequacy of domestic financial resources and institutional capacity make internationalization of conservation efforts the only viable option in many developing countries. Internationalization of nature protection can take many forms and can be implemented through incremental steps ranging from simple external financial support of protected areas all the way to formal control, in which a park becomes, in effect, an international enclave. In a concrete case, Antarctica has long been such an internationally guaranteed protected area. Internationalization is implicit in the well-established institutions of UNESCO Biosphere Reserves and World Heritage Sites.

International participation in nature conservation can be regarded as a form of technology transfer in which the developed nations supply financing, training, and inspiration while the recipient nations supply personnel. There is nothing new about this; it is happening in dozens of countries already. Eventually, it will be recognized and accepted that preserving Nature is a global responsibility. In the meantime, there will be skeptics who retort that internationalization is impractical because it entails a loss of sovereignty. Such claims ignore the inescapable fact that the concept of "sovereignty," as practiced in the twenty-first century, is not the same as that practiced in the nineteenth century. Instant communication, globalization of the economy, and collective international action under the banner of the United Nations, to mention but a few recent developments, have transformed the meaning of sovereignty. In a crucial manifestation of this fact, the world community has come to accept the idea of international peacekeeping forces as a normal mechanism for imposing order in societies unable to create order for themselves. Certainly, nothing signals a loss of sovereignty more emphatically than the presence of foreign troops on a nation's soil. If peacekeeping has become uncontroversial, why should we not also have naturekeeping? The time will surely come when we do, even if the world may not be ready for it just yet.

The future will bring many changes in the ways people live and govern themselves, most of which cannot be predicted at present. But one prediction that approaches absolute certainty is that the number of people on the planet will continue to increase beyond the current six billion to eight, ten, or even twelve billion, before population stabilization is achieved. For Nature to have a chance of surviving in a world of such crushing human numbers, the conservation movement will have to return to basics and focus its efforts on parks. Parks are the indispensable cornerstones of the global effort to conserve biodiversity. In a growing number of countries, parks contain the only remaining natural habitat and therefore stand as the final bulwark against wholesale extinction of flora and fauna. Parks must be strengthened and provided with the resources needed to function well, not abandoned as unworkable "Northern" constructs or given over to vague notions of "sustainable use."

A hundred years from now we will know which approaches and policies were successful and which were not. The recent past has taught us that social approaches to conservation via "sustainable development" have been largely ineffective in creating the permanent institutional structures that will be needed to sustain parks into the future. Conservation has thus reached a crossroads at which new paths will be taken. It is an exciting time, because many new ideas are in the air, some of them already in the testing stage. Here in Part III, the authors endeavor to make these ideas accessible in a simple prescriptive way. It will be up to conservation organizations and park managers to put them into practice. We wish them Godspeed, for the institutional structures of conservation will have to be rock solid to withstand the unprecedented pressures of the coming century.

19

Mitigating Human–Wildlife Conflicts in Southern Asia

K. ULLAS KARANTH AND M. D. MADHUSUDAN

Wildlife conservation has three facets: preservation of rare forms of wildlife, wise use of numerically abundant wildlife, and mitigation of wildlife damage. The first of these is the primary goal of parks. However, success in wildlife preservation usually makes conflict mitigation a concurrent necessity. In this chapter, we primarily focus on the human–wildlife conflict that occurs around designated wildlife protection areas in southern Asia (hereafter parks).

Many human activities, such as hunting, logging, animal husbandry, collection of nontimber forest products (NTFP), agricultural expansion, and developmental projects adversely impact wildlife and parks.[1] Although our concern here is with the issue of adverse impacts of wildlife on human interests, we emphasize that such conflicts often follow because of adverse human impacts on wildlife. For instance, overstocking of cattle can lead to ungulate prey being outcompeted, which in turn may increase livestock killing by large carnivores.

We approach the above problem on the basic premise that mitigation of conflicts is desirable for generating support for parks among local communities, or at least to lessen the hostility that communities often feel toward the parks.[2] In this context, we believe that the overriding conservation priority should be to enhance the long-term survival prospect of the park itself rather than the survival of every individual "problem animal" involved in a conflict situation. Therefore, our perspective is conservation at the scale of species and landscapes, and not at the level of individual animals. Thus, for instance, when nonlethal methods of conflict resolution are not practical, this perspective may justify more extreme measures, such as killing an individual problem animal, in the interest of making parks work.

In the following sections, we review the range of human–wildlife conflicts that occur in southern Asia and the effectiveness of common remedies that are applied under different contexts. Finally, we consider future conflict mitigation scenarios and plead for adoption of a core strategy that prioritizes proactive conflict prevention over reactive conflict reduction measures.

Forms of Human–Wildlife Conflict

Most parks in South Asia have human settlements adjacent to or within them. In the larger landscape matrices that harbor these parks, there usually is a lengthy "edge" where wildlife habitats interface with human settlements. At this interface, conflicts inevitably arise because of the nutritional, ecological, and behavioral needs of animals. There is evidence that large-bodied animals are more likely to come into conflict with humans than smaller ones. Species that range widely, such as elephants or cats of the Panthera family may enter human settlements during daily foraging, seasonal migrations, or territorial and dispersal movements.[3] Nutritionally, both cultivated plants and livestock are attractive resources, respectively, for wild herbivores and carnivores.[4] The damage to human interests engendered by contact with such animals can include economic losses of crops, property, or livelihood opportunities. Frequently, human limbs and lives may be lost.[5]

Damage to Agricultural Crops and Pastures

Crop damage by wild animals is probably the most widespread and persistent form of human-wildlife conflict in the tropics.[6] Such damage adversely impacts staple food grains (rice, wheat, maize, sorghum, millet), nongrain food crops (potatoes, peanuts, vegetables, sugarcane, bananas, cassava, coconuts, cacao), and commercial crops (rubber, tea, coffee, spices). Damage results not only from the animals feeding on crops, but also from trampling, rooting, and other forms of wastage.

Taxonomically, the animals involved in crop raiding are varied. They include elephants (grain crops, sugarcane, fruits), wild pigs (almost all crops), nilgai and black buck antelopes (sorghum, wheat, and millet), gaur (rice and rubber), sloth bear and black bear (maize, sugarcane, peanuts), jackals (sugarcane, maize, and fruits), bonnet and rhesus macaques (most crops and vegetables), giant fruit bats (all orchard crops and areca nuts), and porcupines (areca nuts, coconuts, vegetables).

Crop damage results in the loss of staple foods for the poorest class of rural people and in destruction of commercial crops that may take several years to reestablish. Because agriculture usually employs a significant proportion of rural workers, such crop losses lead to indirect loss of livelihood opportunities on a wider scale. Although people generally do not tolerate such crop losses to wildlife, a few communities in northwestern India do show cultural acceptance of crop damage caused by wild antelopes. Even among these communities, however, the traditional levels of toleration appear to be slowly disappearing with recent cultural and economic changes.[7]

Loss of Livestock and Domesticated Animals

Animal husbandry is a major economic and livelihood activity around many parks. Killing of domesticated stock by carnivores is often a serious problem. Such instances of conflict include killing of domesticated bovids, equids, sheep, and goats by tigers, lions, leopards, snow leopards, wolves, dholes, striped hyenas, brown bears, and black bears.[8] Retaliatory killing of "problem predators" by humans is a major consequence of this conflict. The local people's perceptions of the losses incurred, however, often appear to exceed the actual value of the livestock lost to predators.[9]

The variety of other domestic animals that are lost to predators in South Asia include ducks, geese, and chickens killed by smaller felids, viverrids, canids, mustelids, and raptorial birds. Otters and crocodiles are considered serious threats to inland fisheries in many areas. Yellow-throated martens destroy valuable apiaries in the Western Ghats of Karnataka, India. Transmission of lethal diseases to livestock from wild ungulates, which is a major problem in parts of Africa,[10] is not reported as a widespread problem in South Asia.

Killing of Humans by Wild Animals

Human–wildlife conflict attains its most serious form when people are injured or killed by wild animals. Although big cats, bears, and wolves in southern Asia are readily recognized and targeted for such manslaughter, wild elephants probably kill more people than large carnivores in this region.[11]

Persistent predation on humans is the most severe category of conflict. Man-eating tigers, leopards, and (rarely) child-lifting wolves[12] cause panic over entire regions, inducing massive retaliatory killings and antagonism against wildlife. In some regions, such as the Sundarbans of India and Bangladesh, the endemicity and persistence of man-eating tigers[13] suggests that this acquired behavior may be being transmitted culturally across generations of animals.

Approaches to Mitigating Human-Wildlife Conflict

In this section, we summarize the major approaches that have been adopted in the past to mitigate human–wildlife conflicts. Most such responses have been empirically generated in situ. They are often driven by local contingencies rather than by good science and planning. The potential remedies available to local people and authorities vary in scope from the "softest" option of stoically tolerating the damage caused by wildlife, to the "hardest" option of killing the "problem animal."

Because of the wide variety of tactics employed, we report only a few examples under three general strategies: modifying human behavior, modifying wildlife behavior, and conflict prevention through spatial separation. Further, we have also identified the biological, economic, institutional, and cultural factors that need to be in place for each tactic to work effectively.

Modifying Human Behavior

The behavior of people involved in potential conflict situations can be modified to reduce conflicts through several options. These options include reinforcement of traditional toleration of animal damage, conservation education, changing farming and livestock-raising practices, offering financial compensation, and, finally, establishing deterrence through law enforcement.

Tolerating Wildlife Damage. In parts of northwestern India, a few communities have traditionally tolerated crop damage caused by wild antelopes. Similarly, Maldharis of the Gir Forest[14] and Gujars in the Himalayan foothills exhibit high levels of tolerance to large cat depredations on their buffalo herds. However, increasing livestock densities, market-driven economic forces, and breakdown of cultural values are all lowering the levels of such traditional tolerance. Therefore, we argue that merely tolerating wildlife damage cannot be viewed as a serious long-term option.

Educating Humans about Appropriate Behavior. Deleterious encounters between wild animals and humans often occur around parks because of inappropriate behavior on the part of people. Mobbing cornered predators or walking carelessly close to elephants are examples of such behavior that can be modified through education. In Sundarbans of India, large-scale educational programs targeting local fishermen and honey collectors about appropriate behavior when working in tiger habitats appear to have reduced the incidence of tigers killing humans.[15]

Changing Agricultural and Animal Husbandry Practices. Local land use and cropping patterns significantly influence human–wildlife conflict levels almost everywhere. Changes in human behavior, manifested as new agricultural practices, can either reduce or increase the levels of human–wildlife conflict.[16] For example, in the farms abutting the eastern boundary of Nagarahole Park, India, a large-scale switch from millet to cotton crops has rendered the farms less attractive to elephants, thus reducing the incidence of crop raiding. Similarly, increased area under plantation crops on the western side of Nagarahole has resulted in a reduced presence of draft cattle in the park and lower levels of predatory stock killing.[17] In situations where human population density is low, or where shifting cultivation is practiced, it may also be possible to move fields away from areas of high animal damage to reduce conflict.[18]

Similarly, changing animal husbandry practices to switch from cheap, dispensable, free-ranging native breeds of cattle to expensive, high-yielding breeds that are stall-fed can reduce cattle-killing by predators. Mishra reports that recent penetration of commercial demand for meat and dairy products into hitherto inaccessible areas in the Himalayas has greatly increased livestock densities and consequently has elevated the levels of conflict between herders and snow leopards.[19] In some parts of Africa, livestock are immunized against diseases spread by wild ungulates.[20] Although livestock immunization measures are sometimes undertaken in India also, the primary motive in this case is to protect wildlife rather than livestock.

Often, conflicts between wildlife and humans arise over access to water rather than over crops or livestock. In such situations, it may be possible to redirect water in spatially appropriate patterns to reduce wildlife intrusions into agricultural areas. Establishing new water sources away from agricultural areas appears to reduce elephant intrusions into farmlands in parts of southern India.[21]

Innovative changes in land use from conflict-prone farming practices toward more benign alternatives such as ecotourism or safari hunting of game animals have been tried successfully in Africa and South America. A similar experiment in which ecotourism and farm forestry are packaged as financially viable alternatives to traditional agriculture appears to hold some promise around Chitwan Park in Nepal. The ecological and social preconditions needed for this tourism-based approach to work in Nepal have been identified by Dinerstein and others.[22]

However, agricultural and animal husbandry practices are generally driven by macro-scale socioeconomic forces such as market prices, access to transportation, land-holding patterns, human population density, and local culture. Therefore, it is not easy to change these practices solely to mitigate human–wildlife conflicts. For example, although it is now recognized that planting sugarcane adjacent to Dudhwa Park in India may increase the incidence of tigers killing humans, it has not been possible to induce local farmers to switch to alternative crops because of economic reasons.

Providing Financial Compensation and Incentives. The practice of financially or materially compensating farmers for livestock killed by predators or crop damage caused by herbivores appears to be widespread. However, the effectiveness of these schemes varies widely. The major problems in implementing compensation schemes appear to be inadequacy of the compensation, delays, and official corruption faced by claimants, as well as the misuse of compensation schemes through fraudulent claims.[23]

One major problem everywhere appears to be the relatively high cost of administering the compensatory schemes (e.g., the logistics of authenticating claims compared to the monetary value of loss suffered). A recent study of a scheme for compensating owners of cattle killed by tigers and leopards suggests that the schemes are largely ineffective because of inadequate payments, long delays, and unrealistic conditions imposed on claimants.[24] It shows that affected people really do not feel "compensated," and that they often attempted their own clandestine "solutions" to the conflict by poisoning livestock kills or by shooting at crop-raiding elephants.

A related strategy involves paying out "preventive compensation" by providing insurance cover for crops or livestock lost. The low monetary value of the crops or livestock relative to the per capita costs of administering the insurance schemes and lack of education appear to impede implementation of such schemes on a wider scale in developing countries.[25]

Providing Prevention, Enforcement, and Punishment through the Law. Clearly demarcating legal boundaries can reduce human transgressions into parks that arise from ignorance about park boundaries. This is the least intrusive form of law enforcement possible. More-intensive preventive law enforcement or prosecution are harder options for a park manager. In southern India, farmers and planters who shoot elephants that raid crops are usually prosecuted legally. Such enforcement often acts as an effective deterrent, although in the long run a price is paid in terms of increased antagonism toward parks among local people.

Modifying Wildlife Behavior

It is sometimes possible to modify the behavior of wildlife species involved in conflict situations so that their contact with human settlements is minimized or even eliminated. Often these measures are easier to implement than measures that involve modifying human behavior.

Establishing Barriers. Establishing physical barriers against animal movement into human settlements is an effective technique deployed for centuries. Such barriers may include trenches, moats, walls, and ordinary or electrified fences. The elephant-proof trenches in southwestern India, rubble walls in northern India, and electrified and ordinary fences used worldwide are all examples of such structures. The investments required for establishing such barriers are usually high, and therefore parks or other local authorities are often reluctant to invest in them.[26]

A related problem is continued maintenance of the barriers. The beneficiaries of such structures are often unwilling to pay for such maintenance costs. In some cases, individual beneficiaries selectively "disable" barriers at specific locations in order to gain personal access to resources like fuel, timber, and fodder. In this way, they maximize their own profits at the expense of their communities. Poor maintenance of barriers by government authorities compounds the problem. For such reasons, barriers appear to work most effectively when they are maintained and enforced by landowners or communities themselves, rather than by park authorities.

The effectiveness of various barrier types depends on several factors: the animal species to be excluded, climate, topography, and institutional mechanisms in place for maintenance. For example, in southwestern India, although electric fences work reasonably well in excluding elephants, the periodic disconnection of government-maintained fences by local people to gain access to forests makes them ineffective in practice. On the other hand, electric fences maintained by private landowners work relatively efficiently.[27] Deep trenches, which are costlier to establish initially, seem to work better than fences under government management because they are harder to disrupt.[28]

If barriers are not placed after carefully considering the overall topography and animal movement patterns, they can potentially prevent or disrupt natural migrations and dispersal. Yet, on the whole, when barriers are maintained properly, they are among the most effective techniques for modifying animal behavior and reducing conflict.[29]

Guarding Crops and Livestock. Usually farmers or their employees guard crops against wildlife damage. Sometimes the government or park authorities may assign their staff for the task. Similarly, livestock are protected from predators by employing human labor and guard dogs. In addition, a variety of devices for scaring animals away, including clever local innovations, are also deployed to guard crops or livestock. Such devices may use auditory or visual cues as scaring tactics.

Generally, physical guarding is a nonviable option where labor is scarce and expensive. As a result, in many rural communities of the developing world only elderly or juvenile (low-productivity) labor is entrusted with guarding tasks. Despite practices of guarding, a substantial proportion of crops and livestock is typically lost anyway. In some Indian parks, such as Spiti, Sariska, and Bhadra, annual livestock losses are generally around 12–15 percent of the herds, and rates of crop losses are even higher despite guarding activities.[30]

Removing Problem Animals. Physical removal of an individual "problem" animal that finds its way into human settlements is often the only option available for the affected people or park authorities. The animal is usually driven away from the site, or captured and translocated to a new site or into captivity.

The possibility of driving problem animals away is governed mainly by local topography, landscape linkages, and availability of adequately skilled labor for the task. The gathering of large excited mobs at the site of conflict sometimes hinders drives. Moreover, the same ecological factors that compelled the problem animal to initially come into human settlements may force it to return again.

Before translocation, a problem animal must be safely caught and handled, if necessary, by using chemical capture methods.[31] Successful capture of wild animals requires a sound knowledge of animal behavior, capture techniques, and, if chemical capture is involved, local availability of competent technical persons and drugs. One common problem encountered in such captures is that animals are seriously injured during the process due to a lack of expertise or control over the situation. The presence of excited mobs is a major hazard during attempts to capture problem wild animals, often leading to deaths of both animals and humans.

Such factors can make it unpractical to employ chemical capture, particularly in the case of big cats and elephants.

A related issue is the subsequent fate of the captured problem animal. Although elephants and ungulates are difficult to safely transport, even under sedation, their subsequent release may be relatively less problematic. With large predator species that have territorial social organization and whose densities are governed by prey abundance, there is little evidence that such translocations actually work. Release of captured carnivores into wild populations of conspecifics is likely to lead to social disruptions. In such cases, the released animal, another individual, or both, may be injured in aggressive intraspecific encounters, creating more "problem" animals.[32] On the whole, translocations are more likely to merely transfer the "problem" from one site to another, rather than resolve it.

High costs and technical problems involved in holding wild-caught animals in extended captivity also do not favor the use of zoos as reservoirs for problem animals. However, in special cases involving rare endangered species, augmenting the genetic makeup of captive stocks by using wild-caught problem animals may be an option worth further exploration.

Killing of Problem Animals. In reality, because of the above-mentioned difficulties in effecting live removals, most problem animals involved in conflicts with humans are simply killed. For seriously injured animals and habitual man-eating predators, such killing is often the only option. In the case of man-eaters, it is sometimes suggested that only *that* individual problem animal should be killed and not other "innocent" individuals of the same species. In practice, such prior identification of "guilty" and "innocent" individuals in a population is not possible. For example, in the Chikmagalur district of India in 1995, a prolonged incidence of leopards killing eleven people resulted in the extermination of seventeen leopards before the problem was eliminated. The presence of human settlements inside protected areas that harbor large cats makes it extremely difficult to deal with man-eaters.

Preventive Spatial Separation

The two strategies outlined above for conflict mitigation—modifying human or animal behavior—can be considered proximate "reactive" responses that are essential but do not necessarily address the root cause of the problem. Ultimately, the biology of the species and the levels of human impact on wildlife determine conflict levels. Therefore conflicts are biologically inevitable, particularly when extractive pressures on parks intensify. At the same time, limits of human tolerance for conflict are diminishing.

We have reviewed above the difficulties involved in dealing with human–wildlife conflicts after they occur. We argue that in addition to such "reactive" solutions, there is an urgent need to find ways of preventing conflicts. Consequently, "proactive" prevention of such conflict by achieving spatial separation between humans and wildlife appears to be an attractive proposition.

With many wildlife species, spatial coexistence imposes great costs on both human societies and animals. Because of the much greater concern for human welfare that exists in all societies, wildlife typically is eliminated if the conflict goes unresolved. For example, over the last few centuries, most conflict-prone wildlife species in India have suffered range contractions of over 90 percent.[33] Therefore, at least in wildlife parks, where conservation concerns are of primary concern, achieving spatial separation through voluntary human resettlements has to be considered as a serious option.

Because human populations are very large outside protected areas, such resettlements are not usually a practical option for conflict reduction on park boundaries. Moreover, this option becomes relevant only when there is a serious clash of human interests with the ecological needs of conflict-prone species, such as big cats and elephants. Consequently, the voluntary resettlement strategy is relevant primarily where smaller human enclaves are located in the interiors of parks. Given these caveats, however, we believe that spatial separation is a powerful conservation strategy under appropriate circumstances. Such circumstances include the availability of alternate land and reliance on incentives rather than coercion to motivate people.

We note that the idea of resettlement of humans has opprobrium attached to it because it has sometimes been used as a coercive, socially disruptive tool in executing developmental projects for irrigation, power generation, and mining. Although not on a comparable scale, a small number of wildlife conservation projects in South Asia have also involved resettlement of villages, and not always in a sensitive and fair manner.[34]

However, there are currently many settlements marooned in the interiors of parks whose inhabitants are demanding greater access to social amenities such as agricultural land, roads, communication, education, health care, and employment. As a result, there even appears to be a substantial incipient demand for voluntary relocation.[35] Therefore, incentive-driven resettlement projects appear increasingly to be feasible conservation options to reduce future human wildlife conflicts in southern Asia.

Because conventional park managers are not usually equipped to handle resettlement projects, it may be necessary to create new institutional mechanisms to sensitively interact with local people, raise necessary funds, and implement the projects. In some cases, outright purchase of privately owned land inside protected areas is also an option.

We believe that preventive spatial separation as a cost-effective, humane, and practical solution to the problem of human–wildlife conflict in parks deserves a greater degree of attention from both conservation and development agencies than it has received so far.[36]

Future Directions

During the past two decades, the emphasis on more "inclusive" policies[37] with respect to parks advocated by most conservation and development agencies have rested on the central assumption that human activities such as raising crops and livestock, collecting forest products, and even hunting can "coexist peacefully" with wildlife conservation goals. However, as this review shows, interspersion of human settlements within parks that harbor big, fierce animals inevitably leads to unacceptable levels of conflict.[38] Even if we ignore, for the moment, the issue of adverse impact of such human activities on wildlife and parks,[39] it is still clear that a dogmatic adherence to the idea of coexistence[40] actually has the potential for *escalating* the levels of conflict in the future.[41] Such enforced "coexistence" may sometimes be unavoidable due to local demographic, geographic, and social compulsions. However, we do not find any evidence that it is beneficial for either conservation or human welfare.

Advancing consumerism and rising economic expectations, combined with loosening of cultural ties to the land, will provide new windows of opportunity to implement strategies based on voluntary, incentive-driven spatial separation in parks where the number of people involved is small, alternate land is available, and the degree of conflict severe. However, to seize such opportunities, park-specific actions that promote spatial separation[42] have to fit within the overall regional developmental policies. Therefore, we urge that international and national agencies, pursuing both conservation and development agendas, should reexamine their current apathy and hostility toward this approach. They must seize emerging opportunities for integrating conflict reduction through voluntary resettlement into their overall conservation or development strategies. We argue that such integration can be best accomplished under a framework of "sustainable landscapes,"[43] rather than under conservation paradigms that advocate interspersion of human settlements and wildlife parks.

Acknowledgments

K. Ullas Karanth thanks the Wildlife Conservation Society, New York; Centre for Wildlife Studies, Bangalore, and Karnataka State Forest Department, for supporting his fieldwork in India. M. D. Madhusudan would like to thank the Chicago Zoological Society and the Wildlife Conservation Society for supporting his fieldwork and the National Institute of Advanced Studies for logistical assistance. We are also grateful to Nigel Leader-Williams, Arthur Mugisha, James De Bakey, Rosie Ruf, Madhu Rao, Chaurdutt Mishra, two anonymous reviewers, and the editors for several useful suggestions and comments.

Notes

1. E. L. Bennett and J. G. Robinson, "Hunting for Sustainability: The Start of a Synthesis," in *Hunting for Sustainability in Tropical Forests*, ed. J. G. Robinson and E. L. Bennett (New York: Columbia University Press, 2000), 499–519; R. A. Kramer and C. P. van Schaik, "Preservation Paradigms and Tropical Rain Forests," in *Last Stand: Protected Areas and the Defense of Tropical Biodiversity*, ed. R. A. Kramer, C. P. van Schaik, and J. Johnson, (New York: Oxford University Press, 1997), 3–14; J. G. Robinson, "Limits to Caring: Sustainable Living and the Loss of Biodiversity," *Conservation Biology* 7 (1993): 20–28; J. Terborgh and C. P. van Schaik, "Minimizing Species Loss: The Imperative of Protection," in Kramer et al., *Last Stand*, 15–33.

2. M. Gadgil and R. Guha, *This Fissured Land: An Ecological History of India* (New Delhi: Oxford University Press, 1992); A. Kothari, S. Suri, and N. Singh, "People and Protected Areas: Rethinking Conservation in India," *Ecologist* 25 (1995): 188–194.

3. R. Sukumar, "Wildlife–Human Conflict in India: An Ecological and Social Perspective," in *Social Ecology*, ed. R. Guha (Delhi: Oxford University Press, 1994), 303–317; R. Woodroffe and J. R. Ginsberg, "Edge Effects and Extinction of Populations inside Protected Areas," *Science* 280 (1998): 2126–2128.

4. K. U. Karanth, "Sacred Groves for the Twenty-first Century," *Seminar* 466 (1998): 25–31; M. D. Madhusudan and C. Mishra, "Why Big, Fierce Animals Are Threatened: Conserving Large Mammals in Densely Populated Landscapes," in *Battles Over Nature, Science and the Politics of Wildlife Conservation*, ed. V. K. Saberwal

and M. Rangarajan (New Delhi: Permanent Black, in press, 33–57); R. Sukumar, "Management of Large Mammals in Relation to Male Strategies and Conflict with People," *Biological Conservation* 55 (1991): 93–102; Sukumar, "Wildlife–Human Conflict."

5. C. McDougal, "The Man-Eating Tiger in Geographical and Historical Perspective," in *Tigers of the World: The Biology, Biopolitics, Management and Conservation of an Endangered Species,* ed. R. L. Tilson and U. S. Seal (Park Ridge, New Jersey: Noyes Publications, 1987), 435–448; K. S. Rajpurohit, "Child Lifting: Wolves in Hazaribagh, India," *Ambio* 28 (1999): 162–166; Sukumar, "Wildlife–Human Conflict."

6. J. A. S. Blair, G. C. Boon, and N. M. Noor, "Conservation or Cultivation: The Confrontation between the Asian Elephant and Land Development in Peninsular Malaysia," *Land Development Digest* 2 (1979): 27–59; M. D. Madhusudan, "Living among Large Wildlife: Livestock and Crop Depredation in the Forest Villages of Bhadra Tiger Reserve, India" (manuscript); C. Nath and R. Sukumar, *Elephant–Human Conflict in Southern India: Distribution Patterns, People's Perceptions and Mitigation Methods* (Bangalore: Asian Elephant Conservation Centre, manuscript, 1998); W. D. Newmark, D. N. Manyanza, D. M. Gamassa, and H. I. Sariko, "The Conflict between Wildlife and Local People Living Adjacent to Protected Areas in Tanzania: Human Density as Predictor," *Conservation Biology* 8 (1994): 249–255; N. U. Sekhar, "Crop and Livestock Depredation Caused by Wild Animals in Protected Areas: The Case of Sariska Tiger Reserve, Rajasthan, India," *Environmental Conservation* 25 (1998): 160–171; R. Sukumar, "Ecology of the Asia Elephant in Southern India: Feeding Habits and Crop Raiding Patterns," *Journal of Tropical Ecology* 6 (1990): 33–53; A. C. Williams and A. J. T. Johnsingh, *Status Survey of Elephants (Elephas maximus), Their Habitats and an Assessment of Elephant–Human Conflict in Garo Hills, Meghalaya* (Dehradun, India: Wildlife Institute of India, manuscript, 1996).

7. V. D. Sharma, personal communication.

8. R. Chellam and A. J. T. Johnsingh, "Management of Asiatic Lions in the Gir Forest, India," *Symposium of the Zoological Society of London* 65 (1993): 409–424; R. S. Chundawat, N. Gogate, and A. J. T. Johnsingh, "Tigers in Panna: Preliminary Results from an Indian Tropical Dry Forest," in *Riding the Tiger: Tiger Conservation in Human-Dominated Landscapes,* ed. J. Seidensticker, S. Christie, and P. Jackson (Cambridge: Cambridge University Press, 1999), 123–129; C. Mishra, "Livestock Depredation by Large Carnivores in the Indian Trans-Himalaya: Conflict Perceptions and Conservation Prospects," *Environmental Conservation* 24 (1997): 338–343; M. Oli, I. R. Taylor, and M. E. Rogers, "Snow Leopard *Panthera uncia* Predation of Livestock: An Assessment of Local Perceptions in the Annapurna Conservation Area, Nepal," *Biological Conservation* 68 (1994): 63–68; V. K. Saberwal, J. P. Gibbs, R. Chellam, and A. J. T. Johnsingh, "Lion–Human Conflict in the Gir Forest, India," *Conservation Biology* 8 (1994): 501–507; G. B. Schaller, J. Tserendeleg, and G. Amarsanaa, "Observations on Snow Leopards in Mongolia," in *Proceedings of the Seventh*

International Snow Leopard Symposium, July 25–30, 1992, Xining, Qinghai, China (Seattle: International Snow Leopard Trust, 1992), 33–42; Sekhar, "Crop and Livestock Depredation."

9. Mishra, "Livestock Depredation"; Sekhar, "Crop and Livestock Depredation."

10. A. Dobson, "The Ecology and Epidemiology of Rinderpest Virus in Serengeti and Ngorongoro Conservation Area," in *Serengeti 2: Dynamics, Management, and Conservation of an Ecosystem*, ed. A. R. E. Sinclair and P. Arcese (Chicago: University of Chicago Press, 1995), 485–505; H. McCallum and A. Dobson, "Detecting Disease and Parasite Threats to Endangered Species and Ecosystems," *Trends in Ecology and Evolution* 10 (1995): 190–194.

11. Sukumar, "Wildlife–Human Conflict."

12. Y. V. Jhala and D. K. Sharma, "Child-Lifting by Wolves in Eastern Uttar Pradesh," *Journal of Wildlife Research* 40 (1997): 161–199; Rajpurohit, "Child Lifting."

13. McDougal, "Man-Eating Tiger"; P. Sanyal, "Managing the Maneating Tigers in the Sundarbans Tiger Reserve of India: A Case Study," in Tilson and Seal, *Tigers of the World*, 435–448.

14. Saberwal et al., "Lion–Human Conflict."

15. Sanyal, "Maneating Tigers."

16. Sukumar, "Wildlife–Human Conflict."

17. See chapter 14.

18. A. Mugisha, personal communication.

19. Mishra, "Livestock Depredation."

20. Dobson, "Ecology and Epidemiology."

21. Nath and Sukumar, *Elephant–Human Conflict*.

22. E. Dinerstein, A. Rijal, M. Bookbinder, B. Kattel, and A. Rajuria, "Tigers as Neighbours: Efforts to Promote Local Guardianship of Endangered Species in Lowland Nepal," in Seidensticker et al., *Riding the Tiger*, 316–333.

23. Madhusudan, "Living among Large Wildlife."

24. Madhusudan, "Living among Large Wildlife."

25. Madhusudan, "Living among Large Wildlife."

26. Nath and Sukumar, *Elephant–Human Conflict*; Sukumar, "Wildlife–Human Conflict."

27. Nath and Sukumar, *Elephant–Human Conflict*.

28. K.U. Karanth, personal observations.

29. Sekhar, "Crop and Livestock Depredation"; Sukumar, "Wildlife-Human Conflict."

30. Madhusudan and Mishra, "Big Fierce Animals."

31. D. B. Pond and Bart O'Gara, "Chemical Immobilization of Large Mammals," in *Research and Management Techniques for Wildlife and Habitats*, ed. T. Bookhout (Be-

thesda: The Wildlife Society, 1994), 125–149; S. D. Schemnitz, "Capture and Handling Wild Animals," in Bookhout, *Research and Management Techniques*, 107–124.

32. K. U. Karanth, unpublished data.

33. Karanth, "Sacred Groves."

34. K. U. Karanth, M. E. Sunquist, and K. M. Chinnappa, "Long Term Monitoring of Tigers: Lessons from Nagarahole," in Seidensticker et al., *Riding the Tiger*, 114–122; Kothari et al., "People and Protected Areas."

35. Karanth, "Sacred Groves"; see also chapter 14.

36. Karanth, "Sacred Groves"; Karanth et al., "Long Term Monitoring"; see also chapter 14.

37. Gadgil and Guha, *This Fissured Land*; Kothari et al., "People and Protected Areas"; D. Western and R. M. Wright, *Natural Connections: Perspectives in Community-based Conservation* (Washington, D.C.: Island Press, 1994).

38. Karanth, "Sacred Groves"; Madhusudan and Mishra, "Big Fierce Animals."

39. M. D. Madhusudan and K. U. Karanth, "Hunting for an Answer: Local Hunting and Large Mammal Conservation in India," in Robinson and Bennet, *Hunting for Sustainability*, 339–355; see also chapter 14.

40. IUCN, UNEP, and WWF (The World Conservation Union, United Nations Environmental Programme, World Wildlife Fund), *Caring for the Earth: A Strategy for Sustainable Living* (Gland, Switzerland: IUCN, UNEP, and WWF, 1991); Kothari et al., "People and Protected Areas."

41. Madhusudan and Mishra, "Big Fierce Animals."

42. See chapter 14.

43. Kramer and van Schaik, "Preservation Paradigms"; Robinson, "Limits to Caring."

20

Enforcement Mechanisms

WARREN Y. BROCKELMAN, MICHAEL GRIFFITHS,
MADHU RAO, ROSIE RUF, AND NICK SALAFSKY

Parks are a relatively new phenomenon in many parts of the world, as most individual parks have been in existence for only one or two decades. To many citizens of developing countries, the park concept is as unfamiliar as the restrictions on access and resource use that go with it. Efforts to enforce these restrictions are therefore often met with resentment, if not outright resistance.

Park guards often live in the same communities as the people most impacted by parks, and hence can be subject to strong social pressures to overlook infractions. Where park guards are unarmed and not allowed to make arrests, enforcement falters. Under these circumstances, the best strategy for a park guard is to ignore illegal activities and make peace with the neighbors.

Opinions on how to remedy this impasse range from employing more guards and raising penalties to abandoning enforcement altogether on the grounds that it should not be a part of natural resource management. Of course, the latter opinion is a completely unacceptable dereliction of responsibility. Enforcement of park regulations is unequivocally necessary and is universally practiced in developed countries. In less developed countries, enforcement is even more necessary because pressures on natural resources are intense and because lawlessness is prevalent in many frontier areas.

From the creation of the world's first modern national park—Yellowstone, in 1872—parks and other protected areas have been plagued by enforcement problems, even Yellowstone. Shortly after its establishment, cattle ranchers began encroaching on the park and the United States Cavalry was called in to secure it. Inevitably, parks in other parts of the world are going to face similar challenges, but few will ever benefit from such resolute protection.

Several factors make the problems of enforcement in developing countries especially difficult. One is a lack advance planning to ensure that local residents receive proper notification and compensation for any loss of land or resources. Another is the generally marginal status of local residents compared to elites in the national government, their international advisors, and most of the tourists who will benefit from the park.

After experiencing numerous failures in park enforcement, international agencies began to redress the injustices inherent in park establishment. A number of prominent voices advocated a more development-responsive approach to park management at the Third World Congress on National Parks and Protected Areas held in Bali, Indonesia, in 1982, which stressed "the role of protected areas in sustaining society."[1]

An important product of the Bali Congress was a manual entitled *Managing Protected Areas of the Tropics.*[2] Although heavy emphasis was placed on understanding and working with local villagers, especially in the context of Africa, several sections were devoted to management activities such as patrolling and enforcement.

The socialization of conservation reached new heights at the Fourth World Parks Congress in Caracas, Venezuela, in 1992. Participants stressed that measures were needed for resolving conflicts over protected-area establishment, including the building of broader constituencies for conservation in all sectors of society, increasing benefits to local communities, and enhancing participatory management. The report quite bluntly and correctly concluded that "protected areas cannot coexist with communities which are hostile to them."[3] The congress did not entirely ignore management issues, however. Recommendation four dealt with "Legal Regimes for Protected Areas." Under "National Legal Strategies" the recommendation states:

> The legal status of many protected areas remains uncertain and in some countries the quality and implementation of protected areas legislation remains poor. Existing laws often do not give sufficient attention to societal customs and norms. Regulations, where promulgated, are often not enforced. Many countries do not have sufficient staff or resources to enforce the law.[4]

The frustration of trying to enforce park regulations in the face of persisting conflicts with local communities has given rise to the notion that abridgement of local interests is basically unfair. An extension of this view is that locals should primarily benefit from conserving protected areas, and if this is not possible they should be compensated for forgone opportunities.[5]. Such a parochial focus on local residents challenges the basic premise that parks are for the benefit of everyone. It also ignores the fact that local communities rarely have either the incentives or the expertise to manage resources of national or even global significance.

It is now widely accepted that communities situated near protected areas must have economies based on sustainable use of natural resources before the exclusion of people from core protected areas can be justified.[6] Sustainable use economies should be designed with local participation and managed to maximize local incentives for long-term conservation. The parallel need for enforcement within core conservation areas, however, usually receives only lip service. For example, W. J. Lusigi points out:

> The national park should be the core of this land use system and should be managed strictly in accordance with normal criteria, which should include manned gates, antipoaching activities, tourism, park interpretation, education, training, and research.[7]

The current lack of favor of enforcement by international funding agencies is in part a backlash to the notable lack of success of past efforts and in part the reflection of a feeling that enforcement is not a politically correct concern of aid agencies.

Although enforcement may be unpopular, it is essential to effective conservation. Enforcement will become more acceptable as the constituency for conservation grows and as conservation is increasingly recognized as socially beneficial. In the United States, for example, where a great majority of citizens believe in the basic fairness of their government, considerable resources are devoted to enforcement of wildlife laws at both national and state levels.[8] In many developing countries, however, there is only grudging acceptance of enforcement, and wildlife poaching is not regarded as a criminal activity.

Appropriate and fair enforcement is as basic to park management as public education, local support, and the forging of partnerships for conservation. A socially sensitive approach to enforcement needs to be taken, so that it becomes more efficient and generates less antagonism.

What are the best methods of enforcement? How are they implemented most effectively? Enforcement is commonly envisioned as apprehending poachers at gunpoint, marching them to headquarters, arresting them, and charging them in court. These measures alone are often not effective. In this chapter, we will outline a broader concept of enforcement and propose an expanded set of activities designed to respond to a wide spectrum of violations.

A Diversity of Settings

Enforcement activities must be tailored to each particular cultural or national setting. Communities and cultures differ so much that it is almost impossible to prescribe approaches that will work everywhere. In some places, local residents will be well informed and compliant; in others, they will be hostile and resist arrest. Any manual on enforcement procedures must take such variability into account and advocate a flexible approach. It is therefore essential to analyze the particular setting in terms of the degree of awareness and compliance of park users and local people, and the social and cultural context that determines which enforcement procedures are tolerated by society and are most effective.

The Local Community

Local people need to understand the value and need for conservation as a prerequisite to their acceptance of an enforcement program. In turn, park managers must understand whether poachers are locals or outsiders and how much they depend on poaching for their livelihood. The commonly held assumption that parks can be protected only if local communities receive sufficient benefits to offset all lost opportunity costs is neither always borne out in practice nor even justified in principle. Moreover, as we will argue, even if compensation for lost opportunities is provided and the value of conservation is appreciated by all, villagers will *still* have incentives to continue poaching park resources in the absence of effective enforcement.

In many areas of the world, as villagers develop economically and obtain jobs in the mainstream economy, they come to accept enforcement of park regulations as a fact of life. But such acceptance depends on an understanding of the value of the park, and on at least tolerable relations with park personnel. To be sure, it is extremely helpful if *some* villagers obtain direct benefits from the park, perhaps as employees or rangers, and that local people not be excluded from its educational and recreational attractions.

An important qualification needs to be made at this point. The term "local community" is not intended to include all tribal or subsistence peoples whose traditional livelihood depends on hunting and gathering or other extractive activities, such as many of the tribes in Amazonia. The best option in these cases, short of relocation outside the protected area, is to devise a management strategy that promotes a transition from subsistence to nonconsumptive activities. Reserves containing indigenous people practicing traditional subsistence are best treated as "anthropological reserves."[9]

Although poaching takes place within park borders, it is often linked with activities that occur well outside the borders, or even in foreign countries. If poaching is a subsistence activity, the crime ends when the meat is eaten at the poacher's dinner table. But where poaching is driven by international markets for ivory, rare woods, or tiger bone, it may be linked to a succession of criminal activities involving purchase of the products by middlemen, smuggling across borders, processing into salable products, and finally, purchase in a foreign country. Crimes may be committed at each step, and collusion of officials is often necessary.

Expanding the Scope of Enforcement

Traditional enforcement entails the use of armed force to apprehend violators, and punishment appropriate to the violation. However, unless prospective violators respect the power and jurisdiction of park guards, enforcement will be ineffective. Use of armed might is a last resort in an orderly society, so less-stringent mechanisms should be employed to deter potential violators, or to achieve voluntary compliance. Such mechanisms may be considered components of an expanded concept of enforcement. Some examples follow below.

Promote awareness. Park regulations and penalties for violations must be publicized widely, on signs, in brochures, and through visits of park personnel to villages and local groups. In this respect, enforcement activity is not sharply distinguished from education and interpretation.

Maintain a visible presence. If park rangers and officials are seldom seen in areas susceptible to violations, then violations will increase. Presence should be coupled with nonthreatening duties such as interpretation, guiding, and the like. Guards at check points should not become lax in checking vehicles entering and leaving the park. Frequent patrols serve not simply to catch poachers, but also to deter poachers from entering.

Set prominent examples. Enlist the support of influential people in extolling the values of the park and in urging people to obey regulations. People who enjoy wide popularity, such as singers, TV personalities, priests, shamans, or athletes, will be most effective. Invite them to help stage recreation or entertainment events near or (if appropriate) in the park.

Use village leaders and community sanctions. Convince community leaders of the importance of obeying park regulations and enlist their support in convincing villagers. Of course, this is easier if the community derives some direct or indirect benefits from the park.

Enlist the support of police, military, and other enforcement agencies. Enforcement often fails from lack of cooperation from police, courts, or other legal authorities. In the worst situations, the police themselves may be involved in poaching or smuggling. Such cases require the attention of the highest possible levels of government. It certainly helps if the head of the parks agency is a high ranking or otherwise influential official.

Use nongovernmental organizations. Conservation nongovernmental organizations (NGOs) can help carry out a wide variety of activities that aid enforcement. These may include increasing awareness and helping local communities derive benefits from the park. Other useful activities include guiding tour groups, making presentations to local communities, and reporting violations. NGO personnel can also alert the news media to violations and corruption, something that park officials will generally hesitate to do.

Obtain information from researchers. Scientists carrying out research in a park can often provide valuable information about poaching or other violations. Researchers usually avoid provoking poachers whom they chance to meet in the forest, so most will decline to participate in enforcement operations. On the other hand, researchers are usually highly motivated to conserve wildlife and will readily help with "intelligence" operations. Researchers can also be recruited to help with monitoring of human impacts as well as animal populations. Monitoring is an important adjunct to protection, and park personnel rarely have sufficient time and resources to do it effectively.

Use media pressure. In countries having a free press, the media can be a surprisingly effective deterrent and punitive agent against corruption and other high-level crimes. In an open political system, news writers and opposition politicians are constantly on the lookout for exposés to use against officials who may be guilty of illegal activities such as logging, favoritism, kickbacks, and lax enforcement. Exposure in the media, especially on the front pages of local papers, is often the only "punishment" that influential violators ever receive, and it can be embarrassing and painful in its own way. Park officials and other conservationists therefore should always cultivate the favor of local and national media.

Go global. Experience has shown that market-driven hunting for high-value products cannot be effectively stopped through enforcement within park boundaries. Prevention of such market-driven poaching demands cooperation with national and international agencies responsible for combating trade in endangered species, such as TRAFFIC, CITES (Convention on International Trade in Endangered Species), and the U.S. Fish and Wildlife Service. Carrying out enforcement at the international level requires highly trained investigators, lawyers, and established contacts with counterparts in foreign countries. At present, park agencies in most developing countries have no professional training in investigative or legal operations, much less in international operations.

Types of Violations and How to Deal with Them

We will now describe some examples of park violations, in increasing order of severity, and discuss enforcement measures that seem appropriate. The examples are intended to be indicative, not exhaustive. Enforcement measures should be administered flexibly, with due consideration of the types of persons committing the violations as well as the nature of the violation. Flexibility should not imply unfairness. Ideally, most "enforcement" activities should consist of measures to deter or prevent violations.

Petty Infringements

Littering. "No littering" signs often state the amounts of fines for violations, but in practice, fines are almost never imposed for littering. The primary purpose of aggressive signs is to convey the notion that littering is a minor crime against society. In rural and poor urban areas throughout the world, litter is dropped on the roadside or in natural areas without the slightest compunction. A good practice is to inform the violator immediately and ask him or her to pick up the litter and dispose of it properly. Tour leaders should always instruct visitors on how to dispose of litter. Fines are desirable for major offenders who should know better, for example, tour bus drivers or food concessionaires, whose actions would set particularly bad examples. Fines are also in order for persons who deliberately dump loads of trash in natural areas, but such persons are seldom caught. One of the best methods of instilling a nonlittering ethic is to organize voluntary trash clean-up campaigns with schoolchildren, and reward them afterward.

Picking plants, collecting shells, rocks, and the like. Minor violations of collecting regulations made in innocence are best dealt with in the same way as minor littering violations. Removal of plants or other materials in quantity may merit a fine. The easiest way of discovering such violations is by searches of vehicles at checkpoints.

Excessive noise. Clear regulations must be posted at wildlife viewing spots, wilderness trails, campsites, and other high-use areas. Verbal warnings are usually sufficient. Loudspeakers and "boom-box" radios should be outlawed altogether in parks.

Vandalism and theft. Damaging park property such as signs or locks, or stealing from other visitors, are violations that may be dealt with by a stern lecture, a demand for compensation, expulsion from the park, or by calling in the police, depending on the age of the violator and severity of the offense.

Subsistence Violations

These violations are defined as poaching and extraction of products for household use, and not commercial trade. Typical subsistence products are small game animals, forest vegetables, fruits and medicinal plants, firewood, honey, tool handles, and construction wood. Subsistence violations are best prevented by working with local village leaders to identify alternative sources and to enlist their support in prevention. Cooperation will likely depend on some compromise and provision of benefits to the village, because minor subsistence violations by villagers crossing the borders of a park on foot are typically impossible to prevent. In some protected areas, some types of harvest for household use are allowed (or ignored), such as of fruits, vegetables, honey and medicinal plants, and fish from local streams. Cutting trees for wood and hunting with firearms, however, should be completely prohibited. The creation of buffer zones outside park borders for limited use by villagers is intended to alleviate this problem. Park officials must be clear about what types of violations will be strictly enforced, if they cannot all be enforced. Confiscation of harvested goods in the first instance, and perhaps fines for repeat offenses, are appropriate penalties.

Local villagers are often agriculturists who do not depend heavily on park resources for subsistence but who do wish to improve their farming methods and find better markets for their crops. As their economic situation gradually improves, their need for natural products extracted from the park will decline.

Cattle herders pose a more serious management problem if there are no barriers to the movement of domestic stock in and out of the park.[10] Parks are invariably tempting to herders because of their tendency to overgraze communally held land. There is no way to reduce the incentives for clandestine intrusions other than using local community agreements to limit the size of herds. Wherever practical, it is best to keep cattle some distance from the park boundary and out of a buffer zone. Cattle that wander into the park should be rounded up, driven to a holding area, and kept until the owner comes to retrieve them, perhaps after paying a fine.

Market-driven Poaching and Harvest

By local villagers. If market hunting is carried out by local villagers, it is best dealt with in the same way as subsistence hunting but with more severe sanctions. The most effective way of reducing market hunting may be to eliminate the markets or arrest the buyers.

By outsiders. Poachers who live outside of the local community cannot be sanctioned unless they are caught in the act of poaching or transporting game. Sanctions should begin with the confiscation of any bounty along with weapons and accessory equipment, such as boats. Fines or short prison terms are appropriate for serious offenders. Arrests should be followed by investigations to determine where the markets or traders are. The police should be brought in to make arrests and to make charges under the law, if possible.

By illegal product traders. Dealing in protected products should be treated as a serious violation. Traders are typically better off than hunters or collectors, so the penalties should therefore be heavier. Too often, the penalties are set too low to be a deterrent. Illegal trading is difficult to stop without covert investigations and patient cultivation of sources of information. Prosecution should then be handled by competent lawyers. Stiff fines, confiscation of illegal products, and exposure in the media are the main types of penalties.

By international illegal product traders. The enforcement mechanisms employed to apprehend and prosecute international traders are similar, but the participation of international agencies, foreign governments, and NGOs is required, as suggested previously.

Illegal Sport Hunting

In tropical countries, sport hunting is primarily a pastime of the privileged elite, such as police, military officers, or high-ranking government officials. The overall impact of sport hunting is usually not great, although it can be when endangered species are involved. The most serious aspects of illegal sport and trophy hunting is the flaunting of impunity by those who do it and the bad example it sets for the rest of society. It should therefore be combated vigorously. Arrest should be accompanied by exposure and publicity in order to embarrass the poachers and their agencies or employers. Violators should therefore be prosecuted even though the likelihood of conviction or punishment may be low.

White-collar Crimes

This category includes various quasi-legal acts that involve manipulation of the law, use of political influence, or bribery. Such practices are commonplace in many societies and seldom exposed. In our context, an official might "look the other way" (for a price) while illegal logging proceeded in a protected area. Or, a "legal" concession could be approved in a park. More generally, approval of anything, from dumping wastes to building roads on park land, can be given legal trappings. Needless to say, such "crimes" are rarely punished under the law, but they can sometimes be stopped by vigorous exposure and publicity. NGOs and the media are the most potent enforcers.

Summary of Principles Regarding Enforcement Mechanisms

Below we summarize the most important points regarding enforcement mechanisms. If these are taken seriously, enforcement should become easier, even in understaffed parks.

Enforcement means prevention. The basic thrust of increasing enforcement capability within parks is not to catch and prosecute ever larger numbers of poachers but to prevent or deter them from poaching. This basic principle of effective law enforcement is underappreciated in conservation area protection. Most national governments, however, do not commit nearly enough resources and personnel to achieve effective deterrence.

Fairness. Enforcement should be fair and evenhanded. The ability of well-connected individuals in many societies to flaunt the law with impunity creates resentment and encourages emulation. A few high profile prosecutions can help restore confidence in the enforcement system. Fairness also applies to the treatment of violators after capture or arrest. A proper demeanor and etiquette in enforcement situations is crucial to gaining the respect and trust of violators, and in some situations it could save lives. The administrative beating or punishment of violators only creates hostility and scorn toward law enforcers. The primary purpose of arrest and punishment in civil society is to induce voluntary compliance with regulations.

Flexibility. The punishment should fit both the crime and the criminal. Violations based on ignorance or dire need should carry less severe sanctions than those motivated by arrogance or greed.

Enforcement beyond the borders. "No park is an island" certainly applies to the need for enforcement. Strongly motivated poachers cannot be controlled by a park's normal staff, as the rampage of ivory poaching in the 1980s clearly demonstrated. Unless the motivation for poaching is reduced, or the demand for illegal products is eliminated, it will benefit poachers to persist. In such cases, efforts to curtail the buying, selling, and smuggling of illegal products are likely to prove more productive than the pursuit of armed poachers on the ground.

Hypotheses to Be Tested

Law enforcement entails a large psychological element, which can be turned to good effect by an astute management agency. But because psychological reactions are likely to be culturally determined, we present the next series of suggestions as hypotheses to be evaluated.

Strict enforcement against small crimes leads to more effective deterrence of larger crimes. For example, vigorous application of the law against littering could help deter dumping of trash; similarly, action taken against small-scale poachers could help deter market hunting. If so, the benefits could be substantial, because serious violations by armed poachers are the most dangerous for rangers to enforce.

The certainty of punishment is as important as the severity of punishment. A high probability of punishment can be a powerful deterrent and sets a psychological tone that can carry beyond the level of petty infractions. However, increasing the fine for a given violation rarely deters violators, if only because the greater the penalty, the lower the chance of a firm conviction.

In principle, the psychological power of deterrence can be broken down into the likelihood of being caught times the penalty imposed if one is caught. As the relation between the two components of deterrence is multiplicative, deterrence can be enhanced either by increasing the penalty or by increasing the level of enforcement. The nature of penalties is often public knowledge whereas the chance of being caught is never known with certainty. Villagers would probably have a better idea of this probability than protected-area personnel, because they know how many of their friends and relatives are engaged in poaching, and the number caught each year.

Offsetting deterrence is the benefit to be gained by engaging in the illegal activity. If the benefit is sufficiently high, then poaching will be "worth the risk" of being apprehended. Enforcement typically fails in situations where the benefit of poaching is high and the probability of receiving any penalty is low. The goal of any enforcement regime should thus be to reduce the incentives and/or increase the disincentives so that poachers will decide that other activities are more profitable. When this happens, enforcement has achieved its main objective.

Perceived collective benefits depend on the effectiveness of enforcement. A rational citizen will obey a law that confers collective benefits on the community, provided that enough citizens obey it so that the collective benefits materialize. In the absence of enforcement, rational and well-meaning citizens will not decide to obey it, because there is no escape from a "tragedy of the commons" scenario, or, in other words, "What's the use of obeying the law, since all will be lost anyway?"

Application of this logic to protected areas results in some startling conclusions. First, if we assume rational but selfish behavior, villagers receiving benefits such as compensation payments or alternative income from tourism will have no particular incentive to obey park regulations because there is no direct feedback between an individual's actions and the benefits received. Second, rational villagers receiving benefits that depend on effective park management and enforcement will not necessarily obey the regulations merely because they receive benefits. They must be assured of obedience by all others, either at the village level or more generally. If there is more than one village near the boundary, enforcement may not be effective except in the unlikely case that agreements and trust extend over the whole network of villages. Villagers then must have a love–hate relationship with park authorities. Their freedom to exploit must be restricted, but failing this, the incentive to obey regulations will be destroyed by a loss of collective benefits.

Many conservationists hold the view that in order for enforcement to work, villagers must receive benefits. The argument presented above reverses the logic—in order for villagers to benefit, park regulations prohibiting exploitation must first be enforced. Frequently, however, enforcement problems originate outside the realm of resource conservation and involve inadequacies of land distribution and tenure. This brings us to the last, rather unhappy, argument.

Enforcement problems may not be solvable. All too often in densely populated parts of the world, the number of local residents is simply too high to permit sharing of the benefits provided by parks. Such situations are especially common in Asia and Africa. Under these circumstances, it is hardly possible to devise an incentive structure that encourages local people to abstain from exploiting park resources. Enforcement under these conditions becomes a nearly hopeless Sisyphean task.[11] The problem is not one of resources per se but of festering social and economic conditions outside protected areas. These conditions usually result from social and political inequity—and hence cannot be solved by resource planners.[12] Poverty alleviation is a moral imperative of essential importance to global stability, but it is not an efficient use of scarce conservation dollars.

Acknowledgments

We thank Ullas Karanth, Philip Dearden, and J. F. Maxwell for their comments and discussion.

Notes

1. J. A. McNeely and K. R. Miller, eds., *National Parks, Conservation, and Development: The Role of Protected Areas in Sustaining Society* (Washington, D.C.: Smithsonian Institution Press, 1984).

2. J. MacKinnon, K. MacKinnon, G. Child, and J. Thorsell, *Managing Protected Areas in the Tropics* (Gland, Switzerland: IUCN, 1986).

3. IUCN (The World Conservation Union), *Parks for Life: Report of the 4th World Congress on National Parks and Protected Areas* (Gland, Switzerland: IUCN, 1993), 35.

4. IUCN, *Parks for Life*, 32.

5. See, for example, W. J. Lusigi, "How to Build Local Support for Protected Areas" in *Expanding Partnerships in Conservation*, ed. J. A. McNeely (Washington, D.C.: Island Press, 1995); M. Munasinghe, "Economic and Policy Issues in Natural Habitats and Protected Areas," in *Protected Area Economics and Policy: Linking Conservation and Sustainable Development*, ed. M. Munasinghe and J. A. McNeely (Washington, D.C.: World Bank, 1994).

6. See, for example, Munasinghe and McNeely, *Protected Area Economics*; J. A. McNeely, *Economics and Biological Diversity: Developing and Using Economic Incentives to Conserve Biological Resources* (Gland, Switzerland: IUCN, 1988); J. A. McNeely, *Expanding Partnerships*; R. E. Saunier and R. A. Meganck, eds., *Conservation of Biodiversity and the New Regional Planning* (Washington, D.C. and Gland, Switzerland: Organization of American States and IUCN, 1995); M. Wells, K. Brandon, and L. Hannah, *People and Parks: Linking Protected Area Management with Local Communities* (Washington, D.C.: World Bank, World Wildlife Fund, and U.S. Agency for International Development, 1992).

7. W. J. Lusigi, "Socioeconomic and Ecological Prospects for Multiple Use of Protected Areas in Africa," in Munasinghe and McNeely, *Protected Area Economics*, 89.

8. See, for example, W. F. Sigler, *Wildlife Law Enforcement*, 4th ed. (Dubuque, Iowa: W. C. Brown, 1995).

9. MacKinnon et al., *Managing Protected Areas*.

10. MacKinnon et al., *Managing Protected Areas*.

11. But see chapter 14.

12. J. Vandermeer and I. Perfecto, *Breakfast of Biodiversity: The Truth about Rain Forest Destruction* (Oakland, Calif.: Institute for Food and Development Policy, 1995).

21

Ecotourism Tools for Parks

LISA DAVENPORT, WARREN Y. BROCKELMAN,
PATRICIA C. WRIGHT, KARL RUF, AND
FERNANDO B. RUBIO DEL VALLE

Ecotourism is often hailed as one of the few indisputable examples of sustainable development at work, because it not only helps to ensure the in situ preservation of wilderness and wildlife but it also generates economic revenue from land set aside for conservation.[1] In addition, ecotourism helps to educate the general public on conservation issues and creates a natural alignment between business and conservationists in advocating for better management of protected areas.

Revenue generation from ecotourism is particularly relevant to tropical developing countries whose incomes largely depend on revenues derived from their natural resources. Governments of such countries are under great pressure to maximize rents from all lands, and without tourism revenue they can rarely justify allocating adequate levels of funding for biodiversity conservation.

But what, really, is the primary value of ecotourism to parks? What should be its role in the context of protected area management? Obviously, tourists visit parks to enjoy wildlife and nature, but does this imply that all such tourists are engaged in "ecotourism"? The impact of tourist visits is directed by the availability of facilities (both within and outside the park), as well as by policies and regulations of the park and the nation. Thus, ensuring that visitation to parks is compatible with biodiversity conservation is in part the responsibility of park administrators through policies governing public use and in part a function of the larger society. Our discussion will focus primarily on management tools that aid in planning and promoting true ecotourism within parks. Our working definition of ecotourism is *nature-based visitation to parks that is compatible with biodiversity conservation and promotes long-term acceptance of the park as a legitimate institution.*

Other means of promoting sustainable development, such as providing educational, economic, and revenue-sharing opportunities for local inhabitants, are also touched on in this chapter. But because these often involve external social and economic conditions and tend to be complex and highly variable from park to park, the "extra-park" tools we suggest are more speculative and necessarily less specific than those for ecotourism. Certain of the tools described are well-established techniques developed specifically for use by park managers in the United States or elsewhere, whereas others are new approaches suggested by case studies and the authors' own observations.

The Role of Ecotourism in Parks

We wish to stress that ecotourism in parks should not be viewed merely as a means of maximizing revenue with respect to competing forms of land use. Recent studies of tropical ecotourism reveal that it does not always compete favorably with other more intensive forms of land use.[2] Nevertheless, biodiversity protection, park creation, and ecotourism offer the advantage of perpetual benefits. Supporting parks is a legitimate role for governments, akin to their responsibility to provide healthy environmental conditions for citizens.

Fortunately, ecotourism is capable of providing win–win situations for natural areas and local economies under certain circumstances, and it often is a major component in the development strategies of developing countries. Tourism is currently the world's fastest-growing industry, and ecotourism is widely believed to be the fastest-growing sector of the industry (although reliable statistics on the proportion of tourism that constitutes true ecotourism have not yet been sufficiently collected).[3] Ecotourism is particularly significant in developing nations, as indicated by a 12.5 percent annual growth rate in nonindustrialized countries compared to a 7.0 percent rate for the Organisation for Economic Co-Operation and Development (OECD) countries.[4] In addition, the ratio between international tourism receipts and gross national product (GNP) is significantly higher for developing nations than for industrialized nations in the OECD.[5] Such statistics contribute to the optimism felt by many in government agencies and conservation organizations interested in bringing increased ecotourism to developing countries.

Unfortunately, despite its rapid growth in developing nations, ecotourism is not a panacea for all that might ail them, as cautioned by numerous recent articles.[6] The principal criticisms of ecotourism are described here along with parenthetical references to relevant sections in this chapter that discuss these criticisms.

- Unregulated ecotourism causes degradation of the very natural areas it claims to aid (see Zoning Systems, Carrying Capacity, and Limits of Acceptable Change).
- Park management agencies are not capable of managing foreign eco-tourism effectively (see Diversifying Tourism Infrastructure).
- In the great majority of protected areas, tourism revenue does not or cannot cover management costs (see Optimizing User Fee Structures).
- Even when ecotourism revenues are shared with local residents, the amounts are rarely sufficient to offset opportunity costs or to stop poaching and encroachment (see Diversifying Tourism Infrastructure and Revenue Sharing).
- International tourism is both seasonal and fluctuational, creating unstable local economies (see Diversifying Tourism Infrastructure).
- The notion that parks are only for wealthy foreign tourists causes re-sentment among poor local residents (see Increasing Domestic Tour-ism).
- Ecotourism is not very successful in tropical forests because wildlife there are difficult to observe, and annoying and dangerous conditions are prevalent (see Interpretation and Public Education).

Ecotourism Tools

Table 21-1 provides a list of the ecotourism tools discussed in this chapter. For each tool, the table lists the likely instigator or responsible party; re-quired and best practices; and expected advantages and disadvantages from the perspectives of conservation, visitor experience, and park man-agement. Most of these tools can be implemented in full or in part ac-cording to the needs of each park. For example, a well-funded park system could implement a comprehensive management plan with complex zoning systems for educational facilities, hotels, automobile routes, wilderness, scientific study areas, and the like. However, even if implementation of the full plan is impractical, individual components, such as the zoning system, can applied in a useful way. For instance, a zoning system can be set up al-lowing certain trails to be reserved for use only with a trained guide, while others might be hardened and made accessible to all. Deciding which tools

Table 21-1.
Ecotourism Tools for Parks.

Tool	Responsible Party	Requirements for Best Use	Ideal Components	Conservation Advantages and Disadvantages	Visitor Advantages and Disadvantages	Management Advantages and Disadvantages
Zoning system	Head of park system, with input from scientists, specialists	Implementation of plan for restricting access at high/medium/low levels	Sensitive features (soil, water, species) protected	Proactive system needed to maintain high-quality habitats	Provides for a variety of wilderness experiences (intensive to extensive)	Maintains best balance between visitor access and biological needs
	Park manager	Enforcement free of corruption	Visitor access varied between different zones	Concentrates impacts in least sensitive habitats	*May limit access to some prime wildlife viewing sites*	Can diversify tourism opportunities by creating diverse market niches
			Habitats accessible to visitors should be varied (if feasible while simultaneously protecting sensitive areas)			Can be used in concert with other tools listed in this table
						Initial expense to design may be costly

Carrying capacity	Park manager	Site-by-site analysis Enforcement Good understanding needed of most sensitive features	Biological requirements considered Frequent revision Seasonal variation of carrying capacity numbers	*Usually less tied to needs of biology than to management* *Nearly always impossible to determine biological carrying capacity completely and objectively*	*May result in visitor dissatisfaction because of limited access* *May favor access to large tour groups where reservations would be required*	Can cater to actual management capacity Simple to enforce *Often result in poorly implemented reservation systems and enforcement* *Can invite political pressure to increase carrying capacity above known limits*
Limits of acceptable change	Park manager	Some training of personnel	Designed with indicators tailored to reveal major threats or biodiversity concerns (e.g., no. of scats, no. of bullet casings)	Under strong management, may allow quickest response to any problems	*Unexpected changes in management may limit access to favored sites with little advance notice*	Long-term monitoring provides strong understanding of changes, threats, and park needs

(continues)

Table 21-1. *(continued)*

Tool	Responsible Party	Requirements for Best Use	Ideal Components	Conservation Advantages and Disadvantages	Visitor Advantages and Disadvantages	Management Advantages and Disadvantages
	Rangers with monitoring skills	Maintenance of monitoring records	Incorporated within a zoning system	*Under weak management, may permit impacts later deemed unacceptable*		Can target specific goals of individual park
		Power granted to park manager to authorize remediative measures				Adaptable and comprehensive when fully implemented
						Can involve local people, and increase conservation involvement and interest
						Higher level of education and management capacity required

Increasing Domestic Tourism	Park manager	Feasible even in parks with very low visitation	Train and involve local guides	*May attract more people to the area for economic opportunities created by tourism*	Provides educational and recreational opportunities for local people at low travel cost	Accelerates creation of a local constituency
	Local NGOs	Some trails and educational materials	Plan and manage proactively as for high-use areas (zoning, etc.)	*May allow illegal users of park resources better familiarity with the site*	International visitors' experience may be enriched by greater contact with local cultures	Local groups more likely to support park in difficult political situations than foreign constituencies would
	Local businesses	Low user fees for nationals; If park has few facilities, focus should be on intensive rather than extensive visitor experience				*May increase demands on some natural resources and facilities (firewood, water, sanitary facilities); Difficult to implement if park very remote from population centers*

(continues)

Table 21-1. *(continued)*

Tool	Responsible Party	Requirements for Best Use	Ideal Components	Conservation Advantages and Disadvantages	Visitor Advantages and Disadvantages	Management Advantages and Disadvantages
Optimizing User Fee Structure	Head of park system with input from park manager and tourism specialists	Most useful with high and stable visitation rates	Based upon willingness-to-pay analyses	May provide funds for conservation needs that are otherwise insufficiently funded	*May increase costs, especially for lowest-cost travelers (backpacker, etc.)*	May provide more reliable source of funding than government budget process
		Good understanding of economics of tourism markets	Broad range of potential user fee structures considered (see text)			*May require new, complicated administrative processes*
		Return high percentage of new funds directly back to parks for conservation projects				*May be subject to political pressure to raise or lower fees to suboptimal levels*
		Consider in advance how to spread revenue between parks in				

(continues)

		...system with high and low visitation				May reduce conflicts with local peoples
Revenue Sharing	Head of park system with input from park manager	Most useful with high and stable visitation rates	Well-defined groups of people with legitimate claim to benefits specifically targeted	May aid in reducing threats to park from local populations	Visitors may be glad to contribute to local economies through reliable mechanism	May raise national awareness of parks as sources of revenue
	Local NGOs	Good understanding of local social and economic conditions	Revenue benefit tied to some added form of conservation in or around the park	*May attract more people to the area if benefits are excessively inviting*		*May require new, complicated administration*
			The role of enforcement maintained and possibly increased			*May invite considerable politicization of park management*
						May invite corruption in park and local personnel

287

Table 21-1. *(continued)*

Tool	Responsible Party	Requirements for Best Use	Ideal Components	Conservation Advantages and Disadvantages	Visitor Advantages and Disadvantages	Management Advantages and Disadvantages
Integrated Conservation and Development Projects (ICDPs) based on ecotourism	NGOs with participation of park manager	Link development benefit to success of conservation	Issue of scale of project to the scale of related problems considered	*Often monitoring conservation benefits sacrificed to attending development*	Visitors may acquire richer understanding of local communities	Conservation and public relations benefits may accrue if properly managed
	Tourism entrepreneurs		Conservation and development returns carefully monitored			*May increase demands on some natural resources (firewood, water)*
						Often projects cut off after short period, leaving expectations for park managers to fill
Investment in tourism infrastructure and advertising	National government	Coordinated with parks officials to target most appropriate parks and to comply	Best Practice Tourism standards applied	Visitor impact can be reduced while allowing better access and facilities	Better facilities and access will possibly improve visit options,	May lower seasonal variability of visitation

Actor	Conditions for success	Advantages	Disadvantages
	with their management plans and zoning systems	May strengthen park institutions within the government and the public eye	length of stay, and quality of visit *Excessive access levels of visitation may lower quality of visit* *May create new conservation and management problems for park managers*
Tourism industry	Adequate management capacity in place within parks Building and permitting process free of corruption Access issue carefully considered	A focus on infrastructure most needed to achieve conservation and other goals of the park	*Mass tourism development can have strongly negative effects on park habitats* *May detract management focus from conservation to visitor impact management* *May increase visitor demand above management capacity* *May significantly raise cost of visit*

a Disadvantages are italicized.

could best be put to use in a specific park and at what scale will depend heavily on the existing facilities, the current level of visitation, conservation priorities, threats to biodiversity, budgeting mechanisms, and the skills of park employees.

Zoning Systems

Implementing a zoning plan is probably one of the most important first steps toward improving overall park and tourism management. The process itself makes it easier to assess resources and solidify park objectives and priorities. Park resources (flagship species, scenic landscapes, natural habitats, infrastructure, etc.) must be evaluated regarding their status, uniqueness, sensitivity, and nature and degree of threats. In addition, understanding the dynamics of park interactions with local peoples and their land-use practices may also be important.

Cataloging park resources should be conducted with an eye toward determining the best use of each area, because final zoning decisions often involve a complex weighing of competing goals. Habitat protection is often the prime consideration; however, public access and enforcement needs may also be relevant. It is nearly always desirable to showcase features that draw visitors, although this may conflict with protecting sensitive environments. Careful attention to the principles of conservation biology should govern the decision-making process.[7]

A good example of successful zoning can be seen in the Manu National Park and Biosphere Reserve in southeastern Perú. The park encompasses an entire watershed and includes a wide range of environments from alpine grassland to lowland Amazonian rainforest. Road access is limited, and all lowland access is by river, allowing for relatively inexpensive enforcement from guard stations placed where rivers exit the protected area. The lowest, most accessible section of the river is open to tourism, and restrictions are applied progressively as one proceeds upstream. Visitors are thus excluded from the upper watershed, which remains the redoubt of uncontacted indigenous groups. The zoning is easily implemented, thanks to the one-dimensional access afforded by the river.[8] Other parks may not benefit from such fortunate accidents of geography and may have to consider compromises that don't jeopardize their primary objectives. To promote visitor satisfaction, it is often desirable to zone for a variety of experiences. Some tourists shun the hardships of camping and trekking and want greater accessibility with basic facilities. Still others seek a "nature experience" in remote wilderness, requiring little but foot trails. The two types of wilderness experiences have been termed *extensive* and *intensive,* and their availability is determined by zoning and infrastructure.[9] Parks that thoughtfully integrate zoning for conservation with zoning for a variety of visitor experiences will attract a broader spectrum of tourists, keeping biodiversity protection compatible with visitation.

Zoning should be completed early in a park's development, preferably before major investments are made in its infrastructure. Failure to implement zoning in a timely manner has marred several famous African parks with luxury hotels that unwisely blight the landscape and even abuse sensitive park resources (e.g., by introducing exotic vegetation, extracting water from vital rivers, or disturbing fragile hillside soils).[10] The authors urge governments and park authorities to implement zoning plans and establish the legal authority of park zoning initiatives well in advance of development initiatives.

Carrying Capacity

Studies to determine park carrying capacity have been touted as a cure-all for visitor management in parks. Such studies attempt to determine the maximum number of visitors a park can accommodate without suffering deterioration. A variety of methodologies for calculating park carrying capacities have been proposed for use in First World parks and wilderness areas.[11] Three main types of carrying capacity are recognized: the site's physical carrying capacity, the management capacity of park personnel, and the social carrying capacity (i.e., the number of visitors past which crowding diminishes the visitor experience).[12] Unfortunately, following attempts to put these concepts into practice, most of the authors of this chapter have reached the conclusion that carrying capacity methodology is too site specific to offer much general applicability. Very often the desired goals can be achieved by applying common sense or the techniques of adaptive management.[13]

This said, we nevertheless feel it is important to consider the still-widespread need to enact effective reservation systems for parks where carrying capacity limits are in effect. This may appear to be a simple and obvious task, but many parks in developing countries lack adequate communication and computer systems, and have devised reservation systems which are so nefariously counterproductive that they serve as impediments to ecotourism without providing any clear conservation or management benefits.

Frequently, visitors to parks in the developing world are required either to travel with large package tours or to arrange all permits and fees to be paid at a central office, usually in the nation's capital. Visitors to the park without the proper permits are turned away at the gate. Such systems are usually enacted to avoid entrusting park personnel with handling money and engaging in graft, but the system has the effect of strongly discouraging local residents and young (often foreign) backpackers from visiting.

Other deleterious situations arise where carrying capacity is either never instituted or insufficiently enforced. Failure to regulate campsite visitation can result in unsightly and unsanitary conditions, although officials are often loath to limit the number of campers for fear of complaints from excluded tourists, profit-seeking tour operators, or both. In Parque Nacional Huascaran, Perú, steep entrance fees for backcountry use and a 5 P.M. closing time have resulted in tour operators actively promoting trekking trips that enter the park after closing when tour operators can bribe their way past the night guard. Either an electronic gate or a twenty-four-hour attendant would probably more than double park entrance fees.

While these types of situations are all too common throughout Third World parks, the good news is that with new communications technologies becoming cheaper and more widely available, some carrying-capacity concerns can be easily and permanently solved with only minor investments and training. With cheap solar, computer, shortwave radio, and cellular and satellite phone technologies, even the most remote places on Earth can now be connected to reliable communications systems and even the Internet. This area is thus ripe for investment by governments, aid programs, or small donors interested in improving management capacity of Third World parks.

Limits of Acceptable Change and Visitor Impact Management

The *limits of acceptable change* (LAC) *methodology* has been proposed as an alternative to carrying-capacity methodologies for monitoring and mitigating damage to natural resources in parks. Instead of asking, How much use is too much? LAC methodology asks, What natural conditions are desired here?[14] LAC explicitly employs a form of zoning for varied visitor experiences, delineating different zones as different visitor "opportunity classes." Within each area of the park, the conditions desired are considered, resources inventoried, and indicators chosen for monitoring. Indicators may include multiple biotic and abiotic factors as suggested by park objectives and visitation rates. Possible indicators include

- frequency of encounters with other visitors
- amount of erosion or compaction on trails
- water quality
- die-off of vegetation around campsites
- abundance of sensitive wildlife species
- amount of refuse encountered

The decision-making process is diagrammed in Figure 21-1.[15] This methodology has been used widely within wilderness areas in the United States.

Visitor impact management (VIM) entails procedures similar to those of LAC methodology. A standards-based monitoring program is employed, although with less emphasis on designing the visitor opportunity classes of LAC methodology. Instead, emphasis is placed on comparing standards with existing conditions, determining probable cause of any

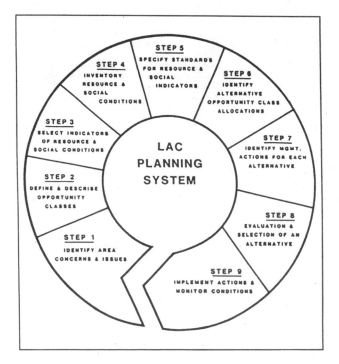

Figure 21-1. Limits of Acceptable Change. From Stankey et al., 1985. *The Limits of Acceptable Change (LAC) System for Wilderness Planning* (Ogden, UT: USDA Forest Service).

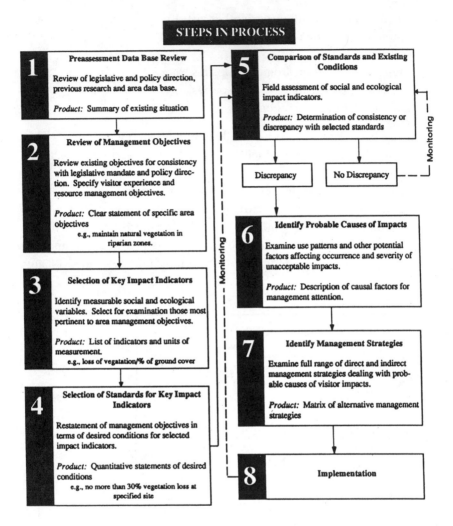

Figure 21-2. Visible Impact Management Planning Process. Reprinted with permission from Graefe et al., 1990.

unacceptable impacts, and then with appropriate management actions (Figure 21-2).[16]

Both systems depend on choosing appropriate indicators and monitoring them. We know of no examples in which these methods have been implemented in developing countries, although certain parks with biological stations do regularly monitor and manage wildlife populations (e.g., Serengeti National Park in Tanzania and Ranomafana National Park in Mad-

agascar). Many parks could benefit from a monitoring program, even a
very modest one. However, for all but the most visited parks, the need to
monitor visitor impacts will be greatly overshadowed by the need to monitor threats to biodiversity. The issue of monitoring is taken up in greater
detail in chapters 2 and 28.

Diversifying Tourism Infrastructure

Within parks, visitors may be forced to accept lower-than-desired standards or, conversely, presented with no alternative to high-priced luxury
accommodations. Neither situation encourages extended visits. Yet, one
of the main ways in which public acceptance of park institutions is
strengthened is through the increased economic opportunities ecotourists
bring by their need for accommodation, food, and entertainment in surrounding areas. Parks themselves often present visitors with limited
choices of routes, attractions, dining, and accommodations, yet such attractions may be better encouraged outside of the protected area itself.

One way to reduce the alienation of local peoples from parks is to encourage small business development that diversifies the choices available
to tourists. Possibilities include campsites, home stays, and restaurants,
plus handicraft cooperatives, musical performances, traditional dance
programs, and travel with local guides versed in the natural or cultural attractions of the area.

In Thailand, an entrepreneur-friendly country, many small ecotourism
businesses have sprung up when small groups or individuals (often resident expatriates) have trained themselves in the local lore and biology
needed for guiding tours. These businesses usually work in collaboration
with particular national parks or wildlife areas, and they may rent their
own accommodations or utilize those available in the park. The small entrepreneurs who run these businesses understand the foreign ecotourist
clientele much better than do government officials, and hence fill a special niche. Similar stories exist for Zimbabwe, Venezuela, Costa Rica, Australia, and probably a multitude of other countries.[17]

Small-business development can be facilitated through local or national programs, and by governments or nongovernmental organizations
(NGOs). Small loans, or financing of start-up costs and training, could
help catalyze the founding of such businesses elsewhere. Besides providing opportunities for local ownership, active investment in tourism can
help increase the level of domestic tourism (see discussion below), extend
and enrich tourist visits, and expand local economies.

Optimizing User Fee Structures

A variety of user fee structures can be applied and optimized to enhance the economic returns from parks thereby making them more attractive to governments (see also chapter 26). Where the majority of park visitors are foreigners, there is considerable justification for establishing a "user pays" system, usually involving a multitiered entrance fee. In developing countries, there is little reason to subsidize the cost of visits by foreigners. Foreigners neither pay the taxes that support park budgets nor do they pay the opportunity cost of leaving land undeveloped.[18] In a Costa Rican study, both national and foreign visitors felt that a fee structure that charged more for foreigners than for nationals was fair and reasonable.[19]

Very commonly, foreigners visit developing country parks as part of a prepaid package tour in which park fees constitute a negligible percentage of the total cost. For countries lacking a substantial share of national ownership of tourism services, "leakage" of ecotourism dollars (the percentage spent that eventually is returned to developed countries) can commonly be 80–90 percent of the cost of a tour.[20] To counter such excessive leakage, the visitor's willingness to pay can be assessed through direct fees or tourism taxes.[21] A 1995 study conducted in Tarangire National Park, Tanzania, determined that park fees accounted for only 5.1 percent of the cost of the average tour. Although many respondents stated that their willingness to pay was premised on the assumption that the entrance fees would benefit park conservation, the queried tourists indicated they would pay $36 per day for entrance to the park, or nearly double the $20 fee being charged. Only 48 percent of the respondents were even aware of the size of the entrance fee they had paid, as most had purchased all-inclusive tour packages.[22]

Rarely are such fees set at efficient levels for foreigners. Yet, in addition to gate fees, there are a number of mechanisms though which governments can earn revenue via tourism, including increasing revenues through tourism-specific levies; increasing revenue from indirect expenditures; minimizing loss of revenue by leakage; increasing efficiency through decentralization and public–private partnerships; and earmarking revenues for park maintenance and community development.[23] The suitability of these options in a given case will vary.

Revenue Sharing

The flip side of efficiently setting tourist user fees is sharing of tourism revenues. Revenue sharing is not a management tool per se, although it may improve public support for parks, especially where parks and local communities are in conflict. Revenue sharing is often instituted where nearby populations demand compensation for lost access to park resources (e.g., firewood and building materials) or for damage done by wildlife originating in the park (see also chapter 19). In this section, we compare some existing revenue-sharing programs for the lessons learned.

In 1995, the first author studied three revenue-sharing programs already in operation at Tarangire National Park. The comparison, although from a small sample, helps to demonstrate potential pitfalls of revenue sharing. The three programs included

- Bundu Safaris, a hunting safari camp on the eastern border of the park. In an informal and sporadic manner, business profits were shared with local people to help garner local support.
- Paul Oliver Safaris and Dorobo Safaris, two private, highly exclusive walking safari operators. In a jointly operated program, these two safari companies each collected a flat $6 per tourist per day "conservation fee" to be paid to a village account in return for restricting farming activities in the wildebeest migration route between the park and the Simanjiro Plain.
- The park's own SCIP program (Support for Community Initiated Projects), supported projects conducted by the park's community service warden. The community service warden's salary and project funds were supported by the African Wildlife Federation (a conservation NGO), with the aim of building better relations with local people by supporting small-scale development projects. Communities had to propose their own projects to park administrators and donate labor in return for logistical and financial support.

The analysis exposed major problems with all three programs. Table 21-2 summarizes the projects, their links to conservation, problems with their implementation, and lessons learned.

The Paul Oliver/Dorobo Tours program stood out as the most successful program of the three we observed. The businesslike arrangement ensured that all parties knew what could be expected from the arrangement, and the program benefited the park by keeping open one of the last signif-

Table 21-2.

Benefit-sharing programs at Tarangire National Park (TNP).

Program	Locations	Benefit Type	Conservation Link	Community Input	Decision-Making	Dependence on Community Leadership
Community Conservation Service (CCS) SCIP Projects	All villages adjacent to TNP eligible	Small-scale infrastructure projects	Loose agreements: no farms in buffer zones, antipoaching support	primarily labor	Strong degree of control over project decisions, implementation rest with park	*Low*
Paul Oliver and Dorobo Safaris	Loiber Soit Emboreet	$6-per-client cash payments to village council	Strong contracted business agreement: no farming in walking safari areas	General land-use limitations in certain areas	*None*	*High*
Bundu Hunting Safaris	Loiber Serrit	Various schemes, depending on whim of owner	None	*None*	Variable	*Variable*

icant migrations of Tarangire wildebeest herds. However, even there, mis-understandings that threatened the continuity of the program arose largely because the local villagers were unused to handling such large sums of money.

The SCIP project was well intentioned, with the goal to improve "good-neighborliness," but it produced only modest benefits for a few of the better-organized communities that agreed to work with the park. From 1995 data, financial value of Tarangire SCIP projects, averaged over the whole surrounding population, benefited locals by only $1 per person per year. The villages surrounding Tarangire were also widely dispersed and belonged to several tribes with differing social and land-use systems. Some were intrinsically better suited for participation in the SCIP program. It was unclear whether the people who benefited most from the program were also those most deserving of compensation. In addition, by improving village infrastructure, such as wells and schoolrooms, the program had the unintended effect of attracting migrants from afar, thereby adding to the local population and diluting the distribution of benefits.

A problem common to all the projects was local political discord that arose over the issue of who benefited most from the funds and infrastructure projects. With the loosely structured Bundu Safaris program, rampant rumors of blatant corruption and misuse of funds pitted local people against their leaders (some community members reputedly starved to death during a severe drought while funds donated by Bundu Safaris went to build new homes for tribal leaders).

Occasional calls for parks to share a percentage of their profits with local people are heard, especially in this region of Africa where tourism is big business. However, many mechanisms for revenue sharing have yet to be worked out, especially for large-scale transfers of funds. In the case of Tanzania, the National Parks Department (TANAPA) is a parastatal organization that is charged taxes equal to corporation taxes. It remains unclear why TANAPA should essentially be taxed at a higher rate than an industry on its "profits."

In addition, human population growth and migration patterns, compounded by foreign aid promises and activities in the region, greatly complicate the expectations local people have for assistance in and around parks. Rarely are revenue-sharing plans designed with explicit goals and under definite terms. Since subsidies once granted are notoriously difficult to withdraw, revenue-sharing programs can raise open-ended expectations that will continue beyond any reasonable compensation for past losses. It may be preferable to propose solutions that resolve a problem equitably and completely with one-time lifetime lump payments rather than by long-term revenue sharing. More work certainly needs to be done to establish mechanisms for compensating legitimate claimants, but the "quick fix" of flat revenue sharing is only rarely the most desirable compensation mechanism.

Where long-term revenue sharing is nonetheless implemented, proceeds intended to foster development would probably be better handled by NGOs or government institutions whose expertise is development than by a mixture of park administration, conservation, and development groups. Most importantly, development projects should be located away from park boundaries and in lands with the best capacity to support human populations. In general, the most intensive forms of land use should not be encouraged adjacent to parks.

In summary, we are sympathetic to the idea that ecotourism revenues should benefit the populace of developing countries and help compensate legitimate claimants. In certain special instances, the case can be made that direct revenue sharing is appropriate and feasible (see chapter 9). However, open-ended revenue-sharing programs are fraught with pitfalls, and other means should be sought to achieve economic and development goals. Direct revenue sharing for local development is probably only rarely the most manageable, effective, and equitable option.

Increasing Domestic Tourism

A vital question for the future of parks is how to increase domestic tourism within tropical parks. Yet most studies on ecotourism barely mention domestic tourism much less offer suggestions for how to stimulate it. Nevertheless, domestic tourism has some advantages that international tourism lacks:

- Domestic tourists may be better informed and better prepared to travel in off-seasons and even during times of war and political instability, thus helping to stabilize visitation rates.
- The expectations of domestic tourists for services usually conform more closely to those actually available.
- Domestic tourists can become an important political constituency in support of parks.

Beyond the societal issues of increasing urbanization, affluence, and leisure (matters not under the control of park or tourism officials), there are two important factors that encourage domestic tourism: enhanced awareness and accessibility.

Raising Interest and Awareness

Even in the world's poorest countries there are affluent citizens who visit their nation's parks if opportunities are available. Similarly, people who have little prospect of visiting remote parks will often support them once they have seen them featured in television documentaries.[24] Nature programs are popular almost everywhere, yet most of them are produced and broadcast in foreign countries. Domestically produced programs featuring a country's parks and wildlife can raise awareness and interest almost overnight.

Other kinds of entertainment can be designed to raise awareness of parks while proffering information about natural history. For example, each year, officials of Khao Yai Park in Thailand promote a huge Woodstock-style rock concert for teenagers just outside the park. Although the tie to direct conservation may be minimal, this activity has brought the park thousands of supporters and organizers.

Developing media contacts and granting media access to parks are two strategies that managers can adopt to stimulate domestic tourism. Too often, members of the media face difficult and expensive permitting procedures in order to film wildlife and produce stories about parks. Similarly, more effort needs to be made in exploring and understanding the vast biodiversity in tropical forest parks in order to better attract the interest of ecotourists and educational groups, especially nationals. Local biologists and foreign researchers can provide significant help in this effort.

Providing Access

The idea of parks as popular attractions for residents needs to be better promoted and facilitated. Some parks should be located close to major centers where urbanites can enjoy them on holidays and weekends (see also chapters 16 and 28).

The simple cost of renting a vehicle, which is required for touring most of Africa's savanna parks, is prohibitive to most nationals. One solution to this dilemma is being practiced in several U.S. parks. Although visitors were once encouraged to sightsee by car, they are now encouraged to park outside and ride shuttles to interior locations. This practice reduces traffic and pollution, allows better control over inappropriate visitor behavior, and refocuses the visitation experience from extensive (car-based) to intensive (foot travel). In recent years, a handful of African parks, including ones in Botswana, South Africa, and Tanzania, have begun offering walking safaris for tourists. Many tourists now specifically seek out parks that provide this unique opportunity. Providing low-cost shuttle service to sites where walking safaris are conducted by park personnel would both diversify the options open to tourists and encourage more domestic tourism, potentially improving the park experience for domestic and international visitors alike.

Local NGOs are often well suited to promote ecotourism in protected areas. They frequently have members who are biologists or other experts capable of leading tours such as forest walks. Park managers should reach out to NGOs and provide cooperation and seek collaboration in extending opportunities to other groups. Such activities, especially for children, are long-term investments in conservation, as children almost universally respond to nature, are impressionable, and are still forming the values that will shape their adult behaviors.

Interpretation and Public Education

Perhaps the most important social function of parks is to educate the public about natural history and the environmental services provided by natural ecosystems. Interpretive programs are thus one of the most important yet inexpensive investments that can be made in the promotion of ecotourism. Investments in public education can double for tourists, and for local residents and children, with appropriate use of multilingual exhibits.

Visitors typically enter a park already knowing something about what it offers. Yet once inside the gate, they need to know where and how to find its natural attractions as well as the availability and locations of visitor services. Unfortunately, in many tropical parks, visitor information is dispensed predominately by tour company guides. Low-budget tourists who cannot afford a tour are thrust into an information vacuum. A priority in the development of domestic tourism should therefore be the creation of well-designed and informative materials in the language of the country, and which can be dispensed at a nominal price.

A majority of tropical parks still lie beyond the reach of organized tourism. Many of these parks have the potential to attract tourists and to provide a satisfying experience if their attractions were more widely publicized and if at least minimal accommodations were available. Lack of information and knowledgeable guides are serious impediments to the expansion of ecotourism in tropical forest areas, where animals cannot be observed on demand.[25] Unguided tourists in the forest often fail to see wildlife and are characteristically oblivious to the fascinating world of small-scale natural history that surrounds them.

A training program that creatively tackled this problem involved the native KéköLdi people of the Talamanca region of Costa Rica. A local NGO (The KéköLdi Development Association) established an education and nature guide training program that accredited young KéköLdi to act as tour guides in their forest homes. A number of traditionally styled rest huts were built along established trails, and tourists entering were required to hire one of the locally accredited guides who had been tutored in languages and guiding skills that incorporated KéköLdi knowledge of animals and medicinal plants. Even when few animals are seen, the guides provide an informative and satisfying tour. Conservation is directly benefiting from the process. In cooperation with governmental development groups, the KéköLdi are using tourism revenues to secure land titles and to increase the size of the existing KéköLdi Reserve.[26]

In general, more emphasis should be placed on plants than is normally done in ecotourism, where spectacular animals are usually the main if not sole attractions. Plants are easily examined and are the foundation of the diversity of the tropical forest, but unfortunately there are relatively few people in most tropical regions who can identify plants and excite interest in them. Involving native guides is one way of injecting greater interest into plant-based excursions. An important but originally unforeseen benefit of the KéköLdi guiding program has been a boost to the KéköLdi people's pride that comes from realizing that their traditions and knowledge are valued by the outside world.[27]

Conclusions

Ecotourism is a rapidly growing global industry with great potential for generating revenues for developing countries and for raising public awareness of the value of conservation. Despite high promise, expansion of ecotourism in many tropical countries has lagged far behind its potential for lack of elementary requirements, such as information, transportation, accommodations, and guides. The simple suggestions we offer here can be implemented, usually at low cost, to improve park management of tourists and encourage domestic ecotourism.

In the end, ecotourism tools are simply a subset of park management tools, and their implementation should improve parks by (1) ensuring that park goals are clearly defined and central to planning and management; (2) identifying limitations and needs of the park; (3) clarifying the roles that employees should play, and possibly making those roles more interesting and participatory; and (4) making the contribution of the park to society clearer, more widely understood, and better appreciated. Ecotourism cannot solve many of the more serious problems frequently faced by parks in developing countries. Nevertheless, implementing sound ecotourism within parks can aid in making parks work better both internally and in the larger interest of the host country.

The main concern of protected-area management, apart from protection, should be in promoting educational activities and recreation among the nation's own people, including poor villagers, schoolchildren, and the wealthy classes. Such ecotourism should be seen as a long-term investment in conservation and education. It may be the principal local and national benefit of protected-area conservation and the primary role that ecotourism plays for biodiversity protection in parks.

Acknowledgments

We thank Jame DeKay and the Gilman Foundation, all conference participants, and the staff of White Oak Plantation for making the lively discussions at the "Making Parks Work" conference possible. The study of Tarangire user fees and revenue-sharing mechanisms was supported by a grant from the Africa Technical Department of the World Bank.

Notes

1. K. Brandon, *Ecotourism and Conservation: A Review of Key Issues*, World Bank Environment Department Paper No. 033, 1996; E. Boo, *Ecotourism: The Potential and Pitfalls* (Washington, D.C.: World Wildlife Fund, 1990); K. Lindberg, *Policies for Maximizing Nature Tourism's Ecological and Economic Benefits* (Washington, D.C.: World Resources Institute, 1991); H. Ceballos-Lascuráin, *Tourism, Ecotourism, and Protected Areas: The State of Nature-based Tourism around the World and Guidelines for Its Development* (Gland, Switzerland: IUCN [The World Conservation Union], 1996); K. Ziffer, *Ecotourism: The Uneasy Alliance* (Washington, D.C.: Conservation International, 1989).

2. D. Wilkie and J. Carpenter, "The Potential Role of Safari Hunting as a Source of Revenue for Protected Areas in the Congo Basin," *Oryx* 33, no. 4 (1999): 339–345.

3. WTO (World Tourism Organization), *Tourism Economic Report* (Madrid: WTO,

1998); D. B. Weaver, *Ecotourism in the Less Developed World* (New York: CAB International, 1998).

4. WTO, *Tourism Economic Report*.

5. WTO, *Tourism Economic Report*.

6. Boo, *Ecotourism*; R. Butler and T. Hinch, eds., *Tourism and Indigenous Peoples* (London: International Thomson Business Press, 1996); Brandon, *Ecotourism*; Ceballos-Lascuráin, *Tourism*; Ziffer, *Ecotourism*.

7. M. Soulé and J. Terborgh, eds., *Continental Conservation: Scientific Foundations of Regional Reserve Networks* (Washington, D.C.: Island Press, 1999).

8. C. Peres and J. Terborgh, "Amazonian Nature Reserves: An Analysis of the Defensibility Status of Existing Conservation Units and Design Criteria for the Future," *Conservation Biology* 9, no. 1 (1995): 34–46.

9. J. L. Sax, *Mountains Without Handrails: Reflections on the National Parks* (Ann Arbor: University of Michigan Press, 1980).

10. C. Clark, L. Davenport, and P. Mkanga, *Designing Policies for Setting Park User Fees and Allocating Proceeds Among Stakeholders: The Case of Tarangire National Park, Tanzania*, Report to the World Bank, (Washington, D.C.: World Bank).

11. L. Malin and A. Z. Parker, *Ecological Carrying Capacity Research: Yosemite National Park. Part 3. Subalpine Soils and Wilderness Use*, U.S. Department of Commerce, National Technical Information Service, PB-27-957 (Springfield, Va.: U.S. Department of Commerce, 1976); A. R. Graefe, F. R. Kuss, and J. J. Vaske, *Visitor Impact Management: The Planning Framework* (Washington, D.C.: National Parks and Conservation Association, 1990); A. M. Cifuentes, *Determinación de Capacidad de Carga Turística en Areas Protegidas* (Turrialba, Costa Rica: CATIE, 1992).

12. Graefe et al., *Visitor Impact*; Ceballos-Lascuráin, *Tourism*.

13. C. Clark and L. Davenport, "Integrating Ecological and Sociological Aspects of Tourism Management in the Curú National Wildlife Refuge, Costa Rica" (master's project, Duke University School of the Environment, 1994).

14. Ceballos-Lascuráin, *Tourism*; G. H. Stankey, D. N. Cole, R. C. Lucas, M. E. Peterson, and S. S. Frissell, *The Limits of Acceptable Change (LAC) System for Wilderness Planning*, USDA Forest Service, Intermountain Forest and Range Experiment Station, General Technical Report INT-176 (Ogden, Utah: USDA Forest Service, 1985).

15. Stankey et al., *Limits of Acceptable Change*.

16. A. R. Graefe, F. R. Kuss, and J. J. Vaske, *Visitor Impact Management: The Planning Framework* (Washington, D.C.: National Parks and Conservation Association, 1990).

17. Commonwealth Department of Tourism, *A Talent for Tourism: Stories about Indigenous People in Tourism* (Canberra: Commonwealth of Australia, 1994).

18. Ceballas-Lascáurin, *Tourism*.

19. Ibid, 114.

20. Brandon, *Ecotourism*.

21. Lindberg, *Policies*; R. G. Cummings, D. S. Brookshire, and W. D. Schulze, eds., *Valuing Environmental Goods and Assessment of the CV Method* (Totowa, New Jersey: Rowman and Allanheld, 1986); S. Navrud and E. D. Mungatana, "Environmental Valuation in Developing Countries: The Recreational Value of Wildlife Viewing," *Ecological Economics* 11 (1994): 135–151.

22. Clark et al., *Designing Policies*.

23. Lindberg, *Policies*.

24. I. Sanchez-Moreno Bayarri, *El Turismo y el Periodismo en el Perú de Hoy* (Lima: S. M. Aserprensa, 1991).

25. W. Brockelman and P. Dearden, "The Role of Nature Trekking in Conservation: A Case-study in Thailand," *Environmental Conservation* 17, no. 2 (1990): 141–148.

26. P. Palmer, J. Sanchez, and G. Mayorga, *Taking Care of Sibö's Gifts* (San Jose, Costa Rica: Editorama, 1991).

27. Palmer, personal communication.

22

The Problem of People in Parks

JOHN TERBORGH AND CARLOS A. PERES

One of the most intractable problems faced by park managers is the presence of human residents within protected areas. The problem is exacerbated when the residents are indigenous people whose rights to occupy the area are legally or tacitly recognized by the government. People of all stripes, whether indigenous or not, pose a grave threat to the biological integrity of any park when they must derive their livelihoods from the park's natural resources. Much research confirms that humans and wild nature are incompatible except where humans practice a low-impact premodern lifestyle at densities of no more than a few individuals per square kilometer. People damage the ecological system by clearing land, hunting, fishing, persecuting predators, and commercializing natural resources.

Here we address the people-in-parks issue, but with special emphasis on "indigenous" people. Who is an "indigenous" person? In the New World, the answer is simple: it is an Amerindian or an Inuit. In the Old World, the question is often obscured by a blurred distinction between native and immigrant groups. In general, the groups least integrated into national economies are considered "indigenous" whereas agricultural groups with a more hierarchical and formalized social structure are not. Even more broadly, the term "indigenous" has been defined to include any second-class citizens who have strong ties to the land but who are now dominated by other peoples.

The presence of indigenous people in and around strictly protected nature preserves presents major challenges to conservation because of the special circumstances that pertain to such people. (By "strictly protected nature preserves" we refer to formal protected areas falling within The World Conservation Union (IUCN) Categories I, II, and III, which expressly exclude exploitation of natural resources, including even presumptively benign activities carried out under the rubric of "sustainable development.") With respect to indigenous people, there is first a moral issue. With the gradual progress achieved over the last century toward the recognition of human rights all over the world, the prerogatives of indigenous people have risen to the top of the political agenda. This is as it should be. As a consequence, long-frustrated or ignored indigenous land claims are finally being honored by governments, especially in the Americas, but also in parts of Africa, Asia, and Australia. Second, indigenous claims to the land often (but not always) have deep historical roots. Third, unassimilated indigenous people often pursue low-impact traditional lifestyles and live largely or completely outside the money economy, making them highly vulnerable to disruption. Fourth, if such people are not to be consigned to "living museums," ways must be sought to ease the inevitable transition to modernity and assimilation.

Because of these special circumstances, and the fact that indigenous people are nearly ubiquitous within the earth's remaining wildlands, it has been the common practice of managers to ignore them on the grounds that "they are part of the ecology," or that "for centuries they have been living in harmony with nature." When examined in the light of facts, such claims are often revealed to be little more than convenient excuses behind which managers hide in the hope of avoiding politically awkward issues.[1] Even when the facts do support a claim that a certain group of people has not materially damaged the environment, the validity of the claim applies only in retrospect. The accelerating pace of change we are witnessing in today's world ensures that the future will not be a continuation of the past.

Much of the land that is currently included within tropical protected areas, or that will be included within future protected areas, is occupied by indigenous people or can be claimed as hunting grounds or ancestral territory. This unavoidable fact confronts conservationists with a dilemma that currently threatens to polarize the conservation community.[2]

On one side of this debate are those who assert that all indigenous claims to the land ought to have priority over any proposed nature preserves and that indigenous peoples living within already-declared preserves should receive title to the lands they occupy, regardless of the circumstances. On the other side lies the heavy-handed practice of expelling aboriginal people from newly created reserves, exemplified by the notorious case of the Ik in Uganda. As is often the case, when debates escalate to a strident crescendo, the truth, or in this case, common sense, is drowned out in the dissonance. It will thus be our goal in this chapter to avoid polemics and to seek common-sense solutions to what are admittedly complex and emotionally charged issues.

Ground Rules

To set the tone and context of the discussion, we shall begin with some observations that we trust will be relatively uncontroversial.

First, the presence of permanent extractive communities, indigenous or not, within core nature preserves is antithetical to the area's long-term conservation goal, and in most countries is in conflict with the legal definition of "national park" and other categories of strict protected areas. Authorized visitors, tourists, official personnel, and scientists are exempted and, in any case, are not permanent residents.

Second, we recognize that indigenous people, no matter what their current state of assimilation or economic development, have the same intrinsic "right" to improve their standards of living and to participate in the modern world as anyone else, provided they choose to do so.

Third, the frequent management practice of ignoring indigenous inhabitants of parks ("because they are part of the natural system") inevitably relegates them to the disadvantaged side of a double standard, and in the process leaves their "hands tied," if the purposes of the reserve are even nominally respected. For example, for more than twenty-five years it has been the policy of Manu National Park in Perú that indigenous people living within the park may not possess firearms or motorized conveyances and are prohibited from commercializing natural resources. These restrictions deny them "rights" enjoyed by their tribal brethren who happen to live just outside the park's boundary.[3] Such policies cannot be considered "fair," nor do they offer a long-term solution to the dilemma posed by the presence of developing communities inside the park. Arbitrary restrictions on economic activity and the use of technology represent the "living museum" approach, which, in our view, is a nonsolution, at least for the long run (but with qualifications spelled out below).

Fourth, if such restrictions are not applied and maintained, consider the alternative. Within a generation, even pre-modern people can acquire the dominant language of the country they inhabit and can begin to participate in the money economy. As once-isolated communities increase their contacts with the outside world, they will begin to demand and receive education, health care, and other services, as they should if they are so inclined. Even when the national government fails to provide these services, it is likely that missionaries or nongovernmental organizations (NGOs) will step into the breach and provide them instead. Thus, it is inevitable that even the most traditional societies will eventually be awakened to the modern world and, when that happens, there is no natural stopping point other than full assimilation into the dominant culture.[4] The end point of acculturation is a lifestyle like ours—replete with towns, communications and transportation infrastructure, and a market economy—a lifestyle that is incompatible with the concept of a park or nature preserve. Indigenous people living inside a protected area thus cannot join the social and economic mainstream without transgressing legal definitions and severely compromising the area's intended purpose of conserving nature.

The people-in-parks dilemma is a time bomb that affects an estimated 70 percent of all parks in the developing world. Deteriorating situations are typically allowed to fester because managers frequently lack either the authority or the means to act. Politicians shy away from the problem. When pressure builds, the action taken may be decided by the outcome of a nasty political struggle rather than by a rational optimization process. This is an unsatisfactory situation in which most solutions result in harm to parks and/or to the people unfortunate enough to be caught in them.

Minimizing Human Impacts

If these are the realities, what then do we propose to do about it? As a matter of principle, people-free parks should always be the ultimate goal. It is the only goal that over the long run is consistent with the requirements of biodiversity conservation. Thus, all relevant policies should be directed to reducing the human presence within parks.

Even when the presence of residents within a park does not currently appear threatening, it will eventually become so as their numbers increase and as their lifestyle changes. Policies should therefore be proactive if progressive degradation of protected areas is to be avoided. Any and all proactive policies to minimize human impacts on protected areas must counter the ineluctable tendency of human populations to increase over time.

The impact of a human population on the environment is represented in the following formula:[5]

Impact = (number of humans) x (per-capita consumption of resources) x (a "technology factor")

From the formula, it is evident that human impact can be reduced in only three ways: (1) by reducing the number of humans, (2) by lowering the per-capita consumption of resources, or (3) by restricting access to technology (e.g., requiring stone axes instead of chainsaws). We have already ruled out, as a long-term solution, the restriction of technology, because doing so locks people into a living museum. Lowering the per-capita consumption of people who are already likely living at a subsistence level is morally repugnant and therefore also not an option. That leaves only the first of the three variables—the number of humans living off the land.

A program designed to reduce the number of humans occupying a park, especially if they are considered "indigenous," would be decried by many as an attempt to perpetrate ethnocide. But if we can put our ethnocentric bias aside for a moment and seriously address the question of how to reduce the environmental impact of a human population that legally occupies a protected area, it is obvious from the above analysis that none of the options are attractive. For reasons already explained, it would be unethical to deprive people of access to technology or limit their per-capita resource consumption. The only alternative remaining is to limit their numbers. Limiting population growth is painless, leads to increased per-capita availability of resources, and is morally acceptable in most societies (everyone who uses birth control has made this judgment).

Some readers may be surprised to learn that programs to reduce population growth among indigenous groups inhabiting national parks already exist. An example familiar to us involves the government of Perú, which is making a concerted effort to deliver family planning services to all its citizens through the national public health program. Included among the citizens of Perú are Machiguenga villagers who are legal residents within the Manu National Park, the flagship of the nation's protected-area system. Public health workers were sent to Machiguenga villages in the park to announce the availability of Depo Provera, an injectable contraceptive taken by women.

It is unthinkable in Machiguenga culture for a woman to discuss the topic of reproduction with a male stranger, much less one that belongs to another culture. The public health workers therefore assembled the men of each village and explained the program to them. The men were then instructed to explain what they had been told to their wives. No pressure was applied. Each couple was to decide for itself whether it wished to join the program.

A good number of the couples decided that they had already had enough children, and the wives are now receiving periodic injections of Depo Provera. More couples will surely follow when the effectiveness of the treatment has been demonstrated. In our view, programs such as this are the only hope if indigenous people are going to continue indefinitely to occupy parks and reserves that were established to protect nature. The alternative is unregulated population growth leading to poverty and the gradual degradation of the park's resources.

Relocation

The most direct and effective way to reduce human impacts within parks is through active relocation programs. A number of governments have quietly and successfully carried out such programs (see chapters 14 and 28). Ideally, land of equal or better quality than available in the park should be purchased and distributed to agriculturists. Alternatively, compensation could take the form of employment, housing, and improved access to schools, medical services, and transportation.

Relocation programs require both political will and adequate resources, conditions that are all too often lacking. It is expressly because of the high cost of relocation programs and the politically sensitive issues involved that governments have so consistently ignored the presence of internal residents when decreeing new parks. Indeed, the tendency of governments to ignore all implementation costs is what lies behind the vast number of "paper parks" already in existence (see chapter 23).

Voluntary Resettlement

As premodern societies become aware that they are surrounded by a more-powerful, technologically advanced culture, they typically experience strong intergenerational tensions. The older generation tends to be comfortable with the traditional lifestyle and uncomfortable with adopting new ways. To the younger generation, however, the "lure of civilization" can be irresistible. The influence of elders wanes as their skills and knowledge are seen to be irrelevant to the challenges of acquiring an education, earning money, and buying a tractor or a television set. The young consequently begin to view "the old ways" as hopelessly anachronistic. At this point, the young may begin to emigrate voluntarily, provided the outside world offers attractive opportunities.

Park managers can take advantage of these social pressures by adopting policies that enhance a "push–pull" process. Regulations, such as those mentioned above, which have turned Perú's Manu National Park into a living museum, coupled with rejection by the young of the traditional lifestyle, can provide the "push." Simultaneously, opportunities offered by the outside world (employment, education, marriage, access to markets) will exert a "pull" on the younger generation. By working with NGOs or international assistance programs, managers can potentially take advantage of both sides of this equation.

"Pull" can be created in many ways: schools can be built outside park boundaries; legally titled land can be made available; health services can be provided; training programs can be offered. Without a formal education or even full proficiency in the national language, young people from tribal backgrounds can be trained as park guards, guides, mechanics, drivers, cooks, and the like. Forest dwellers, such as the Caboclos of Brazilian Amazonia, are often avid for such opportunities and may willingly migrate to unprotected areas, provided the incentives are attractive.

The compelling advantages of the push–pull mechanism for alleviating demographic pressure within parks is that it is passive, cost effective, strictly voluntary, and therefore less prone to controversy than active relocation. What is most critical is that any relocation program, whether active or voluntary, be executed in a way that is perceived as fair and unobjectionable to all concerned.

Fallback Strategies

Increasingly, parks in the world's more populous countries are becoming islands of natural habitat embedded in a matrix of intensively managed land. Under such circumstances, relocation of a park's internal residents may be prohibitively expensive and therefore impractical. To address these situations, we now consider several "fallback" strategies that can help to mitigate human impacts while not alleviating them altogether. These fallback strategies do not solve the people-in-parks problem but may serve to buy time until more propitious circumstances may arise. Fall-back strategies rest on expedience but entail a high risk, because inevitably there will always be a point of no return at which the sheer number of residents in a park forecloses any practical means of reducing human impact. Avila National Park in Venezuela, to cite an extreme example, is estimated to have more than 500,000 people living within its boundaries. In extreme cases such as this, degazetting the park or redrawing the boundaries offer the only practical means of bringing the reality on the ground into conformity with the legal definitions of what a park is (see chapter 28).

The Living Museum

We view the living-museum policy as at best an expedient step on the way to a people-free park; it can buy time but is emphatically not a permanent solution. In effect, the living museum is a pure "push" policy. Even in the absence of a formal relocation program, aversion to restrictions may persuade park residents to live elsewhere if opportunities beckon.

Ecotourism

Given that it will not be practical to remove all people from all parks, the goal of any fallback strategy should be to wean park residents from an economy based on the extraction of natural resources. So-called "sustainable development" is being promoted in and around many tropical protected areas, and where the "people problem" is otherwise insoluble, a nature-friendly development model is certainly preferable to more destructive alternatives. However, one is skating on thin ice here, because the fostering of low-impact lifestyles comes perilously close to advocating the living museum.

The only development model of which we are aware that does not entail significant impacts on natural resources is ecotourism. If managers could devise ways of incorporating a park's indigenous inhabitants into an ecotourism economy, it could well result in a win–win situation. We know of one outstanding example, which we shall now briefly describe.

Venezuela's Canaima National Park, comprising 3 million hectares, is one of the world's largest. All of Canaima rests on the Guiana Shield, a geological formation that produces some of the least fertile soils in the world. Consequently, the human density of Canaima was extremely low, even before it became a park. The motive for creating the park was to build a tourism industry around several spectacular waterfalls, including Angel Falls, the world's highest.

The remoteness of the main tourist destinations in Canaima made it difficult to attract employees, a condition that was especially pronounced in the heyday of Venezuela's oil boom in the 1960s and 1970s, when tourism at Canaima first got under way. Even today, the only access to the main visitor center is by air. Concessionaires soon discovered that local Pemon tribespeople were good, reliable workers and that they were quite willing to accept jobs as boat drivers, cooks, guides, and mechanics.

Now, a generation later, the Pemon live in an attractive modern village situated a few hundred meters from the principal tourist hotel. The Pemon we have spoken with took evident pride in their skills and in providing a high-quality experience to the tourist. They openly acknowledged that their business was tourism. Many have even made the effort to learn English, German, Italian, or other foreign languages to enhance their professional skills.

The Pemon of the town of Canaima now live completely in the money economy (although there are others living elsewhere in the vast park who still pursue more traditional lifestyles). The men of Canaima work in the tourism industry, as we have described, while many of the women dedicate themselves to producing handicrafts, which are sold to tourists. Most of them neither hunt nor engage in agriculture. Effectively, they act as concessionaires.

We recognize the difficulty of replicating the Canaima model, but it nevertheless illustrates how indigenous people living inside a formal park have willingly changed their lifestyles and economy to adapt to new circumstances and opportunities. Now, they no longer depend on local natural resources, and their impact on the park is therefore as close to zero as it could be.

But the case of Canaima is admittedly special—that of a flourishing tourist industry which sprung up in a tight labor market after the completion of an all-weather airport in a remote natural area. Despite the improbable combination of circumstances, the Canaima case holds a lesson. It demonstrates that the traditional skills possessed by many indigenous people can readily be applied to service in the tourism industry. Cases like that of Canaima are rare because indigenous inhabitants are commonly looked down upon by members of the dominant culture and are the last to be hired. But managers do not have to heed local prejudice and, where practical, can act to catalyze indigenous engagement in tourism.

Do Nothing

In densely populated regions, the option of relocating a park's indigenous inhabitants may be impractical. Elsewhere, the option may be closed by financial limitations or prevailing political sentiments. In either case, managers are faced with an overwhelming temptation to do nothing: to ignore internal populations and focus attention on reducing external threats. If the external threats are perceived as more severe than the internal ones, and resources are limited, then a policy of doing nothing about the indigenous residents of a park may be the most rational. But to claim that a policy of doing nothing is a policy without consequences would be wrong. The long-term consequences of people in parks are bound to be negative, but in the short term, there may even be benefits.

Indigenous people can serve as highly vigilant and effective protectors of parks, and when possessed of the means, they will defend the territory that provides their livelihoods.[6] The Kayapó Reserve in Brazil provides a stunning example. Within the last decade, the rapidly advancing agricultural frontier of southeastern Amazonia has reached the reserve and continued around it, nearly engulfing it in amoeboid fashion. Outside the reserve, primary forest has been replaced with a checkerboard of heavily logged areas, cattle pastures, and agricultural plots. However, forest disturbance currently stops dead at the boundaries of the reserve, which secures over 10 million hectares of intact primary forest, the most important stronghold of undisturbed forests in this corner of Amazonia.[7] The boundaries between the Kayapó reserve and the open frontier are often ramrod straight, testifying to the Kayapó's determination to maintain their territorial integrity. To defend their boundaries, the Kayapó have taken up arms to expel trespassing loggers and gold miners and have taken possession of nonconforming cattle ranches. Overflights have aided them in detecting unauthorized activities within the boundary.

Of course an indigenous people's reserve is not a park. The Kayapó are acting in their own best economic interest by protecting the reserve from encroachment. The big question is what the Kayapó Reserve will look like in fifty or one hundred years. The Kayapó are masters of their own domain, and they, not a park administrator, will make the decisions that answer this question. For the time being, forest habitat is being protected inside the reserve but not outside, but that may not be more than a temporary condition.[8] On a more global scale, the role of indigenous people as stewards of natural resources has not been one to inspire confidence, and many Indian reserves in more developed parts of Brazil (as well as those of the United States) have long been severely degraded.

Nevertheless, indigenous reserves are potentially important for biodiversity conservation in the Amazon because they account for over one-fifth of the region.[9] They should not be seen as substitutes for parks but instead as complements to parks in a regional system of conservation areas (see chapter 10).

The largely benign presence of indigenous people in Amazonia stands in sharp contrast to post-frontier parts of South America where groups of largely acculturated "Indians" have repeatedly invaded public parks under the pretext that traditional territories are being reclaimed.[10] Such cases underscore the need for firm government policy toward the issue of human occupation of protected areas, whether by indigenous people or others.

Zoning

Many park agencies engage in the practice of "zoning." For example, the Manu Biosphere Reserve in Perú is composed of a number of formally recognized zones for tourism, scientific research, indigenous communities, and nonindigenous colonists. Such zoning schemes are characteristic of UNESCO biosphere reserves and formalize the distinctions between the highly protected core area and peripheral buffer areas within which a variety of resource-based activities may be permitted.

Biosphere reserves benefit from a benign form of zoning. However, zoning can also be employed by managers in a thoroughly pernicious way to paper over embarrassing cases of nonconforming land use. An example is described in chapter 28 in which "special use zones" are employed by the managers of a Venezuelan park to exempt villages and other occupied land from many park regulations.

The use of zoning to create enclaves of development within a park is bad policy because it (1) effectively reduces the size of the park, (2) exposes the park's interior to detrimental human activities, and (3) sets a dangerous precedent. But bad policy or not, in worst-case scenarios it may be preferable to define zones of nonconforming use as part of a strategy to contain them rather than simply to ignore them.

Conclusions

The typical response of park managers to the presence of legal or illegal internal residents is to turn a blind eye. But neglect is the worst-possible policy because the problem will inevitably worsen with time as the human population increases in size and acquires the technology (e.g., guns and chainsaws) to amplify its per capita impact on the environment. Human impact thus does not simply grow in proportion to population but rather it grows much faster in an accelerating rush that, once unleashed, is almost impossible to control. Moreover, vacant land in which to relocate people outside protected areas is a rapidly dwindling commodity in many regions. In dealing with the people-in-parks problem, it is therefore imperative to act sooner rather than later.

The people-in-parks problem admits no satisfactory long-term solution other than reducing demographic pressure. The only completely painless way to do this is by introducing family planning. Other more assertive policies include imposing restrictions to discourage continued residence and offering incentives to relocate. Worst-case scenarios may call for drastic measures such as negotiated agreements or the creation of human enclaves, hopefully as interim solutions.

Eventually, the world's current demographic "crunch" will ease. What will remain of wild nature when that time comes? If wild nature is to survive, it must be recognized that the matter of people in parks is a make-it-or-break-it issue that will determine the fate of much biodiversity in the world of the future.

Notes

1. J. Terborgh, *Requiem for Nature* (Washington, D.C.: Island Press, 1999).

2. S. Schwartzman, A. Moreira, and D. Nepstad, "Rethinking Tropical Forest Conservation: Perils in Parks," *Conservation Biology* 14 (2000): 1351–1357; J. Terborgh, "The Fate of Tropical Forests: A Matter of Stewardship," *Conservation Biology* 14 (2000): 1358–1361; K. H. Redford and S. E. Sanderson, "Extracting Humans from Nature," *Conservation Biology* 14 (2000): 1362–1364; C. A. Peres and B. Zimmerman, "Perils in Parks or Parks in Peril? Reconciling Conservation with and without Use in Amazonian Reserves," *Conservation Biology* 15 (2001): 793–797.

3. Terborgh, *Requiem*.

4. J. Terborgh, "A Dying World," *New York Review of Books* 47 (2000): 38–40.

5. P. R. Ehrlich and J. Holdren, "The Impact of Population Growth," *Science* 171 (1971): 1212–1217.

6. M. Colchester, "Self-determination or Environmental Determinism for Indigenous Peoples in Tropical Forest Conservation," *Conservation Biology* 14 (2000): 1365–1367; Peres and Zimmerman, "Perils in Parks."

7. Schwartzman et al., "Rethinking Tropical Forest Conservation"; B. Zimmerman, C. A. Peres, J. Malcolm, and T. Turner, "Conservation Alliances with Tropical Forest Indigenous Peoples: The Case of the Kayapó of Southeastern Amazonia," *Environmental Conservation* 28 (2001): 10–22.

8. K. H. Redford and A. M. Stearman, "Forest-dwelling Native Amazonians and the Conservation of Biodiversity: Interests in Common or in Collision?" *Conservation Biology* 7 (1993): 248–255.

9. C. A. Peres, "Indigenous Reserves and Nature Conservation in Amazonian Forests," *Conservation Biology* 8 (1994): 586–588. F. Ricardo, *Terras Indígenas na Amazônia legal,* report to PRONABIO, (Programa Nacional de Diversidade Biológica) (Brasilia, D.F.: PRONABIO, 1999); Zimmerman et al., "Conservation Alliances."

10. M. Galetti, "Indians within Conservation Units: Lessons from the Atlantic Forest," *Conservation Biology* 15 (2001): 798–799.

23

Political Will for Establishing and Managing Parks

MARC J. DOUROJEANNI

The process of creating parks is severely hampered by the fact that proposed parks frequently have more opponents than advocates. It is only later, when a park has been in existence long enough to build up a popular mystique and clientele, that its supporters begin to outnumber its detractors. Each act of creating a park is therefore a manifestation of political will. This chapter inquires into the sources of political will for establishing parks and on possible ways of enhancing that will. The geographical context will be that of Latin America and the Caribbean (LAC), especially Brazil, but most of the relevant principles should apply to other regions as well.

This chapter begins by explaining why politicians are so much more given to creating parks than to providing funds for their management. A widespread disinclination of legislators to invest in management is, in brief, why there are so many "paper" parks. Evolving fashions in conservation are another concern. Lately, the trend has been to emphasize the establishment of "soft" protected areas (condoning multiple use in various forms) and away from strict nature preserves. This confounding of goals is largely attributable to the rise of social environmentalism in the 1980s and to the accompanying zeal for "sustainable development." There is an urgent and compelling need for advocates of social environmentalism to reach an accommodation with the requirements for biodiversity conservation. The chapter concludes with suggestions on how the actual and perceived costs of protected areas can be reduced and how to soften the costs of management to make them more palatable politically.

Establishment versus Implementation of Protected Areas

It is essential to understand that there is more political will for establishing parks than for managing them. Creating a park is a highly visible act that draws attention to the political founders. Voting funds for management, however, attracts no attention and wins few votes. As a result, the problem of parks in developing countries is much more one of management than one of establishment. This basic fact is often overlooked.

Political will, for the purpose of this discussion, may be defined as a public decision "to pay the cost" of establishing and managing parks. The mere passing of legislation establishing parks is only a weak indicator of "political will." Political will is demonstrated in the legislation and/or in the public budget by the adoption of measures to finance the required actions over time. Most LAC environmental legislation, especially as related to protected areas, totally disregards financial implications, revealing a "limited political will" that does not extend to the core issue of paying the price of establishment and management.

Political will regarding protected areas is a direct consequence of the level of public education, especially the depth and quality of environmental education, and the level of activism in the voting population. A generally low level of environmental education is certainly at the root of the feeble political will displayed by most LAC countries in regard to protected areas.

Generating Political Will for the Establishment of Parks

The political will to establish parks is affected by several issues, including both economic and political costs. New park proposals may languish if they spark a legislative debate on the tradeoff between "new parks" versus "well-managed parks." New "social environmental" concepts; local, national, and international political pressures; national and international legal obligations (e.g., treaties); and issues of social and economic viability can all be considerations. The following discussion reviews available options for co-opting these issues in favor of the establishment of new parks.

Reducing Reluctance to Assume Economic Costs

Some LAC governments are still so unaware of what parks are about that the question of costs related to implantation (establishment studies, land purchase or land expropriation, and demarcation) and implementation (basic management infrastructure, visitor facilities, equipment, staff, training, and research) is not even discussed or mentioned. In some countries, the governments are aware of the cost issue but unwilling to consider it. Typically, it is assumed that the regular annual budget of the institution in charge of parks is sufficient. Within such institutions, however, the authorities are keenly aware of the costly implications of new parks but often fail to persuade higher levels of the need for expanded budgets. Frequently, they prefer to remain silent so as not to jeopardize the establishment process.

Land acquisition is always a major consideration in park establishment. In some LAC countries, it is still possible to create parks in areas where the land is fully state owned, thereby avoiding the huge cost of purchasing the land. However, it is increasingly difficult to find large tracts of uncommitted public land. Consequently, the political resistance to establishing strictly protected areas tends to increase in proportion to the commercial value of the land. For example, a 1991 analysis revealed that US$524 million would be necessary to implement the already established parks in the Brazilian Amazon (82 percent of the total was required to purchase private inholdings). In contrast, the yearly maintenance costs were estimated to be only US$27 million.[1] In other, longer-settled regions of Brazil, the situation of parks with regard to land acquisition is even more dire.

Special funds earmarked for acquisition of parkland have been established in a number of countries, but politicians find the temptation to divert the revenues to other purposes almost irresistible. In one such case, the Brazilian agency for federal parks (IBDF, now IBAMA) had authority to buy parkland out of a fund originating in stumpage fees. The revenue was relatively modest but sufficed to regularize land tenure in a number of parks. The fund is still nominally available but has been gradually allocated to the states that are not using it to purchase land in federal parks.

Several LAC countries have already instituted financial mechanisms that contribute to park establishment and management, such as special trust funds, debt-for-nature swaps, entrance and concession fees, tax deductions for private citizens that establish protected areas, and so forth (see also chapter 26).[2] Their existence helps blunt economic arguments against the establishment of new parks. However, the creation of these mechanisms depends on the same political will that is often lacking in the case of individual parks.

In any event, it is important that new park proposals be accompanied by an analysis of land tenure and of costs related to land tenure regularization, although in the past this has rarely been done. Superficially constructed cost estimates are often overblown. More credible estimates of cost can help in obtaining positive political decisions.

Reducing Political Costs

Political risks, as well as economic costs, are implicit in creating new parks. Political risks are obviously related to opposing private interests, whether legitimate or not. Well-organized local or regional opposition will nearly always block the establishment of a park. Fortunately, popular opposition is seldom a major factor. More often, opposition comes from isolated but influential landowners who can deny support in future elections or move other political factions against the proposal.[3] Hostile landowners can sometimes be placated by the promise of substantial economic compensations[4] obtained by selling their land or through procedures in the judiciary. Local opposition may arise in nearby communities that hold rights to some of the area or that view the park as foreclosing future development opportunities. Whatever the source of opposition, it is certain to be amplified by doubts that the state will provide just and timely compensation for the land.

Of course, the most effective way to overcome political resistance to new parks is to organize proponents, putting their electoral power on display through a highly visible campaign. This is a major role to be played by local, national, or international NGOs (nongovernmental organizations). Publicity campaigns can benefit from press involvement, provided it is early and well informed. Recruiting influential "godfathers" as advocates and making strategic alliances with green political parties can also enhance the cause.

"New Parks" versus "Well-Managed Parks:" An Unending Debate

Some environmentalists strongly oppose new parks, arguing that it is not sound to accumulate obligations while established parks are bereft of adequate management. They also rightly argue that neglected parks encourage violations and set a poor example. Without disagreeing with the merits of either argument, the fact remains that, if not protected as fast as possible, the world's remaining wildlands will soon be gone forever. The correct response, of course, is common sense applied to each specific case. Experience in LAC shows that formal, even if phantom, legal protection is much better than no protection at all. In any event, it is crucial that environmentalists present a united front on the matter of new parks. Every crack on their side of the debate creates an enormous advantage for the opposing forces.

Blunting the Negative Side of the Social-Environmental Movement

The last two decades have seen a major expansion of the environmental movement, as disparate groups have become aware of the relevance of the environment to their interests. Among the new players, a group of social professionals has been exceptionally influential. Regarding parks, its influence has been beneficial in many ways, promoting better harmony between humans and nature, as well as promoting healthy societal participation in nature conservation.

However, social environmentalists have also been the cause of several major problems regarding the establishment and management of parks. Seduced by the generous but vaporous allure of the "sustainable development" concept, and woefully ignorant of biological processes, some social-environmentalists are currently major advocates of the extinction of parks, often described by them as "dinosaur institutions."[5] Many social-environmental organizations also promote the "sustainable utilization" of parks by "traditional populations,"[6] while ignoring the tremendous difficulties and risks such concessions impose on parks. Social-environmentalists are also largely responsible for the explosive growth of "soft" protected areas, where, in theory, development goes along with protection.

Politically, it is far easier to establish "soft" protected areas, where utilization of natural resources is allowed, than it is to establish "strict" protected areas. For policy-makers, soft protected areas are ideal, because they involve no economic or political costs. Consequently, the proportion of strict parks in the LAC region is declining every year. Until the late 1970s, well over 80 percent of LAC protected areas were strictly protected. Today, more than 43 percent of the region's protected areas correspond to IUCN categories 4 and 5, allowing some form of exploitation of natural resources. However, this percentage is much higher if other categories are included.[7] Today in Brazil[8] there are 47 million hectares of soft protected areas[9] and only 22.2 million hectares of strict protected areas,[10] not including in the former category either biosphere reserves or indigenous reserves. Even in the Brazilian Amazon, where public land is not scarce, more than 65 percent of the protected areas are "soft," excluding indigenous land.[11]

"Environmental Protection Areas" (Áreas de Proteção Ambiental or APAs) that allow almost any human activity became very popular in Brazil in the 1980s. There are currently twenty-one APAs in the Brazilian

Amazon, covering 9.6 million hectares (17 percent of the total protected area in the region). UNESCO's biosphere reserves have followed a similar trend. There are now twenty-seven biosphere reserves in Latin America covering 51 million hectares. The Mata Atlantica Biosphere Reserve in Brazil nominally "protects" 29 million hectares. Most of the included land is heavily affected by human activities. Remnant forests receive almost no protection outside of a few, mostly small parks. However, this biosphere reserve is listed in official statistics as a fully protected area.

There is no simple way to rectify the situation of soft protected areas. More dialogue between environmentalists and social-environmentalists is clearly needed, so that both forces can focus on an agreed-upon set of long-term goals. Above all, social environmentalists need to appreciate the pervasive threat of extinction and the conditions that act to prevent it in the natural world. Minimizing extinction will inevitably require keeping a small percentage of the earth relatively free of human intervention.

Often it seems that social professionals believe that social problems may be solved simply by opening parks to "sustainable" exploitation. These opinions are often arbitrary and ignore the offsetting social gains to be realized by keeping these areas natural. A long-term solution would be to improve the ecological training of social professionals. Environmentalists and natural scientists, for their part, are frequently too extreme in their "protectionist" positions, such as in Brazil, where most strict protected areas are not even open to visitors.[12]

Local and Regional Political Pressure

In some cases it is possible, especially as a consequence of a sustained promotional campaign, to achieve a local, regional, or even national quasi-consensus for the establishment of a park. In such cases, passing of the corresponding legislation is enormously facilitated. The secret resides in how to generate the consensus. The optimal approach depends on the character of the target population. Environmental arguments are effective when citizens are educated, but economic arguments resonate better among the poor. In general, a balanced mix of arguments is the best option. The NGO movement is crucial to managing this kind of campaign in which success requires the engagement of the mass media (see chapter 3).

International Pressure

International pressure is a double-edged tool. While some countries are susceptible to international exhortation to establish new parks, others react very negatively. However, if diplomatic contacts are low key and discreet, most LAC countries will give a special look at the issue of establishing a park when this is promoted by developed countries. Quiet pressure works even better when applied in the context of international outcries about environmental destruction within a country that simultaneously is negotiating its international debt or any other financial problem.

Another situation that synergizes international pressure to establish parks is the negotiation of loans from multilateral development banks (MDBs), such as the International Bank for Reconstruction and Development (IBRD) and the Inter-American Development Bank (IDB), or the solicitation of technical assistance from the United Nations or other bilateral institutions. Since the greening of the MDBs in the late 1980s, hundreds of new protected areas have been established and/or implanted with international financing all over LAC. This has been a collateral benefit of projects that specifically address environmental issues, and it reflects the green conditions now required for public works financed by these institutions. These banks support proposals originating in the environmental public sector or civil society that otherwise would not be considered seriously by the governments. Awareness of MDB lending programs can be a great advantage for those promoting new parks, as it already has been in a number of cases.[13] However, MDBs are not allowed to finance the purchase of land for new parks, even if the government is ready to include this cost in the loan. The land must be purchased with local counterpart funding, which imposes a major obstacle. An obvious solution would be to lobby for a change in the rules being applied by the MDBs. Alternatively, international private donors working in collaboration with local NGOs could fill the breach (see chapter 24).

In 1998, the government of Brazil set an example that may serve as a global precedent. President Cardozo offered to reserve 10 percent of the Brazilian Amazon as strictly protected areas. By making this pledge, he created an advantageous moment to promote a United Nations General Assembly resolution setting a similar goal for the rest of the world. The World Conservation Union (IUCN) and other organizations should take the lead in this endeavor.

Taking Advantage of Legal Instruments

Some legal provisions in Brazil's constitution, such as the declaration of "national heritage" for the Pantanal, the Amazon, and the Atlantic Forest, are helpful for proposing special protection measures such as the establishment of new parks. There are similar legal texts in almost every LAC country, some of which have been successfully used in the past. For example, the 1940 Pan-American Convention for the Protection of Wildlife and Natural Landscapes has been helpful in justifying and underpinning local proposals for new parks.

International treaties become law in the countries that sign them and thus carry a moral weight that can assist in overcoming political resistance. Currently, there are several international conventions, treaties, and other legal instruments that advocate for nature conservation in one way or another. The existence of such a plethora of documents containing overlapping or vague concepts diminishes their impact on policy-makers. Even so, they remain useful if well exploited.

The Importance of Well-constructed Proposals

Too often, proposals for new parks are poorly prepared. Supporting studies, if any, are conducted hastily and are frequently under pressure to meet deadlines for a ceremonial event. Consequently, field studies are often lacking, the ecological justification is not clear, and the social and economic implications of the proposal are not well evaluated. Presented with such proposals, policy-makers find little difficulty in framing arguments to oppose the park. Worse, it is all too common that scientists, pseudoscientists, and special-interest groups promote the establishment of a park to further their own specific goals, provoking negative reactions from other environmentalists. When the resulting controversy becomes public, policy-makers react negatively to the proposal, even if it is sound and important. It is thus essential that the feasibility of a proposal be fully tested before it is submitted to a government or legislature. The social implications of establishing a new park must be fully assessed (for instance, how would resident indigenous peoples be affected?); Costs of expropriation or land purchase, as well as the cost of initial protection and implantation need to be disclosed. And the new park's potential for achieving some level of economic sustainability should be analyzed.

Valuing the potential environmental services of a new park is essential to creating political will, but this is rarely emphasized in proposals. Instead, the arguments for new parks rely on traditional themes: the area's natural beauty, the occurrence of species at risk of extinction, or, more recently, the presence of exceptional biodiversity. Policy-makers would prefer to see a balance sheet, with the costs of the park on one side and a realistic estimate of economic benefits on the other. Implications of the proposal for business (hotels, restaurants, transportation, tourist services), and new employment (in tourism, transport, specialized agriculture [growing food for park visitors]) should be emphasized. There should also be a balance sheet for environmental implications, such as the volume of water originating in the park and its replacement cost if not conserved, or potential costs of natural disasters (i.e., floods or avalanches) if the area is not protected, In short, the establishment and management of a park must be represented as an economically sound investment, and not only as an ethical act.

When Political Will Is Lacking

Private efforts to preserve nature are gaining momentum in many countries (see chapters 13 and 24). In one celebrated example, a rich American acquired 289,000 hectares of forests near Puerto Montt, Chile, to create the Pumalin Natural Reserve.[14] In Brazil, a private foundation (SESC, the Brazilian Commercial Social Service) purchased 90,000 hectares in the Pantanal of Mato Grosso to create a private natural reserve. More recently, the Fundação Biotropica purchased an additional 70,000 hectares with funding from The Nature Conservancy, an American NGO, to establish another private natural reserve. Elsewhere, in the State of Parana, the Fundação Boticario bought 2,700 hectares to establish the Salto Morato Private Natural Reserve. Currently, there are some 500,000 hectares of strictly protected areas in Brazil under the regime of private natural reserves. In exchange for exemption from property taxes, the owners must sign a public declaration affirming preservation of the land in perpetuity. Owners are permitted to sell the land, but it remains under covenants that prohibit any form of direct exploitation.

Private conservation initiatives are free of political pressures and are increasingly useful, especially in countries such as Brazil, where the cost of land (i.e., in the Amazon or in the Pantanal) is still on the order of US$25–50 per hectare.[15]

Generating Political Will for Better Management of Parks

In many developing countries, there is scant political will for financing park management. High cost is only one factor; lack of visibility and political return are others. But at a deeper level, the disinclination to provide better support for management reflects a lack of public concern about parks. A frequent contributory factor is that the public institutions responsible for parks lie deeply buried in the bureaucracy, where they lack both prestige and visibility. Park administrations are commonly subsumed within forestry agencies, which, in turn, fall within the agriculture ministry. Forest services are more inclined to spend their limited budgets on reforestation projects and research than on park management. More generally, the low status accorded to park agencies reflects a lack of public concern that is rooted in the fact that most parks are not accessible to the ordinary citizen.

Opening Parks to Visitors

Underlying a lack of political willingness to establish and especially to manage parks in most developing countries is a pervasive view among lay people that parks look like useless land. This impression is reinforced by policies that exclude visitors from parks. Only a handful of Brazil's national parks are open to the public, for example. The most visited is Iguazu National Park, but visitors are allowed only to view the falls; the rest of the park is off limits. Even some parks that have management plans and infrastructure are closed. It is only recently, in 1997, that IBAMA, under pressure from the tourism sector, declared its intention to open parks for visitors in an effort to promote ecotourism and recreation. Public service concessions in parks are now being considered.

The Brazilian government is currently developing PROECOTUR, an ecotourism program that may soon open the most famous parks of the Brazilian Amazon for visitation (Amazonas, Serra do Divisor, Pico da Neblina, Araguaia). Other projects in planning, such as the Pantanal Program and the PRODETUR-Sul, will contribute to the same goal in their respective regions.[16]

In Brazil, as in other countries with categories of protected areas that do not even allow public visitation, it is advisable to re-categorize them as national parks or, at least, open them for limited visitation. Zoning is a powerful enough instrument, when applied within a park, to ensure complete protection wherever it is required.

Encouraging a close association of the environmental movement with both public and private tourism sectors is an excellent way to reinforce the efforts of two usually weak sectors and to increase political awareness in favor of parks. This strategy has produced excellent results in Costa Rica and has not required compromising conservation principles. As shown above, it is also being applied successfully in Brazil.

Management Plans That Are Less "Perfect" but More Useful

Policy-makers deeply dislike spending money on "making paper," a term they apply to studies of all kinds. They prefer to make investments that are visible, thus providing a tangible demonstration of how well the government is using public funds. Some studies are obviously necessary, but environmentalists of many LAC countries have gone to excess, especially in the case of park management plans.

A sound management plan is an indispensable tool for the administration of a park. However, all too often management plans are published and then ignored. Many of them have little applicability to conditions on the ground, or recommend actions for which the necessary resources are lacking. At worst, they present outsider views that sometimes disregard basic principles of park management.

The production of management plans has become a formalistic exercise that generates business for consulting firms. Predictably, the cost has escalated. During the last two decades, the contracted price of management plans in countries such as Brazil has gone up from a few tens of thousands of dollars to several hundred thousand dollars and even up to a couple of million dollars.[17] In the worst cases, more is spent on the management plan for a park than on the first five years of management.

Grossly inflated management plans possess little utility as practical tools. Huge paper monuments stuffed with theoretical information of doubtful value to managers—their fate is to gather dust until forgotten. What is needed instead are concise descriptive documents that apply common sense and local experience. A few pages of practical advice and recommendations can be extremely valuable to a manager, especially during the initial life of a park. Good-quality maps and/or aerial photography of the area can be particularly helpful. Information on the attitudes and habits of local people is indispensable, although recent documents often exaggerate the role of local participation.

Creating Political Pressure for Better Park Management

Local or national support for improved park management is as essential as popular support for creating a new park. NGOs are well positioned to organize this support, but for reasons not always clear, they are often less effective than they could be. One possible reason is that NGOs lack of a "sense of ownership." Parks are frequently regarded as a mere government problem and not as a public problem.

It would be helpful to have "watch dog" organizations for parks, in the mold of the U.S. National Park and Conservation Association, in every country (see chapter 20). In Brazil, the new "Rede de Unidades de Conservacao" has been organized along this line, being integrated by environmental NGOs. In its short existence, it has been useful in deterring all kinds of transgressions against parks.

Local and/or national support committees have a proven record as useful mechanisms for engaging citizens in park management and generating political pressure. Such groups are particularly effective when they work in partnership with park authorities. Local businesses can benefit through better understanding of opportunities presented by a park, and local municipal authorities can look forward to increased tax revenues.

Finally, it is important to create an "esprit de corps" among park workers by encouraging exchanges among park rangers and professional managers. Short training courses can also boost morale. Clearly, a united and energized staff will perform better than a demoralized one.

Reducing the Need for Political Will

Few LAC park systems, if any, have achieved even limited administrative autonomy. Entrance and concession fees, fines, donations, book and souvenir sales, and any other incidental income must be forwarded to the central government. This practice, rooted in fears of corruption, greatly discourages park managers and limits park income to the annual budget coming from headquarters. This budget may reflect, but never in equivalent proportion, the funds raised locally. It is therefore desirable to promote legislation that will confer more autonomy on park managers, allowing them to raise funds and spend them in discretionary ways, under of course, adequate supervision and control.

One way to circumvent a lack of administrative autonomy is through contractual agreements with NGOs. In Perú as well as in Brazil, a number of national parks are being successfully administered by NGOs (see chapter 11). Pró-Naturaleza of Perú is managing eleven parks, covering some 5 million hectares, and employing eighty rangers and twenty-six professional staff.[18] In Brazil, the Serra da Capivara National Park is managed by FUNDHAM and may be the best equipped and managed park in all LAC. Other parks managed by NGOs in Brazil include Grande Sertao Veredas National Park (FUNATURA) and Jau National Park (Vitoria Amazonica Foundation).

Sources of funding for these NGOs vary greatly. Pró-Naturaleza and

Vitoria Amazonica receive funding from The Nature Conservancy and World Wildlife Fund, among other donors. FUNDHAM was financed by a dozen donors, but primarily through IDB technical cooperation grants. FUNATURA finances the Grande Sertao Veredas Park with the only debt-for-nature swap consummated in Brazil. NGOs have the advantage of being able to raise funds from a variety of sources and are also much more efficient in managing money. They may pay better salaries to staff but can also expeditiously replace poor performers. NGOs are also more efficient in purchasing goods and services because they do not have to comply with the amazingly complex routines necessary to expend public funds. Finally, NGO personnel tend to be more highly motivated than public officers.

Despite these obvious advantages, consigning park management to NGOs is not a panacea, because NGOs have no legal authority to represent the park and even less to exercise police functions. Therefore, a public servant must always be at least nominally in charge. Dual authority is often a source of serious conflict, as the public servant has no staff or operating capacity whereas the NGO has the means but not the authority (see chapters 11 and 15). Moreover, NGOs are generally not allowed to recover costs by retaining entrance fees or other park income.

An innovative formula is contained in a law passed in Brazil in 1998 allowing the creation of "social organizations."[19] These are private organizations that can be established for the specific purpose of managing an individual park or group of parks within a region. The law calls for heavy government representation on the boards of "social organizations." Like any NGO, these organizations can receive donations but are also allowed to receive and manage public funds (annual budget, entrance, and other fees) with full autonomy, while respecting rules for the use of public funds. Rules governing federal parks will continue to be issued from the federal park service (currently IBAMA), but otherwise, IBAMA's role will be limited to supervision, technical assistance, and international affairs. As of this writing, the law has not yet been implemented, so how well these concepts can be applied in practice remains to be seen.

Financing Park Management

Financing of parks is a subject addressed elsewhere in this book. It is enough to say here that there are several mechanisms in place for financing parks in LAC countries, especially in Costa Rica,[20] none of which are currently adequate for supporting high-quality management. However, the park-finance mechanisms are being improved and may ultimately resolve the heretofore intractable issue of paying the costs of management. Involvement of the private sector in public parks management is also essential, as has already been demonstrated in a number of cases.

Notes

1. FUNATURA, Custo de implantação de unidades de conservação na Amazônia Legal (Brasìlia: Fundação Pró-Natureza, 1991).

2. M. J. Dourojeanni, "Financing Protected Areas in Latin America," in Anais Congresso Brasileiro de Unidades de Conservação, vol. 1 (Curitiba, Brazil: IAP/ UNILIVRE/Rede Nacional Pro Unidades de Conservação, 1997), 237–261.

3. There are, currently, two examples of this situation in Brazil: (1) the proposed Serra dos Pirineus State Park, in Pirenópolis, Goias, is not being implemented due to the opposition of the main owner of the land, and (2) the future Serra da Bodoquena National Park, in Mato Grosso do Sul, is facing violent opposition from landlords and especially from loggers that are illegally exploiting the area. In both cases, financial resources to pay for the land come from large infrastructure compensation funds.

4. This has been the case, in 1998, for a new park in the southern coast of Bahia (Descobrimento National Park).

5. M. J. Dourojeanni, "Areas protegidas: problemas antiguos y nuevos, nuevos rumbos," in Anais Congresso Brasileiro de Unidades de Conservação, vol. 1 (Curitiba, Brazil: IAP/UNILIVRE/Rede Nacional Pro Unidades de Conservação, 1997), 69–109.

6. The Brazilian Congress is discussing a new law for the national system of protected areas. The social wing of the environmental movement proposed several articles that may seriously erode or even eliminate national parks. These include (1) requiring that up to 5 percent of national parks be opened for living and for "sustainable" exploitation to undefined traditional populations not now residing within or using the area; (2) distributing part of the meager incomes of the parks to neighbors, and; (3) delaying for land tenure regularization after which the area not regularized must be transformed in a "soft" protected area.

7. World Resource Institute/United Nations Environment Programme/United Nations Development Programme/World Bank, *World Resource 1996–97* (New York: Oxford University Press, 1996).

8. Brasil. Ministério do Meio Ambiente, Primeiro Relatòrio Nacional para a Convenção sobre Diversidade Biològica: Brasil (Brasìlia: Ministério do Meio Ambiente, 1998).

9. Áreas de Proteção Ambiental (APAs), national forests, extractive reserves, and sustainable uses reserves. In APAs and sustainable uses reserves, the land is private.

10. National parks, biological reserves, and ecological stations. This has been the case in 1998 for a new park in the southern coast of Bahia (Descobrimento National Park).

11. Information provided by the Instituto SocioAmbiental (Brasilia), based on IBAMA and state reports, 1998.

12. Only the national parks can be opened for visitors (and even so, only a few actually are). Visitors are prohibited in biological reserves (over 3 million hectares) and ecological stations, which are restricted to those conducting scientific research.

13. The State Park Serra do Conduru, in the state of Bahia, Brazil, was established when Conservation International and local NGOs requested the IDB to include this park as a condition for the paving of a nearby road financed by IDB.

14. V. Perera, "He Saves the Rain Forest by Buying It," Los Angeles Times, Sunday, 16 March 1997, sec. M, p. 1–2.

15. M. J. Dourojeanni, "Condominio natural: Una nueva estrategia para establecer reservas naturales privadas," Medio Ambiente 11, no. 68 (1996): 44–51.

16. These three projects are being developed with assistance of the Interamerican Development Bank.

17. As in the case of the Jaú National Park, in the Brazilian Amazon.

18. G. Suarez de Freitas, "Cooperation between NGOs and Government: A Successful Experience in Perú," Parks 5, no. 3 (1995): 36–40.

19. The Law No 9.637 of May 1998 was not passed exclusively for parks but for several public functions (i.e., hospitals, museums) that may be better developed with more autonomy.

20. IDB, Investing in Biodiversity, Proceedings of a Workshop (s.l.: Inter-American Development Bank, Environment Division, 1997).

24

The Role of the Private Sector in Protected Area Establishment and Management

RANDALL KRAMER, JEFF LANGHOLZ, AND NICK SALAFSKY

In many aspects of economic activity, there is a trend toward privatization. In countries that traditionally were socialistic or had large government sectors, many government-owned industries have been sold to the private sector.[1] In other countries that have a strong market tradition, there has been a reexamination of the public provision of services such as waste management and prison operation.[2] Increasingly, these functions are being contracted to the private sector. This transformation has been justified on the basis of effectiveness and cost efficiency.[3] It has also been motivated by the generally poor performance of public agencies providing the functions. At its best, the private sector harnesses market incentives to reduce costs and encourage innovations.

The privatization trend is now making its way into nature conservation as well.[4] Privatization of conservation can take many forms. It can range from contracts to provide specific services such as food and lodging, to public–private partnerships for park management, to full private ownership and operation. There are several advantages that the private sector can potentially bring to protected-area establishment and management. Businesses and NGOs (nongovernmental organizations) can provide financial and technical resources that would otherwise not be available for conservation. This is particularly important in developing countries where park authorities are often seriously underfunded. Also, concession contracts and associated user fees can contribute to sustainable self-financing of protected areas.[5] Another advantage is that the private sector may be more successful than the public sector in providing the marketing and operational expertise necessary to compete in the highly competitive international nature tourism industry. Although these approaches have advantages in theory, it is important to consider under what conditions they may actually result in improved conservation of protected areas.

The process of developing our understanding of these conditions ultimately requires an analysis of many different examples of private-sector conservation. But before embarking on such an analysis, it is useful to frame the problem. Here, we present a simple conceptual framework derived from an initial assessment of experiences with private-sector conservation experience. We then apply the framework to a set of four case studies. We conclude with suggestions for further exploration.

Conceptual Framework

In this section we present a theoretical structure for examining the effectiveness of different organizational constructions in establishing and managing protected areas.

Framework Outline

The first step in developing a conceptual framework involves defining a taxonomy of the different strategies being considered (see chapter 29). A key distinction is made in the privatization literature between the privatization of ownership and the privatization of management functions and services.[6] Accordingly, as shown in Table 24-1, we divide organizational effectiveness in implementing a protected area strategy across two dimensions:

1. Ownership of land and resources in the protected area.
2. Ownership of the organization(s) responsible for carrying out management functions and services necessary to establish and operate the protected area.

Within both these categories, there is not a hard and fixed dichotomy between public and private ownership. Instead, ownership can be classified along a spectrum ranging from fully public to fully private ownership as shown in Figure 24-1. The most traditional arrangement is to have a national, provincial, or local *government agency* assume ownership (represented by the box on the far left-hand side of the diagram). Moving along the spectrum, some countries have chosen to create *parastatal agencies,* such as park authorities who benefit from a certain degree of independence from political influence. Moving to the center of the spectrum, the next type is the *local stakeholder organization,* which in some senses is public (the lowest level of government) and in other senses is private (a

Table 24-1.

Two dimensions of protected-area ownership.

	Ownership of Organization Providing Management Functions	
Ownership of Land and Resources	*Public*	*Private*
Public	Traditional national parks	Tourist concessionaires in national parks
Private	Lands bought by NGOs and managed by state agencies	Private safari parks

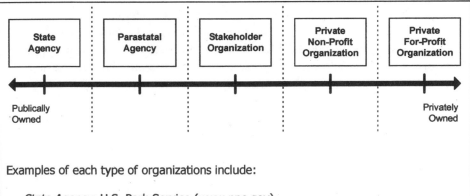

Examples of each type of organizations include:

- *State Agency*: U.S. Park Service (www.nps.gov)
- *Parastatal Agency*: ADMADE Zambia
- *Stakeholder Organization*: Crater Mountain Wildlife Management Area (Papua New Guinea) (www.bcnet.org/projects/crater97.htm)
- *Private Non-Profit*: The Nature Conservancy (www.tnc.org); Trustees of Reservation (Massachusetts, USA) (www.thetrustees.org); Research and Conservation Foundation (Papua New Guinea)
- *Private For-Profit*: The Conservation Corporation - Africa (www.conscorp.co.za)

Figure 24-1. A spectrum of organizations involved in implementing protected areas.

small group of individuals). Since stakeholders are typically a diverse collection of individuals and groups, there may be multiple organizations to represent them. Next in the public–private continuum is the private *nonprofit* organization, which can range from foundations established to manage a particular piece of land to large international organizations that purchase huge areas of land and work with governments to provide support activities for park management. Finally, at the end of the spectrum are *for-profits*—private businesses that may purchase land as part of a business venture or provide contract services for a publicly owned park.

Beyond the question of public versus private ownership, the size of the organization must also be considered. Agencies and organizations at each point along the spectrum can range from small local groups to large international ones. Although there may be some variation in our assessments related to the size of the agency or organization, for the most part our framework is independent of scale. Yet it is important to bear in mind that some organizations may be too small to take on certain tasks, such as establishing a park where none existed before.

Major functions related to establishing and managing protected areas are outlined in the leftmost column of Table 24-2. Traditional conservation functions include establishing the protected area, demarcating borders, detecting and punishing violations of protected-area regulations, and planning and implementing management activities such as proscribed burns or game culling. Integrated management functions include raising money from government agencies and private foundations, attracting private investments, collecting user fees, maintaining relations with local (e.g., resident populations) and external (e.g., nonresident resource users, conservationists) stakeholder groups, carrying out administrative functions, providing tourist services, and facilitating research.

Pros and Cons of Different Management Models

Each type of agency or organization described above has inherent strengths and weaknesses. In Table 24-2, we offer an assessment of how each type of organization can be expected to perform a series of functions relative to the others. Pluses or minuses indicate comparative advantage or disadvantage. In some cases, a mixture of pluses and minuses were assigned when varying circumstances could result in either positive or negative influences.

Table 24-2.

Summary of theoretical strengths and weaknesses of different organizations in different protected-area functions.

Function	Government Agency	Parastatal Agency	Local Stakeholder	Private Nonprofit	Private For-Profit
Traditional Conservation					
Establishment	++	–	– –	+	+/–
Demarcation of boundaries	–	–	+	+	+
Detection of encroachment	+/–	+	++	+	++
Enforcement of sanctions	+	+	+/–	– –	+
Planning resource management actions	–	+	–	++	+
Implementing resource management actions	+/–	+	+/–	–	+/–
Integrated Management					
Revenue generation—external donors	++	++	–	++	– –
Revenue generation—investment	–	+	– –	+	++
Revenue generation—internal user fees	+/–	+	+/–	+/–	++
Local stakeholder relations	– –	–	++/– –	+	+/–
External stakeholder relations	–	+	–	+	+/–
Administration	– –	+/–	– –	+	++
Tourism services	– –	–	–	+	++
Research	+	++	– –	++	++

A plus (+ or + +) indicates the organization type is thought to generally conduct a given function well.

A minus (– or – –) indicates the organization type generally conducts a given function poorly.

Traditional Conservation Functions

In this section, we examine the relative effectiveness of different organizational types in carrying out traditional conservation functions such as boundary demarcation, enforcement, and managing wildlife resources. As a rule, state agencies should have a comparative advantage in establishing reserve areas and enforcing sanctions, because these functions stem from powers vested in state organizations. In particular, with regard to park establishment, state agencies have the ability to set aside lands under eminent domain and to help relocate or compensate local residents who bear the costs of protected area development. State agencies should normally be able to detect violations of protected area rules but may fail where poorly paid guards may be vulnerable to corruption when asked by resource pirates "to look the other way." Public agencies may also be inefficient at performing specific tasks such as demarcating boundaries and implementing resource management actions, because of rigid job descriptions and the relatively high cost of public sector employees.

We presume that parastatal organizations should be relatively less effective at establishing and demarcating protected area boundaries, because it may be difficult for them to overcome stakeholder conflicts. However parastatals should be relatively effective at the other major traditional conservation functions. In part this is because they are to some degree buffered from political forces and may be less bureaucratic than their government agency counterparts.

The relative advantage of stakeholder groups might be in detecting violations of protected-area rules because of their intimate knowledge of the site and the people using it (assuming, of course, that they have a vested interest in the protected area). Stakeholder groups might be effective in enforcing sanctions against outsiders but less-effective in enforcing sanctions against themselves. They might also have a mixed ability to implement resource management actions depending on their level of organization. On the negative side, stakeholder organizations might have difficulty in planning large-scale resource management actions. We also imagine that they might not be effective in establishing protected areas, since they typically include the people who would have to bear the opportunity costs inherent in limiting access to resources (exceptions to this being game reserves or marine protected areas that can potentially increase harvest rates in adjacent habitat).

Private nonprofit organizations might be particularly effective in planning resource management actions because they have access to trained resource managers. And since their focus is on conservation, NGOs might also be relatively effective in establishing and demarcating protected areas and detecting encroachment. On the other hand, we assume that nonprofits might have difficulty implementing resource management actions in a cost-effective way and will likely have extreme difficulties in enforcing sanctions because of their lack of political "clout" with local governments.

Finally, we presume that for-profit firms should generally be able to undertake most tasks in an effective and cost-efficient manner. In particular, private firms have a strong motivation to detect encroachments. A key condition behind all of these assessments, however, is that the country or society in which the protected area is being implemented has a tradition of strong and enforceable private property rights. If not, then it should be difficult for private firms to undertake such functions, including, in particular, establishing protected areas. For-profit firms may lack incentives to implement management actions affecting resources that are not commercially valuable.

Integrated Management Functions

In this section, we discuss integrated management functions that are a part of modern protected-area management and require a broader set of expertise than the traditional conservation functions. The integrated functions include such activities as relations with local communities, revenue generation from internal and external sources, tourism development, and ecological and socioeconomic research.

State agencies should be particularly effective at attracting funds from external donors, including especially multilateral institutions and bilateral development agencies. State agencies can also be effective in promoting research and, where corruption is low, in collecting user fees. We expect that state agencies are less effective in maintaining relations with local stakeholders and in providing administration and tourism services because of their bureaucratic and nonresponsive tendencies.

Parastatals should have a relative advantage in generating all kinds of revenues because of their dual public–private nature. Where they are less bureaucratic than governments, they may be effective at administration; however, in many cases this assumption may not hold. They may encounter the same difficulties as state agencies in maintaining local stakeholder relations and in providing tourism services.

For obvious reasons, stakeholder groups should be effective at maintaining stakeholder relations (although this may be problematic for protected areas managed by competing stakeholder groups). Similarly, they could have either a positive or negative ability to collect user fees from themselves. However, stakeholder organizations are unlikely to include trained managers and administrators, and thus can be expected to be ineffective in carrying out almost all other management functions.

Private nonprofits should, in principle, be effective in carrying out almost all integrated management functions. Their particular strengths are in soliciting grants from donors and in promoting research. Nonprofits are less suited for collecting user fees.

Finally, for-profit firms should generally be able to perform many functions in an efficient manner. They do bring some weaknesses, however, in that they are generally unable to solicit grants from external donors. They may have little incentive to promote good stakeholder relations, particularly if the relations do not affect the resources providing the firm's profits. Finally, for-profit firms are unlikely to make scientific research a major priority unless it is research that will directly improve their bottom line (e.g., bioprospecting).

Case Studies

In the following section, we attempt an initial vetting of our framework. We focus on four of the five organization types (all but state-owned, traditional parks). The case studies represent innovative and distinct approaches to protected-area institutional design and are drawn from Asia, Africa, and Latin America.

Parastatal Organization: Administrative Design Management Program of Zambia

The Administrative Management Design (ADMADE) program in Zambia is an example of a parastatal organization with responsibilities for park management. The ADMADE program was established in 1988 by the National Parks and Wildlife Services (NPWS) in response to concerns about increasing pressure on the biological resources of the country's national parks, coupled with complaints from local communities that they were not receiving benefits from the parks. The program was established following a successful pilot project in the Lower Lupande area supported by the Wildlife Conservation Society.

ADMADE vests responsibility for management of wildlife resources in local communities that reside inside Game Management Areas. In exchange for protecting habitat, communities are allowed to derive revenues from legal harvest of wildlife populations through safari hunting. ADMADE has implemented its activities by appointing NPWS staff as extension officers to advise local communities on their management responsibilities.[7] Local residents are selected by their communities to work as scouts. Traditional leaders have help from local authorities in managing the resource and determining how to allocate program revenues to support community activities. In addition, a national institute was created to provide capacity building for the local communities and technical services, including resource monitoring and computer mapping.

The startup phase of ADMADE was not without problems. The task of decentralizing wildlife management and facilitating community participation was perhaps larger than the founders recognized. Local authorities were not organized into defined structures, and this led to concerns about community participation and transparency in the use of local funds. Reforms have been instituted to address these concerns and new legislation has been passed to give national support to ADMADE and its system of local community participation.

The ADMADE experience supports several of our presumptions about management functions. ADMADE has been successful in seeking outside sources of revenue, with both USAID and the Wildlife Conservation Society providing substantial funding support. It has improved its abilities in detection of violations, enforcement, and planning. Although it initially had problems with stakeholder relations (as we hypothesized), it has improved in this area by taking on many of the characteristics of a stakeholder organization through devolving much of its decision making to the local level.

Stakeholder Organization: Crater Mountain Wildlife Management Area

Crater Mountain Wildlife Management Area (CM-WMA) is located in the highlands of Papua New Guinea (PNG).[8] CM-WMA covers 2,600 square kilometers, an area about the size of Rhode Island. The area spans a wide range of habitats, including primary forest at lower elevations and alpine scrub and grasslands on the ridgetops. These habitats are home to 220 bird species of which forty-nine are endemic to that region of PNG, and eighty-four mammal species of which fifteen are endemic. CM-WMA is composed of the lands owned by residents of several small villages totaling less than two thousand people. Major threats to the area include overhunting by local community members, expansion of local agricultural gardens, and industrial logging, mining, and oil drilling. The industrial threats are particularly problematic, because the international companies behind them are offering the local residents relatively large amounts of money compared to their current incomes.

To help address these threats, the local community members came together with two environmental NGOs—the Research and Conservation Foundation (RCF) and the Wildlife Conservation Society (WCS)—to propose the CM-WMA and preempt the corporations.[9] At the time, PNG had no statutes that recognized a wildlife management area. The first step, therefore, was to work with national and provincial agencies to create the law. CM-WMA was formally gazetted as the first such protected area in the country, and it is run by management committees from each of the main villages. Management committee members come together each year for an annual meeting at which policies and regulations are discussed and enacted. Each village is charged with establishing resource management schemes for its traditional lands. These management actions include designating no-hunting zones for conservation, deciding which species are protected (for example, some species of birds-of-paradise), and developing eco-enterprises such as nature tourism, research, and handicrafts production.[10]

Although we proposed above that stakeholder groups would have trouble establishing protected areas, CM-WMA is one of the interesting exceptions that proves the rule. The local communities were able to establish a protected area in large part because in PNG (as in other Melanesian countries but unlike almost everywhere else in the world), traditional landowners have constitutionally guaranteed tenure over land and aboveground natural resources. In addition, the communities had major support from both WCS and RCF, their NGO partners, a fact that gave them a voice in establishing policy and passing the legislation required to gazette the WMA. As predicted, community members actively patrolled their lands and excelled at detecting poachers. For example, management committee members from one village detected a group of visiting government officials who had illegally used shotguns to hunt a cassowary. The committee members intervened and fined the officials.[11]

In line with our hypothesis, the community members have, however, had difficulties in enforcing sanctions against their own members. Likewise, it is "hard for committee members to take a stand in a decision ruling against a relative, because then his clan members will not stand by him in times when he is in trouble."[12] Finally, the local committees have taken some steps toward planning and implementing resource management actions, but by dint of a great deal of work and, at best, mixed success.

The CM-WMA experience generally confirms our expectation with respect to integrated management functions. The CM-WMA has received some support from external foundations, but only through its NGO partners. The project has attracted little or no investment (save one early and failed venture to build an ecotourism lodge). User fees have generated only minimal revenues because it has been hard for local people to tax themselves. The village committees have had some success in dealing with the government and other external stakeholders (for example, persuading the forestry authority to remove the WMA from its logging plans), but this has largely been accomplished by working with RCF and WCS.

The Crater Mountain experience highlights the extreme advantages and disadvantages of stakeholder organizations. Management committee members have spent countless hours dealing with inter- and intra-clan conflicts over resources—conflicts that have at time threatened to lead to physical violence. Finally, with regard to providing tourism and research services, the WMA project is again an interesting exception that proves the rule. The WMA has been able to set up both ecotourism and research support services, largely under a major grant to WCS and RCF that was aimed specifically at setting up eco-enterprises. Although these enterprises are owned and operated by the communities, it is overwhelmingly clear that they could not have developed these businesses on their own and need intensive support from their NGO partners.

Overall, the CM-WMA experience shows that under the right conditions, local communities can establish and manage protected areas. The lesson learned is that unworldly villagers need extensive support from both government agencies and civil society institutions.

Private Nonprofit: The Children's Rainforest

The history of protected natural areas worldwide suggests that only the largest organizations, such as national governments, can mobilize sufficient resources to establish and operate large protected areas.[13] The case of The Children's Rainforest casts doubt on this conventional wisdom.

The Children's Rainforest is located high in the Tilaran Mountains of northwest Costa Rica. More than 60 percent of the reserve is covered in primary rain forest, with the remainder being secondary forest in various stages of regeneration. The reserve is owned and administered by the Monteverde Conservation League (MCL), a 165-member nonprofit NGO based in Monteverde (see chapter 12 for details on the reserve's history). Membership is split about evenly between foreign expatriates and Costa Rican nationals. Although most revenues originally came from international donations, the reserve is slowly moving toward self-sufficiency. MCL Director Johnny Rosales notes that since 1995, "most of our income has come from domestic sources, especially government incentives and ecotourism."[14]

With over 17,000 hectares, The Children's Rainforest is the largest private reserve in Central America. It is larger than most of Costa Rica's national parks. But unlike most, The Children's Rainforest continues to expand, using a trust fund specifically earmarked for acquisition of adjacent lands.

The reserve is not only large, but also well protected. "As a private reserve, we have to provide our own protection. It's a very expensive activity," says Rosales. "Guards. Trucks. Horses. Paying overtime for guards who spend the night in the reserve. Our protection program costs approximately $70,000 per year"—out of a total budget of $250,000 to $400,000. It supports a staff of eleven in the Monteverde Conservation League protection branch, five of whom are full-time forest guards. With such a large area, a high level of protection is not only expensive, but also necessary. "We are constantly chasing poachers," says Rosales.

In addition to its sheer size and high level of protection, the reserve contributes to conservation in a variety of other ways. As noted elsewhere in this book (see chapter 12), MCL supports reforestation on local farms and promotes regional conservation as part of the larger Monteverde reserve complex. MCL has also sponsored numerous floral and faunal studies in the park, and operates a community outreach and education program. Behind the program is a long-standing policy of allowing local residents free access to the reserve and its facilities.

Private For-Profit: Game Lodges and Ranches in South Africa

Given its diverse, captivating, and readily observed wildlife, it is no surprise that the Republic of South Africa has seen extensive attempts to combine biodiversity protection with financial profit. Abundant land and wildlife have led South Africans to establish roughly nine thousand privately owned game reserves and game farms, covering some 8 million hectares in South Africa.[15] A growing number of these private enterprises cater to high-end tourists in an effort to integrate ecology with economics.

Perhaps the most notable for-profit example is the Conservation Corporation–Africa (CCA), which develops and sustains wildlife sanctuaries across several countries in southern and eastern Africa. Dedicated to the twin goals of conservation and profit, CCA maintains a thriving network of upscale lodges and reserves catering largely to affluent foreign visitors seeking a traditional African safari-like experience.

Although some may question the motives and conservation track record of the private game ranches, few can doubt the contributions and credibility they have established within the region. As one scholar notes, "Even though they consist mostly of a myriad of small operations, these private reserves and ranches are so large in aggregate that they make up an important component of wildlife conservation in South Africa."[16] South African park officials, in fact, have removed the fences once separating famed Kruger National Park from Ngala and other adjacent private reserves. This decision has expanded the effective size of Kruger, providing additional high-quality habitat for wide-ranging species. It has simultaneously augmented the tourism value of Ngala's 14,000-hectare private reserve, and others. According to another scholar, the agreement provides CCA with exclusive rights for operating tourist activities in that area.[17] In exchange, CCA pays dues to the park, which uses the money for wildlife management, research, educational programs, and community-based projects.

The single largest barrier to establishing a private for-profit conservation enterprise is access to land. Unlike national governments, private individuals and groups cannot expropriate land for parks. Furthermore, in most parts of the world, land prices are prohibitively high to justify acquisitions on an ecologically significant scale. A result is the establishment of smaller more fragmented conservation areas that are assembled in a piecemeal manner. Most of Africa's large game ranches have been passed down in families over several generations, thus bypassing the need for a major capital outlay. The reputed high profitability of such areas, however, is attracting financial investors (as we surmised) who bring sufficient capital to create new reserves, as well as expectations of financial return.

The proffering of high-quality tourism services to an elite clientele is a hallmark of private for-profit conservation organizations worldwide, and the standards are especially high in southern Africa. Londolozi, for example, provides air-conditioned chalets, private pools, bars, lounge areas, gift shops, guided walks, and gourmet meals for US$550–900 per person per night. The profitability of such ventures remains unknown, partly because as private ventures they are under no obligation to share financial records and partly because no serious attempt has been made to study them.[18] As noted elsewhere, the conservation community would benefit from detailed investigation into the economic potential and trade-offs of privately owned protected areas.[19]

Policing privately owned for-profit protected areas presents a major dilemma. National governments are hesitant to commit public resources (e.g., park guards) to patrol a private for-profit venture. Yet private guards lack legal authority to arrest poachers and others found on the premises, and many people are uncomfortable with the idea of heavily armed park guards who have no legal authority or law enforcement training. The stakes are high given that profitability often depends on the very megafauna that attracts poachers. Consequently, it is not uncommon for poachers to escape while private park guards summon public authorities and wait for them to arrive. An innovative compromise is found in Costa Rica's system of COVIRENAs, in which citizen vigilante forces are authorized to monitor and report illegal activity.

Stakeholder relations can be a flashpoint for privately owned, for-profit reserves. On the positive side, for-profit status leads to creation of high-paying and long-lasting jobs, which benefit locals.[20] On the other hand, local residents are often resigned to being employees of private reserves rather than owning such ventures themselves.[21] Even when the owners are nationals, they frequently belong to a comparatively wealthy and white minority. Compounding the problem is a phenomenon researchers have documented in South Africa whereby wealthy landowners place lands into conservation status as a means to avoid land redistribution schemes designed to assist the black majority.[22] A similar phenomenon may be occurring in Costa Rica, where an innovative program to encourage establishment of private wildlife refuges could potentially pit the popular goals of biodiversity conservation and social justice against one another.[23]

Next Steps

We have provided a framework for anticipating the strengths and weaknesses of different types of organizations in performing both traditional conservation functions and more integrated conservation functions associated with protected areas. The case studies we have presented suggest that more careful analysis is needed to identify the conditions under which each type of organization can most effectively contribute to protected-area establishment and management.

The second step in developing a conceptual framework involves determining these conditions by indicating specific assumptions that can be tested and developed into general and yet nontrivial guiding principles (see chapter 29). For instance, one critical factor determining whether a private firm will be able to establish a protected area is the security of property rights. Thus, the prospect of setting up privately owned protected areas in countries like Indonesia, where the land is owned by the state, or in Papua New Guinea, where it is owned by traditional landowners, is likely to be poor.

Another key factor is the ability to enforce property rights. Private organizations will more likely succeed in establishing or managing protected areas in societies that have strong legal systems that support private ownership. Greater private sector involvement is unlikely in countries that lack strong judicial and police systems willing to take action against encroachment and other forms of property rights violations.

Further work is needed to develop a comprehensive set of assumptions or hypotheses that can be tested against real-world cases. We hope that the framework we have formulated in this chapter will encourage more careful analysis of the conditions under which innovative approaches to protected area institutions will improve conservation and help achieve other social goals.

Acknowledgments

The authors thank Mike Griffiths, Carlos Peres, and Barry Spergel for their suggestions during the privatization working group at the Making Parks Work Conference, August 1999.

Notes

1. J. O. De Castro and K. Uhlenbruck, "Characteristics of Privatization: Evidence from Developed, Less-Developed, and Former Communist Countries," *Journal of International Business Studies*, First Quarter (1997): 123–143.

2. W. Z. Hirsch, "Contracting Out by Urban Governments: A Review," *Urban Affairs* 30, no.3 (1995): 458–472.

3. J. D. Donahue, *The Privatization Decision: Public Ends, Private Means* (New York: Basic Books, 1989).

4. N. Salafsky, B. Cordes, J. Parks, and C. Hochman, *Evaluating Linkages between*

Business, the Environment, and Local Communities: Final Analytical Results from the Bio-diversity Conservation Network (Washington, D.C.: Biodiversity Support Program, 1999). Available online: http://www.bcnet.org.

5. World Tourism Organization and United Nations Environment Programme, *Guidelines: Development of National Parks and Protected Areas for Tourism* (Madrid: World Tourism Organization and United Nations Environment Programme, 1992).

6. S. Kikeri, J. R. Nellis, and M. M. Shirley, "Privatization: Lessons from Market Economies," *World Bank Research Observer* 9, no.2 (1994): 241–272.

7. ADMADE, *Administrative Management Design for Community Based Wildlife Management in Zambia* (May 2000).

8. Biodiversity Conservation Network, *Evaluating Linkages between Business, the Environment, and Local Communities: Final Stories from the Field* (Washington, D.C.: Biodiversity Support Program, 1999); Biodiversity Conservation Network, *Evaluating Linkages between Business, the Environment, and Local Communities*, a web site at http://www.bcnet.org.

9. A. Johnson, *Measuring Our Success: One Team's Experience in Monitoring the Crater Mountain Wildlife Management Area Project in Papua New Guinea. Lessons from the Field, Issue BCN-3* (Washington, D.C.: Biodiversity Support Program, 1999); M. Pearl, "Local Initiatives and the Rewards for Biodiversity Conservation: Crater Mountain Wildlife Management Area, Papua New Guinea," in *Natural Connections: Perspectives in Community-based Conservation*, ed. D. Western, R. M. Wright, and S. Strum (Washington, D.C.: Island Press, 1994), 193–214.

10. J. Ericho, R. Bino, and A. Johnson, "Testing the Effectiveness of Using a Conceptual Model to Design Projects and Monitoring Plans for the Crater Mountain Wildlife Management Area, Papua New Guinea," in *Measuring Conservation Impact: An Interdisciplinary Approach to Project Monitoring and Evaluation*, ed. K. Saterson, R. Margoluis, and N. Salafsky (Washington, D.C.: Biodiversity Support Program, 1999), 21–40.

11. Biodiversity Conservation Network, *Evaluating Linkages*.

12. Biodiversity Conservation Network, *Evaluating Linkages*.

13. A. Runte, *National Parks: The American Experience* (Lincoln: University of Nebraska Press, 1979); D. Western and M. Pearl, eds., *Conservation for the Twenty-first Century* (New York: Oxford University Press, 1989); IUCN (The World Conservation Union), *1993 United Nations List of National Parks and Protected Areas* (Gland, Switzerland: IUCN, 1994).

14. Personal communication with J. Langholz, April 1998.

15. M. Wells, *Economic Perspectives on Nature Tourism, Conservation, and Development*. Environmental Economics Series, no. 55 (Washington, D.C.: World Bank, 1997).

16. Wells, *Economic Perspectives*.

17. G. Borrini-Feyerabend, *Collaborative Management of Protected Areas: Tailoring the Approach to the Context* (Gland, Switzerland: IUCN, 1996).

18. Wells, *Economic Perspectives*.

19. J. Langholz, J. Lassoie, D. Lee, and D. Chapman, "Economic Considerations of Privately Owned Parks," *Ecological Economics* 33, no. 2 (2000): 173–183.

20. C. Alderman, "The Economics and the Role of Privately Owned Lands Used for Nature Tourism, Education, and Conservation," in *Protected Area Economics and Policy: Linking Conservation and Sustainable Development*, ed. M. Munasinghe and J. McNeely (Washington, D.C.: IUCN and World Bank, 1994), 273–305; J. Langholz, "Economics, Objectives, and Success of Private Nature Reserves in Sub-Saharan Africa and Latin America," *Conservation Biology* 10 (1996): 271–280.

21. J. Langholz and K. Brandon, "Ecotourism and Privately Owned Protected Areas," in *The Encyclopedia of Ecotourism*, ed. D. Weaver (Oxon, United Kingdom: CAB International, in press), 303–313.

22. T. Brinkate, *People and Parks: Implications for Sustainable Development in the Thukela Biosphere Reserve. Presentation at the Sixth International Symposium on Society and Natural Resource Management* (University Park: Pennsylvania State University, 1996); M. Cohen, "The South African Natural Heritage Program: A New Partnership among Government, Landowners, and the Business Sector," in *Expanding Partnerships in Conservation*, ed. J. McNeely (Washington, D.C.: Island Press, 1995), 252–260.

23. J. Langholz, J. Lassoie, and J. Schelhas, "Incentives for Biodiversity Conservation: Lessons from Costa Rica's Private Wildlife Refuge Program," *Conservation Biology* 14, no. 6 (2000): 1735–1743.

25

Anarchy and Parks: Dealing with Political Instability

CAREL VAN SCHAIK

Parks must be defended against exploitation, otherwise they become open-access areas whose valuable resources will be exploited for profit and eventually depleted. Some form of patrolling and law enforcement is therefore needed. Where protection is deficient, some solution needs to be sought as soon as possible lest the park be significantly damaged. Inadequate park protection may have a variety of causes. Government institutions may be weakly represented in the frontier areas where we find most parks, they may be hopelessly corrupt, or they may have collapsed.

This chapter focuses on one important reason for inadequate protection: the temporary or permanent loss of the central government's reach due to political instability (anarchy, civil war, or war). For the present purpose, political instability is defined as the absence of an effective role of the national government in law and order. As a result, conventional law enforcement mechanisms are no longer in place, and there is an increase in violations of national laws, including conservation regulations in general and parks in particular.

The challenge is how to maintain an effective conservation presence under such exceedingly arduous circumstances. In this chapter, I will first describe the general impact on park defenses and changes in pressures and players inherent during political instability. Then I will review several cases that serve both to confirm these general expectations and to highlight the sometimes surprisingly effective protection of parks maintained during the trying times of anarchy. That review forms the basis for the final section, in which I try to derive generalizations as to which conservation structures are likely to be most effective in areas where anarchy is expected. This chapter is meant to complement chapter 7, which discusses the situation in Congo (formerly Zaire), by providing additional examples and drawing further general lessons.

Before reviewing the cases, it is worth addressing a commonly heard and understandable reaction in the West. Some exasperated conservationists argue that the only reasonable response in such situations is to take out the critical endangered species and breed them in captivity. Captive breeding of unique endangered species that are especially vulnerable to overkill makes good sense as insurance against inevitable losses. However, when an entire biogeographic assemblage is at risk, ex situ conservation is unlikely to be as cost effective as in situ protection and will save only a small fraction of the endangered species.[1] Moreover, there is a risk that an emphasis on captive breeding creates a trade-off between in situ and ex situ conservation efforts.[2] Ex situ captive efforts should not diminish the international community's determination to preserve habitat. On the contrary, if the ultimate aim is to reintroduce animals, synergism is optimal, because in situ efforts ensure that there is habitat left into which to reintroduce animals. We cannot let temporary anarchy in a biogeographically unique area lead to permanent biodiversity losses so long as there is hope that some effective in situ conservation can be achieved.

General Expectations

During instability, park defenses are bound to suffer. Even when park guards remain dedicated and armed, they may be outgunned by poachers or disarmed by insurgent forces. In areas where guards are unarmed and must rely on the police or military to arrest trespassers, they will almost certainly lose their ability to maintain order without the presence of supporting law enforcement. They also tend to lose basic resources (such as fuel and, often, their vehicles) needed to carry out their jobs. Often, salaries are no longer paid, and as a result some guards may turn to park exploitation themselves to make a living.

International aid, especially bilateral government-initiated projects and multilateral donor programs, tend to suspend their activities or to pull out altogether at the first sight of instability. At the very least, no new activities or increases are to be expected in these situations.

At the same time, pressures are likely to rise. Anarchy produces a rapid increase in all illegal activities not dependent on capital investment, such as market hunting, artisanal mining, and pitsawing, in part because demand for forest products increases. Large-scale, organized, high-investment activities are occasionally taken over by armed groups. Pressures sometimes increase further due to movements of refugees fleeing from fighting, or because rebel groups move into the reserves, using them as a hideout. In some cases, however, the pressures actually decline because people leave the surroundings of parks, companies close, and no new initiatives are taken.[3]

During anarchy, there are three main classes of exploiters in parks: local people, refugees, and armed outsiders. Local people who exploit parks do so opportunistically in order take advantage of the lack of park defense; they are often emboldened by the widespread availability of firearms made possible when fleeing armies abandon their weapons (usually in order to pass for civilians in territory held by opposing forces). Once encroachment starts, an open-access situation ensues in which anybody not joining in falls behind, and a run on the resources quickly results. This response is of course especially likely where people were hostile to the park to begin with and did not accept its existence even during the preceding period of stability.

Refugees, on the other hand, come to settle in the area and may see parks as the only available space to do so because in densely settled landscapes private individuals or concerns have claimed all other land. This has especially been the case in West and central Africa.[4] At the very least, they need firewood, but more often they take up farming or begin keeping cattle.

Invading forces are the third type of exploiters that take advantage of lower park defenses during periods of anarchy. Professional armies are generally more disciplined, with a tendency to concentrate on strategic areas and move through others quickly. They may, however, leave control to ragtag, undisciplined bands following in their wake; it is such groups who pose a distinct danger to parks.

During such periods of political instability, then, protection of parks is especially important because old pressures increase, new ones arise, and the defensive mechanisms are rendered ineffective. Yet, remarkably, there are examples where parks remain largely intact during such dark times. We will now examine some of these cases.

Congo (Formerly Zaire)

A number of scholars describe the response in the parks in eastern Zaire (now Democratic Republic of Congo) to the massive influx of refugees following the outbreak of Rwanda's bloody civil war in 1994.[5] Although large numbers of heavily armed refugees moved in, the damage remained remarkably limited despite the lack of an institutional presence of the central government in this remote corner of the country and in spite of the absence of well-connected and well-supplied foreigners. Determined local conservation staff, with limited but reliable resources, persuaded refugees and international aid agencies to locate refugee camps away from sensitive areas and managed to minimize poaching. This effective response had been made possible by long-term internationally funded on-site conservation partnerships in which promising nationals had been trained, equipped, and supported throughout the crisis.

Chapter 7 describes how this system was able to cope with the complete collapse of the country and the ensuing civil war. This was achieved using the same formula of well-trained, dedicated, and independent local staff; strong local contacts and support; and devoted foreign individuals who persuaded international nongovernmental organizations (NGOs) to maintain their support throughout the crisis.

Uganda

Chapter 8 chronicles the conservation status of Kibale Forest in Uganda between 1970 and 1988.[6] Uganda, independent since 1962, was one of the most prosperous and literate countries in Africa. After a military coup in 1971, followed by civil war, Idi Amin established a brutal military dictatorship until he was toppled in 1979. During this period, Uganda's economy and institutions fell apart. Wildlife was poached to extinction or severely diminished, especially in savanna parks. Forest clearing for farming was rampant. High-level corruption led to the release of parts of protected areas for logging.

The invasion by Tanzania that overthrew Amin was accompanied by a brief period of near anarchy and record poaching stopped only by strong international pressure arising from persuasive coverage by the international media. It was not until Museveni's troops overthrew the last of several equally brutal governments in 1986 that some semblance of order returned to the country, and economic recovery could begin.

During these fifteen years of instability, a Kibale Forest research team led by a few dedicated foreigners supported law enforcement logistically and financially, systematically reported violations, lobbied at all levels of government, provided research findings to the forestry department, trained students, had an extension program, and promoted ecotourism. At the team's request, local army troops sometimes accompanied the forest guards on their patrols. Consequently, Kibale suffered only minor losses, perhaps largely because most poaching of timber and wildlife was by locals. The main exception was elephant poaching by outsiders armed with AK-47s. One of the few positive impacts of those fifteen years of chaos was that foreign companies were effectively discouraged from establishing large-scale logging programs.

Rwanda

Researchers describe a very similar experience in the Nyungwe Forest of Rwanda.[7] In spite of a civil war of almost unprecedented brutality in 1994, local project staff continued with remarkably effective protection activities after all foreign and national senior project staff were evacuated. These individuals were members of a long-term conservation project that involved training of local staff and community outreach. The senior staff continued to support the local efforts as much as possible from abroad, managing to raise modest amounts of money after intergovernment funding was terminated. The project continued after the civil war ended and, as the only formal conservation effort in the country at the time, served as a model for subsequent efforts.

Sierra Leone

Having gained independence from Britain in 1961, Sierra Leone was politically stable under one-party rule by mildly authoritarian presidents, although gradually the economy stagnated and the central government weakened. Tiwai Island was established as a center for research, education, and ecotourism in 1982.[8] It is a tiny island, but it contained some of the last rain forests in the country with a mammalian fauna that was not depleted by commercial hunting. Because national institutions were increasingly ineffective and regarded with suspicion by the local people, local involvement was essential. However, official permission remained equally important. Steered by enthusiastic foreign conservationists, the area became an official sanctuary in 1987 with the blessing of both the national government and local chiefs.

The economy steadily weakened during the late 1980s, creating conditions in which insurgency thrives. War spilled over from neighboring Liberia in 1991, and civil war lasted the rest of the decade, with alternating governments and continuing foreign military involvement. Various waves of government and rebel forces terrorized, mutilated, and raped local populations, stole crops, mined diamonds, and shot monkeys in the former conservation area. Although foreign military intervention restored the civilian government in 1999, rebel activity remained. In the atmosphere of general terror and unspeakable atrocities, and because of the rapid turnover of local leadership among the various rebel factions, it was impossible to maintain conservation and the income from tourism. The area had to be abandoned, and although many people had fled the countryside, hunting soon affected wildlife.

In this case, then, little conservation action was possible due to the general level of terror (several people involved with the conservation project lost their lives, although not in attempts to protect the area). As in Rwanda, no conservation work can be done in a country where violence is rampant and all rules of civilization are suspended. Nonetheless, even here, a small group of people, supported by modest donations from outside, remains committed to restarting the conservation program as soon as conditions allow some return of stability.

Panama

After the American invasion of Panama in 1990, a brief period occurred during which there was no functioning government. During this brief period of anarchy, some 50,000 hectares were cleared in the Panama Canal Zone, all in the span of a few weeks.[9] This example is so powerful because it shows how fast the consequences of lawlessness can become evident.

Indonesia

In the Indonesian province of Aceh, relations between the Acehnese and the national government have become increasingly tense over the past twenty years, both because of increased immigration, especially from Java, and because revenues from resource extraction (oil, gas, wood) are being siphoned off to the rest of the country. Logging in Aceh's extensive forests came in the form of legal timber concessions and illegal logging, the latter organized by local entrepreneurs with the passive or active involvement of the local forestry staff and armed forces.

Since the fall of the Suharto regime, lawlessness has increased throughout the country, resulting in many violations in parks, especially illegal logging and poaching. Since park guards in this province may not carry arms, they have to rely on the police or army to make arrests. In areas with rebel activity, the armed forces no longer move around freely, which only further promotes an atmosphere of anarchy.

The mounting pressure on parks demonstrated that the locals had long since lost respect for the authorities, many of whom were heavily involved in clandestine operations and had only acknowledged their authority for fear of punishment. A frequently heard justification was that large-scale resource exploitation by outsiders had taken access away from local people and that they now had the right to take back their resources.

Thus, gradually rising since mid-1998 and reaching a crescendo during 1999, the province was swept by a pandemic of illegal logging and of forest clearing to grow profitable cash crops and woody crops, and to develop industrial-scale oil palm plantations. The legal status of the land was irrelevant. The only criterion was the availability of the desired resources in an economically attractive way, leading to serious degradation of all forests within 1–2 kilometers of roads or waterways.

At the same time, a conservation program funded by the European Union and the government of Indonesia was active in the Leuser area in Aceh (see chapter 15). It was implemented by enthusiastic Indonesians and foreigners, many of whom had a long-term involvement in the area. In addition, the presence of foreign and local researchers and their staff, spread throughout a network of research stations, had already helped to keep some of the most valuable areas intact during the initial period of anarchy. At that time, the program stepped up its involvement with local communities to help form local conservation action groups, and also increased its involvement with students, customary law groups, and local NGOs, all of whom to some extent could help to minimize the damage. Thus, even when, in later stages of the armed conflict, the presence of foreigners in the area was considered too dangerous, the activities could still continue to some extent due to the network of contacts and the financial support that was established before the pullout. Although much forest was lost or harmed considerably, these activities significantly limited the damage, at least in some of the most important places.

One of the other consequences of the insurrection was that most non-Acehnese have left the province. In particular, thousands of Javanese transmigrants fled, making it difficult for plantations to find enough workers. This development may provide opportunities for regaining recently converted land and letting forests regenerate.

Preparing for Anarchy

As shown by these examples, even short periods of political instability or anarchy can affect parks. In many cases, the instability lasts long enough that without countermeasures parks will become severely degraded. However, the cases we just reviewed show that the situation is not always hopeless.

The following analysis examines features that best prepare a park for inevitable anarchy and lists measures to implement should anarchy become a possibility. Thus, in areas where anarchy is anticipated, the conservation strategy to be followed should ensure a smooth transition to "anarchy mode" to minimize damage.

Preparation

Parks likely to remain effective in the event that a country is plunged into instability are identified by several key traits. These traits are summarized in Table 25-1.[10]

First, when the national infrastructure crumbles, park-based rather than countrywide projects will be most effective. Second, park projects should be some form of private–public partnership. Although a project may fall under the jurisdiction of a government agency, downplaying this association will make it possible to retain some local credibility in times of civil war. This independence also creates an autonomous—and therefore more flexible and responsive—organization that can react quickly to changes on the ground. Moreover, it makes the project independent of funding from government, bilateral, or multilateral aid, all of which are

Table 25-1.
Features ensuring park effectiveness during periods of political instability.

- *Projects based at specific parks rather than programs serving the country as a whole*
- *A project structure independent of the central government and not likely to lose bilateral aid in times of instability (usually implies some involvement of an international nongovernmental organization)*
- *Continuous source of international funding*
- *Long-term presence of domestic staff (and conservationists, where possible) with high morale, discipline, and integrity*
- *Long-term presence of foreign conservationists who can lobby for the project*
- *Good contacts with local people and local leadership through extension and assistance activities and quid pro quo agreements (classic ICDP)*

---

likely to be suspended at the first sign of political turmoil or human rights violations. Obviously, this means some form of funding must be found that guarantees cash flow during the instability. The most obvious source is an independent, international NGO, but internationally based and supervised trust funds are probably the most reliable guarantee for continuing cash flow.[11]

A third desirable feature is project permanence. The better established a project is, and the longer it has been around, the more credibility and moral authority it commands. In addition, a well-established project has had time to build up capable and loyal staff that can be relied upon during difficult times. This is best achieved by building a tradition of integrity and fairness, job permanence, and reward for performance, and by creating a structure that will continue to pay and provide for workers during periods of political upheaval. Often, maintaining regular payments during such times is essential for retaining staff loyalty.

A fourth feature is the motivating presence of dedicated foreigners who have established a local presence, served as role models for local conservationists, and undertaken the training. In some cases, foreigners can more easily achieve conservation objectives than governments can. Also, the institutional presence of foreign NGOs, critical for funding, is only guaranteed because of the individual commitment of these experienced people.

A fifth feature of effective projects is a good rapport with local communities and their leadership. It is important to establish an authority based on respect and trust. Such a thing is not easy to attain and requires extensive contacts and extension efforts maintained over long periods, along with conservation-linked support in the form of medical services and other activities (all done on a scale that does not attract outsiders to the villages).

The regions in which anarchy is most likely to occur are also those in which basic services such as education and health care are most likely to be deficient. Such a situation, however, in which significant local impact can be made with only modest input, is ideal for traditional integrated conservation and development projects (ICDPs), which will provide these services in exchange for conservation guarantees from local communities. In many respects, the projects resemble traditional missionary activities, and many of their techniques to maintain operations in difficult conditions may be usefully copied.

Immediate Response

Often, local park staff can remain on duty during periods of active conflict and with strong local support can, to some extent, continue to function effectively. In some cases, it is possible to generate understanding for conservation needs among the newly dominant forces. Foreign staff are frequently pulled out, but even so must continue to support conservation efforts from outside by providing financial and moral support. They can also attain results at the international level in a variety of ways through political pressure and publicity campaigns. Even if conservation on the ground is no longer possible, the other avenues of support (regional, international) remain open.

Aftermath

Terrible as conditions are during political instability, they can present important opportunities for conservation. Sometimes, the opportunity is entirely passive: the situation may become so bad that all exploitation stops because investors pull out or transportation to markets is no longer possible. Such a reprieve from exploitative pressures may benefit wildlife, as was seen in parts of Africa and Central America.[12] Likewise, many people may leave the stricken areas, leading to reduced pressures on wildlife and land.

For instance, if a conservation project is one of the few operative institutions in an area during times of political chaos, it has an advantage when the situation returns to normal. A project that has weathered the turmoil is usually well positioned to influence conservation policy for the better after the fighting ends, perhaps leading to improved protection or enhanced park sizes or numbers.

Another possible benefit is the opportunity to buy up land or lobby for official changes of land status when companies have closed and human populations have permanently moved away. When armed conflicts lead to strips of disputed land or demilitarized zones without human populations, the international community could propose to turn these areas into wildlife reserves (ensuring proper compensation of the original owners). These reserves could have a positive impact on relations as well.

Finally, if in some future conflict, the international community sends in peacekeepers, the foreign conservationists can lobby to ensure that the international community recognizes conservation as one of the priorities of the mission.

Discussion

Situations such as those described in the examples above are bound to continue to characterize several countries that are currently in crisis, notably parts of central Africa.[13] They are also likely to become increasingly more common in other parts of the world. Resource shortages due to high population densities and overuse will arise with increased frequency. Similarly, the impact of global climate change is beginning to be felt. These two developments combine to make "natural" disasters more frequent and more severe. Hence, the insights gained in the cases reviewed above (see Table 25-1) may be useful for conservation planning in the developing world.

As stressed in Table 25-1, one of the more important features of potentially anarchy-proof conservation models is a site-based approach involving international, national, and local players. Another rationale for this approach is that in the countries predictably subject to instability, the national infrastructure and institutions are so weak that conservation can only be effectively implemented through strong local involvement. As we noted above, such conditions are ideally suited for a classic ICDP.

Inevitably, however, despite all good efforts, some conservation projects will collapse during political instability. In single ecoregions, parks should wherever possible be supported by multiple countries to offset the potential loss of a single country's conservation efforts.[14] This "duplication approach" is likely to be more successful than the "triage approach," which is to save what is possible but abandon a country expected to slide into anarchy. The reason is that political developments are hard to predict on time scales of more than a decade or so—the time scale relevant for long-term conservation efforts.

This chapter focused on anarchy, but other forms of political change are conceivable and they may require different action to achieve effective conservation. Where two countries are at war, or where there is a large-scale uprising against foreign occupation, clearly identifiable central authorities remain or arise, and the measures needed to ensure continued conservation are justifiably different.

We should always approach general recipes with circumspection, including the one presented here, and always test whether the main premises hold in a particular case. In countries where the central government is likely to lose its grip, park projects should be designed to remain operational and effective when anarchy rules. The reverse is also true, however. The best project design for periods of anarchy may be ineffective under a stable central government. For instance, wholesale privatization of parks, while effective during times of anarchy, may not be the best strategy when a country is politically stable. Thus, some formal links with public bodies should probably be maintained whenever possible.

Acknowledgments

I acknowledge the valuable input of the participants at the White Oak conference, in particular Gernod Brodnig, Terese Hart, Jeff Langholz, John Oates, Carl and Rosie Ruf, Barry Spergel, and Tom Struhsaker. I thank Terese Hart, Lisa Davenport, and Paul Steinberg for insightful reviews of a draft. My own experience in Aceh was made possible by consistent support of the Wildlife Conservation Society. I also thank the staff of the Leuser Management Unit, especially Mike Griffiths and Yarrow Robertson, for many fruitful discussions.

Notes

1. M. E. Soulé, "Conservation Tactics for a Constant Crisis," *Science* 253 (1991): 744–750.

2. J. F. Oates, *Myth and Reality in the Rain Forest: How Conservation Strategies Are Failing in West Africa* (Berkeley: University of California Press, 1999).

3. See, for example, J. A. Hart and J. S. Hall, "Status of Eastern Zaire's Forest Parks and Reserves," *Conservation Biology* 10 (1996): 316–327.

4. See, for example, Hart and Hall, "Status"; Oates, *Myth and Reality*.

5. T. B. Hart, J. A. Hart, and J. S. Hall, "Conservation in the Declining Nation State: A View from Eastern Zaire," *Conservation Biology* 10 (1996): 685–686; Hart and Hall, "Status."

6. T. T. Struhsaker, *Ecology of an African Rain Forest: Logging in Kibale and the Conflict between Conservation and Exploitation* (Gainesville: University Press of Florida, 1997), and personal communication.

7. C. Fimbel and R. Fimbel, "Conservation and Civil Strife: Two Perspectives from Central Africa," *Conservation Biology* 11 (1997): 308–314.

8. The following account is distilled from Oates, *Myth and Reality*, and personal communications.

9. J. Terborgh, *Requiem for Nature* (Washington, D.C.: Island Press, 1999).

10. See also Hart et al., "Declining Nation State."

11. Confer Hart et al., "Declining Nation State;" confer chapter 26.

12. See, for example, Oates, *Myth and Reality*.

13. Hart et al., "Declining Nation State."

14. Confer Soulé, "Conservation Tactics."

26

Financing Protected Areas

Almost universally, parks in tropical developing countries are severely underfunded, with considerable detriment to their biodiversity a predictable result. Average budgets for protected areas in developing countries are
only around 30 percent of the minimum amount required for conserving
those areas.[1] In some regions that are exceptionally rich in biodiversity,
such as Central Africa and Indochina, budgets are less than 3 percent of
the global average per hectare.[2] In many developing countries, budgets for
managing protected areas have actually declined by more than 50 percent
over the past decade due to financial and political crises.[3] International
donor assistance for biodiversity conservation in developing countries
reached a peak at the 1992 Rio de Janeiro Earth Summit and has been declining ever since.[4] Many officially gazetted parks in developing countries
have become "paper parks" that lack the funds to pay for staff salaries,
uniforms, equipment, or vehicle fuel.

How can funding be increased for protected areas in developing countries? This chapter examines a range of potential options (or financing
tools) to increase the funding for protected areas in developing countries.
There are three basic ways to finance protected areas: (1) annual allocations from a government's budget; (2) user fees and environmental taxes
that are earmarked for parks and nature conservation; and (3) grants and
donations from individuals, corporations, foundations, nongovernmental
organizations (NGOs) and international donor agencies. This includes
the use of financial mechanisms such as "debt-for-nature swaps" and conservation trust funds, which can be used to stretch grants over a longer
period of time or multiply the local currency value of hard-currency
grants from donors.

Developing countries should try to tap all three of these sources for funding protected areas, since it is unlikely that any single one of them alone will suffice. Although it is not possible in this chapter to prescribe solutions appropriate for all parks, the goal is to describe in considerable detail a number of potential financing tools for consideration.

Annual Governmental Allocations

Most governments in developing countries give higher priority to funding economic development and social programs than parks and wildlife conservation. But governments may be persuaded to increase their budget allocations for protected areas if it can be demonstrated that protected areas provide substantial economic benefits. In Kenya, for example, nature-based tourism has become the country's second-largest source of foreign exchange earnings. In Ecuador, the Galapagos Islands National Park annually attracts around eighty thousand foreign tourists, each of whom must pay a US$100 park entry fee, thereby generating more than $8 million per year. Associated expenditures by these tourists contribute more than $100 million annually to the country's economy.

Wildlife and nature-based tourism can become an important engine of economic growth and job creation in many developing countries. But this will only happen if governments allocate enough money to conserve wildlife, adequately maintain roads and other tourism infrastructure, and effectively enforce laws against illegal logging, hunting, fishing and agricultural settlement inside of protected areas.

In addition to tourism, protected areas can also provide economically valuable ecological services for which the government might otherwise have to allocate money. These include protecting watersheds (to ensure the supply of drinking water and hydroelectric power); protecting spawning grounds for fish that can later be commercially harvested; conserving plants and genetic resources that may become the basis for valuable new medicines; and conserving forests that can sequester and store carbon emissions from industrial countries (an ecological service for which developing countries may become eligible to receive financial compensation, under the Climate Change Convention).

However, even these reasons may not be enough to persuade a government to increase spending on protected areas if the government is unable (or unwilling) to make decisions based on a relatively long-term view of economic costs and benefits.

User Fees and Taxes Earmarked for Conservation

Many countries collect fees and taxes from people who "use" protected areas. This includes fees for entry, fishing, hunting, diving, climbing, hiking, boating, camping, photography, scientific research, and "bioprospecting." These fees also include concessions and taxes paid by businesses operating in protected areas, such as visitor lodges, stores, and tour operators. In many cases, however, only a small part of such revenues is used to support protected areas and biodiversity conservation. More commonly, the revenue from these fees and taxes simply flows into the government treasury and then is allocated for other budgetary purposes. A second problem is that these fees and taxes are often set much lower than what many people would be willing to pay. International visitors who have spent thousands of dollars on air transportation and lodging are unlikely to change their travel plans because of higher park entry fees or hotel taxes that are earmarked for conservation. Surveys have shown that most park visitors are willing to pay significantly higher fees and taxes if this money is used solely for conserving the parks.

Park Entry Fees

Some of the ways of increasing revenues from protected area fees and taxes are by collecting higher entry fees for foreigners than for local citizens, higher entry fees during peak visitation periods, and separate fees for newly developed attractions inside of protected areas, such as illuminated underground caves, rainforest canopy walkways, or guided nature walks. Parks may also collect permit fees for particular kinds of recreational activities inside of a protected area, such as scuba diving, mountain climbing, or river rafting; higher concession fees and taxes from businesses operating inside a protected area, such as visitor lodges, stores, restaurants, and tour companies; or by auctioning off these concessions to the highest bidder (provided that detailed environmental standards are established for operating such concessions and stiff penalties are imposed for failure to meet the standards).[5]

International tourists may be willing to pay high entry fees to visit protected areas that have highly unique ecosystems, like the Galapagos, or that have large numbers of "charismatic mega-fauna," such as gorillas, lions, and elephants. To give one example, after Botswana raised its park entry fees for foreigners by 900 percent (from US$3 to around US$30 per person per day) in 1989, the number of foreign visitors actually rose 49 percent. This led to such a dramatic increase in total revenues that "it effectively eliminated the subsidy being provided by the central government to game reserves and national parks."[6] The increase in park entry fees was part of a deliberate government policy of promoting high-cost luxury tourism. It led to a decrease in the number of low- and medium-budget visitors to Botswana's parks (mostly from South Africa) but a large increase in the number of higher-spending visitors from Europe and the United States. Surveys conducted three years after the fee increases in Botswana showed that most visitors not only approved of the new fees but were also willing to make additional donations to a wildlife conservation fund.[7]

Higher park fees have their limitations, however. First, tourists may not be willing to pay such high entry fees to visit protected areas that are less unique or that do not have large numbers of easily observable "charismatic" wildlife. Visitor surveys should be conducted in each protected area to determine the maximum "willingness to pay" of different categories of visitors, and then fees should be raised to approach those levels. Second, visitor numbers are only likely to increase when revenues from entry fees are "earmarked" to support protected areas and biodiversity conservation. For example, the law raising the entry fee at the Galapagos National Park to $100 per person for foreigners specifies in detail how the revenues are to be allocated to various conservation goals.

Another less specific approach for earmarking park entry fees and user fees is to declare that individual protected areas may keep (and decide how to allocate) some fixed percentage of the entry fees that they collect from visitors, with the balance of the revenues remitted to the national park system's head office or to the national treasury. Nepal recently adopted this approach, and in 1997 the U.S. National Park Service instituted a similar system in four of its most famous parks—Yellowstone, Grand Teton, Yosemite, and Grand Canyon. Vehicle entry fees for these four parks were raised from $10 to $20, and each park is now allowed to keep 80 percent of the total fees that it collects. A recent survey revealed that 85 percent of the visitors to these parks were "satisfied" with the higher entry fees, or thought that the fees should be raised even higher.[8]

Tourist Fees and Taxes

In 1996, the country of Belize enacted a law requiring all foreign tourists to pay a US$3.75 "conservation fee" in addition to the regular $11.25 airport departure tax. When tourists pay the conservation fee at the airport, they are given a separate receipt and an explanatory brochure. Revenues from the conservation fee are deposited directly into a new Protected Areas Conservation Trust (PACT) that is independent of government. The PACT's board of directors is composed of three voting members from Belize government ministries and four voting members from outside of government. The PACT is legally required to spend all of its funds on conservation projects in (or adjacent to) the country's protected areas. The number of foreign visitors to Belize has increased each year since the conservation fee was first imposed. A number of other countries are now considering proposals to collect fees at the airport for parks and conservation.

Several other ways to raise money for parks exist. Examples of recently instituted fees in developed countries are road tolls for scenic drives and cruise ship waste disposal fees (to finance environmental cleanup and marine conservation). On various islands, scuba divers are charged a diving fee to pay for coral reef conservation. Surcharges on hotel room taxes have been used in various places around the world as a way of raising funds for conservation. The U.S. federal government imposes an 11 percent excise tax on all sales of hunting weapons and ammunition, which generates more than $300 million each year for conservation of wildlife. A 10 percent federal excise tax on motor boat fuel and sports fishing equipment is used to fund the U.S. Aquatic Resources Trust Fund.

Fees and Taxes on Resource Extraction

Using natural resource rent for conservation has a powerful logic: compensating for the extraction of one type of natural resource by conserving another.[9] The best example of this is the U.S. Land and Water Conservation Fund, which is financed by fees paid by oil companies to the U.S. government for offshore oil and gas leases. Since 1964, the fund has provided almost $9 billion for the purchase of more than 3.4 million acres of land for national parks and reserves, and financed thirty-seven thousand grants to state and local governments for nature conservation.[10] The state of Michigan has a similar program, based on a 1984 constitutional amendment. Over the years, the trust fund has provided over $300 million in funding.[11]

A recent study[12] has argued that mining and oil companies operating in developing countries should formally agree (in their own economic self-interest) to contribute a fixed percentage of their revenues for conservation to mitigate the company's risk of being expropriated or nationalized. This is because one of the most common reasons for expropriation is the public perception (whether justified or not) that multinational oil and mining companies are making "excessive" profits while not caring about the country's environment.

Some countries, such as Norway and the Philippines, require that a percentage of the money paid to the government as timber royalties or logging concession fees must be allocated for the conservation of protected areas (rather than merely for reforestation of logged-over areas). Other countries, such as Namibia, collect a natural resource levy on commercial fishing vessels based on the number of tons of particular species of fish that they catch and then use this to finance scientific research on the management of commercial fishing stocks. However, there is no reason why the revenues from a fish catch levy (or the revenues received from auctioning off fishing quotas) could not also be used to finance the conservation of marine biodiversity and marine protected areas. A particularly compelling argument could be made in cases where protected areas serve as the spawning grounds for fish that are later harvested commercially.

Watershed Protection Fees

Colombia's 1993 Environment Law requires hydroelectric plants to transfer 3 percent of their revenues to regional governments (and an additional 3 percent to municipal governments) to carry out watershed conservation projects and urban sanitation projects. The law also requires any entity that invests in water projects to use 1 percent of the amount invested to pay for watershed protection. Provincial and municipal governments are required to spend 1 percent of their budgets to purchase lands that protect municipal water sources. In Quito, Ecuador, water consumers pay a small surcharge on their monthly water bills to finance the cost of maintaining the forest cover of the watershed that supplies the city with drinking water.

In Laos, the developers of the proposed $1.3 billion Nam Theun hydroelectric dam have agreed to pay $1 million per year for thirty years into a "watershed conservation fund" to protect the pristine forests and endangered wildlife on the steep mountain slopes above the dam. Conserving the forests is also a way of preventing the dam from silting up, thereby extending the dam's economic life by more than 50 percent.

Carbon Emissions Trading

The Climate Change Convention (the Kyoto Protocol) obligates developed countries to reduce their carbon emissions by significant percentages. Forests can serve to store or sequester such emissions. The parties to the Climate Change Convention may soon decide to approve rules that will allow developed countries to achieve part of their required reductions in carbon emissions by paying developing countries to conserve (or to plant) forests. This type of "carbon emissions trading" is technically referred to as the "Clean Development Mechanism." It can be viewed as the payment of a "user fee" for one of the vital "ecological services" provided by forests. Carbon emissions trading could result in the payment of many millions of dollars to developing countries that conserve large areas of forests. However, there is also a risk that the Clean Development Mechanism could be used to finance the establishment of new forest plantations composed of fast-growing nonnative species such as pine and eucalyptus, rather than to conserve existing natural forests.

Property and Gasoline Taxes

More than forty states in the United States impose some kind of surcharge on property taxes in order to generate revenue for acquiring privately owned land and turning it into parks and permanent "open spaces." In France, local governments are authorized to impose a surcharge on real estate transfer taxes in order to acquire privately owned land or development rights in specially designated "scenic areas" that would otherwise be threatened by excessive development. Many of these areas have also been classified as biosphere reserves or some other category of protected areas.

New Jersey has proposed increasing its state gasoline tax by seven cents per gallon and earmarking this revenue to acquire additional private land as parks and open spaces. Costa Rica imposes a "carbon tax" on gasoline and other fossil fuels to finance an environmental fund called "FONAF-IFO." This fund makes payments to small landowners who are willing to sign contracts not to cut the trees on their land for a five-year period. After that, they can receive a second payment for extending the contract for an additional five years.

Other Forms of Revenue

In Oregon, 15 percent of the proceeds from the state lottery go to fund the "Oregon Plan for Salmon and Watersheds." In Colorado, state lottery revenues have raised more than $60 million for the "Great Outdoors Colorado" fund, the object of which is to acquire and manage "conservation lands" ranging from state parks to historic sites to wetlands. And in 1967, voters in the city of Boulder approved an additional one-cent sales tax, 40 percent of which is earmarked for acquisition of undeveloped "natural lands." This percentage was later increased to 73 percent because of strong popular support. Part of the revenue from national lotteries in the Netherlands and Britain is used to fund nature reserves and conservation projects.

Ten years ago, California voters approved Proposition 117 authorizing the state to issue $900 million in new bonds to purchase habitat for the conservation of mountain lions and other endangered native species. The repayment of these bonds is financed by fees for personalized automobile license plates and by a tobacco tax increase. In March 2000, California voters approved an additional $2 billion state bond issue to finance state parks.

Many U.S. states raise money for parks and conservation by selling special automobile license plates that display pictures of native wildlife and cost $10 to $20 more than regular license plates. This can generate millions of dollars for parks and wildlife conservation. Germany and other European countries have issued special wildlife conservation postage stamps that cost more than regular postage stamps in order to raise money for biodiversity conservation projects in developing countries.

Hunting Fees

There are various examples of conservation programs financed by trophy hunting fees or sport fishing fees. Most of these are not in parks and are therefore not relevant to this chapter. However, hunting fees have been used to finance conservation on privately owned nature reserves in the United States, South Africa, and other countries. For example, the state of New Mexico allocates a certain number of elk-hunting permits each year to local landowners based on estimates of the elk population and the land's carrying capacity. The landowners are free to sell these permits to hunters, charging thousands of dollars per animal. Landowners may now find it more profitable to let their land remain in (or revert to) its natural state, with an abundance of elk and other wildlife, rather than using the land for cattle ranching.

Hunting fees on private land can only be effective conservation tools if they satisfy three conditions. They must involve (1) nonendangered species of wildlife, (2) for which there are scientifically based (and strictly enforced) limits on the annual allowable catch, and (3) for which hunters or fishermen are willing to pay substantial amounts of money.

Fines

In some countries, part or all of the fines for illegal logging, hunting, and fishing inside of protected areas are used to help pay the budgets of the government conservation agencies responsible for managing those areas. In other countries, proceeds from the sale of confiscated, illegally harvested timber, fish, and wildlife are also used for this purpose. However, this practice must be specifically authorized by law, since fines and money from the sale of confiscated illegal merchandise usually must be paid directly into the government treasury and cannot be earmarked for any other purposes.

Another way of raising money for protected areas and biodiversity conservation is by earmarking a percentage of the money from pollution fines and "pollution charges" (i.e., payments for permission to emit specified amounts of particular pollutants). Many eastern European countries have established national environmental funds that are financed by the collection of tens or hundreds of millions of dollars in pollution fines and pollution charges each year. In some cases, such as Poland, a fixed percentage (around 5 percent) of the amount collected may be allocated for nature conservation.

In the United States, judges have sometimes approved out-of-court settlements that obligate industrial polluters, in lieu of paying a fine, to establish a multimillion-dollar trust fund for the long-term conservation of the river or lake that they have polluted. Polluting companies have paid millions of dollars to establish nature conservation trust funds for New York's Hudson River, Virginia's James River, and rivers in Nebraska and Massachusetts. This was done pursuant to judicially approved out-of-court settlements of lawsuits brought against those companies by conservation organizations and government environmental agencies. Part of Exxon Corporation's multibillion-dollar payment in settlement of damage claims arising out of the huge oil spill caused by its ship *Valdez* was used to buy pristine forests on nearby Kodiak Island and to convert the land into a wildlife preserve for the endangered Kodiak Bear. The land was owned by native Alaskan tribal corporations that would otherwise have sold the land to logging companies as their only way of earning money.

Funds from Privatization of State-Owned Enterprises

In Perú, part of the proceeds from the privatization of a formerly government-owned mine was used to fund the conservation of a nearby nature reserve. In Ecuador, the government used $1 million raised from the privatization of state-owned companies to endow a new environmental conservation fund. This approach to funding parks and conservation could be adopted by other countries engaged in privatizing state-owned companies.

Caveat on User Fees

Notwithstanding the large revenue-generating potential of earmarked user fees, taxes, and fines, they should not be relied upon to cover the core costs of managing protected areas. Since many user fees depend on tourism, they can suddenly and dramatically decline as a result of domestic or international political or economic crises, such as the Gulf War, or civil turmoil in a neighboring country, or even as a result of increasing street crime. The revenues generated from user fees and taxes on natural resource extraction (such as logging or mining) can also fluctuate dramatically as economic conditions change, or as the resource itself becomes depleted. User fees and earmarked environmental taxes should therefore be regarded as a supplement to regular government budget allocations and international donor funding rather than a replacement for those two funding sources.

International Donor Contributions

The third main source of financing for protected areas and biodiversity conservation is grants and donations from individuals, corporations, foundations, NGOs and international donor agencies. In most developing countries, contributions from private individuals and corporations constitute a relatively insignificant source of funding for parks and conservation. This is probably because these countries often provide little or no tax incentives for individuals and corporations to make charitable donations, and also because many countries lack a cultural tradition of "cause-related" charitable giving other than to religious or social welfare institutions.

By contrast, some of the large foundations established by wealthy individuals in the United States contribute many millions of dollars each year to support parks and conservation projects in developing countries. International NGOs such as WWF, The Nature Conservancy, and Conservation International, which are financed by donations from their millions of individual members, also contribute tens or even hundreds of millions of dollars each year to support protected areas and conservation projects in developing countries.

However, by far the largest source of international funding for parks and conservation in developing countries is international donor agencies such as the World Bank and the Global Environment Facility (GEF), the U.S. Agency for International Development (USAID), the German Technical Cooperation Agency (GTZ), the Dutch International Cooperation Agency (DGIS), the European Union (EU), the Danish and Norwegian government aid agencies (DANIDA and NORAD), the UK's Department for International Development (DFID), the Canadian International Development Agency (CIDA), and the United Nations Development Programme (UNDP). Each of these donor agencies has particular policies and priorities (including priority countries) that may often change.

Conservation Trust Funds

International donor agencies generally provide funding for short-term projects of two to five years. But unless funding is sustained over a long period, conservation impacts are likely to be only transitory. A steady source of long-term funding facilitates long-range planning, training, recruitment of personnel, and institution building, all of which contribute to more effective biodiversity conservation.

Conservation trust funds are an increasingly common way of providing long-term funding for parks and conservation in developing countries. Conservation trust funds have been established in more than forty countries, and many others are now in some stage of development. Conservation trust funds have been set up to finance a single protected area; a country's entire protected area system; a trans-border park; a particular wildlife species; or a wide range of small environmental projects executed by local communities and NGOs.

A trust fund can be broadly defined as money or other property that (1) can only be used for a particular purpose; (2) must be kept separate from other sources of money, such as a government agency's regular budget; and (3) is managed by an independent board. Trust funds can take a variety of different legal forms and may vary from country to country. In countries whose legal systems are based on English or American models, conservation funds are often set up under statutes codifying "common law" trusts. In civil law countries (which includes all of the French- and Spanish-speaking countries), similar results can often be achieved by setting up a "foundation" or "fideicomiso." In some countries, conservation trust funds have been established by a special act of the national legislature (as in Belize) or the head of state (as in Bhutan).

There are three main types of conservation trust funds, viewed from a financial perspective:

1. *Endowment funds* are the most common type and are intended to last in perpetuity. An endowment fund spends only the income that it earns by investing the capital originally contributed by donors. The capital is usually invested in some combination of bank deposits, government treasury bonds, and corporate stocks and bonds, so as to earn a steady stream of income (usually around 5 to 10 percent annually) over a long term, while minimizing risk. Most endowment funds also try to increase the size of their capital by seeking new donations, and often reinvest a small percentage of their income in order to offset for inflation and maintain the same "real" value of the trust fund's capital. The conservation funds with largest endowments (in the first half of the year 2000) are those in Mexico ($45 million), Bhutan ($35 million), the Philippines ($30 million), Indonesia ($25 million), Colombia ($30 million), Panama ($25 million), Brazil ($15 million), Madagascar ($12 million), Perú ($10 million), and Uganda ($7 million).

2. *Sinking funds* not only spend the income which they earn each year from investing their capital, but they also spend part of their capital each year until it gradually "sinks" to zero over a predefined period of time (usually ten to twenty years). Then the fund either goes out of existence or is replenished from other sources.

3. *Revolving funds* continually receive new revenues, most commonly from user fees, fines, or specially earmarked taxes. Revolving funds spend most of their revenues relatively quickly rather than investing them in order to generate a long-term stream of income. Belize's Protected Areas Conservation Trust is a good example of a revolving fund, since it receives a continual stream of revenues from the "conservation fee" paid by all foreign tourists.

A trust fund's basic legal document (which depending on the country may be called its charter, bylaws, or articles of incorporation) should clearly set forth the trust fund's goals and objectives in order to define and to limit the types of projects for which the board can make grants. The trust fund's goals and objectives should be based on consultations with many different "stakeholders" *before* the trust fund is legally established. If the trust fund's goals and objectives are too general, then the board may be flooded by grant proposals and end up making ad hoc grants for numerous unrelated projects and activities. In order to prevent this from happening, a conservation fund's charter or bylaws should also specify what kinds of projects and activities will *not* be eligible for grants.

Some trust funds have very specific rules for how their funds are allocated. For example, the articles of incorporation of The Mgahinga and Bwindi Impenetrable Forest Conservation Trust (which was established to fund two national parks in Uganda that are home to some of the last remaining mountain gorillas) require that 60 percent of its annual budget must be used for grants to local communities to implement projects integrating conservation and development; 20 percent to fund the two parks' operating expenses; and 20 percent to fund scientific research and wildlife monitoring.

Donors to a trust fund may sometimes try to "earmark" their contributions for very specific conservation projects and activities. This should be avoided to whatever extent possible, because it may require complex and burdensome accounting procedures to keep track of contributions from different donors.

Conservation trust funds can provide the following important benefits:

• *Long-term sustained funding.* This is the single most important benefit of conservation trust funds. However, conservation trust funds should not be used simply to replace existing government funding for protected areas and conservation agencies. Donors often rightly insist that their contributions only be used to pay for conservation activities that are *in addition* to those currently being financed by the government. Otherwise, setting up a trust fund is a zero sum game. International donor agencies also frequently require national governments to make some form of matching contribution, either in cash or in kind, to demonstrate the government's commitment to achieving the trust fund's objectives and to create a greater sense of local "ownership" of the trust fund.

• *Small-grant-making capacity.* International donor agencies generally prefer to make a few large grants rather many small ($5,000 to $50,000) grants, because the cost of administering a small grant is often the same as administering a large grant. However, many conservation objectives can be more successfully achieved through a large number of small grants (ranging from $5,000 to $50,000). Conservation trust funds can be a way of resolving this dilemma by splitting up a large international donor grant into many small local grants.

• *Improving absorptive capacity.* Trust funds enable large donor contributions to be spread out over an extended period, which makes it easier for a government conservation agency or an NGO to effectively spend (i.e., "absorb") a single large grant. For example, the Bhutan Trust Fund focused spending in its early years on staff training and institutional restructuring and thereby built up its capacity to successfully execute larger numbers of field projects in later years. Such a strategy is often far more effective in achieving conservation goals than requiring that a large grant be spent in a short period.

• *Financing recurrent costs.* A trust fund can be used to help pay recurrent costs for which it may otherwise be very difficult to obtain grants from donors. Such costs include salaries, equipment, vehicle maintenance, fuel, and administration.

• *A catalyst for policy reforms.* The establishment of conservation funds can lead to environmental policy reforms, restructuring of government conservation agencies, expanded activities to protect the environment, and increased cooperation between government conservation agencies and local NGOs, especially in cases where the trust fund is used to pay part of the costs of such initiatives.

• *Strengthening the role of civil society.* Conservation trust funds can provide an institutional framework for representatives of civil society and government to work together as equal partners. In contrast to the "command and control" approach of many government agencies, conservation trust funds are run by an independent board that makes decisions by a vote of a majority of the members. The board members usually include representatives from nongovernmental conservation organizations, the private business sector, academic and scientific institutions, as well as government agencies. Some international donor agencies, such as USAID, even have an explicit policy of not contributing to conservation funds that are "government-controlled," and require that at least 50 percent of a fund's board of directors must come from outside of government. Another way that conservation trust funds strengthen civil society is by making grants directly to NGOs and local communities to carry out conservation activities.

• *Decentralization.* In order to further increase local participation and decentralize decision making, some conservation trust funds have established regional councils or boards whose function is to review all grant proposals from a particular region of a country and then make recommendations to the national-level board of directors. The environ-

mental foundations in the Philippines and Colombia have both established such regional councils or boards. The Mgahinga and Bwindi Impenetrable Forest Conservation Trust in Uganda has achieved a high
degree of grassroots participation through "local steering committees"
composed of locally based park staff and people living near the national
parks. These local steering committees have independent authority to
make small grants for community-based conservation activities that fit
within certain categories and guidelines established by the trust fund's
board of directors.

Deciding on the composition of a trust fund's board of directors is often a very political process. Board members should be selected based on
what they can personally and actively contribute to the achievement of
the trust fund's objectives. However, it is often necessary to include representatives of a particular government ministry or donor agency in order
to gain their political or financial support for the trust fund, even if they
lack the necessary time or qualifications. Some trust funds have established complex voting rules in order to ensure checks and balances among
board members.

The most common problems that may be experienced by conservation
trust funds are a lack of a clear focus or clear criteria for making grants,
excessive political interference, high administrative expenses, and low investment returns. A lack of focus and excessive political interference are
usually indications that the fund was not designed properly in the first
place, either because important stakeholders were not involved in the
process or because the trust fund's legal documents were poorly written.
The problem of high administrative expenses may result from high start-
up costs (which donors are sometimes willing to fund through a separate
grant), or may result from the endowment being too small, so that administrative costs consume a larger proportion of the fund's relatively small
annual income. This can be avoided by waiting to set up an endowment
fund until a certain minimum amount of money is raised (in most cases,
at least US$5 million). The problem of low investment returns is often the
result of investing too much of a trust fund's endowment in safe but low-
yielding investments such as bank accounts or government bonds, rather
than in stocks, which are more volatile in the short term but yield higher
total returns in the long term.

There is no single model or set of "best practices" for an ideal conservation trust fund. Each trust fund needs to be custom designed to fit a coun-

try's political circumstances, its legal code, its human resource capacity, its environmental problems, and the requirements of the fund's donors. This can be a process lasting two or more years, involving a great number of meetings and frequent revising of documents.

Debt-for-Nature Swaps

The Latin American debt crisis of the 1980s led to the introduction of the debt-for-nature swap, a financial mechanism that has enabled developing countries to reduce external debt while generating funds for conservation activities. Debt-for-nature swaps can take three forms: (1) swaps of debt owed by developing country governments to international commercial banks; (2) swaps of debt owed by developing country governments to the governments of developed countries (usually to their bilateral agencies for international development aid, such as USAID, DGIS, or GTZ); and (3) swaps of debt owed by corporations or commercial banks in developing countries to international commercial banks ("private to private" debt swaps).

Commercial Debt-for-Nature Swaps. Most debt-for-nature swaps have been three-party swaps involving external commercial debt owed by sovereign governments ("public debt"). Typically, an international conservation organization purchases a certain amount of a developing country's foreign debt from international commercial banks at a discount from the debt's face value using money that the conservation organization has raised from private donors or from international (bilateral) aid agencies. In a few cases, rather than selling the debt, international commercial banks have been willing to simply "donate" the debt to conservation organizations. After acquiring the debt, the conservation organization then negotiates with the debtor government and agrees to cancel the debt in exchange for the government's commitment to allocate local currency (and/or other resources) for specific conservation projects or a conservation trust fund.

For example, in 1993, WWF was able to purchase US$19 million worth of Philippine government debt from the international commercial banks that originally made the loans for a purchase price of only $13 million, which was given for this purpose by USAID. In exchange for WWF's agreement to cancel the debt, the government of the Philippines agreed to allocate an amount of Philippine pesos equivalent to US$17 million (i.e., 90 percent of the debt's face value) for the purpose of establishing a conservation trust fund called the "Foundation for the Philippine Environment." USAID thereby achieved the same on-the-ground conservation impact that would have otherwise cost US$17 million.

Bilateral Debt-for-Nature Swaps. In a bilateral debt for nature swap (which is a type of bilateral debt conversion), one government agrees to cancel debt that another government owes it in exchange for the debtor government's agreement to allocate a specific (lesser) amount of local currency for conservation projects. The negotiation of bilateral debt swaps requires coordinated action among the two countries' ministries of finance, the debtor government's agency for parks and conservation, and the creditor country's foreign aid agency. It often also involves the participation of conservation organizations or other local agencies as intermediaries and/or beneficiaries.

A number of bilateral creditors have formally established debt conversion programs, such as the U.S. government's Enterprise for the Americas Initiative. The U.S. Congress voted to appropriate $90 million in order to buy back debts (from the U.S. Treasury) having a total face value of $875 million that were owed by seven Latin American and Caribbean governments. In exchange, each of the debtor countries agreed to take certain measures to liberalize their economies and to create local currency endowment funds (using the interest that these seven countries would otherwise have had to pay to the U.S. Treasury) that make grants to local conservation organizations. The local currency endowment funds in these seven countries have a total value equivalent to US$150 million.

In 1999, the U.S. government launched a similar bilateral debt conversion program called the Tropical Forest Conservation Act to finance the establishment of foundations for tropical forest conservation in any developing country (not just countries in Latin America) that has globally significant tropical forests and can also meet certain other conditions (such as having a democratically elected government and an open market economy). It was originally hoped that the U.S. Congress would appropriate hundreds of millions of dollars under this program, but thus far only $26 million has been appropriated.

Private-to-Private Debt-for-Nature Swaps and Blocked Local Currency Funds. Although almost all of the debt-for-nature swaps up to now have involved government debt (also referred to as sovereign debt), some conservation organizations are now trying to swap private debt. This involves purchasing at a discount the debt that a corporation in a developing country owes to an international commercial bank. The conservation organization will then negotiate an agreement with the debtor corporation to either (1)

swap the corporation's hard currency debt in exchange for a larger equivalent amount of local currency, which the conservation organization will
use for conservation projects, or (2) swap the hard currency debt in exchange for a specific asset of the debtor corporation, such as a piece of
land with high biodiversity value, or a government-awarded concession to
log particular forests. The conservation organization will then be able to
dedicate the land for conservation purposes.

Sometimes conservation organizations may be able to purchase at a discount or obtain as a donation the "blocked local currency funds" of a multinational corporation. Certain developing countries prohibit multinational companies from converting their local currency earnings into
hard currency or taking them out of the country. But a conservation organization may be able to use this local currency for conservation projects. This is very similar to a three-party commercial debt-for-nature
swap, except that in this case the government plays no role.

Although the preceding discussion has focused on some of the technical
complexities of the debt swap process, the ultimate success of a debt-for-
nature swap depends on the success of the conservation programs that it
finances.

Notes

1. A. James and M. Green, *A Global Review of Protected Area Budgets and Staffing* (World Conservation Monitoring Center, 1999), 17.

2. James and Green, *Global Review*, 4, 10.

3. H. T. Dublin, T. Milliken, and R. F. W. Barnes, *Four Years after the CITES Ban: Il-legal Killing of Elephants, Ivory Trade and Stockpiles* (IUCN and WWF, 1995).

4. James and Green, *Global Review*, 4.

5. On the other hand, when visitor lodges, restaurants, and other park conces-sions are operated directly by park managers rather than by the private sector, these facilities frequently end up losing money. Few park managers are capable of acting like private entrepreneurs, not only because they often lack business expe-rience and training, but also because their business decisions are often con-strained by civil service regulations and political considerations. Some parks and reserves in southern Africa are now trying to identify what kinds of services can more efficiently be performed by private contractors, such as vehicle mainte-nance, road repair, erection of fences, eradication of exotic species, and even car-rying out wildlife censuses and scientific research.

6. J. I. Barnes, "Wildlife Economics: A Study of Direct Use Values in Botswana's Wildlife Sector," (Ph.D. diss., University College, London, 1998), 106.

7. Barnes, "Wildlife Economics," 6.

8. A. Lundgren, *Monitoring Park Visitor Reactions to the National Park Service* (1997), available from http://www.nps.gov/feedemo/visitor.htm.

9. Corinne Schmidt, "Reinvesting Natural Resource Rent," paper prepared for The Nature Conservancy, Arlington, Va. (1999), 7.

10. However, it should also be noted that a substantial portion of the payments for offshore oil and gas leases has been diverted to other areas of the federal budget, such as deficit reduction. Without a constitutional amendment requiring that specified oil and mining revenues can only be used for conservation, governments may find it hard to resist temptations to use these revenues for other purposes.

11. Schmidt, "Resource Rent," 16.

12. Schmidt, "Resource Rent."

27

Internationalization of Nature Conservation

JOHN TERBORGH AND MARIO A. BOZA

Nature is under siege over much of the tropical world. Habitat, once lost, cannot be regained in a satisfactory time frame. Recovery, via the process of plant succession, can take centuries. Conservationists are faced with having to defend what is left of nature against powerful forces that stand to gain from destroying the environment. Everywhere, there will be continuing losses, even in the most prosperous and enlightened countries.

Some cause for optimism in the face of these discouraging prospects can be found in evidence that the tide of history is running in favor of reining in the excesses of the past. There is hardly a person on the streets of Washington or Stockholm who has not at least heard of "sustainable development" and who doesn't in principle think it is a good thing. Nature programs on television draw huge audiences, and membership in such organizations as The Nature Conservancy and the World Wildlife Fund (WWF) have been growing steadily for decades. In the Netherlands, one person in twenty is a member of WWF, whereas in the United States the figure is about one in two hundred, indicating ample room for further growth.

Visitation at national parks is on the rise everywhere. U.S. parks now accommodate more than 270 million visitors per year, a number equal to the entire population of the country. Tourism has become the largest industry on the planet, and ecotourism is the fastest-growing component of the tourism industry.

Another positive development is seen in the burgeoning ranks of nongovernmental organizations (NGOs) in the developing world. In 1980, Perú had one conservation-oriented NGO; by 1990, there were more than seventy, including local ones in most regional capitals. Tiny Costa Rica boasts more than three hundred. Grassroots concern about conservation and the environment has veritably exploded in Latin America, and other developing regions of the world are not far behind. All these are hopeful signs that the caring people of the world will close ranks and come to the aid of nature before it is too late.

What conservationists must do in the meantime is erect a line of defense in the form of well-designed and effectively managed parks. The defense of nature has to be a concerted international effort. Many tropical developing countries possess neither the will nor the means to manage parks effectively, but there is reason to hope that the current lack of capacity is only temporary. However, the job of rescuing nature has to be done now; it can't wait until the developing countries have fully developed, as some social scientists insist. By default, responsibility for rescuing nature must fall on the so-called "international community," consisting largely of the major industrialized nations.

To a significant degree, internationalization of nature protection is already a fact. International conservation organizations such as the World Wildlife Fund, Conservation International, Wildlife Conservation Society, and The Nature Conservancy operate in scores of countries around the world through individual staff members, field offices, or local NGO affiliates. These organizations and many smaller ones are engaged in a myriad of conservation-related activities that range from the simple financing of projects, to hands-on project management, to unabashed lobbying and politicking in national capitals. In short, international influences in conservation throughout the developing world are ubiquitous and pervasive. Indeed, it is fair to say that the admittedly bleak situation of conservation efforts in many countries would be far worse were it not for the persistent interventions of international organizations.

Nevertheless, the lamentable condition of many parks in the developing world—many of which are mere "paper parks"—makes it clear that the current level of effort on the part of both national and international organizations is not sufficient. Obviously, more funds are needed, but not all of the shortcomings of tropical parks can be attributed to insufficient funds. Huge allocations, totaling billions of dollars over two decades, have been poured into integrated conservation and development projects (ICDPs) with little lasting effect. More recently, the GEF (Global Environment Fund) of the World Bank has weighed in with billions more. But these funds are so inefficiently managed that the lion's share disappears into administration, overhead, planning workshops, consultancies, and other nonproductive expenditures. World Bank policies require that GEF funds go predominately to governments, notoriously inefficient organizations for getting things done on the ground (see chapter 23); NGOs are thrown a few table scraps.

Globally, substantial sums are being spent on "environmental protection" by the major donors (a collective term for bilateral agencies such as USAID, and multilateral agencies such as UNESCO and the World Bank). Enormous gains could be made in strengthening parks around the world if only the funds of these organizations could be directed more effectively to operations on the ground. A breakthrough could be made by relaxing bureaucratic restrictions that limit the funds that can be directed to NGOs. As explained elsewhere in this book (see chapter 24), NGOs have many advantages over governments as action organizations, and what conservation urgently needs are actions, not more reports, studies, workshops, planning conferences, and other such sterile exercises that constitute the lifeblood of bureaucratic institutions.

Another urgently needed reform in the way international support to conservation is administered involves the time scale. Nearly all donor organizations, whether NGOs like WWF, bilateral agencies like USAID, or multilateral institutions like the World Bank, organize their activities around projects. A strong instinctive aversion to entering into long-term commitments has instilled a "project mentality" in the culture of nearly all such institutions (see chapter 2). The project format is appropriate for building a bridge, constructing a dam, or even subduing an outbreak of infectious disease, but it is entirely inappropriate for conserving nature. Conserving nature requires an open-ended commitment that in principle extends forever.

Of course, there are compelling reasons why institutions are so reluctant to make long-term commitments, even to programs that are fully in line with their missions. Long-term commitments restrict their options for responding to future opportunities. Boards of trustees need to be assuaged by evidence of progress from meeting to meeting, engendering short-term thinking among executive staff. Demands of directors for accountability and indicators of performance almost preclude embarking on open-ended ventures. Campaigns to increase membership or to raise funds are fueled by a continuous drum roll of novelties, emergencies, and triumphs. And, not the least, individual staff members feel compelled to show evidence of accomplishment as the means of advancing their own careers. In short, the psychology of human institutions, whether governmental or private, runs contrary to the goal of sustaining an effort in perpetuity.

There are, however, human institutions that have survived for centuries. Among them are churches, governments, museums, and universities. Foundations constitute another type of enduring institution, although they are relative latecomers and few have been in existence for more than a century. Conservationists should be informed by such institutions and learn how to structure their organizations more appropriately for the purpose at hand. The recent establishment of conservation trust funds offers encouragement in this context (see chapter 26).

International Conservation Assistance

Now, let us imagine that there were more funds flowing into international efforts to conserve nature, or that the funds currently allocated to environmental projects by the major donors could be more effectively channeled into actions on the ground. The particular measures that would strengthen conservation around the world are discussed in more specific terms in many chapters in this book.

General Assistance

We begin by considering a set of issues that are directly amenable to international lobbying and intergovernmental assistance but are not linked to any park in particular:

- *Provide assistance to governments for the purpose of creating orderly and legally backed systems of land tenure.* Ambiguities in land tenure, including open access to state lands, ill-defined traditional rights, conflicting claims, private inholdings, divergent rights to above-ground versus below-ground resources, and the like are plaguing conservation efforts in dozens of countries.
- *Lobby for independence and professionalization of national park agencies.* Park agencies demonstrably suffer when they are buried deep in a bureaucracy, as for example when they are but one of several divisions of a forestry directorate, which, in turn, is but one of several divisions of a ministry of agriculture. Along with higher status and greater independence should come a better ability to oppose the actions of other ministries that might desire, for example, to build a road through a park, or to sign an oil production contract covering park lands.

• *Lobby for police authority for park guards.* All too often, park guards have no legal authority and can only report infractions to local police who often disdain taking action.

• *Promote the establishment of scientifically designed protected areas.* Well-designed protected areas are a rarity anywhere in the world (see chapters 10, 12, and 15). Redesigning protected area systems in accord with the precepts of conservation biology will require thinking and planning on large spatial scales—country, ecoregion, continent. The parks-as-islands approach of the past is patently inadequate to prevent extinctions.

• *Promote family planning.* A vigorous family planning component should be linked to all socioeconomic development programs such as ICDPs. Attempts to promote sustainable development while ignoring population growth constitute an oxymoron.

• *Lobby for improved environmental legislation* covering not only protected areas but also forests, frontier zones, and natural resources in general.

• *Attribute value to biodiversity* by promoting valuation of environmental services, such as potable water and the mitigation of environmental disasters.

• *Urge governments to recognize more protected areas as World Heritage Sites and/or UNESCO Biosphere Reserves.* International recognition adds cachet to a park and helps persuade administrators and legislators of its global significance.

International Standards for Parks

Even if all the innovations that are currently being applied to international conservation were implemented on a global scale, there would still be major obstacles to conserving nature in many parts of the world. Nature must be conserved in perpetuity, here defined as the foreseeable future and beyond, or conservationists might as well look for another profession. Hence, it is imperative to ask, "Where do we go from here?"

Ensuring the survival of nature in many of the more troubled and unruly parts of the globe entails extraordinary challenges (see chapters 7 and 25). Demonstrably, there are countries in which strong, resilient, and enduring conservation institutions are painfully lacking. In such countries, impediments in the way of creating strong institutions appear overwhelming: pitiful budgets, a lack of trained professionals, weak national institutions, political instability, corruption and often dictatorship at the top, and, worst of all, a high probability that civil war or a breakdown of social institutions will occur within any given decade (see chapters 5, 7, and 25). By not coming to grips with these facts of life, what we are doing, in effect, is trusting the future of nature on earth to faith and blind luck— whistling in the dark. But is this the best that can be done? We think not.

Overcoming the daunting challenges presented by nature protection in some of the poorest and least stable countries will require a mind-bending rethinking of assumptions. Let us begin by considering the matter of "rights." Numerous organizations passionately and righteously advocate "human rights" as a fundamental principle of civilization, but the underlying logic is blindly anthropocentric. Is it not equally reasonable to assert that chimpanzees, whales, and other sentient beings have a "right" to exist? What self-evident principle is it that confers "rights" on humans but excludes all other organisms? We are not aware of any such principle.

If it is conceded that other beings have a "right" to exist, what institution guarantees that right? The rights of citizens in many human societies are guaranteed by a constitution, but there is no constitution that defines the rights of species other than ourselves. Conservation in most countries is governed by laws, a less-robust mechanism than a constitution, because laws can be legislatively modified or rescinded at the whim of politicians. But our concern here is for conservation in countries where at best the rule of law is tenuous and at worst, nonexistent. What do we do when laws are ignored or violated with impunity? Do we write off nature protection as hopelessly unattainable, as some authors have asserted? Or do we put our ingenuity to the task of designing mechanisms capable of overcoming some of the obstacles? Inevitably, such mechanisms would have to be implemented by the international community.

The prospect of internationally implemented solutions immediately raises questions about sovereignty. Sovereignty is a sacred cow in a world of nation states. But examined dispassionately in the light of recent history, the concept of sovereignty is a moving target. What is the meaning of sovereignty, for example, in a country at war with itself, a country with no functioning institutions, one in which tides of refugees surge this way and that, even spilling over international borders, to avoid being massacred or mutilated by marauding bands of rebels? By sending peacekeeping troops into such situations, the international community is tacitly subscribing to a new definition of sovereignty, one that is subordinate to "human rights." Under these revisionary practices, sovereignty is reduced to a recognized set of international boundaries and the right of self-determination. But even the right of self-determination is a qualified one, for when a country plunges into civil war, the inherent "self" to which that concept refers is no longer readily definable. International peacekeeping missions have, de facto, become the accepted mechanism for redefining that self.

Every time a country signs an international agreement or treaty, there is an implicit loss of sovereignty. Treaties and international protocols now regulate transport, communications, trade, use of the sea, production of chlorofluorocarbons, and even the conduct of warfare. This growing web of formalities establishes the rules for what we term globalization. No thoughtful observer of today's world can imagine that such rules will be fewer in the future. The assertive, often belligerent, sovereignty of the nineteenth century was a self-serving construct of the European powers; it did not apply at all to the vassal states of their colonial empires. It was thus fundamentally hypocritical, a concept now clearly outmoded. What has replaced it is the concept of self-determination within recognized international boundaries. But is the current convention merely another way station in a continuing evolution of concepts of sovereignty?

We cannot see the future, but Europe may be leading the way by merging into a superstate, one in which sovereignty is diffused between fading nation states and the superstate. Even now there are heated policy debates taking place within the European Union, as Brussels begins to apply uniform environmental standards across all member states. Most of the questions at issue have little to do with nature; they concern air and water-quality standards, permissible levels of emissions, use of environmental chemicals, genetically engineered crop plants, and other such matters that fall into the realm of the Environmental Protection Agency in the United States. But is it jumping too far into the future to begin considering internationally approved environmental standards for nature protection?

The beginnings of such a system already exist in the form of internationally sanctioned World Heritage Sites and UNESCO Biosphere Reserves. What does not yet exist is any mechanism for guaranteeing the environmental integrity of such areas. The biggest stick in the compliance arsenal of the international community is disaccreditation. Intended to be coercive, the threat of disaccreditation is ultimately self-defeating in the rare instances when it is applied. Stronger, more effective mechanisms are obviously needed, as well as a system of international standards for nature preserves to complement the existing standards for other kinds of environmental protection.

We shall not attempt to describe the structure of such a set of standards here. That should be the work of a properly constituted international body. However, it will help to be clear about what we mean. Standards should be detailed and specific, not limited to vague platitudes and definitions. They should also provide targets for compliance. The IUCN (The World Conservation Union) has long employed a system for classifying protected areas, from those afforded the strictest protection (Category I) to those in which a wide range of human activities is permitted (Categories IV and above). In practice, however, the IUCN categories are paper constructs. Newly established protected areas are classified in accordance with the terms of the legislation that created them. Beyond that, there is nothing to ensure compliance, not even the threat of official downgrading, if the reality on the ground does not conform to the stated ideal.

If the creation of a set of formal standards for protected areas is not to be similarly meaningless in practice, it must be accompanied by a systematic monitoring program (see chapter 28). Monitoring and reporting by an independent agency will be essential, unless the continued biological wellbeing of World Heritage Sites and other such areas is simply to be taken for granted, a patent absurdity. The monitoring agency should issue periodic status reports, accompanied by quantitative measures of compliance and change. Management should be linked to monitoring reports via systems of incentives and disincentives designed to guide individual managers as well as the politicians above them.

Foreign Assistance or Foreign Intervention?

Standards and monitoring are much-needed ends in themselves but should be understood as essential contributions to the greater goal of better managing the world's protected areas. Ultimately, what is needed is conservation with teeth. The big question is how to achieve it. Middle-income developing countries with vigorous NGO communities can do much for themselves if provided with financial assistance. But no one can reasonably expect that either domestic conservation organizations or the governments of the world's poorest countries will be up to the job. By default, in some parts of the world the task will fall to the international community, or it will be left undone at the cost of thousands of extinctions.

Internationalization of nature protection can be instituted in myriad ways, of which we shall mention only a few, just to indicate the range of possibilities. Perhaps the most simple and obvious expedient is for hard-pressed governments to assign the management of protected areas to NGOs. This can result in dramatic improvements in the quality of management and in the morale of personnel but is likely to provoke mistrust and even hostility from the government agencies ultimately responsible for natural resources (see chapter 11). But the overriding disadvantage of NGO management is that it alienates the enforcement function, when often lack of enforcement is the crucial issue (see chapter 20). That NGOs will be empowered as independent enforcement agencies seems unlikely in the short run (but see below). However, NGOs can effectively substitute for or complement government management agencies in law-abiding countries possessing effective enforcement institutions.

A far greater challenge will be presented by countries with weak domestic institutions that are experiencing political instability or social disorder. In these worst-case scenarios, local NGOs are unlikely to be able to protect parks even if they are generously financed from abroad. Facing down rebels armed with AK-47s is not a job for the unarmed, no matter how dedicated (see chapter 7). It is a job for a defense force. Several countries in Africa have lost most of their wildlife to the ravages of warfare: Uganda, Angola, Mozambique, Liberia. Hopefully, some of these are now on the road to recovery (Uganda, Mozambique), but it will be a miracle if other countries do not collapse into chaos in the future.

What should the rest of the world do in such cases? Sit back and wait for events to take their course, or intervene on humanitarian grounds? This question is one of the great policy issues of our era, and a matter of intense debate. The debate is renewed each time a new crisis bursts upon the world stage: Cambodia, Somalia, Yugoslavia, Sierra Leone. A decade ago there was no established policy for responding to such crises. Then, and still now, the industrialized countries hold a strong aversion to intervening in places of little strategic importance.

Many hoped that the end of the Cold War would usher in an era of peace, but no one any longer harbors such illusions. Instead, it is increasingly recognized that if there is to be peace in the world, it will have to be an enforced peace. Instead of fighting wars, many armies will increasingly be called upon to impose peace, an operation unfamiliar to most generals and therefore resisted by them. Nevertheless, each new crisis provides another learning experience and another incremental expansion of the envelope of what is internationally acceptable.

Why is this foreign policy discussion relevant to conservation? It is relevant because countries that cannot impose order cannot protect their parks any more than their citizens. Civil war, even more than simple anarchy, is frequently disastrous for conservation, because warring groups sell natural resources to support their causes. The Khmer Rouge in Cambodia and rebel groups in Liberia sold timber; UNITA in Angola and RENAMO in Mozambique sold ivory; and rebels in the Democratic Republic of Congo and Sierra Leone are selling diamonds as this is written. Moreover, soldiers in the bush tend to live on wild game. In war, nothing is sacred. If wars were rare, this discussion might be superfluous, but unfortunately, wars are distressingly common, affecting about a quarter of the world's countries at any given time. As old wars are resolved, new ones spring up in an unending cycle. If wars, both civil and transnational, are simply ignored by the rest of the world, over a few decades they will seriously degrade the environments of scores of countries, with dire consequences for biodiversity. Therefore, conservationists should be in the vanguard of the movement to create a global security system charged with imposing order where national institutions have failed.

As collective international action increasingly becomes the means for resolving humanitarian emergencies, including earthquakes, floods, famines, and epidemics, as well as wars, it does not take a great leap of faith to imagine that nature protection will also increasingly be seen as a collective responsibility. It already is in a financial sense, as is abundantly documented in this book. But we need to go beyond finances and grapple with the enforcement issue, for that is the toughest challenge of all, and the sine qua non for successful implementation of protected areas.

Forms of Internationalization

If a government proves incapable of preventing gross violations of the nation's protected areas, how might the international community come to the rescue? We shall suggest three possible courses of action. These depart from current norms to degrees that range from the incremental to the dramatic.

An incremental step would be to sign an agreement that turned over responsibility for a country's protected areas to an international organization. The agreement could be for a fixed or indefinite term. The contracting organization, let us say an international NGO, would explicitly acquire enforcement powers as a key term of the agreement. For most kinds of offenses, judicial proceedings would not be an issue. The penalty could simply be confiscation of the equipment used in committing the offense (firearms, boats, chainsaws, etc.). In most situations this would be sufficient. NGOs already manage protected areas under contract in many countries; the incremental step here would be the inclusion of enforcement powers. It can be assumed that the enforcement personnel would normally be citizens of the country in question.

A further step toward internationalization would be the deployment of a corps of armed guards modeled after international peacekeepers. Let us call them *naturekeepers*. Like peacekeepers, they would be sent to a country only upon request of the government, and only as an interim measure (keeping in mind that some peacekeeping missions have lasted a decade or more). A corps of naturekeepers would be under international authority, although it might be made up largely of nationals. They would be appropriately armed to respond to any anticipated threat and would be empowered to defend themselves and the park they were charged with protecting. In the best of all worlds, young people might even be able to serve as international naturekeepers in lieu of military service in their own countries.

Finally, coercion would be the measure of last resort, to be used only in the absence of more palatable options. Coercion need not be violent and could be applied through incentives as well as disincentives, either political or economic. Uninvited international intervention might be approved on humanitarian grounds, as described above, to quell chaos or civil war. In such an event, troops could be assigned to guard protected areas, as well as the usual kinds of civil installations, such as bridges, airports, and power plants (see chapter 25).

Beyond the problem of how to wrest control of the enforcement issue, there are other mechanisms for increasing international participation in nature conservation. The world is full of young people who would jump at an opportunity to spend a year or two in the service of conservation. Precedents abound and have been quietly in existence for several decades. One well-known example is the U.S. Peace Corps, which for many years has been sending volunteers to assist in the management of understaffed protected areas in developing countries. Various European organizations also send volunteers. These programs are extremely valuable and could profitably be expanded at a relatively trifling cost. Committed young people set an example for local park guards; they bring new skills, such as computer literacy; they promote cross-cultural exchange, which increases understanding on both sides; they can serve as watchdogs; but most importantly they bring a set of values and a passion for nature that can be contagious. The world needs a Nature Corps!

The state of nature in much of the developing world is precarious but not yet hopeless. Business-as-usual for the major international conservation organizations has brought us to the "Silent Crisis," in which vast sums of money are poured into rural development projects in the name of conservation, while the parks these projects are nominally designed to serve are suffering degradation, downsizing, and even degazetting. The status quo is clearly unsatisfactory, and increasing the funds available to do more of the same is not the answer. What is urgently needed are fresh ideas and a boldness of purpose that has been extinguished in organizations that have become stultifyingly bureaucratic and for which saving nature all too often takes a back seat to donor relations. What international conservation needs today is a counterpart to start-up companies with the venture capital to encourage new ideas and test them on the ground. The authors of this book have proposed a wealth of such new ideas. What is needed now are people to carry the ball.

28

Monitoring Protected Areas

JOHN TERBORGH AND LISA DAVENPORT

One reason protected areas are so routinely neglected by governments is found in the "out-of-sight, out-of-mind" principle. So long as protected areas have weak national constituencies and are situated far from the capital city, they will fall below the horizon of officials and budget managers and will be last in line in the competition for scarce financial resources. That situation can potentially be turned around by exploiting another principle: "the squeaky wheel gets the grease." By appropriately publicizing the threats faced by parks and the management handicaps under which they operate, public opinion can be brought to bear on an otherwise invisible situation. Accurate and credible information on the current state of parks will be necessary to incite public opinion. Such information can best be generated through an organized monitoring process. The point seems obvious, yet we know of no systematic program to monitor the status of protected areas anywhere in the developing world.

Despite its name, the World Conservation Monitoring Center (WCMC) in Cambridge, UK, is not primarily a monitoring organization. WCMC performs a valuable service to the international conservation community by compiling government-sanctioned statistics on the names, locations, areas, and other basic quantifiable features of protected areas the world over. It makes the information available in publications and on the Internet. What WCMC does not do is conduct systematic on-the-ground investigations of the current condition of protected areas and the processes threatening them. The data compiled by WCMC are largely static, whereas the actual condition of parks and the forces that threaten them are moving targets that require periodic updating.

Watchdog organizations dedicated to promoting the well-being of protected areas have existed for a long time in some developed nations. In

North America, for example, the National Parks and Conservation Association (NPCA) operates within the United States, and the Canadian Parks and Wilderness Society (CPAWS) plays a counterpart role in that country. NPCA is a $20 million organization founded in 1919 that publishes a widely respected journal. Based in Washington, D.C., NPCA devotes much of its energy to lobbying the U.S. Congress on behalf of the national park system. Among the concerns that it brings to the attention of congressional committees, beyond budgetary issues, are problems of overvisitation in certain parks, threats of inappropriate development around the boundaries of others, inadequate facilities and maintenance, and policy issues, such as how to regulate snowmobiles, jet skis, and off-road vehicles in various units of the national park system.

Generally speaking, neither NPCA nor CPAWS perceives the need to finance a major investigative program to expose illegal activities within U.S. and Canadian parks. The presumption is that mechanisms already in place make such efforts unnecessary. By and large, North American parks are adequately financed and professionally administered, and their problems pale in comparison with the problems created by illegal activity in many tropical parks.

Several impediments exist to the successful implementation of park monitoring in developing countries. First, there may be ambiguities in a park's legal status. Often, the legislation that establishes protected areas is deficient as, for example, when it ignores prior or competing claims on the land. In Mexico, for example, all national parks overlie preexisting land rights, amounting to what would be considered a "taking" among conservatives in the United States. The government holds title to none of the land, yet restrictions on land use are imposed on landowners. A similar situation exists in Brazil, where much of the land within what are nominally national parks remains privately owned.

Second, the need for monitoring is not always recognized. The concept of watchdog organizations operating in the public interest is still a novel one in many developing countries, where transparency and public accountability are still new and largely untested concepts. Where there is no established tradition of grassroots activism, the idea that governments can be influenced by citizen pressure (short of mob action in the streets) is an unfamiliar one that is slow to be grasped and put into practice. Of course, in nondemocratic societies, public watchdog organizations are simply not permitted to exist.

Third, methods for systematically monitoring protected areas have yet to be perfected. Indeed, park management involves so many administrative levels that it is by no means clear how to assign priorities in a monitoring program. For example, until one has investigated a situation thoroughly, it might not be obvious whether a particular failing was attributable to flawed administrative directives issued from the central government or to a demoralized or corrupt staff on the ground. But unless the cause of a problem can be accurately identified and its source pinpointed, a plan for alleviating it cannot be devised. Effective monitoring thus requires a rather sophisticated systems-level analysis of how the entire budgetary and administrative chain operates within a given system of protected areas. Different categories of problems and threats will consequently have to be addressed at different levels of the system.

The precipitous worldwide rise of nongovernmental organizations (NGOs) makes it likely that watchdog and advocacy groups focused on parks will soon appear in many countries that currently lack them. In this chapter, we shall consider the agenda that such an organization might adopt. An effective agenda for monitoring protected areas must build upon the answers to four questions: (1) Who should do the monitoring? (2) How should monitoring be conducted? (3) What should be monitored? (4) How should the resulting information be disseminated? There is presently no formula that answers these questions, so monitoring organizations will be obliged to break new ground as they develop their programs. Here we will offer preliminary answers to questions one, three, and four. The answer to the second question, concerning how monitoring should be conducted, is too technical for this book and, in any case, will differ from one country to another, in accordance with varying levels of access to official information.

It is axiomatic that monitoring will serve a valuable purpose only if it leads to increased public awareness of parks and their problems, and to actions that diminish these problems. The goals of monitoring should thus be, first, to diagnose the status and condition of individual protected areas and, second, to arrive at recommendations for reducing threats and remedying deficiencies of management or administration.

In generating information relevant to these goals, a well-designed monitoring system should attempt to satisfy two somewhat different objectives. The first is that of standardization. Periodically updated, scientifically validated accounts of conditions pertinent to the well-being of formal protected areas should be gathered according to a uniform set of criteria so that the data can be compared between parks within a country and between park systems in different countries, as well as over time within a park. But because conditions vary so much from one country to another, the uniform application of a standard monitoring formula may not prove practical, at least initially. Few developing country organizations will possess the capacity to monitor everything listed below. Some data will always be relatively easy to obtain, whereas other kinds of data may be difficult or impossible to acquire. In some countries, for example, park budgets, staffing levels, and other such basic information is a matter of public record, whereas in others it is held by secretive ministries that do not respond to public appeals for information. As for illegal activities, large-scale violations of park boundaries are readily seen in satellite images or air photos, whereas small-scale violations, such as poaching and single-tree hijacking, are not detectable except by on-the-ground surveys and/or interviews with local residents.

The second objective is that of achieving appropriate emphasis within the socioeconomic context of the target country. NPCA, for example, does not find it useful to investigate the occurrence and extent of illegal activities, such as mining and logging, because such blatant assaults on U.S. parks are rare and can be dealt with by law enforcement at the local level. In many developing countries, however, such flagrant assaults on parks are commonplace and constitute major causes of park degradation. In these cases, the detection and documentation of illegal activity should be a principal objective of monitoring. Levels of need and urgency for any given type of information will therefore vary greatly. We do not wish to be excessively prescriptive in suggesting how individual monitoring programs should be structured or carried out. The local organizations doing the work will be in the best position to make the necessary decisions.

Having made the case for why monitoring is important, we shall continue by first addressing the three questions posed above and then presenting preliminary observations derived from a pilot project to monitor Venezuelan parks.

Who Should Conduct Monitoring?

The question of what kind of organization is best suited for carrying out monitoring activities is not a trivial one. The most crucial criteria in this context are independence and credibility. An organization that is seen to be too closely allied to the government and/or to the agency that administers parks can be suspected of favoritism or whitewashing statistics. On the other hand, an outspoken advocacy group will have axes of its own to grind. Neither may be wholly free of bias. The best solution would be a freestanding organization with a policy of rigorous objectivity and neutrality that would engender the confidence of both the government and local advocacy groups. Ideally, the information gathered should be of value to all sides.

On-site monitoring and the conducting of interviews are not expensive activities, but they are labor intensive. It should not be necessary that paid staff do all the work. Trained volunteers can be extremely useful if engaged under close supervision. Universities are excellent potential sources of volunteers. Students tend to be more aware of conservation issues than members of the general public, and during vacations they may have time available for volunteer service.

Of course, there are risks involved in publicly exposing negative or even scandalous information. Predictably, the messenger will be blamed for bad news. An embarrassed government might refuse to cooperate with the monitoring organization. In countries unaccustomed to transparency and public accountability, monitors could find themselves in physical jeopardy. However, to abandon an effort in the face of adversity is not an acceptable option. The greatest need for monitoring is often in the most closed societies, those in which official information is withheld from the public and where criticism of the government is not tolerated. One strategy for avoiding conflict with a hostile government is to post information anonymously on an internationally sponsored website. Another, which should be employed only as a last resort, is for the monitoring program, or parts of it, to go underground, but we do not recommend clandestine activities except under the most aggravated circumstances.

What to Monitor?

The following is a preliminary list of monitoring targets, grouped by theme. Some areas of concern are global (climate change), some are national (enabling legislation, budget, law enforcement), some are regional (certain threats, such as fire), and others are local (quality of management, many illegal activities). The ease of acquisition of information pertinent to the various categories will vary greatly.

Socioeconomic Setting

- Demographic pressure around boundaries
- Attitudes of local populace, both around and inside park (where appropriate)

- Local economy and dependence on extractive activities
- Presence of large-scale resource extraction operations
- Prevalent land-tenure system

Threats Posed by Legal Activities

- Presence of legal residents within boundaries
- Legally sanctioned "sustainable use" of protected-area resources
- Tourism
- Concessions
- Recreational activities
- Waste management

Threats Posed by Illegal Activities

- Poaching
- Logging
- Mining
- Livestock grazing
- Invasion of squatters
- Commercialization of natural products

"Invisible" Threats

- Deficient documents of establishment
- Lack of unencumbered title to the land
- Lack of title to below-ground resources
- Lack of political will to enforce regulations
- Lack of inter-institutional cooperation (police, courts)
- Existence of private inholdings
- Hierarchy of ministries (e.g., omnipotence of petroleum ministry)
- Pending legislation detrimental to the park (e.g., a proposal for degazetting)

Administration and Management

- Budget
- Staffing, including educational levels of personnel
- Equipping of personnel
- Enforcement capability
- Management of tourism
- Indications of corruption
- Definition and posting of boundaries

Natural Resources

- Biological indicators, flagship species, endemics, and so forth
- Species of exceptional commercial value
- Water quality

Trans-boundary Threats

- Global climate change
- Air and water pollution
- Fire
- Invasions by alien species

The above lists are not intended to be exhaustive but rather to represent the range of circumstances, constraints, and threats under which parks are obliged to function. For further information, the reader is referred to the ParksWatch website: http://www.parkswatch.org.

Dissemination of Information

Just as the acquisition of accurate information about protected areas presents challenges and questions, so does dissemination of the information once it is in hand. The first question to be answered is, What group or groups constitute the clients of the monitoring process? Should the information be targeted to the administrator of a particular park, the director of the nation's park service, the public of the country in question, the principal international donors, the world at large, or all of the above?

The question, of course, has no fixed answer, but as a first consideration there should certainly be a world clearinghouse of monitoring information. Ideally, all local organizations conducting monitoring programs should report their findings to the clearinghouse, which would then post the information on the Internet and use it in other ways, as appropriate. Information made available on the Internet is typically nonthreatening, and poses minimal risk to the individual monitor or park administrator.

On the other end of a spectrum of openness, information derived from a monitoring process could be used to spearhead publicity campaigns or even public demonstrations on behalf of a threatened park. In some political contexts, public protest is one of the few means citizens have of influencing public policy. The law provides another mechanism, but only in countries where the courts exhibit independence and impartiality. In the United States, groups such as Earthjustice Legal Defense Fund have been established to use the law as an instrument for compelling the government to live up to its legal obligations. But in many countries, governments simply do not allow themselves to be sued in the courts, so citizens must resort to other tactics to make themselves heard.

Sensitive information should be managed carefully to avoid aggravating public officials and provoking political backlash. Different individuals in the same agency can have very different perspectives on the same issue. There may be many dedicated conservationists filling the ranks of a parks agency, for example, who would welcome public exposure of threats to parks and deficiencies of management in the hope that publicity might lead to reform. However, the top administrator of the agency, likely a political appointee, will almost certainly feel threatened. Ideally, information derived from monitoring should serve the needs and interests of both the government and local advocacy groups. For that to be the case, the independence and credibility of the monitoring organization should be beyond question.

Local conservation activist groups are weak or nonexistent in a number of developing countries. Even if monitoring could be conducted in such a country, there would be no obvious client group at the national level, other than perhaps the government park agency. In general, we think that monitoring will be most productive when there are strong local organizations to publicize or otherwise make use of the information. In the absence of local organizations, international organizations, such as the World Wildlife Fund or Conservation International often fill the vacuum. Even in some nominally democratic countries, politicians may be more responsive to international pressure (and/or financial inducements) than they are to appeals from their own constituents (see chapter 23).

Increasingly, the major international conservation organizations are opening local offices staffed by local people in the countries where they operate. This policy creates channels of communication so that information developed locally can reverberate in real time within the international conservation community. Major international donors, such as the World Bank, can be brought into the picture through their own well-developed links to large conservation organizations. Eventually, the donors themselves might use monitoring information to set priorities and/or to design remedial programs.

A final goal that will be achieved only through experience is that of optimizing feedback between the monitoring process and reduction of threats to parks. If monitoring does not lead, more or less directly, to improved management, then it is hardly worth doing. But it is not obvious how to forge all the feedback links between monitoring and mitigation of the problems identified by the monitoring. Quietly sharing information with a manager without public exposure might be sufficient to bring a satisfactory response in some situations. But more often the problems that beset the parks of developing countries lie beyond an individual manager's capability and require intervention at higher levels of authority. An elementary problem of paper parks, for example, is that there is no manager. A lot of experience and additional thought will have to go into forging effective feedback loops between monitors, managers, park agencies, international organizations, and major donors. But one thing should be clear. Without the information provided by monitoring, festering problems will not rise to the attention of governments, activist groups, donors, or anyone else until they become crises or until it is too late.

An Example: Parks Monitoring in Venezuela

The ParksWatch Organization of the Duke University Center for Tropical Conservation (CTC) has embarked on a pilot project to monitor national parks in Venezuela. The project is being sponsored by CTC and is being carried out by Sociedad Conservacionista Audubon de Venezuela, a Caracas-based NGO. Limited results are available at this time because the project has been under way for less than a year and fewer than half of Venezuela's forty-three national parks have been visited. Yet, even the preliminary glimpse afforded by these initial efforts has been highly instructive, revealing that the condition and needs of different parks can vary greatly, even under the nominally uniform administration of IN-PARQUES, the government agency responsible parks.

We present thumbnail accounts of the situation of three Venezuelan national parks: Mochima, El Guacharo, and Guatopo. The three represent a diversity of settings and purposes—coastal-marine (Mochima), special biological feature (El Guacharo), and a scenic, mountainous region near the capital city (Guatopo). The authors visited these parks in March 2000 and came away with the impressions described below after interviewing INPARQUES administrators and other knowledgeable people in and around each of the three parks.

Although Venezuela has some "paper" parks in the remote and unpopulated south, the three parks we visited are all fully implemented, each having a staff consisting of twenty or more administrators, guards, and other personnel, all of whom hold career positions in the government service. All INPARQUES personnel we interviewed were courteous, well informed, and willing to discuss a wide range of issues with strangers who arrived with no formal documents or prior introduction. Each park has a modern administrative office equipped with computer and communications facilities. Enforcement and vigilance capability is represented by up to nineteen guard posts positioned around the boundaries. Two parks had visitor centers, and all were equipped with vehicles and/or boats.

Mochima National Park

Located on the Caribbean coast between two regionally prominent port cities, Barcelona and Cumana, Mochima was created in 1973 to preserve an archipelago of scenic islands. The park encompasses 94,935 hectares of estuaries, islands, and inland terrestrial habitat. Lacking endangered species or narrow endemics, the park has only minor significance as a repository of biodiversity. Several key elements of the fauna, including jaguar, tapir, and the American crocodile, are already extinct.

Mochima offers a good example of the almost insoluble dilemmas that can arise when a park is arbitrarily superimposed on a preexisting pattern of land tenancy. The region in which Mochima is located has been populated by nonindigenous settlers since the seventeenth century. Families living inside the boundaries when the park was established were told that they could continue to live in their homes and pursue their normal livelihoods but that they must respect certain restrictions (e.g., no hunting, no construction of new buildings). At that time, most coastal residents were artisanal fishermen and most interior residents were small-scale farmers. Today, many commute to jobs in one of the nearby towns.

At the outset, Mochima's administrators were confronted with a blatantly contradictory situation. The legal definition of a "national park" under Venezuela's statutes did not anticipate private property and legally established residents. Legally and financially unable to initiate a resettlement program, Mochima's administrators chose to reconcile the situation by formally designating "special use areas" to include all preexisting farms, homesteads, and villages.

In principle, no new structures were to be built inside the park, but in practice, park administrators have tended to look the other way. Municipalities adjacent to the park boundary have plans to supply public sewer and water to communities within the park. Bending to pressure, INPARQUES is developing plans to increase the number and size of formally designated "special use areas." If projected into the future, the end point of this process is painfully obvious.

There is no easy way out of this impasse. Is Mochima truly to be a national park in which nature protection enjoys the highest priority, or is it destined to become one large "special use area" in which the residents remain implacably at odds with INPARQUES?

The answer may not be that difficult. As is, the terrestrial portion of Mochima has no great biological significance and is too populated, too degraded, and too small to be a first-class national park. Given these realities, it is better to recognize Mochima for what it is: a failed park. The cost of resettling Mochima's thousands of legal (and illegal) residents would be prohibitive relative to the pursuant conservation gain. Although, on principle, we oppose degazetting any national park, in this case it seems better to face unalterable facts and downgrade the status of the terrestrial portion of the current park. The marine portion could be reclassified as a national recreation area, special coastal management zone, or something similar.

Although entailing a sobering (and one hopes, therapeutic) admission of defeat for conservation, these steps would produce major benefits: resolving a hopeless situation, eliminating "special use areas," which we view as inappropriate within a national park, and relieving most of the sources of tension that plague interactions between INPARQUES and local residents. Most importantly, reclassification of Mochima would remove a glaring example of nonconformity to legal statutes from Venezuela's generally outstanding national park system and would eliminate a situation that could be used by politicians or administrators in the future to excuse similar awkward situations in other parks.

El Guacharo National Park

El Guacharo is one of the few units of Venezuela's national park system created to preserve a biological phenomenon—a population of twenty thousand oil birds that inhabits an extraordinary cave near the northeastern city of Caripe. The oil bird is one of the world's most unusual. It resembles a large nightjar, eats nothing but fruit, especially the oily fruits of palms and laurels, and nests exclusively in caves, where it navigates in total darkness using echolocation. The oil bird was discovered and described scientifically by the renowned German explorer, Alexander von Humboldt, who discovered the cave at Caripe in 1799. Subsequently, for more than two hundred years the oil birds were exploited by local residents who harvested the chicks for their fat.

The cave was designated as the Alexander von Humboldt Natural Monument in 1975, and a larger mountainous area surrounding it became the El Guacharo National Park. The cave and its oil birds are the central attraction. Arriving tourists pass through a modern visitor center that offers a small museum with informative exhibits, a gift shop, restaurant, and lecture theatre. A campground and other facilities are available nearby. Organized groups limited to twenty are escorted through the cave by superbly informed guides. Included on the park's staff is an engaging public-use specialist who interacts with local communities.

Scientific knowledge of the extraordinary biology of the oil bird was negligible until Venezuelan Roberto Roca undertook a Ph.D. dissertation on the species in the early 1980s. One of his findings, obtained by attaching tiny radio transmitters to the birds, was that they sometimes travel enormous distances to find fruit, even as far away as the gallery forests of the Orinoco River, some 200 kilometers from Caripe. To reach such distant feeding areas, the birds are obliged to fly up to four hours one way, and return, all within the span of a single night. Research showed that birds from the cave routinely foraged over a much larger area than was provided by the existing national park, raising concerns that the birds might disappear if the surrounding forests were cleared. In response to these concerns, the government approved a major expansion of the national park, substantially increasing the protected area to 62,700 hectares.

Although popular and successful in some ways, and supported by a competent and dedicated staff of INPARQUES personnel, El Guacharo National Park is not without its share of problems. One of them is fire. Farmers living around the boundaries are accustomed to burning off the dead grass in their pastures in the dry season. Occasionally these fires escape and burn upslope into the park. In especially dry years, fires can even propagate through primary forest. Several such fires have destroyed thousands of hectares of habitat the park intended to conserve. Much of the park's remaining primary habitat remains vulnerable, yet INPARQUES lacks the capacity to implement a strong fire prevention program.

El Guacharo faces another serious problem in the delineation of its boundary. The boundary was arbitrarily set at the 900-meter contour without regard to existing land use. Farms and villages that happened to lie above that elevation were included within the park, whereas natural forests that extended to lower elevations were excluded. Fortunately, most of the human residents of the park live just within the boundary; most of the park's interior is too steep and rugged to be farmed and remains heavily forested.

The problems of El Guacharo are not insoluble, at least in principle. Fire breaks and other control measures could be installed along vulnerable sections of the boundary. And the boundaries themselves could be redrawn to exclude most human inhabitants without compromising the park's natural habitat. Of the two problems, reducing the threat of fire is probably the easier to solve because an NGO could implement a control program in collaboration with INPARQUES. Redefining the boundaries would be more difficult, because it would require approval by the legislature, a political process that could have unforeseen consequences. Nevertheless, a proposal to relocate the park's boundaries would be highly popular among the people who now find themselves living in a legal contradiction.

Guatopo National Park

Guatopo National Park is situated only an hour's drive south of Caracas and protects 122,000 hectares of the Cordillera del Interior. Guatopo is a gem of a park. It boasts a complete fauna, including the species most sensitive to area restriction and hunting (jaguar, puma, spider monkey, tapir). The habitat is evergreen forest, much of it second growth but now substantially recovered and pleasing to the eye. A scenic road bisects the park and offers panoramic vistas of forested mountains and ravines, unmarred by any signs of human activity.

Guatopo is a full-service park, offering a spectrum of visitor attractions and amenities, including a visitor center, historical site, picnic and campgrounds, trails, and recreation areas.

One of Venezuela's first protected areas, Guatopo was created in 1958. In establishing Guatopo, the government made a concerted effort "to do it right this time." The included area was occupied by rural smallholders and some larger properties (haciendas). A government-financed program was set up for the purpose of buying out and relocating the inholders, all of whom were moved, often to nearby locations in the surrounding lowlands. A number of former residents were hired as guards. Now, despite being an island in a settled landscape, Guatopo has no serious "people problems" other than the inevitable irritation of low-level poaching. It could benefit from an increased budget, as some of its facilities are a bit run down, but fundamentally Guatopo functions as a viable park, protecting nature as it serves the public.

Conclusions

One thing we learned from our first tentative steps to put ParksWatch into practice is that there were unexpected contrasts within a government-managed protected-areas system. Mochima has essentially failed as a national park; El Guacharo has promise but is burdened by serious legal and environmental problems; Guatopo is a success. In retrospect, it is obvious that many of the problems faced by both Mochima and El Guacharo are intrinsic to their designs.

Through analyzing the situation of parks for the express purpose of arriving at a diagnosis of deficiencies and threats, and a corresponding tailor-made prescription for alleviating them, it may be possible to usher in a new era of support for protected areas. A new approach is urgently needed, one that can replace the ineffective ICDP model now in fashion. Only rarely are ICDPs designed to address specific park problems such as those described for El Guacharo. What is needed now is a new generation of projects based on informed prescriptions and designed specifically to meet the goal of "Making Parks Work."

29

Breaking the Cycle: Developing Guiding Principles for Using Protected Area Conservation Strategies

NICK SALAFSKY AND RICHARD MARGOLUIS

Over the past few decades, conservation efforts in developing countries have cycled back and forth between two paradigms. In the 1960s and 1970s, conservationists in these countries tried to duplicate the protected-area model that had been developed in the United States and parts of Africa.[1] They soon found, however, that protected areas were difficult to implement in countries where boundaries were not enforceable due to inadequate government resources, weak management capacities, remote sites, and ineffective legal systems. Furthermore, many protected areas were proposed on lands or in waters legally or customarily owned and managed by local people. It became impractical, illegal, and immoral to declare these lands off-limits to use by destitute people living nearby.[2]

In response to these limitations, conservationists shifted paradigms and began working with local communities to promote economic development in conjunction with protected areas. One of the earliest models was the biosphere reserve.[3] In a biosphere reserve, people are entitled to use biological resources according to defined spatial buffer zones around a core protected zone. Over time, these biosphere reserve projects evolved into more complex integrated conservation and development projects (ICDPs) that include enclaves for local communities, corridors for wildlife, and various income-generating schemes for people.[4]

Here again, however, conservationists found that ICDP approaches were also difficult to implement.[5] Perhaps the biggest problem was that in many cases, development activities were not directly tied to conservation behavior. Local people often continued to use resources in the core re-

A Practitioner's Guide to Understanding the Debate on *Protected Areas* vs. *Community-Based Conservation*
(Warning - Understanding May Not Occur)

Text: Nick Salafsky   Artwork: Anna Balla   Concept/Design: Adapted from a cartoon by Tom Tomorrow

Figure 29-1. The debate over protected areas versus community-based conservation.

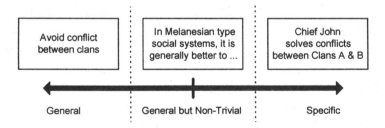

Figure 29-2. General and yet nontrivial guiding principles. Adapted from N. Salafsky and R. Margoluis, *Greater Than the Sum of Their Parts: Designing Conservation Programs to Maximize Impact and Learning* (Washington, D.C.: Biodiversity Support Program, 1999). Also available online: http://www.bcnet.org or http://www.bsponline.org.

serve even if prohibitions were posted or otherwise made public. These approaches also did not seem to provide local people with the incentives to stop external threats to the biodiversity, such as a logging company clearcutting the forest from the other side of the reserve or a foreign fishing boat unsustainably harvesting marine resources.[6] There often seems to have been no local constituency to monitor the development of these threats and take action on behalf of the biodiversity.

As a result of these and other problems, the pendulum swung back as a number of prominent conservationists began to call for a return to a strict protected-area strategy.[7] And almost immediately thereafter, a backlash began to form arguing against the protected-area strategy.[8] Although Figure 29-1 is obviously a gross oversimplification, it demonstrates how we seem to be collectively locked in an endless debate, going in circles while all around us biodiversity is lost at ever-increasing rates.

As is the case with almost any polarized debate, if there are solutions, developing them probably involves incorporating elements from both sides of the argument. To break this cycle, we need to stop looking at generalities and instead focus on developing our understanding of the specific conditions under which a protected strategy works, the conditions under which it does not work, and why. We need to use scientific processes to help practitioners determine *general and yet nontrivial guiding principles* for using a protected-area strategy, as well as all other conservation strategies.

We do not claim to have any specific answers as to what these principles might be. In this chapter, however, we would like to first discuss what these principles might look like in the abstract. We then discuss *learning portfolios* as one method that the conservation community can potentially use to find them for different conservation strategies. Finally, we conclude with a discussion of three challenges that these learning portfolios might be able to meet.

What Are General and Yet Nontrivial Guiding Principles?

The best principles are those that apply at a wide range of sites but are not so trivial that practitioners will disregard them. As shown in the right side of Figure 29-2, at any given site there are *specific* principles that are of great use to people working at that site. For example, project team members working at a site in Papua New Guinea might develop a principle such as:

P *Use Chief John to help settle conflicts that arise between different clans.*

Unfortunately, these site-specific principles do not really help a person working at the next site over, let alone at a site halfway around the world. On the far-left side of the diagram are *general* principles that apply to most or all sites as illustrated by the example:

P *Avoid conflict between clans.*

Unfortunately, these principles tend to be trivial—they are true but not very helpful to practitioners. Are there *general and yet nontrivial* guiding principles as shown in the center of the diagram? It is most likely that, if these guiding principles exist, they will take the form of conditional probability statements. For example, we might develop the principle:

P *In Melanesian type social systems, it is generally better to work with the big man to solve conflicts, unless he is corrupt.*

This principle applies to more than one place (throughout Melanesia) but not everywhere. Furthermore, it refers to a specific strategy to undertake (work with the big man to solve conflicts), outlines specific conditions under which the principle will hold (if the big man is not corrupt), and leads to specific and measurable outcomes (solving conflicts). This principle is not guaranteed to work in all instances, so the user must be smart enough to apply it to his or her own situation. Our task thus becomes determining not just what the principles are, but also under what conditions and with what probability of success each principle is likely to work.

The best principles are those that have been tested in many different situations. Until a principle has been fully tested, it is probably better to state it as an assumption:

A *In Melanesian type social systems, it is generally better to work with the big man to solve conflicts, unless he is corrupt.*

Testing Conservation Strategies Using Learning Portfolios

As shown in Figure 29-3, from an operational research perspective, conservation takes place in complex systems with many pieces that interact in a dynamic fashion. A typical project, the basic unit of conservation, involves a group of practitioners using one or more intervention strategies

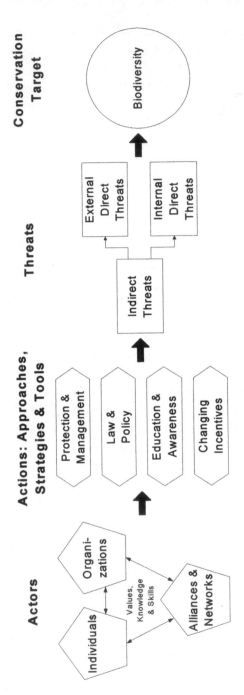

Figure 29-3. A general model of a conservation project. The *biodiversity* of the project site can be defined in terms of species, habitats, and ecosystem functions. *Threats* are the pressures that affect the biodiversity of the project site. *Internal direct threats* are caused by the stakeholders living at the project site and *external direct threats* are caused by outsiders. These proximate direct threats are in turn affected by ultimate *indirect threats*. Although not shown, the model can also include *opportunities*, which are the inverse of threats. *Actions* are the responses that the project can use to counter the threats to the biodiversity. Finally, *actors* are the *individuals and* organizations that are responsible for implementing interventions. Adapted from N. Salafsky and R. Margoluis, "Threat Reduction Assessment: A Practical and Cost-effective Approach to Evaluating Conservation and Development Projects," *Conservation Biology* 13 (1999): 830–841.

to counter threats to biodiversity at a defined site.[9] There are basically four more or less mutually exclusive types of actions that can be undertaken to promote conservation. Each of these four types of intervention contains a number of specific strategies. For example, the Protection and Management category includes various forms of protected area strategies as well as ex situ conservation strategies. The Changing Incentives category includes strategies that focus primarily on income generation and economic incentives for local people.

Effective conservation action depends on practitioners having the information that they need to make important management decisions. Practitioners need to understand the specific local conditions at their project site, both at the start of their project and as they change over time. They thus need to be able to collect the right information, analyze it, use it, and learn from it. At the same time, practitioners also need to know more generally about the costs and benefits of each conservation strategy under different conditions. They must be able to draw on the experience and learning of other practitioners.

Drawing on the principles of adaptive management,[10] we believe that one of the most effective ways to help practitioners develop and obtain this information is through a *learning portfolio* approach.[11] As shown in Figure 29-4, a learning portfolio involves bringing together project teams that are all using a similar strategy to share their experiences, pool their knowledge, and enhance their collective understanding of how best to use the strategy. The practitioners become both researchers who can work together to test assumptions about the strategy and teachers who can help each other develop their individual and institutional capacity.

This approach seeks to achieve conservation at a few sites, and at the same time leverage learning from these experiences to develop general principles that can affect many sites. One of the first examples of a learning portfolio was the Biodiversity Conservation Network (BCN). BCN was established specifically to test an enterprise-based strategy for conservation.[12] BCN compared the experiences of thirty-nine project sites to develop guiding principles about the conditions under which an enterprise-based strategy might be effective.[13]

Three Challenges for Using Learning Portfolios

There are three fundamental challenges that learning portfolios can help meet. We believe that meeting these challenges is the foundation for success in conservation.

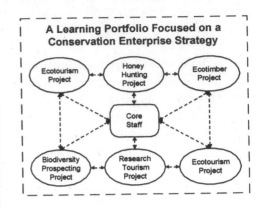

Source: Adapted from Salafsky and Margoluis (1999b).

Fig 29-4. A learning portfolio is greater than the sum of its parts. A typical *results-only portfolio* involves implementing or funding a group of projects that are loosely clustered around some theme to achieve a conservation goal. For example, you might develop projects in a certain country or perhaps even near a specific national park. The key point here is that, as is shown in the left side of the diagram, each project in a portfolio is selected more or less independently of the others and there are, thus, few if any synergies. The net benefit of the portfolio is the sum of the impacts of successful projects plus any capacity developed in the organizations implementing the projects. Failed projects can only be written off as losses. The portfolio's net impact is at best the sum of its parts.

A *learning portfolio* is a special kind of program that has two types of goals. The first involves achieving specific conservation objectives. The second involves systematically learning from actions taken to determine what works, what does not work, and why. Under a learning portfolio approach, a group of projects is deliberately selected to test a specific strategy as shown in the right side of the diagram. This portfolio should be designed in such a way that it enables lessons to be learned by comparing the projects to one another. Ideally, a learning portfolio may also want to invest some resources in a core staff that can bring the different project teams together. In this case, benefits may still be derived from successes, but failures are no longer wasted. Instead, they provide important information regarding assumptions made—as much or more may be learned from the failures as from the successes. Furthermore, the project teams in the portfolio can readily exchange ideas and share experiences to develop more effective guiding principles. The portfolio's net impact thus becomes far greater than the sum of its parts.

Define Clear and Measurable Conservation Goals

The first challenge for using learning portfolios is to develop a better understanding of what we are trying to achieve. Much of the confusion in the seemingly endless debate shown in Figure 29-1 stems from projects that combine conservation and development objectives. Both conservation and development are worthy goals. Unfortunately, they are not the same thing and at best are necessary, but not sufficient, conditions for each other. If the goal of a project is conservation, then one set of strategies may be appropriate. If, however, the goal is local people's empowerment, then another set of strategies may be appropriate. Learning portfolios thus should be used to assist practitioners to define what conservation is and to develop practical and cost-effective indicators of whether conservation is occurring or not.

Traditionally, measurements of conservation success have focused primarily on biological indicators.[14] In effect, these measurements have focused on the state of biodiversity in Figure 29-3. There is, however, a growing trend among conservation practitioners to design projects by identifying threats to the biodiversity at a site and then developing interventions that address these threats.[15] The threat reduction assessment (TRA) approach to monitoring project success seeks to identify threats not only by designing projects, but also by monitoring them and using this information as a proxy measurement of conservation success.[16] The theory behind TRA is that if a project team can identify threats to the biodiversity of a region, then the team can assess its progress in achieving conservation by measuring the degree to which these threats are reduced.

The TRA approach is based on three key assumptions. First, all biodiversity destruction is human-induced. Second, all threats to biodiversity at a given site can be identified, distinguished from one another, and ranked in terms of their scale, intensity of impact, and urgency. Third, changes in all threats can be measured or at least estimated either quantitatively or qualitatively. When compared to biological methods of measuring success, the TRA approach is practical and cost effective because it is based on data collected through simple techniques, is directly related to project interventions, is readily interpreted by project staff, and can be done in retrospect.[17]

Determine General and Yet Nontrivial Guiding Principles

The second challenge for using learning portfolios is to work with practitioners to determine guiding principles for protected areas and for all other conservation strategies. We must use science to build a solid understanding of the specific conditions under which each intervention strategy works, does not work, and why.

To develop effective principles, we first need to clearly define the specific intervention strategies or substrategies that we are focusing on. The first row of Table 29-1 shows one partial taxonomy of different kinds of protected-area substrategies. Depending on the focus of the work being done, this taxonomy can be fairly simple or it can be as complex as the listing of different types of protected areas cataloged by The World Conservation Union (IUCN).[18] The key is to make sure that everyone involved in producing and using the principles is speaking a common language and referring to the same strategies or substrategies in the same way.

Table 29-1.

Examples of different protected-areas substrategies and their assumed effectiveness in mitigating different types of threats.

	Substrategy			
Threat	Protected Area (State Owned)	Protected Area (Privately Owned)	Biosphere Reserve	Ex situ Conservation
Poaching of high-value species	–	+	– –	+ +
Expansion of swidden agriculture	+	+ +	–	– –
Overharvesting of forest products	–	+	+ +	–
Acid rain	+	– –	–	?

Note: this table is incomplete and is presented only as an example.
A plus (+ or + +) indicates the substrategy is useful to mitigate the threat.
A minus (– or – –) indicates the substrategy is not useful to mitigate the threat.

One possible next step is to postulate general assumptions about the effectiveness of each substrategy against different types of threats. For example, as shown in Table 29-1, these general assumptions can be represented by plus and minus signs that indicate whether a given strategy is effective against a given threat.

Although these general assumptions are a good starting point for analysis, ultimately they are not specific enough to be of real use to practitioners. It thus probably makes more sense to select a given strategy and develop more specific assumptions about the conditions under which it may or may not mitigate a given threat. These assumptions can then be experimentally tested over time as shown in Table 29-2. This process is based on the scientific method that researchers have been using for centuries, and the work should ideally undergo scientific peer review to ensure accuracy. In addition to meeting the scientific "peer review" test of accuracy, however, principles also have to pass the practitioner "peer review" test of utility. This is not an easy test to pass.

Table 29-2.

Two dimensions of experimental design. Experiments can use data that have been collected either *passively* (by using existing data and information from ongoing projects) or *actively* (by implementing projects and then monitoring the results of deliberate management actions). Furthermore, analytical designs can be either *cross-sectional* (comparing members of a group of projects to each other, thus allowing only tests of association) or *longitudinal* (comparing projects to themselves over time, thus allowing tests of causality).

	Analytical Design	
Experimentation	*Cross-sectional*	*Longitudinal*
Passive	Relatively easy, and thus common, but tends to lead to trivial principles	Difficult to do and thus not common
Active	Doable with sufficient investment; some examples exist (e.g., BCN)	The "gold standard," but expensive and difficult and thus not common

For example, in 1999 researchers conducted an admirable review of twenty-one ICDPs in Indonesia (a cross-sectional passive study).[19] By comparing these twenty-one sites they were able to determine characteristics of successful ICDPs as well as the problems faced by unsuccessful efforts. Practitioners can undoubtedly learn a great deal from reading the specific case studies. Many of the report's conclusions, however, are on the "general" side of the spectrum. For example, the authors note that law enforcement is a problem in many ICDPs. They go on to state:

> The extent to which the effective enforcement of laws and regulations is a basic requirement for successful ICDPs is deeply under-appreciated.... Without major improvements in law enforcement, both large and small actors will continually intrude into protected areas and further destroy habitat. Without more effective sanctions and penalties for illegal use of protected area resources, the alternative and less environmentally destructive ways of making a living offered through ICDPs will not be effective.

These conclusions are an important first step in developing guiding principles. Furthermore, it is clear that the authors are trying to state their conclusions in a careful fashion so as to maintain scientific objectivity and not create political problems. Unfortunately these conclusions are also fairly general—most practitioners would not find them useful.

In a similar fashion, BCN examined enterprise-based approaches to conservation across thirty-nine sites in Asia and the Pacific (a cross-sectional active study).[20] Here again, some of the principles that are developed (e.g., "Communities need to have the power to defend resource rights whether they are legally held by themselves or by the state," or "Promote local stakeholder involvement in the ownership and management of the enterprise") would not be useful to most practitioners. Our point here is not to criticize these authors but to demonstrate how difficult it is to come up with good guiding principles that are scientifically rigorous but also useful to practitioners.

To solve this challenge, it is helpful to start with a more specific set of assumptions that can be tested. The starting point for good guiding principles might be assumptions such as the following:

A *Establishing checkpoints can control poaching of low- to mid-value plant and animal species if the park is not too large and/or can only be accessed through specific routes.*

Table 29-3.

An example of a practitioner's guide for using a publicly owned protected area strategy. To use this guide, compare the conditions at your site with the factors listed in the far left-hand column. If you get even one entry in the "Forget It!" column, then you might want to consider another strategy. If most of your criteria are in the "Think Hard" or "Maybe If . . ." columns, then you should consider the comments in the far right-hand column. If you can resolve the problems, then it might make sense to use this strategy. Finally, if most of your criteria are in the "Go For It!" column, you are home free, assuming all your assumptions are true.

Factor	Conditions at Your Site				Comment on "Maybe If . . ." Column
Biophysical					
Size of protected area	Huge	Large	Moderate	Small	. . . if boundaries can be clearly delineated and patrolled
Accessibility	Easy	Moderate	Restricted	Difficult	. . . if through limited checkpoints where guards can be posted
Economic					
Market demand for poached species	Very high	High	Limited	None	. . . if there are also campaigns to reduce demand for illegally harvested products
Social					
Pay available for guards	Very low	Low	Moderate	High	. . . if higher than other jobs
Legal system enforcement	None	Weak	Moderate	Strong	. . . if courts are willing to consider environmental issues
Implication	**Forget It !**	**Think Hard**	**Maybe If . . .**	**Go for It !**	

Adapted from N. Salafsky et al., Evaluating Linkages between Business, the Environment, and Local Communities: Final Analytical Results from the Biodiversity Conservation Network (Washington, D.C.: Biodiversity Support Program, 1999). Also available online: http://www.bcnet.org or or http://www.bsponline.org.

Note: This table is incomplete and is presented only as an example.

A *In countries with weak legal systems, providing high salaries and cash incentives tied to measurable performance objectives to park guards and managers will lead to a reduction in the threat posed by the poaching of low- to mid-value plant and animal species.*

Following the pattern for good principles outlined in Figure 29-2, each assumption proposes a very specific management intervention (e.g., setting up checkpoints and providing high salaries and performance bonuses to park guards and managers). Each assumption also lists specific conditions under which the assumption will hold (e.g., the park is not too large or is in a country with a weak legal system). Finally, each assumption predicts a specific and measurable outcome (e.g., poaching of low- to mid-value plant and animal species can be controlled). If we were to test these assumptions across the ICDP case studies in Indonesia, we might then be able to turn them into guiding principles and perhaps even ultimately develop a chart like the one in Table 29-3 that would help guide practitioners in the selection of the appropriate strategy for their site.

Develop Individual and Institutional Capacity to Learn and Adapt

Finally, the third challenge for using learning portfolios is to help practitioners develop the ability to use science to learn from their own experiences over time. We need to develop learning institutions that can define and solve problems and retain and share the knowledge that they have gained so that it does not have to be relearned over and over again. We also need to create organizations that can encounter new situations and learn how to creatively and effectively deal with them on their own. Only when practitioners have learned how to evaluate different conservation strategies and apply them to the specific problems that they are facing will we truly be able to break the cycle in which we seem to currently be trapped.

Acknowledgments

We thank Cheryl Margoluis and Carel van Schaik for comments on drafts of this chapter.

Notes

1. S. Marks, *Imperial Lion: Human Dimensions of Wildlife Management in Central Africa* (Boulder: Westview Press, 1984); R. W. Sellars, *Preserving Nature in the National Parks: A History* (New Haven: Yale University Press, 1997); R. Kramer and C. van

Schaik, "Preservation Paradigms and Tropical Rain Forests," in *Last Stand: Protected Areas and the Defense of Tropical Biodiversity*, ed. R. Kramer, C. van Schaik, and J. Johnson (Oxford: Oxford University Press, 1997), 3–14.

2. N. Uphoff, "Fitting Projects to People," in *Putting People First*, M. Cernea (Oxford: Oxford University Press, 1985), 359–395; K. Rao and C. Geisler, "The Social Consequences of Protected Areas Development for Resident Populations," *Society and Natural Resources* 3, no.1 (1990): 19–32; N. Peluso, "Coercing Conservation? The Politics of State Resource Control," *Global Environmental Change* 3, no. 2 (1993): 199–217; N. Salafsky and L. Wollenberg, "Linking Livelihoods and Conservation: A Conceptual Framework for Assessing the Integration of Human Needs and Biodiversity," *World Development* 28, no. 8 (2000): 1421–1438.

3. UNESCO, *Convention Concerning the Protection of World Cultural and Natural Heritage* (Paris: UNESCO, 1972); M. Batisse, "The Biosphere Reserve: A Tool for Environmental Conservation and Management," *Environmental Conservation* 9, no. 2 (1982): 101–111; J. MacKinnon, K. MacKinnon, G. Child, and J. Thorsell, *Managing Protected Areas in the Tropics* (Gland, Switzerland: IUCN, 1986); J. Sayer, *Rainforest Buffer Zones: Guidelines for Protected Area Managers* (Gland, Switzerland: IUCN, 1991).

4. J. A. McNeeley, *Economics and Biological Diversity: Developing and Using Economic Incentives to Conserve Biological Resources* (Gland, Switzerland: IUCN, 1988); C. M. Peters, A. H. Gentry, and R. O. Mendelsohn, "Valuation of an Amazonian Rain Forest," *Nature* 339 (1989): 655–656; D. Western and R. M. Wright, eds., *Natural Connections: Perspectives in Community-based Conservation* (Washington, D.C.: Island Press, 1994); N. Salafsky, B. Cordes, J. Parks, and C. Hochman, *Evaluating Linkages between Business, the Environment, and Local Communities: Final Analytical Results from the Biodiversity Conservation Network* (Washington, D.C.: Biodiversity Support Program, 1999). Also available online: http://www.bcnet.org or http:// www. bsponline.org.

5. Sayer, *Buffer Zones*; J. Robinson, "The Limits to Caring: Sustainable Living and the Loss of Biodiversity," *Conservation Biology* 7 (1993): 20–28; J. F. Oates, "The Dangers of Conservation by Rural Development: A Case Study from the Forests of Nigeria," *Oryx* 29 (1995): 115–122.

6. M. Wells and K. Brandon, *People and Parks: Linking Protected Area Management with Local Communities* (Washington, D.C.: World Bank, 1992); K. Brandon, K. H. Redford, and S. E. Sanderson, *Parks in Peril: People, Politics, and Protected Areas* (Washington, D.C.: Island Press, 1998).

7. Kramer et al., *Last Stand*; Brandon et al., *Parks in Peril*; J. F. Oates, *Myth and Reality in the Rain Forest* (Berkeley: University of California Press, 1999); J. Terborgh, *Requiem for Nature* (Washington, D.C.: Island Press, 1999).

8. A. Agrawal and C. B. Gibson, "Enchantment and Disenchantment: The Role of Community in Natural Resource Conservation," *World Development* 27, no. 4 (1999): 629–649; S. R. Brechin, C. Fortwangler, P. Wilshusen, and P. West, "Rein-

venting a Square Wheel: The Backlash to People-sensitive Conservation and the Future of International Biodiversity Conservation Management," *Society and Natural Resources* (2000).

9. R. Margoluis and N. Salafsky, *Measures of Success: Designing, Managing, and Monitoring Conservation and Development Projects* (Washington, D.C.: Island Press, 1998).

10. C. S. Holling, ed., *Adaptive Environmental Assessment and Management* (New York: John Wiley and Sons, 1978); K. Lee, *Compass and Gyroscope: Integrating Science and Politics for the Environment* (Washington, D.C.: Island Press, 1993); L. Gunderson, C. S. Holling, and S. S. Light, eds., *Barriers and Bridges in the Renewal of Ecosystems and Institutions* (New York: Columbia University Press, 1995); N. Salafsky, R. Margoluis, and K. Redford, *Adaptive Management: A Tool for Conservation Practitioners* (Washington, D.C.: Biodiversity Support Program, 2001).

11. N. Salafsky and R. Margoluis, *Greater Than the Sum of Their Parts: Designing Conservation Programs to Maximize Impact and Learning* (Washington, D.C.: Biodiversity Support Program, 1999). Also available online: http://www.bcnet.org or http://www.bsponline.org.

12. Salafsky et al., *Evaluating Linkages*.

13. Salafsky et al., *Evaluating Linkages*.

14. R. F. Noss, "Indicators for Monitoring Biodiversity: A Hierarchical Approach," *Conservation Biology* 4 (1990): 355–364; K. Redford and B. Richter, "Conservation of Biodiversity in a World of Use," *Conservation Biology* 13, no. 6 (1999): 1246–1256.

15. See, for example, The Nature Conservancy, *Designing a Geography of Hope: Guidelines for Ecoregion-based Conservation* (Arlington, Va.: The Nature Conservancy, 1997); D. Bryant, L. Burke, J. McManus, and M. Spaulding, *Reefs at Risk: A Map Based Indicator of Threats to the World's Coral Reefs* (Washington, D.C.: World Resources Institute, 1998); C. Kremen, V. Razafimahatratra, R. P. Guillery, J. Rakotomalala, A. Weiss, and J. S. Ratsisompatrarivo, "Designing the Masoala National Park in Madagascar Based on Biological and Socioeconomic Data," *Conservation Biology* 13 (1999): 1055–1068.

16. N. Salafsky and R. Margoluis, "Threat Reduction Assessment: A Practical and Cost-effective Approach to Evaluating Conservation and Development Projects," *Conservation Biology* 13 (1999): 830–841.

17. Salafsky and Margoluis, *Threat Reduction*.

18. IUCN, *Guidelines for Protected Area Management Categories* (Cambridge, UK: IUCN, 1994).

19. M. Wells, S. Guggenheim, A. Khan, W. Wardojo, and P. Jepson, *Investing in Biodiversity: A Review of Indonesia's Integrated Conservation and Development Projects* (Washington, D.C.: World Bank, 1999).

20. Salafsky et al., *Evaluating Linkages*.

30

The Frontier Model of Development and Its Relevance to Protected Area Management

CAREL VAN SCHAIK AND MADHU RAO

Parks everywhere are threatened by an array of factors that include local communities (small players) as well as large public and private investments (big players). Those hardest to defend are located in rapidly developing regions with high rates of immigration and economies that rely heavily on extraction and extensive uses because of the social and institutional characteristics of such frontier regions. Policy-makers tend to respond to pressures on protected areas by downgrading their status and, encouraged by the prevailing paradigm in international conservation, by calling for sustainable use instead. Similarly, external support to protected-area management often assumes the form of integrated conservation and development projects (ICDPs), which attempt to achieve stable extractive and extensive use of the land at the boundaries of protected areas. We will argue here that such fossilization of what is a dynamic process can only be a stopgap measure and is ineffective from both a conservation and a development perspective.

We first examine the changes in land use and activity characterizing the frontier model of development, at various temporal and spatial scales. We then explore the implications of this model for thinking about park management.

Predictability of Land-use Changes: The Frontier Model

Throughout recent history, many remote and sparsely settled regions have undergone a characteristic set of rapid changes in their land-use spectrum fueled by expanding economic power or by intrinsic population growth. This pattern is based on the formation and gradual dissolution of frontiers.[1] Frontiers are defined here as areas of unstable land use at the edge of wilderness. They replace what can be called the remote pattern, in which local population densities are very low, land use is extensive, commercial trade is modest, and activities are largely for subsistence (Figure 30-1).

In the frontier phase of development in a region, many outsiders are attracted to the region to practice extensive agriculture or commercially harvest species and other natural products from the wildlands that are considered open access.[2] As the frontier matures, many of the extracted resources become scarcer and more valuable. If the exploitation is destructive, the resource will therefore become rarer; perversely, exploitation pressure will then go up as prices rise. In response, people have an incentive to take the resource out of the forest and cultivate it directly on private property, a commonly observed development.[3] This increases efficiency and minimizes theft by other exploiters. The main exception concerns resources that are too difficult to cultivate or take so long to mature that cultivation is not economically feasible until the resource is commercially extinct in the wild (e.g., Brazil nuts).

At the frontier, agriculture is extensive, since land is abundant and freely available for conversion to cropland or grazing. The frontier closes when extractable resources become depleted and free land becomes scarce enough to enforce a lifestyle that requires less land per capita: a change from extraction to cultivation, and from extensive to intensive agriculture. Also, as suitable land becomes scarce due to rising human

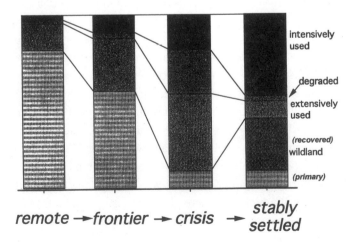

Figure 30-1. The predictable sequence of changes in the land-use spectrum accompanying development.

density or for other reasons, inappropriate or more intensive land use on marginal lands tends to cause an increase in the area of degraded land. Thus, depletion and a high proportion of degraded land become hallmarks of the region in this phase, which can be termed the *crisis phase*. During the crisis phase, when land has become scarce, population growth drives agricultural intensification (increased frequency of cultivation, labor and capital intensification per hectare), land investments (for soil and water conservation, irrigation and drainage) and productivity enhancement.[4]

Because of these activities, the crisis phase grades into the stable and intensive land-use pattern of established regions, where intensive agriculture and horticulture are found on the most suitable lands, degraded land is either restored to productivity or left alone to regrow gradually, and the lower per capita land requirement allows the society to reserve more land for its ecological services and to protect biodiversity. In the stably settled phase, extensive uses are rare, although they need not have disappeared altogether.

The beginning of the stable phase marks the closing of the frontier. Figure 30-1 illustrates this predictable sequence from frontier through a crisis phase to a stable end phase. Although the last phase in this sequence is not stable from an economic perspective, because obviously intensive land uses keep on changing, land use of wildlands stabilizes.

Technological advancement and enhanced institutional capacity are critical factors underlying the stabilization or reduction of land under cultivation. There are two key changes. First, new agricultural technology causes a rise in productivity to the point that it outpaces population growth, so land becomes available for other uses (or no consumptive use at all). Second, this is usually followed by increases in the share of nonagricultural economic activities, which further increases the "yield" per unit of land considerably and thereby the carrying capacity. These two processes inevitably lead to the release of agricultural land to less-intensive forms of land use, such as recreational area or wildland.[5]

We will now illustrate this general model with descriptions of developments in both Western and tropical countries. Although the timing of the changes and the rate at which they take place vary geographically, the trends are remarkably robust, suggesting a law-like progression that must have implications for the practice of conservation.

Land-use Trends in Temperate Countries

The frontier-crisis-stable land-use transitions in Figure 30-1 also characterize recent trends in land use in Europe, summarized in Table 30-1. Similar trends can be discerned in other rich regions or nations, although the details are obviously enormously variable and the timing of major transitions varied as well. However, the main features are similar, and they fit into the model specifying the sequence of remote → frontier → crisis → stable phases in the land-use spectrum.

In Europe, the landscape was completely transformed between A.D. 900 and 1900, as forest clearing and land drainage created pastures and agricultural fields.[6] Agriculture varied in intensity as a function of distance from cities but in general was characterized by several-year fallows and low yields per hectare. Where it was permanent, each hectare of cropland was supported by several hectares of heathland or other pasture land used to produce the dung that fertilized the cropland. In the Netherlands, one of the first countries to reach the crisis phase, serious overexploitation produced desert-like conditions on the poorer soils. Likewise, in Sweden, overall productivity actually fell during much of the nineteenth century. As a result, the area of cultivated land increased for several centuries until it peaked at around 1930 (Figure 30-2).

Table 30-1.
Trends in land use over the past century in Europe, especially accelerated during the post-World War II era.

- Gradual decline in agricultural land, especially in regions with marginal productivity, accompanied by steady rises in productivity on intensively used lands. This trend followed increases in agricultural land during the nineteenth century.
- Continuing (sub-) urbanization, accompanied by gradual decline in population growth.
- Gradual increase in forest area, both for production and protection. This followed steady declines during the nineteenth century.
- Large increase in reserved lands, both for recreation and as original or restored wildlands.

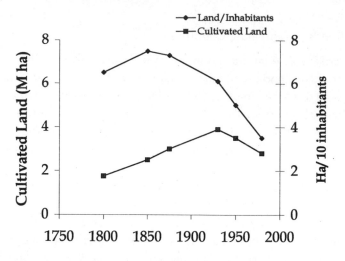

Figure 30-2. Changes in area of cultivated land and intensity of use in Sweden over the past two centuries. After S. Anderberg, "Historical Land Use Changes: Sweden," in F. M. Brouwer, A. J. Thomas, and M. J. Chadwick, eds., *Land Use Changes in Europe: Processes of Change, Environmental Transformations and Future Patterns* (Dordrecht: Kluwer Academic Publishers 1991), 403–426.

Transformation of the European agricultural landscape has been accompanied by marked increases in agricultural productivity. Whereas productivity remained relatively constant for several hundred years prior, crop yields began to increase in the seventeenth century and, in the nineteenth century, wheat yields in England increased by about 50 percent. Early increases in productivity were attributed to a reduction of fallow, deeper plowing with improved equipment, and better drainage. Truly revolutionary increases in productivity have occurred in the last fifty years with the introduction of new plant varieties and large-scale application of fertilizers, pesticides, and herbicides.[7] These significant transformations in the land have supported increasingly dense populations. The intensification of agriculture outpaced population growth, and the acreage allocated to it has steadily declined, especially since World War II.[8] The proportion of the population employed in agriculture likewise showed a steep decline in most countries.

Forestry was almost exclusively extractive until late in the eighteenth century, with a wave of forest depletion and deforestation spreading east and northeast through Europe to support shipbuilding and other industrial needs.[9] The land that became available was mainly turned into (often marginal) agricultural land needed to absorb the population increases. Forest cover was thus very low during much of the nineteenth century in Western Europe. Over the last century, forest area has gradually increased.[10] Most of this forest is actually tree plantation, but reserved forest area and wildland has more recently also begun to increase.[11] At present, virtually all timber production in Western Europe comes from managed forest plantations.

A similar pattern of land transformation is observed in parts of the United States. Originally nearly entirely forested, by the late nineteenth century virtually 80 percent of the New England landscape was under agriculture. A nearly complete reversal has occurred in the subsequent one hundred years. Much of New England is again heavily forested, and in some areas forests again cover nearly 80 percent of the land.[12] Most timber in North America now also comes from managed forests, although logging of old-growth forest is still common in remote regions.[13]

Economically marginal occupations involving extraction and extensive use have become increasingly rare, because regular jobs in the mainstream economy provide far better incomes. Thus, hunters, fishers, shepherds, willow cutters, herb collectors, latex collectors, mushroom collectors, berry pickers, tanners, reed cutters, charcoal burners, and so forth have gradually become so rare that they make up less than 1 percent of the adult population. The main exception to this trend is fisheries, which still remain largely extractive and which are notoriously incapable of avoiding depletion of the stocks.[14]

People increasingly have found occupations not directly dependent on land, in industry and services. The trend toward urbanization has continued in parallel and in turn produced reductions in family size and thus population growth. All these trends away from extensive and extractive uses mean that more land has become available for other uses, including forest, recreation areas, and wildlands. These changes in occupations have also spawned more romantic and less pragmatic attitudes toward nature and gradually produced strong support for the protection of wildlands, both for recreation and conservation. The well-being of increasing numbers of city dwellers depends on access to areas of natural beauty for recreation.

It is of interest to note that these trends still continue. One study estimates that, relative to 1980, agricultural land in Europe will decline by another 33 percent to the year 2030, largely made possible by a continuing rise in productivity (yield per hectare).[15]

Thus, the stable stage in developed countries has produced a highly urbanized landscape in which land uses are polarized between very intensive uses (urban, agriculture, horticulture) and no consumptive use at all,
and is relatively stable (the major transitions are within the intensive-use
category).

Land-use Trends in Tropical Countries

Many regions in the humid tropics, where most tropical forest reserves
are found, have not yet reached the phase of stable land use. However, the
trends found in the temperate zone are also found in the developing
world, and similar changes will also arrive in what are currently developing countries. Indeed, overviews of development trends in a broad
range of tropical and subtropical countries strongly support the frontier
model posited above for the parts of the world that achieved affluence
much earlier.[16]

Many developing countries are still in the frontier phase of development, with continuous increases in the acreage of agricultural land,
largely extensive agriculture, and massive loss of wildlands. To give just
one example, Bruenig describes the following transitions in Sarawak (Bor-
neo) among Iban pioneer communities: "All shifting cultivators in Sarawak are in rapid cultural transition from migratory shifting agriculture to
settled hill-rice cultivation, mixed farming and, finally, intensive agriculture. . . . The young move away from the longhouse and become urbanites." The reason is that they have run out of suitable land.[17]

Many other areas are already entering the stable stage. In both Taiwan
and India, total area devoted to agriculture has remained approximately
constant since the end of World War II, despite enormous population
growth.[18] The total amount of agricultural land remained steady in
densely settled northern Nigeria during 1965–1981, a period of rapid population growth.[19] Finally, in Thailand, the area under cultivation rose dramatically until around 1980, but has begun to stabilize since then.[20]

Country-level trends of course belie much internal variability. The
trend toward intensification usually starts near large urban centers, many
of which are already quite similar in their land-use spectrum to that of the
stable parts of the world. Several countries (e.g., Taiwan)[21] have now
reached the stage where the increase in yields made possible by agricultural intensification outweighs population growth rate, and land can
gradually be allocated again to other uses.

Agricultural transformation is predictably associated with environmental degradation and loss of wildlands, reaching the ecological crisis stage in places. However, in more rapidly developing countries, increasing levels of economic prosperity have already led to positive changes in attitudes toward the conservation of depleted natural resources and protection of wildlands (e.g., Taiwan).[22] Thus, it is only a matter of time until the more slowly developing countries reach the same stage.

The rapid growth of the agricultural sector eventually produces accelerated growth in the nonagricultural sector, which assumes increasing significance in the fast-growing economy in many countries from Taiwan to Mauritius.[23] This transformation to greater reliance on manufacture or services (e.g., tourism) acts as an important sink for the population increase in rural areas, both frontier and stable. The trend has become so strong that globally, urbanization is outpacing population growth (Figure 30-3). Much of the strongest urbanization is taking place in the developing world. If, as is anticipated, family sizes in the developing parts of the world come down, cities may increasingly take over the role of frontiers in absorbing the landless and the poor in established rural areas.

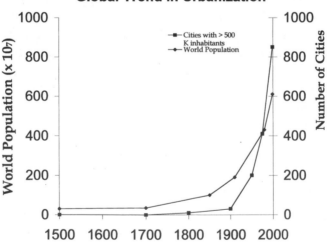

Figure 30-3. Global trend in urbanization showing that the increase in the number of large urban areas outpaces overall population growth. After B. J. L. Berry, "Urbanization," in B. L. I. Turner, W. C. Clark, R. W. Kates, J. F. Richards, J. T. Mathews, and W. B. Meier, eds., *The Earth as Transformed by Human Action: Global and Regional Changes in the Biosphere over the Past 300 Years* (Cambridge: Cambridge University Press, 1990), 103–119.

Thus, pressures on land should decline, and the more remote or unproductive parts of the country can return to extensive uses or, more likely, no productive land use at all.

Implications for Conservation
Park Management in Frontier Zones

The three contexts described earlier (remote, frontier, and stable) require different approaches to protected-area management (see also chapter 31). Frontier zones have certain social and institutional characteristics that make the management of protected areas especially difficult. First, most people in the region, both government officials and common people alike, regard the wildland as empty land waiting to be exploited by the first to come and lay his claim. This attitude is often shared by most agencies in the central government, who consider this the country's foremost development zone in terms of forestry and mining, and as future agricultural production areas. With such "resourcist" or "exploitationist" attitudes predominating, it is difficult to impose policies that assume stable land use and respect of boundaries. Second, frontier zones inevitably have weak institutions. Corruption tends to be more common, law enforcement more lax, and land-use planning less effective than in the more stable parts of the country. These occur for a variety of reasons: the entrepreneurial spirit of the people; weak social control due to the absence of established social networks; and the fact that it takes time to build institutions. The history of the American West provides numerous illustrations of these characteristics and also shows the linkages between social and institutional features, with proudly independent frontiersmen tending to resent authorities meddling in their business.

Hastening the Transition

If we accept that the proper role of conservation assistance is to hasten the transition toward more sustainable activities to reduce pressures on the remaining wildlands, the key question now becomes how such transitions can be accomplished. This is obviously a complex challenge, and one that requires actions at the central level that go well beyond the scope of current park support programs. Nonetheless, it is worth exploring the issue because of the potential for development assistance to be truly integrated with conservation.

Societies will only change toward more intensive land use, in other words, one that requires less land per capita, when they are forced to do so by economic circumstances, such as scarcity of the extracted resource, land scarcity, rising land prices, or are driven to it by the opportunity to trade a surplus and thus accumulate wealth and other desired commodities. Had there been no incentives to change in this direction, we would still be hunter-gatherers in a state of paradise, living off the plenty of the land.

Normally, nature does the forcing. A growing population gradually exhausts certain types of natural resources such as timber, land, game, and freshwater supplies and is forced to reduce its numbers by emigration or change its traditional use of resources and way of life. Thus, the increase of population within an area provides an incentive to replace natural resources by labor and capital.[24] Eventually, most if not all countries will reach the stable state in which agricultural productivity and urbanization outstrip population growth, reducing pressures on land and making it available for other uses, and in which popular attitudes toward conservation will be favorable (see also chapter 3). The bad news is that countries that have not reached this phase yet may take decades to do so, and may have to go through an ecological crisis first. They may lose most or all of their wildland in the process and thus incur irreversible biodiversity losses.

However, there is no reason governments could not do the forcing before nature does. The landscape—the patterns of land use—is the arbitrary side effect of economic decisions of individuals. Hence, the landscape can be steered in a direction more in line with the needs of society at large by policies that affect the economic decisions of individuals. If the political will exists to skip the crisis phase, it can be done. This will obviously bring about better conservation of wildlands for their biodiversity or ecological services, but also improved development.

How can those developments be encouraged that accelerate the transition to the stable land use in which wildlands are safe and development is improved? In general, national governments and donors can encourage economic development that relies less on extensive and extractive activities, making more land available for return to wildland status. The policy measures that should bring about stability of land use, at various time scales, are summarized in Table 30-2.

Park conservation projects can contribute to many of these measures. One of the most important ways is through support of improved protection of wildlands. Intensification is the product of several factors such as better profit margins, the presence of technical knowledge and skills, and a willingness to adopt them. Intensification will receive a boost when the

Table 30-2.
Policy measures promoting faster shifts toward more stable land use by reducing the dependence on extensive uses (shifting agriculture, extraction).

Short-term positive effect:
- Strictly enforce forest protection in protected forests, thus cutting off easy avenues for continuing damaging lifestyles.
- Support intensification efforts by reducing taxes on intensively used land and increasing the tax rate on extensively used land.
- Support the development of nonconsumptive uses, such as ecotourism.
- Make credit available for those people who need support to change their lifestyle.
- Enhance the sustainability of extensive uses by prescribing the use of appropriate equipment (e.g., through less damaging logging techniques, using elephants instead of heavy machinery) and social organization (e.g., by strengthening existing local conventions and reinvigorating the role of communal accountable bodies).
- Direct the flow of spontaneous settlers toward areas most suitable for extensive uses, in other words, where they least compromise biodiversity and ecological services, through road building, land allocation, and settlement schemes.

Medium-term positive effect:
- Stimulate the cultivation, rather than the direct exploitation, of nontimber forest products, such as rattans, fish, monitor lizards and crocodiles, resin-producing trees, songbirds, ornamental plants, butterflies, wildfowl, and the like.
- Stimulate local processing of cultivated products in order to enhance added value and employment options.
- Support family-planning efforts.

Long-term positive effect:
- Continue to improve education at all levels, but especially at primary and secondary levels.
- Improve urban infrastructure and transportation.
- Enhance economic opportunities for non-land-based employment by creating a solid financial system and a regulatory climate in which entrepreneurs can thrive.
- Strengthen institutions governing land use.
- Increase investment in research to enhance agricultural productivity.
- Encourage research to improve energy efficiency in agricultural production and utilization.
- Intensify research on environmentally sustainable farming systems.
- Eradicate corruption.

---

costs of extraction become unrealistically high, something best achieved by strict law enforcement and steep fines, provided positive incentives are in place as well.

Objection and Caveat

One important objection needs to be addressed. Most politicians and economists would argue that the land-use transitions cannot be accelerated since the frontier phase generates the wealth on which intensive uses are built. In the industrialized world, a conservation ethic arose after the easily extractable resources were exhausted, most people lived in urban areas, the generation of frontierspeople had aged, society had reached a certain level of affluence, and the populace had reached a reasonable level of education. History is therefore on the side of the politician from a developing country who exclaims that his country cannot afford the luxury of setting aside land that will not be used, of reserving resources that will not be exploited, of forgoing income that can be used for development; most especially not since the developed countries have built the foundation of their wealth on this exploitation. Realistically, then, we should not expect developing countries to worry about biodiversity protection and to afford a high priority to the establishment or defense of protected areas. Their first priority is to develop economically, not to protect species.

One obvious response to this problem is that outsiders who do value the biodiversity provide support to the developing economies for establishment and management of protected areas. Unfortunately, there is very little political will in the country to undertake biodiversity protection, even where financing is at least in part provided by the international community. Numerous failed conservation projects, funded by foreign donors but basically neglected by national governments, only serve to underscore this conclusion. This assistance should continue, and the political will of the recipient nation should be produced by persuasion.

Another response is to argue that leaping toward the stable land-use phase of development before being forced to do so by exhaustion of suitable land and of extractable resources is actually an economically wise policy. By leaving erosion-prone or unproductive land alone, countries forgo the costs of restoration. By leaving upper watersheds intact, they forgo the costs of restoring silted lakes and of rebuilding infrastructure or restoring agricultural land destroyed by devastating floods. By leaving wildlands intact they forgo the costs of re-creating natural communities desired by future generations of citizens.

A caveat should also be faced. Speeding up the processes of intensification and urbanization are not without their own problems. Agricultural intensification produces pollution and eutrophication of surface water, contamination of foods, degradation of soils (including salinization and erosion), and siltation of water bodies. The severity of degradation associated with intensification may be expected to be more acute than has been experienced in the past. Although traditional systems were able to sustain rates of population growth in the 0.5–1 percent per year range, modern rates of growth in demand are in the range of 1–2 percent per year in the developed countries and often rise to the range of 3.0–5.0 percent per year in the less developed and newly industrializing countries. Rates of growth in demand in this range lie outside the historical experience of presently developed countries.[25] Moreover, gains in agricultural production required over the next quarter century will be achieved with much greater difficulty than in the immediate past and several constraints in terms of declining incremental response to energy inputs can be expected.[26] Rapid and unplanned urbanization has created serious problems in contemporary developing countries, including a tendency for the urban population to concentrate in one or very few major population centers.

Conclusions

The land-use transitions may be real enough, but many may question our ability to advance the arrival of the settled state. Nonetheless, the political support for such measures inside the countries concerned is growing. As a result of the increasingly apparent discrepancy in perception between frontier zones and more established central urban areas, especially near urban areas, there is growing support for buying out communities from the most sensitive areas. Even if we do not succeed in accelerating the transition to stably settled land, the frontier model shows that pressures on parks will eventually decrease. The challenge is to hold on to at least some remnants until that day arrives.

Virtually all development is the fruit of activities that are not extractive or extensive. Development ultimately results from accepting restrictions on activities and thus from intensification of land use or from undertaking activities not depending on land. The stable phase of development produces a segregated landscape in which parts with intensive economic activities, agricultural and otherwise, are separated from parts with no consumptive uses. This is the landscape in which biodiversity is best maintained given current human population levels and standards of living.

HISTORICAL CHANGES IN DEEP TIME

To identify the underlying causes of this predictable sequence of land use and per capita land requirements, it is worth noting that there are also parallels to the history of humanity in general, going back as much as ten thousand years. Major transitions in human history were often precipitated by ecological crises. "Paradise" ended as a direct consequence of overexploitation of wild species, forcing humans to invent agriculture.[27] Later, increasing scarcity of suitable land led to increased intensity of agriculture. Table 30-3 illustrates the major historical transitions in agricultural practices. For instance, instead of rice cultivation in temporary clearings, people developed rain-fed, and later irrigated, cultivation in paddy fields. The paddy field cultivation itself also became increasingly intensive, with yields increasing due to year-round irrigation, the use of fertilizers and integrated pest control, and the use of selected high-yield varieties. Animal husbandry followed a very similar path, where humans first domesticated and later manipulated the genetic stock of the animals through deliberate selection of desired traits, and also started producing artificial environments in which the production was increased, from corrals and stables with feeds directly supplied to the animals to large-scale "bio-industry."

Historically, rising population densities can be linked to agricultural intensification. This development also caused serious environmental degradation, in some cases[28] leading to the end of the culture involved. However, long-term stability of highly intensive land use is also possible, as shown by the following examples. In Mesopotamia, irrigation development was associated with urbanization.[29] Early stratigraphic and archaeological records in

Table 30-3.

Historical transitions in land use during human history.

Extraction →	Extensive Production →	Intensive Production →	Non-land-based Production
Gathering and collecting	Shifting agriculture	Rainfed-paddy	Greenhouse-based plant production
Hunting	Wild animals in enclosures	Domestic animals	Bio-industry

the Tigris basin also reveal successive periods of successful irrigation inter-
rupted by siltation of canals and salinization of the soil, problems resulting
from inadequate application of water, and poor maintenance. In the Indus
valley, extensive irrigation development at Harrapa involved changes in land
use, including the rise of an urban center. In the modern era, in the nine-
teenth-century colonial period in India, large irrigation developments not
only produced large increases in production but also, over time, were
plagued with predicted problems of salinization and waterlogging. Nonetheless, irrigation and new crop varieties have contributed to large increases
in food production in the face of significant population growth.[30]

The Nile valley reflects a similar alteration of the landscape over a period
of thousands of years. Agriculture was initially practiced in natural riverine
wetlands to the south. Over time, natural systems were altered, and several
thousand years ago embankments constructed on the floodplain held water
in place after flooding, permitting extensive basin irrigation.[31] Large-scale
land transformation in the past led to degradation by salinization and waterlogging, but these effects have often been overcome or reversed with technological advancements. Overall, there is little historical evidence to suggest
that the benefits of increased production associated with intensification
were overwhelmed either by population increases or by deterioration of the
environment.[32]

The land-use perspective taken here, and the associated social and institutional characteristics of different developmental phases, may also be useful in providing suitable operational definitions of sustainable development.
Sustainability is notoriously difficult to define, but from the perspective of
biodiversity conservation it is perhaps best defined as stability of land use.
Where stable landscapes include a fair measure of wildlands, we may
achieve sustainability in the sense of limiting the number of species extinctions, or at least maintaining evolution in natural communities unaffected
by humans. Stable land use also implies ecological sustainability in terms of
maintaining services (nutrients, soils, climate, etc.). Imposing stability of
land use may help to bring about sustainability, because it forecloses the
easy options of leaving degraded land behind and moving on, and thus
forces landowners to make the most of the existing land. Thus, sustainable
development can be approached as stable land use to be achieved by favor-
ing intensification and activities not directly dependent on the land. In other
words, the measures advocated here are also measures that contribute to
sustainable development.

Notes

1. W. Cronon, *Changes in the Land: Indians, Colonists and the Ecology of New England* (New York: Hill and Wang, 1983); J. F. Richards, "Land Transformation," in *The Earth as Transformed by Human Action: Global and Regional Changes in the Biosphere over the Past 300 Years*, ed. B. L. I. Turner, W. C. Clark, R. W. Kates, J. F. Richards, J. T. Mathews, and W. B. Meier (Cambridge: Cambridge University Press, 1990), 163–178.

2. E. F. Bruenig, *Conservation and Management of Tropical Rainforests: An Integrated Approach to Sustainability* (Oxford: CAB International, 1996).

3. N. Salafsky, B. L. Dugelby, and J. W. Terborgh, "Can Extractive Reserves Save the Rain Forest? An Ecological and Socioeconomic Comparison of Nontimber Forest Product Extraction Systems in Peten, Guatemala, and West Kalimantan, Indonesia," *Conservation Biology* 7 (1993): 39–52.

4. W. Lutz and E. Holm, "Mauritius: Population and Land Use," in *Population and Land Use in Developing Countries: Report of a Workshop*, ed. Carole L. Jolly and Barbara Boyle Torrey, Committee on Population (Washington, D.C.: National Academy Press, 1993), 98–107; M. Mortimore, "Northern Nigeria: Land Transformation under Agricultural Intensification," in Jolly and Torrey, *Population and Land Use*, 42–69.

5. Mortimer, "Northern Nigeria"; V. W. Ruttan, "Population Growth, Environmental Change, and Innovation: Implications for Sustainable Growth in Agriculture," in Jolly and Torrey, *Population and Land Use*, 124–155.

6. M. G. Wolman, "Population, Land Use and Environment: A Long History," in Jolly and Torrey, *Population and Land Use*, 15–29.

7. D. Grigg, *Population Growth and Agrarian Change: An Historical Perspective.* Cambridge Geographical Studies (Cambridge, England: Cambridge University Press, 1980).

8. S. Anderberg, "Historical Land Use Changes: Sweden," in *Land Use Changes in Europe: Processes of Change, Environmental Transformations and Future Patterns*, ed. F. M. Brouwer, A. J. Thomas, and M. J. Chadwick (Dordrecht: Kluwer Academic Publishers, 1991) 403–426.

9. Richards, "Land Transformation."

10. J. Okuniewski, "Historical Land Use Changes: Poland," in Brouwer et al., *Land Use Changes*, 427–440; H. N. van Lier, "Historical Land Use Changes: The Netherlands," in Brouwer et al., *Land Use Changes*, 379–401.

11. Van Lier, "Netherlands."

12. H. M. Raup and R. E. Carlson, "The History of Land Use in the Harvard Forest," Harvard Forest Bulletin, no. 20 (1941); Cronon, *Changes*.

13. M. Clawson, "Forests in the Long Sweep of American History," *Science* 204 (1979): 1–7.

14. D. Ludwig, R. Hilborn, and C. Walters, "Uncertainty, Resource Exploitation, and Conservation: Lessons from History," *Science* 260 (1993): 17.

15. Brouwer et al., *Land Use Changes*.

16. Wolman, "Population"; A. Bigsten and P. Collier, "Linkages from Agricultural Growth in Kenya," in *Agriculture on the Road to Industrialization,* ed. J. W. Mellor (Baltimore: Johns Hopkins University Press, 1995), 196–208.

17. Bruenig, *Conservation and Management*, 82, 81.

18. E. Dayal, "Agricultural Land and Man–Land Ratio in India: An Analysis of Change," in *Natural Resources in Tropical Countries*, ed. O. J. Bee (Singapore: Singapore University Press, 1983), 346–367; Yu-Kang Mao and C. Schive, "Agriculture and Industrial Development in Taiwan," in Mellor, *Agriculture*, 23–63.

19. U. Lele and S. Stone, "Population Pressure, the Environment and Agricultural Intensification: Variations on the Boserup Hypothesis." Madia Discussion Paper 4 (Washington, D.C.: World Bank, 1989); Mortimore, "Northern Nigeria."

20. A. Saimwalla, "Land-abundant Agricultural Growth and Some of Its Consequences: The Case of Thailand," in Mellor, *Agriculture*, 150–177.

21. Mao and Schive, "Agriculture and Industrial Development."

22. A. Rabinowitz and L. L. Lee, "A Management and Conservation Strategy for the Tawu Mountain Nature Reserve, Taiwan, R.O.C.," COA Forestry Series No. 30 (1990).

23. Wolman, "Population."

24. E. Boserup, *The Conditions of Agricultural Growth: The Economics of Agrarian Change under Population Pressure* (Chicago: Aldine, 1965).

25. Ruttan, "Population Growth."

26. Ruttan, "Population Growth."

27. J. Diamond, *Guns, Germs, and Steel* (New York, W. W. Norton & Company, 1997).

28. C. Ponting, *A Green History of the World: The Environment and the Collapse of Great Civilizations* (New York: Penguin Books USA, 1991).

29. R. M. Adams, *Heartland of Cities* (Chicago: University of Chicago Press, 1981).

30. P. Buringh and R. Dudal, "Patterns of Land Use in Space and Time," in *Land Transformation in Agriculture*, ed. M. G. Wolman and F. G. A. Fourneier (New York: Wiley [SCOPE], 1987).

31. K. W. Butzer, *Early Hydraulic Civilization in Egypt: A Study in Cultural Ecology* (Chicago: University of Chicago Press, 1976).

32. Wolman, "Population."

PART IV

CONCLUSIONS

31

Putting the Right Parks in the Right Places

KATRINA BRANDON

Expanding the number of new protected areas and introducing active management into existing areas where it is lacking are two key actions needed to meet worldwide biodiversity targets. Despite general agreement among conservationists about the need for more protected areas, there is a debate under way concerning whether we can protect biodiversity in situ, whether we should bother to try, and whether these efforts should include any areas that permit some human uses.[1] Critics have claimed that protected areas are hard to manage, that they are too small to make a difference, or that they are socially unfair and unjust.[2]

Evidence is emerging, however, that protected areas are a viable strategy for biodiversity conservation.[3] A recent study looks at how effectively parks have protected biodiversity in the tropics.[4] The study focused on protected areas in IUCN (The World Conservation Union) categories I and II that are over 5,000 hectares in size and more than five years old. The analysis included ninety-three parks from twenty-three countries cumulatively covering 18 million hectares. It also focused exclusively on parks in areas of significant human activity. Although the parks in the study ranged widely in factors such as size, primary ecosystem type, budget, and management strategy, nearly all faced serious pressure due to human activity in their immediate surroundings.

The study provided the following key findings. Creation of the parks, even with low levels of management and a high degree of threat, was enough to stop land clearing. In this study, land clearing ceased in 83 percent of the parks after their establishment. Furthermore, a full 40 percent of the parks permitted the regeneration of native vegetation on land that was cleared at the time of park establishment. Only 17 percent of the parks lost native vegetation to land clearing. On balance, the parks reclaimed more land than was lost to clearing. These are especially impressive achievements given that the average age of parks in the study was twenty-one years. The parks were in better condition than surrounding lands even though they were under considerable pressure: they had less grazing, more commercially used tree species, and higher levels of game animals than nearby areas. For all impacts tested, the parks were in significantly better condition than their surrounding areas. There was an evident spatial distribution of impacts. For instance, some types of impacts were evident inside the park borders but gradually declined farther inside the park where protection was greater;[5] likewise, the impact from burning decreased with distance. There was, however, no significant decline in logging and hunting inward from park boundaries.

What is remarkable about these findings is how well parks are protecting biodiversity even though they have inadequate support for management, are under high levels of threat, and are in the most difficult of contexts.[6] The results of this study are encouraging, since they demonstrate that even parks created to stop transforming forces are having some measure of success. It also suggests that improving both management and enforcement can greatly increase the effectiveness of parks. These findings demonstrate that there is tremendous opportunity to improve the effectiveness of existing protected areas.

Deciding what actions need to be taken in and around a given park has been a subject of debate within the conservation community. Over the past decade, the trend has been to apply a large number of interventions whenever possible—usually under the rubric of integrated conservation and development projects (ICDPs)—that often don't work or that themselves introduce new problems. However, this need not occur. The cases discussed in this volume highlight a number of factors that have proved important to successful park management. These factors, and the cases they are drawn from, are summarized in Table 31-1.

This summary suggests that certain conditions must be in place before effective, long-term management of protected areas can be achieved. Unfortunately, greater emphasis is given to securing a certain level of funding than to determining the actual needs of a site. Applying a stock set of treatments to all parks has led to complaints that large infusions of funding undermine local-level efforts and initiatives. At other more complex sites, the infusion of funds and the level and scale of projects have been dwarfed in comparison to the magnitude of the problem. If any message comes through loudly from the case studies in this volume, it is that to be

Table 31-1.

Factors cited within cases presented in this volume important to maintaining protected areas.

Action Needed for Success	Cases Where Cited
Law enforcement	Kibale, Leuser, Monteverde, Nagarahole
Community involvement in protection	Monteverde, Kibale, Ranomafana, Congo-Zaire
Modest funding for conservation; not for development	Afi (Oates)
Long-term commitment by donors	Kibale, Leuser, OFR (Hart), Congo-Zaire
Long-term commitment by participants	Kibale, Monteverde
Permanent collaborative links with overseas research and funding sources	Kibale, Ranomafana
Training and participation	Kibale, Ranomafana
Long-term scientific presence and ecological monitoring	Kibale, Tiwai (Oates), Nagarahole, Monteverde
Education and public support at local and national levels	Kibale, Tiwai, Monteverde, Nagarahole
Flexible conservation and management plans	Kibale
Professional and dedicated national staff	Kibale, OFR, Monteverde, Congo-Zaire
Local communities with low or varied natural resource use	OFR, Tiwai (Oates)
Ecotourism	Tai (Oates), Monteverde, Nagarahole, Ranomafana

effective, conservation activities should come first, with development activities added if they are directly targeted and highly linked to the conservation objectives based on the characteristics of a given site.[7]

Unfortunately, there has been little uniform or rigorous analysis to determine what actions are most needed, and where.[8] This lack of analysis has led to widely divergent views by conservationists on the necessity and efficacy of protected areas, as well as widely differing advice about how to manage parks effectively. What accounts for these differences? How do we decide which set of management actions might be appropriate for a given site? How do we know which actions are likely to succeed? How do we learn from our past actions and prioritize our goals? Are there principles that can be applied in all circumstances, or must all approaches be site specific?

Recent studies indicate that park projects are more likely to succeed when specific conservation goals are identified and reasonable strategies are developed to achieve them. Complex initiatives that try to cover every eventuality are usually doomed to failure.[9] This chapter identifies key factors for successful protected area design and implementation. Many of the findings here are derived from a study of protected areas in Latin America administered through the Parks in Peril (PiP) program.[10]

A Brief Typology of Protected-Area Types

One of the most powerful findings from the Parks in Peril study is that a few key actions can make significant differences in how effectively a protected area can promote biodiversity conservation. The most significant of these is whether the type of protected area is appropriate given the social context. Serious and lasting problems arise when there is a mismatch between the park type and the social context in the area. Here, we specifically address publicly owned protected areas with biodiversity conservation as a key management objective.[11]

We can define two kinds of protected areas that function very differently: *core protected areas* and *biosphere reserves*. The challenge of managing core protected areas—what we typically think of as a national protected area—is generally twofold: restricting uses inside the area, such as local consumptive resource uses, and stabilizing threats outside the area that can spill inside. In contrast, protected areas based on the biosphere concept differ in that people live within their borders (and in social arrangements that can vary widely among protected areas) and they rely on a system of internal zoning to regulate a variety of uses.[12]

When a protected area is established that is inappropriate for a given social context, the odds that it can protect biodiversity over the long term are greatly diminished. Such misdirected applications of protected areas are dubbed "problems of creation"[13] and are usually the result of fundamental design flaws. For example, Mochima National Park in Venezuela (see Chapter 28) was superimposed on long-standing communities. Because there was no feasible way to manage the area as a national park, administrators tried to manage the area as a biosphere reserve. Yet such actions undermine the meaning and intent of different national categories of protection. Because it was not specifically designed as a biosphere reserve, the legal framework was not in place that would allow the park's residents (or "insiders") to benefit from revenue-generating enterprises such as ecotourism. With the right zoning, and with more intensive use of the park's potentially high-revenue beach areas, enough revenue could have been generated to support park operations while also providing benefits to "insiders" while simultaneously limiting claims by "outsiders." Instead, the result was angry residents, frustrated managers, and lost biodiversity.

Mochima exemplifies how putting the wrong kind of protected area (core rather than biosphere reserve) in the wrong place (overlapping resident populations) has led to problems of creation. In such circumstances, protected areas must be either developed as multiple-use areas or designed as core protected areas that do not overlap existing human populations. When residents are dispersed at low densities throughout a proposed protected area, it may be impossible to have a "conventional" core protected area. Such areas must be thought of as biosphere reserves, because they require a process of consultation with and agreement by residents to help to define, delineate, enforce, and monitor zoning and uses of the protected area.

The second factor to be considered is the social and political context of the area where a protected area was established, at the time of establishment, and when management is being initiated. Protected areas can be divided into two general categories in terms of the social and political context at the time of their creation: stable, or undergoing a process of rapid social change (see also chapter 30). Many of these stable parks were established in remote areas precisely because they were remote, either geographically or in terms of political power. The people were poor and lacked political power, government services and infrastructure were limited, and lands and resources were viewed as having little productive value. In contrast, the second category of protected areas were established to "stop," or at least to control or manage, the effects of rapid regional changes. These regional-level changes are usually generated by forces external to that region that are often rooted in government policies or programs, such as road construction and the consequent changes in land uses.

A matrix (see Table 31-2) combining the two types of protected-area origins (stable and/or remote versus areas undergoing rapid social

Table 31-2.

Common characteristics of four types of sites.

General Characteristic	Stable/Remote		Rapid Change/Frontier	
	Core	Biosphere Reserve	Core	Biosphere Reserve
Drivers of threat	Local	Local	External pushing local	External pushing local
Level of threat	Low	Low	Increasing—medium to high	Increasing—medium to high
Sources of threat	Limited; livelihood-based	Limited; livelihood-based; varies across biosphere reserve	Multiple sources even for same threat; livelihood plus extractive	Multiple sources even for same threat; livelihood plus extractive
Resource dependence	Medium to high	Medium to high	Highly variable	Highly variable
Community cohesion	Generally stable and defined	Generally stable and defined	Social groups in transition; existing communities and local institutions changing with new residents, market access, commercialization	Social groups in transition; existing communities and local institutions changing with new residents, market access, commercialization
Level of access to alternative resources	Often with access to land and resources outside of protected area	Residents throughout an area with dependence on land and resources	Increased livelihood insecurity for existing residents outside area	Increased livelihood insecurity throughout biosphere reserve area for residents and migrants

Table 31-3.

Classification of protected areas in this volume by type and social context and level of complexity.

Stable/Remote		Rapid Change/Frontier	
Core protected area	Biosphere reserve	Core protected area	Biosphere reserve
1[a]	2	3	4
Monteverde, Costa Rica; Ranomafana, Madagascar; Kibale, Uganda; Khao Yai, Thailand; Guatopo, Venezuela		Okapi, Congo (DRC)	Leuser, Indonesia; Nagarahole, India

[a] 1 = easiest; 4 = hardest.

change) with protected-area types (core versus biosphere reserve) shows that we can differentiate among four distinct types of protected areas. Cases discussed in this volume have been assigned to categories on the basis of how they are actually administered rather than on how they were legislatively established (see Table 31-3). This typology is useful in determining the level and intensity of approaches needed at each type of site and is described more fully in the following section.

Stable Areas

There are two types of stable areas: remote areas and densely settled areas that still retain sufficient surplus land to support a protected area (see chapter 30). For both types, the process of social change can be either slow or stable. The key characteristic of both is a lack of rapid changes in resource use.

In *remote areas,* access in and out of the area is limited, rates of migration are low, and integration into the marketplace is generally low. One example of a remote site that is discussed in this volume is Ranomafana National Park in Madagascar. In contrast to these remote areas are areas that have been settled for a long time. Such well-settled areas may still have intact wilderness next to them and—most often because of the biophysical characteristics of the area—tend to be wetlands, have steep slopes or poor soil, or are particularly difficult to access. Sometimes, there has been an impetus to maintain a large, natural area adjacent to a more densely farmed, settled, or urbanized zone. Two protected areas discussed in this volume, Kibale National Park in Uganda and Guatopo National Park in Venezuela, represent stable areas in this second sense. These areas are not remote or sparsely populated areas—Guatopo is near urban areas, and Kibale is "an island within an densely settled area with extensive agriculture." But in both cases transition in land-use intensity from light to heavy is nearly complete so that they can be considered stable in this regard. In terms of social stability, however, Kibale and Guatopo are similar in that the rate of change affecting land-use conversion is low.

The management priority for long-settled stable areas is to identify all local-level characteristics that pose threats (i.e., lead to changes in resource use) to protected areas. Important local-level characteristics include types and patterns of resource use and production, particularly in farming, fishing, and grazing systems; demographic characteristics, such as infant mortality, reproductive rates, and settlement patterns; local tenure security; structure of gender roles in production and resource use; levels of local organization; and access to technical changes and markets. Significant changes in one or more of these local-level characteristics often lead to significant pressures on biodiversity. In the absence of these changes, the pressures on resources are low and the luxury of time exists to build a solid base of community support for parks.

Social stability and low levels of threats mean that long-settled stable areas offer an opportunity for work in both core protected areas and biosphere reserves. It also offers the opportunity to undertake activities slowly, with sufficient processes of local consultation to avoid contentious issues over land and resource ownership and use.[14] Some actions need to be undertaken at the lowest local levels: boundary demarcation, conservation education and public awareness, employment generation, community involvement in protection, and the like. Interactions with local residents need to be open and honest; for example, by being upfront about conservation objectives rather than pretending that the objective is development in order to ultimately achieve conservation—a tactic at many sites. Within this context, both direct and indirect linkages between actions and conservation objectives may be effective. However, hiring large numbers of local people who receive useful training and promised payment in a timely manner (especially if it coincides with periods of low labor demand—for instance, if it can be integrated appropriately into agricultural cycles) can effectively turn local people into conservation advocates. Excellent opportunities often exist for short-term employment in baseline data collection. The cases discussed in this volume demonstrate that if a conservation project is managed properly from the beginning, a local constituency for conservation will exist, even when adverse events occur or changes come to the area.

Managing Core Protected Areas in Stable Social Contexts

Investments in these areas are appropriate if the protected area is large enough to capture key biodiversity values—a scale- and site-dependent judgment. In some parts of the world, particularly in South America, there is still opportunity to create large core areas that support ecosystem and evolutionary processes without human residents. Such areas are rapidly dwindling, however. For more densely populated regions, smaller core protected areas connected by viable corridors may be the best solution. The social context in which such sites are established is paramount; however, the larger the area, the greater the possibility to include key biodiversity components and attributes.[15] Core protected areas established in a stable area do not require a great deal of institutional infrastructure, and efforts can often be successfully based on small-scale research activities and training. Protected areas at remote sites are the best candidates for ICDP approaches in which locally oriented projects reach outside the protected area to stabilize uses and threats and build support for conservation.[16] ICDPs at these sites should emphasize clear and direct connections between the protected area and any actions taken.

Four key assumptions underlying the protection of core areas are that (1) protected areas must be the cornerstone of biodiversity conservation efforts; (2) protected areas themselves are not sufficient to protect biodiversity—areas outside are integral as well; (3) the larger the protected area, the better; and (4) connectivity between areas and processes is vital. One important aspect of developing new protected areas at such sites is that money may be required to buy out or compensate landowners for expropriation; however, apart from this, these areas should not necessarily require high or immediate expenditures of money for protection activities.[17] Although the costs of purchasing inholdings may be high, doing so is essential for effective management of a stable, core protected area. This is well demonstrated in the case on the Monteverde Reserve Complex (see chapter 28).

Protected areas created through a taking of land without providing acceptable compensation are likely to have problems over the long term (unless circumstances are unique and owners *want* to have consumptive uses limited). Carlos Peres (see chapter 10) comments that lack of payment for inholdings is a problem in Brazil. In the state of São Paolo, only 35 percent of land put into nature reserves is under state control—the rest still must be acquired. At the federal level, only thirteen of thirty-two federal nature reserves were wholly in the public domain.

Lasting hostility and problems also result when protected areas are created without proper consultation about boundary location. For example, in El Guacharo, Venezuela, the boundary was arbitrary, slicing through farms (see chapter 28). Yet another case, the Pampas del Heath, demonstrates the difficulties that result when governments and outside organizations attempt to establish management authority over an area without first consulting local communities and gathering their input. An excellent example of consultation is that of Ranomafana, where the final park area, with the input and agreement of each village, and after compromises were made on both side, actually exceeded the area originally proposed (see chapter 9). These lengthy negotiations ensured that the villagers had a voice in decision making and that each knew where the park boundaries were located.

One of the most common scenarios in which management of a core protected area is difficult to achieve is when a core is superimposed over indigenous, tribal, or traditional resident populations. The options in such a case are either to (1) engage in a long-term process of negotiation and persuasion and hope that voluntary resettlement can lead to the creation of a core protected area (see the Nagarahole process in chapter 14), (2) to manage a larger and more extensive area as a biosphere reserve, or (3) to help indigenous groups control their lands and support practices that conserve biodiversity. Historically, the creation of such core protected areas has created long-term problems and resentment. For example, "some villages still exist in a few areas, such as the Karen in Thung Yai Naresuan Wildlife Sanctuary in West Thailand. In their commitment to evict these people, the Forest Department is opposed by many. . . . " (see chapter 16). The most promising solutions are likely to recognize indigenous authority for the areas and for conservation groups to enter a partnership and to train and pay for traditional populations to define use zones, moving an unrealistic unworkable core area into a stable-biosphere reserve category.[18]

Managing Biosphere Reserves in Stable Social Context

Biosphere reserves or multiple-use areas with a stable context are similar to large core areas except that they have people residing within them. The most viable biosphere reserves should be as large as possible, especially if core areas are fragmented or are small and dependent on the larger conservation landscape. In general, biosphere reserves, because they often imply human use of all or part of the area, must be large enough to capture significant biodiversity values. Residential patterns within biosphere reserves vary widely. In some places, people may be widely dispersed at low densities throughout a large area (e.g., Mamirauá Reserve in Brazil).[19] In such cases, it may be possible to designate one or more core areas within the reserve by working with residents there.[20] In other cases, there may be large areas with relatively little human disturbance, and people may be concentrated in population centers. Establishing a series of smaller core areas, with connecting corridors, may be possible.

Biosphere reserves require a more comprehensive approach than core protected areas do. Local consultation and participation, as well as the appropriate policy framework, especially jurisdictional authority, are vital. At these reserves the management objective is to keep the "system" intact—which has led to the persistence of biodiversity in the area. What makes up the "system" at each site involves complex social, cultural, economic, and political issues. In general, however, the "social" side of management activities will seek to reinforce the local patterns that have maintained biodiversity and thus limit practices such as hunting or expansion of slash-and-burn agriculture. This means that most biosphere reserves will be engaged in traditional ICDP activities.[21] However, in all cases, it is essential that formalized agreements with local residents exist and are continually revisited, since certain activities, such as hunting, can have profound effects on wildlife populations.[22]

Although the biosphere reserve concept sounds good on paper, anecdotal evidence suggests that few biosphere reserves follow through on implementation.[23] Managers often overlook the importance of zoning and developing agreements with residents and instead increase enforcement within disconnected core areas (which they have defined but which locals have not agreed to) and promote development activities that have few connections to conservation objectives. This approach is often tantamount to declaring an area with people living in it to be "protected" and hoping for the best.[24]

Although the biosphere model is promoted because it is considered "fairer," evidence suggests that these areas may, over time, impose higher social costs on local populations than core protected areas do. Biosphere reserves must often, over time, and with local acquiescence, promote "sustainable" use, development, or resource extraction, which in reality, may implicitly condemn local populations to lives of poverty. Issues of transparency, social justice, and poverty determination and alleviation are therefore paramount within the biosphere reserve category. Open discussions of livelihood needs, use, and "sustainability" are essential. Residents themselves may often be the first to see that existing patterns are, in fact, not sustainable; this is particularly the case when population density has increased in a localized area. Although stable core areas should primarily undertake "directly linked" activities, biosphere areas must undertake a broader range of activities. Actions that are directly and indirectly linked may be important because from a biodiversity perspective the bottom-line goal is both core area protection and maintenance of areas around the core that can extend the core's wildlife attributes and ecosystem services. Therefore, "sustainability" across the entire biosphere reserve becomes an objective requiring both direct and indirect strategies.

Rapid-Change Areas

Areas experiencing rapid social change will always be more complex to work in than stable areas. In such areas, the forces propelling that change are often nested—local areas are influenced by changes occurring at the regional level, which in turn are influenced by policies set at the national level.[25] Changes are often propelled by unpredictable and changing market forces, such as demand for particular resources (e.g., global demand for shrimp, or North American demand for fresh fruits and vegetables in winter), civil unrest and war (see chapters 7 and 25), and development policies and structural adjustment.[26]

Forces external to a region (often the result of government policies or programs at the national level) can generate changes that in turn affect local areas. One of the most common sources of regional change is road construction, which leads to influxes of migrants who influence patterns of land use and local organization, particularly agricultural production patterns and extractive resource uses. Thus, forces (such as national road-building programs) that promote region-wide changes will eventually influence land-use decisions and resource management activities at a local level as well, sometimes in profound and unpredictable ways. These changes are not always necessarily bad for conservation. For example, the decline in prices for beef and reluctance of U.S. companies to buy cattle from Central America (due to environmentalists' concern over rainforest conversion to pasture), combined with a more educated and urbanizing population, made the creation of a large conservation area in northwestern Costa Rica much easier.[27]

Politics also plays a defining role in areas of rapid change. Core protected areas and biosphere reserves that are established primarily to thwart or slow regional change will succeed only if there is significant political will backing them up. And projects undertaken in such areas require a different approach than those carried out in stable areas. For example, working with local people is still important, but the process is different and tradeoffs are the rule. For example, there may be less time to undertake a participatory process of boundary demarcation, but it may be possible to engage large numbers of local people to become involved in protection activities by proving them with jobs. Amid such change, the greatest threat to local people is to their livelihood, and they may lose out when pressure from outside groups is strong. Conflict in these areas may be high, but it is often between different groups who threaten each other's livelihoods rather than between a particular group and the park. In such areas, protection may be nearly synonymous with legitimizing local claims to certain activities through zoning.[28]

In the context of rapid social change, even strong efforts to involve all parties in decision making may be completely overwhelmed by an influx of new people, leaders, organizations, and the like.[29] In such situations, protected areas can perform a valuable set of ecosystem services that can be easily recognized by long-term residents. Complex ICDPs implemented to address all the needs and interests of the many competing stakeholders[30] most often do not work, as the evidence is making abundantly clear.[31] They are most likely to succeed if their goals are simple, direct, and well focused.

Managing Core Protected Areas in Rapidly Changing Contexts

Establishing and managing core protected areas in the midst of rapid social change is usually more complicated than in stable areas because of the greater technical and financial resources required and the larger geographic areas involved. A system of consistent management must be quickly established, but numerous obstacles can slow the process, such as difficulties in identifying local communities with legitimate stakes in the area and in negotiating park boundaries acceptable to all involved parties. But delaying park protection until such issues are resolved can result in even greater problems. Squatters and resource pirates often move in to take advantage of such delays, and government agencies with priorities of their own may intervene, making claims to land or resources. Actions such as hiring local residents to work in the park can serve several needs at once by increasing local employment and establishing ties with local communities who might otherwise feel that their livelihoods were being imperiled.[32] By having a stake in the success of the park, local residents can gain some security in land, resources, and their livelihoods.

Linking conservation and development can be successful in some circumstances involving core protected areas amid rapid social change, but the root causes of biodiversity loss must be determined so that the resulting plans are linked with conservation goals. Management must not only be effectively administered in protected areas and developed with an eye toward minimizing or mitigating local-level issues, it must also contribute to regional stability. To do so, managers must identify forces and players behind the rapid changes taking place. Devising means of dealing with tenure and resource security on lands adjacent to protected areas may be the best way to gain local support for the protected area and bring a measure of social stability. Regional-level interventions in policy coordination or change, which require political support, are also needed.[33]

Establishing a core protected area amid rapid change is difficult at best. Although as much area as possible should be included, it is also important to minimize social conflict. Therefore, careful assessments are needed before a protected area is established to determine whether surrounding communities are able to protect their remaining nonpark land from competitors. However, amid rapid change, even the process of social assessment may be difficult, as is often the case when road construction brings outside migrants into the area making it difficult to determine who has legitimate claims to local rights and resources. In such cases, unless it is possible to identify and work with long-established resident populations, high levels of social participation may be difficult to achieve. Long-term residents may see protected-area activities as a way of helping them protect their livelihoods and resources.[34] Efforts to improve or change natural resource management practices or agricultural systems are likely to meet with resistance until levels of risk and uncertainty for local populations are reduced.

In such a context, social pressures will affect all aspects of managing a protected area. For example, while the boundaries of parks proposed in areas that are stable can generally be worked out through a participatory process agreeable to both park managers and community leaders, prospective parks in areas undergoing rapid social change must emphasize quick boundary demarcation, information dissemination, and enforcement. Otherwise, the rapid changes occurring on the periphery of the park can quickly transform forests to fields and decimate wildlife populations.[35] In a short time, these changes can reduce biodiversity to isolated "islands" (the *island effect*), resulting in "hard-edge" parks.

Creating new parks in this category, or bringing new ones under management, requires significant levels of political will and relatively high financial investment. As Marc Dourojeanni notes (see chapter 23), it is much easier to attract political will for creating parks than for maintaining them over the long term. However, these parks require just such support for effective and lasting management.

Managing Biosphere Reserves in Rapidly Changing Contexts

The most complex type of protected area is the biosphere reserve in an area undergoing rapid change. Without large amounts of money and political will to address regional issues, these reserves almost always fail.[36] When rapid change is under way, action must be taken simultaneously to protect biodiversity in the core zones and influence the processes of regional change elsewhere. If biosphere reserve boundaries are not promptly defined and zoned, core zones can be quickly reduced to only small, fragmented pieces. But because biosphere reserves by definition include a human element, the needs of stakeholders affected by the creation of a biosphere reserve must be taken into account. While local participation is essential at such sites, it is extremely difficult to define who is local, who has standing, and on what basis. Who can be involved in management? How do you balance the short-term need for immediate protection with participation?

Working within this context of rapid change requires having both sufficient political will and the financing to "do it right." Such projects must go well beyond the scope of traditional conservation projects, and in fact they may more closely resemble regionwide land-use development plans. Such projects require managers to identify and work with local populations but simultaneously take steps to control regional change, particularly those changes that affect local resource use. This can be difficult, since stakeholders come and go, and national and regional forces are continuously transformed. It is unrealistic to assume that the establishment of a protected area will prevent further biodiversity loss. Biosphere reserves amid areas of rapid change are the hardest areas to conserve, because (1) existing systems of social organization and local institutions are often overwhelmed by the changes taking place, and (2) communities are often factionalized, and traditional patterns of organization within communities (including those that govern resources uses) break down under the influx of migrants or changes in resource use, prices, and so forth.

In addition, reaching agreements over zoning within biosphere reserves is often difficult. Even knowing who to negotiate with can be problematical: as discussed in previous sections, differentiating between traditional residents with legitimate rights and new migrants is not always straightforward, and given the transitional nature of rural society it can be difficult to arrive at a satisfactory definition of "local" (see chapter 6). However, one of the first tasks of biosphere reserve managers is to stabilize residency within the biosphere reserve by establishing the rights of legitimate "insiders" versus rights of "outsiders." Equity concerns quickly emerge between these two groups as well.[37] Spending large sums of money on conservation and development projects in these biosphere reserves will have little impact if the projects were poorly conceived and did not consider the processes of rapid social change (especially when political will is lacking).[38] For insiders to "want" to be part of the biosphere reserve, they must receive benefits that are greater than those received by outsiders. Yet such benefits can also act as a magnet for outsiders. At such times, protecting biodiversity and stabilizing threats through improving the lives of long-term residents and recent migrants requires extraordinary levels of technical assistance, local involvement, money, and strong political backing.[39]

Combining the Elements to Make Parks Work

The debates over protected areas seem to be at a false impasse, with academics, practitioners, and conservationists taking an array of positions—"pro-biodiversity conservation" at one end of the spectrum and "pro-people" at the other. Further complicating the debate is that a tremendous amount of money earmarked for conservation is largely spent on initiatives outside protected areas. Critics of ICDPs have noted that in many cases ICDPs have supported development at the expense of biodiversity conservation. Implementing site-specific responses tailored to the specific historical and social context of each site would be the best possible situation, but one that is unlikely to occur.

Although such complexities cannot be resolved in a short chapter such as this, it is possible to identify certain elements, or management actions, that successful cases of park management have in common. These management actions, listed in Table 31-4, are drawn from the cases presented in this book (especially those listed in Table 31-1), from the Parks in Peril study, from Conservation International's review of parks, and from other recent literature.[40] The primary goal in each case is to protect biodiversity, but actions are taken only as appropriate in a given social context. While not exhaustive, these cases provide a starting point for determining the level of action needed depending on the situation. Different types of protected areas, each with a different social context, require different management actions.

The first step in establishing viable protected areas is to keep in mind the idea of "the right park in the right place" by matching areas with management actions appropriate for their social context. When a particular type of protected area is inappropriate for the social context within which it falls, it may never seem to "come together"—and, indeed, it never may if proposed management actions cannot be reconciled with the existing social context. For instance, if a national park is established whose boundaries incorporated existing villages but which forbids humans to live within its borders, what are the alternatives? In such a case, policies must be sufficiently flexible to allow for changes in the legislative framework to recognize local residents and their rights.

Once a management category is determined for the area, then the appropriate corresponding actions can be taken. Table 31-4 clearly shows that there is increasing uncertainty in defining the appropriate set of actions, as the social context is more complex. This indicates that for the long-term viability of protected areas, projects in stable areas are more easily undertaken than projects in areas of rapid change. However, it is important to note that the inherent complexity of the biosphere reserve approach will always require high levels of collaboration with local populations and greater management effort than work in a "correctly" sited core protected area.

In cases where the legislation establishing a park is clearly inappropriate and represents a "taking" of resources, efforts should be undertaken immediately to remedy the situation. For example, Amboró National Park

Table 31-4.

Key social management actions for four types of protected areas.

Change	Stable		Rapid	
Key Actions at Protected Area Sites	**Core Protected Area**	**Biosphere Reserve**	**Core Protected Area**	**Biosphere Reserve**
Boundary demarcation				
High local participation	*	*	*	~
As a visible form of zoning	/	~	*	~
Enforcement and protection				
High local participation	*	*	~	~
Strong, and visible, trained patrols	/	/	*	*
Local/regional strong adjudication system	~	~	*	*
Environmental education and park-centered public relations				
Local and regional levels	*	*	*	~
National level	~	~	*	*
Clear system of zoning and use-level agreements	*	*	~	~
Address tenurial claims				
Within protected area (core first)	*	*	*	*
In surrounding/adjacent lands to stabilize	~	~	~	~
Clear and immediate compensation for lost use or access	*	*	*	~
Research (ecological, monitoring, etc.)				
High local input (field assistants through senior staff)	*	*	*	*
Long-term scientific presence	*	*	*	*
Threat analysis and mitigation: identify and respond to:				
Social/demographic threats	*	~	~	~
Large-scale/external threats	*	*	*	*
Threats to local livelihood security	*	*	~	~

Generation of local revenue and tangible economic benefits (e.g., ecotourism, handicrafts, harvesting)	*	*	~	~
Clear and direct linkage between any development activities and core area/conservation goals	*	*	*	~
Long-term commitment				
Funding projects as identified (follow through)	*	*	*	~
By conservation organizations/ researchers	*	*	*	*
Large-scale project and funding	/	/	~	*
High institutional involvement	/	/	~	*
Political support				
For park creation	*	*	*	*
For ongoing management	*	*	*	*
To stop large-scale threats	*	*	*	*
To manage regional change	~	~	~	*
To grant jurisdictional authority	~	*	*	*
To undertake relevant policy reforms	~	~	~	*
Conflict identification and resolution				
Within protected area	*	*	*	~
Around protected area	*	~	~	~
Creation of professional and dedicated staff				
Locally based	*	*	~	~
Nationally based	~	~	*	~
Key				
Total Definite * - necessary	21	20	19	16
Total Possibly ~site-specific based on context	7	9	13	16
Total / - may undermine project	4	3	–	1

in Bolivia was decreed in such a way that long-present communities fell within its boundaries and were thereby prevented from logging, hunting, and farming on these lands. Through a protracted process, the park boundaries were eventually reduced to exclude these communities, leaving a large core zone intact and placing the communities in less-restrictive "buffer zones" where they could carry out their traditional activities.[41] In this case, either the size of the core had to be reduced or the zoning changed, since the original legislation establishing the park was by definition faulty.

Laws that prevent established groups of people from carrying out traditional activities are unjust. At sites that are more stable, it is often possible to work with communities and involve them in protection activities. In the case of stable core protected areas, communities outside of parks may view compensation for protection activities (e.g., stopping new residents from invading and claiming lands) as a tangible economic benefit. In fact, although the perception is widespread that park creation and enforcement activities result in conflict, the conflict pervasive in many regions is not always directed at protected areas. Increasingly, parks and reserves are using mechanisms such as tenure or other types of rights to differentiate between "insiders" and "outsiders." In such cases, local groups have used and supported protected areas as a way of defending their interests against outsiders, and protected-area guards focus efforts on defending outsiders from using resources.

It is also worth noting that over time, protected areas may change from one category to another as a result of management actions and the prevailing social context. Nagarahole National Park in India is indicative of a protected area that for a long time was managed as a "stable" core protection area. However, as the protected area expanded and tribal peoples were incorporated into the protected area, and as those outside the protected area were allowed to enter and use park resources, the de facto management shifted to a biosphere reserve model that preserved several core areas and zoned others for various local uses. Although most protected-area managers would not think of these fragmented core areas (protected because they were still remote) and surrounding community lands as representing a biosphere reserve, that is in fact how this area was managed. Simultaneously, within the whole region where the protected area and surrounding lands lie, there have been substantial increases and changes in population, infrastructure, forms of land use, and social organization. What appears to be happening is that over time the protected area will shift from a biosphere reserve undergoing rapid change to a stable core protected area. This is possible because there is a program to promote voluntary resettlement of tribal peoples from within the protected area, and economic changes have led to increased employment opportunities outside the protected area. Furthermore, conservation education and public relations have led to greater support for the protected area overall. In social terms, such a change is likely to be welcomed by the poor, legally landless tribal peoples who, through voluntary resettlement, can greatly improve their standard of living and have access to secure livelihoods, both in economic terms and in physical terms (e.g., by residing outside the protected area, they are less likely to be stalked by tigers).

It may be possible to devise activities aimed at moving parks away from the more-complex biosphere reserve model. For example, imagine a scenario in which a road is cut through a formerly remote biosphere reserve, leading to rapid in-migration and colonization—even in areas that are under some form of legal protection. Increased emphasis would need to be placed on protecting the core area, and over a period of ten years the whole biosphere reserve could, in reality, be transformed into a densely populated "stable" and settled area surrounding a large core park (see chapter 30). Managers who face this situation must determine the degree to which (i.e., how much and where) the condition and management of habitat outside of a protected area must be ecologically compatible with habitat inside the protected area. This situation is serious when there is no large core area but only a series of fragmented areas remaining that must be connected by corridors to ensure species survival.

Unfortunately, we have uncritically embraced development as a way to achieve conservation and have devised and hidden behind an alphabet soup of acronyms such as CBNRMs, CBCs, ICDPs, ICADs, and CCPs.[42] If conservation has a bad name, it is partly our own doing. Each method differs in its approach and in the degree to which it aims to protect biodiversity. Even approaches such as ICDPs that purport to manage primarily for biodiversity protection,[43] have "become all things to all people and a number of labels have been developed to meet the particular objectives of the project."[44] What is now called an ICDP is often simply any conservation project that manages people and promotes improved natural resource management over strict protection. Such uncritical adoption of different approaches, at very different types of sites, has led to projects that aren't working well—when, given their context and the actions implemented, they never could work well.

Our inability to isolate, differentiate, and fix problems at challenging sites—or even to know how to respond well to the challenges—has opened the door for skepticism, even among some conservationists. In reality, our understanding of the ecological, social, and political constraints on biodiversity conservation is quite sophisticated, and we are constantly learning more. But we need to recognize that different types of sites require different responses. Whether the international community can reach consensus on actions and support programs linking the social context, management needs, and adaptive management processes at the level of each park will ultimately determine the fate of biodiversity in much of the tropical world.

Notes

1. See, for example, S. Schwartzman, A. Moreira, and D. Nepstad, "Rethinking Tropical Forest Conservation: Perils in Parks," *Conservation Biology* 14, no. 5 (2000): 1351–1357; K. H. Redford and S. E. Sanderson, "Extracting Humans from Nature," *Conservation Biology* 14, no. 5 (2000): 1362–1365; A. Chicchón, "Conservation Theory Meets Practice," *Conservation Biology* 14, no. 5 (2000): 1368–370. It should be noted that there have been a number of points and counterpoints in numerous journals, including *Conservation Biology, Oryx* (e.g., vol. 32, no. 4, October 1998), and *Land Use Policy* (vol. 12, no. 2, 1995).

2. K. B. Ghimire and M. P. Pimbert, eds., *Social Change and Conservation: Environmental Politics and Impacts of National Parks and Protected Areas* (London: Earthscan Press, 1997); S. Brechin, P. R. Wilshusen, C. L. Fortwangler, and P. C. West, "Beyond the Square Wheel: Toward a More Comprehensive Understanding of Biodiversity Conservation as a Social and Political Process," (under review; available from authors at the School of Natural Resources and Environment, University of Michigan, Ann Arbor, Michigan).

3. A. G. Bruner, R. E. Gullison, R. E. Rice, and G. A. da Fonseca, "Effectiveness of Parks in Protecting Tropical Biodiversity," *Science* 291, no. 5501 (2001): 125–128; G. A. Sanchez-Azzofeifa, C. Quesada-Mateo, P. Gonzalez-Quesada, S. Dayanandan, and K. Bawa, "Protected Areas and Conservation of Biodiversity in the Tropics," *Conservation Biology* 13, no. 2 (1999): 407–411; K. Brandon, K. H. Redford, and S. E. Sanderson, eds., *Parks in Peril: People, Politics, and Protected Areas* (Washington, D.C.: Island Press, 1998).

4. Bruner et al., "Effectiveness."

5. Land clearing and grazing declined significantly, with impacts reaching zero at an average of 8 kilometers and 5 kilometers in from the border, respectively.

6. Additional findings showed that most of these parks were able to achieve these objectives despite inadequate support for management. Median annual funding

was US$1.18 per hectare, significantly less than most proposed financial targets for effective management. Respondents also judged that staff lacked critical training and equipment.

7. N. Salafsky and E. Wollenberg, "Linking Livelihoods and Conservation: A Conceptual Framework and Scale for Assessing the Integration of Human Needs and Biodiversity," *World Development* 28, no. 8 (2000): 1421–1438; K. Brandon and M. Wells, "Planning for People and Parks: Design Dilemmas," *World Development* 20, no. 4 (1992): 557–570.

8. M. A. Sanjayan, S. Shen, and M. Jansen, *Experiences with Integrated-Conservation Development Projects in Asia*. World Bank Technical Paper no. 388 (Washington, D.C.: World Bank, 1997).

9. R. Margoluis and N. Salafsky, *Measures of Success: A Systematic Approach to Designing, Managing, and Monitoring Community-Oriented Conservation Projects* (Washington, D.C.: Island Press, 1998).

10. Brandon et al., *Parks in Peril*. The PiP program includes over sixty protected areas in eighteen countries, covering an area of over 30 million hectares. PiP is administered by The Nature Conservancy through its partner organizations in each of the eighteen countries, largely with financial support from USAID.

11. The section does not address private reserves (see chapter 13) nor does it discuss indigenous territories or reserves, which may be extremely important for biodiversity conservation but which represent a very different management context (see J. Mansour and K. Redford, *Traditional Peoples and Biodiversity Conservation in Large Tropical Landscapes* (Arlington, Va.: The Nature Conservancy, 1996); K. Brandon, "Policy and Practical Considerations in Land-Use Strategies for Biodiversity Conservation," in *Last Stand: Protected Areas and the Defense of Tropical Biodiversity*, ed. R. Kramer, C. van Schaik, and J. Johnson (Oxford: Oxford University Press, 1997).

12. M. Batisse, "Developing and Focusing the Biosphere Reserve Concept," *Nature and Resources* 22 (1986): 110.

13. K. Brandon, "Perils to Parks: The Social Context of Threats," in Brandon et al., *Parks in Peril*.

14. P. D. Little, "The Link between Local Participation and Improved Conservation: A Review of Issues and Experiences," in *Natural Connections*, ed. D. Western and R. M. Wright (Washington, D.C.: Island Press, 1994), 347–372.

15. B. Richter and K. Redford, "Conservation of Biodiversity in a World of Use," *Conservation Biology* 13, no. 6 (1999): 1246–1256.

16. Brandon and Wells, "Planning."

17. Expropriation in this context is assumed to be from nonresident populations.

18. J. Mansour and K. Redford, *Traditional Peoples and Biodiversity Conservation in Large Tropical Landscapes* (Arlington, Va.: The Nature Conservancy, 1996).

19. Sociedade Civil Mamirauá, National Council for Scientific and Technological

Development, Environmental Protection Institute of the State of Amazonas, *Mamirauá Management Plan* (Brasília, Brazil, 1996), and J. M. Ayres, personal communication, August 2000.

20. A. Lehnhoff and O. Núñez, "Sierra de las Minas Biosphere Reserve, Guatemala," in K. Brandon et al., *Parks in Peril*, 107–141

21. Brandon and Wells, "Planning."

22. J. Robinson and E. Bennett, *Hunting for Sustainability in Tropical Forests* (New York: Columbia University Press, 2000).

23. Brandon et al., *Parks in Peril*; E. O'Neill (master's thesis, University of Maryland, College Park, 2000); M. Panuncio, "Understanding the Challenges of Integrating Conservation and Development: Key Findings from ICDPs in Perú" (master's thesis, University of Maryland, College Park, 2000).

24. Good examples of biosphere reserves are Mamirauá and Sierra de las Minas (see Lehnhoff et al., "Sierra de las Minas"). For examples of areas designated as biosphere reserves but where management has not been applied in this way, see O'Neill.

25. Brandon et al., *Parks in Peril*; P. Stedman-Edwards, *Root Causes of Biodiversity Loss: An Analytical Approach* (Washington, D.C.: Worldwide Fund for Nature, 1998).

26. A. Wood, P. Stedman-Edwards, and J. Mang, *The Root Causes of Biodiversity Loss* (London: Earthscan Publications Ltd., 2000).

27. See D. H. Janzen, "Costa Rica's Area de Conservación Guanacaste: A Long March to Survival through Non-damaging Biodevelopment," *Biodiversity* 1, no. 2: 7–20; K. Brandon, "The Policy Context for Conservation in Costa Rica: Model or Muddle?" in *Biodiversity Conservation in the Costa Rican Dry Forest*, ed. G. Frankie, G. A. Mata, and S. B. Vinson (Berkeley: University of California Press, forthcoming 2002).

28. E. Fiallo and L. Naughton, "Machalilla National Park, Ecuador," in Brandon et al., *Parks in Peril*, 249–285.

29. A. Agarwal and C. K. Gibson, "Enchantment and Disenchantment: The Role of Community in Natural Resource Conservation," *World Development* 27, no. 4 (1999): 629–649.

30. M. Wells and K. Brandon, *People and Parks: Linking Protected Area Management with Local Communities* (Washington, D.C.: World Bank, World Wildlife Fund, and U.S. Agency for International Development, 1992).

31. C. B. Barrett and P. Arcese, "Are Integrated Development-Conservation Projects (ICDPs) Sustainable? On the Conservation of Large Mammals in Sub-Saharan Africa," *World Development* 23, no. 7 (1995): 1073–1084; P. Church and K. Brandon, *Strategic Approaches to Stemming the Loss of Biological Diversity* (Washington, D.C.: Center for Development Information and Evaluation, U.S. Agency for International Development, 1995); P. Larsen, M. Freudenberger, and B. Wyckoff-

Baird, *WWF Integrated Conservation and Development Projects: Ten Lessons from the Field 1985–1996* (Washington, D.C.: World Wildlife Fund, 1998); W. D. Newmark and J. L. Hough, "Conserving Wildlife in Africa: Integrated Conservation and Development Projects and Beyond," *Bioscience* 50, no. 7 (2000): 585–592; Sanjayan et al., *Experiences*; M. Wells, S. Guggenheim, A. Khan, W. Wardojo, and P. Jepson, *Investing in Biodiversity: A Review of Indonesia's Integrated Conservation and Development Projects* (Washington, D.C.: World Bank, 1999).

32. How migrants are viewed depends largely on the county and its culture. For example, in some parts of the world obligations to members of the same tribe, clan, or ethnic group mean that migrants should be welcomed, even if that tips the scales and overpopulates areas.

33. Wood et al., *Root Causes*.

34. See the example of Machalilla National Park in Fiallo and Naughton, "Machalilla."

35. C. Gascon, G. B. Williamson, G. A. B. da Fonseca, "Receding Forest Edges and Vanishing Reserves," *Science* 288 (2000): 1356–1358; Woodroffe and Ginsburg, "Edge Effects and the Extinction of Populations inside Protected Areas," *Science* 280 (1998): 2126–2128; Robinson and Bennett, *Hunting*.

36. Brandon et al., *Parks in Peril*; E. O'Neill, "Rio Platano Biosphere Reserve, Honduras: People, Planning, Progress" (Conservation Biology and Sustainable Development Program, College Park: University of Maryland, unpublished, 2000).

37. S. Sanderson and S. Bird, "The New Politics of Protected Areas," in Brandon et al., *Parks in Peril*, 441–454.

38. See case study of the Osa Peninsula in Costa Rica, where over $25 million was spent with virtually no discernible conservation impact (C. Cuello, K. Brandon, and R. Margoluis, "Costa Rica: Corcovado National Park," in Brandon et al., *Parks in Peril*, 143–192.

39. Cuello et al., "Costa Rica."

40. See cases in Brandon et al., *Parks in Peril*; Bruner et al., "Effectiveness"; and cases in sources cited in note 31.

41. A. Moreno, R. Margoluis, and K. Brandon, "Bolivia: Amboró National Park," in Brandon et al., *Parks in Peril*, 323–352.

42. CBNRMs are community-based natural resource management projects; CBCs are community-based conservation; ICDPs and ICADs are integrated conservation and development projects; CCPs are community conservation projects.

43. Wells and Brandon, *People and Parks*.

44. Sanjayan et al., "Experiences."

32

Making Parks Work: Past, Present, and Future

CAREL VAN SCHAIK, JOHN TERBORGH,
LISA DAVENPORT, AND MADHU RAO

It is an inconvenient but inescapable fact that most of the world's biodiversity, and the parks created to preserve it, are in developing countries, whereas many of the affluent people who contribute personal funds or tax dollars to support biodiversity conservation live thousands of kilometers away. The situation presents a fundamentally new challenge in the process of globalization.

Colonialism, now thoroughly discredited, was once widespread as a mechanism that allowed people in one set of countries to influence how land is used and managed in another set of countries. Now influence is spread by markets and by moral suasion rather than by conquest. Conservation is emerging, along with the encompassing issue of good stewardship of the earth's natural resources, as one of a set of cultural values that are uniting the earth's diverse nation-states into a unitary global system. These values include, among others, democracy, justice, transparency, accountability, individual rights, and freedom from corruption, exploitation, and favoritism. Most people recognize that the practice of these values leads to more secure and comfortable lives for individuals, and to governments that better serve the needs and aspirations of their constituents. Conservation must take a high place among these unassailable values if the earth is ever to achieve the nirvana of sustainable development, which it must, if humanity is ever to prosper and live at peace with itself.

Before any such new era dawns, the earth's peoples and nations will pass through a stressful transition period during which poverty, injustice, and social inequity are gradually alleviated by the spread and application of the self-evident merits of a universal value system. Our concern in *Mak-*

ing Parks Work[1] is how to engage the emerging international system in constructive ways to help conserve nature through the transition period we have embarked upon.

If nature is to be conserved, parks must work. There is no alternative. In country after country, parks encompass all that remains of the natural world and the wildlife that once inhabited it. If the parks of these countries fail, their natural heritage will be lost forever, and ensuing generations of citizens will inherit a world of weeds.

The condition of many parks in developing countries is demonstrably deteriorating. When parks fail, the cause is nearly always attributable to institutional deficiencies, not only at the level of the individual parks, but at higher levels as well. Because parks are a relatively new concept in much of the developing world, lack of success can sometimes be understood as the foundering of inexperienced beginners. Poor performance can also reflect insufficiencies of design, such as small size, indefensible boundaries, or the inclusion of human inhabitants. Parks also fail through sheer neglect. Governments are prone to declaring parks for the international prestige they bring, which they can do with the stroke of a pen. But all too commonly they then fail to follow through by acquiring title to the land and by installing guards and infrastructure. Neglect of the resulting "paper parks" then almost invariably invites poaching, encroachment, and other forms of degradation. Financial constraints are nearly universal, but the ills of many parks go much deeper than mere budgetary woes; their problems are rooted in institutional and social issues. The challenge of "making parks work" is thus a complex one that requires not one solution but many, and that must be met on different terms in different social and cultural contexts.

Through much of the 1980s and 1990s, the most prominent mechanism for extending international support to protected areas in developing countries has been the ICDP (integrated conservation and development project). The underlying rationale was that economic development would reduce the needs of local people for primary natural resources and thereby alleviate pressure on parks. It is now apparent that this premise is only partly true and that frequently the largesse of ICDPs has the perverse effect of attracting more poor people to the neighborhood of parks.

Enthusiastically adopted by much of the international conservation community, the ICDP model, as viewed in retrospect, has only occasionally led to measurable and enduring advances for conservation. Billions of dollars have been spent with negligible or even negative long-term consequences. Underwritten by heavy-hitting donors, such as the World Bank and USAID, the typical ICDP expends funds on a predetermined schedule within a limited target area that often lacks the institutional capacity to assimilate the tidal wave of investment. So great is the imbalance between expenditures and absorptive capacity that the annual budget of a single ICDP may exceed the recipient nation's entire appropriation to protected-area management. The benefits, such as they may be, accrue uniquely to the targeted park and its surroundings, while all other protected areas in the country continue to languish. Does this make sense? Clearly not.

On the positive side, park protection gains political clout by being part of a larger development effort. ICDPs are high-profile projects that command the attention of enforcement agencies and buy the political will to veto destructive government-sponsored activities around or even inside the targeted park. Large development projects, by their sheer financial impact, can coax all players, from a rural community to the regional authority, to accept conservation as a serious element in socioeconomic planning. But it is critically important to emphasize that development assistance is being provided as a quid pro quo for conservation of biodiversity and for protection of the ecological services that ultimately make economic development possible.

Apart from occasional successes and such indirect benefits, two decades of experience with ICDPs have amply demonstrated how not to structure international support for protected areas in developing countries. The lessons learned point clearly in new directions (Table 32-1). International support for nature conservation should be redesigned to focus directly on the central issues of strengthening protected-area management and reducing the internal and external threats to parks.

Strengthening Parks: Reducing Pressures, Improving Defenses
Enforcement

Park managers should be given the tools they need to enforce park regulations. Indeed, maintaining legal processes within park boundaries is the manager's primary responsibility. The goal is to increase the presence and capacity of law enforcement so that it serves primarily a deterrent role, thereby reducing the need to apply heavy-handed methods. Psychological deterrence is adequate to ensure compliance in many law-abiding societies that have accepted the value of nature conservation.

Table 32-1.

Contrasting features of a typical integrated conservation and development project (ICDP) and those of an "ideal" park-support program.

Feature	Typical ICDP	Ideal Program
Focus of program	A single protected area	A nation's protected area system
Primary goal	Development	Conservation
Rate of expenditure of funds	Very high	Low to moderate
Term	Short, five years or less	Long, indefinite
Area targeted	Mainly outside the protected area	Mainly inside the protected area
Direct support to park	Little to none	Primary target
Pre-implementation phase	Long	Short
Adaptability to new conditions	Low	High
Use of fly-in consultants	High	Low to zero
Termination of support	Abrupt	Gradual
Permanence of change	Ephemeral	Institutionalized
Training/capacitation	Some, short-term	Full professionalization of personnel
Emphasis on enforcement	Slight to none	Central/primary
Relocation of internal residents	Not done	High priority
Addressing other problems of management	Haphazard	Systematic
Promotion of ecotourism	Often one activity among many	Should be a high priority
Criteria of success	Economic measures	Biological indicators
Monitoring	Little to none	Systematic
Support of NGOs in target country	Episodic, leads to boom-or-bust cycles, instability of employment	Long-term partnerships
Corrupt practices	Encouraged by over-abundance of funds	Discouraged when park personnel well paid
Interactions with local people	Patronizing; abundance of funds encourages "gold rush" mentality.	Mutual respect
Attitude of local people	Greed, cynicism, "beggar mentality"	Respect for conservation goal and park regulations

A contrasting set of social conditions typically exists in frontier regions. Established traditions are few and social restraints are weak in a largely immigrant population of opportunity seekers attracted by the availability of open-access resources. A lawless attitude typically prevails, so violations such as poaching and logging are often rampant and not easily suppressed. Such conditions logically call for heightened emphasis on enforcement, yet remote frontier parks are often weakly staffed relative to those closer to population centers, putting them at a severe disadvantage. So-called "paper parks" represent the worst case because they are not defended at all. In the absence of authority, local people become accustomed to helping themselves to park resources. Efforts to introduce enforcement into such a situation can be met with strong resentment and even outright hostility.

Nevertheless, a recent worldwide analysis of park effectiveness found that the critical correlates of success were density of guards, demarcation of boundaries, and compensation to locals for damages caused by wildlife.[1] By implication, even modest increases in funding could significantly strengthen many currently understaffed and underequipped parks. Eventually, emphasis on law enforcement can be reduced, as acceptance of the park concept and the accompanying restrictions becomes widespread.

Park administrators, being subject to political influences from above, often do not have the will, courage, or means to take enforcement actions on their own. Nevertheless, there are many ways that enforcement can be strengthened in relatively unobtrusive ways. Most violations of park regulations are furtive; the potential gains are low (e.g., meat in the dinner pot that evening), and the risks perpetrators are willing to assume are correspondingly low. Volunteer guards or even scientific researchers can be of help in these situations by serving in a watchdog capacity and informing park authorities or police of violations. The extra vigilance itself is a deterrent.

But the systematic raiding of parks for high-value resources such as ivory, rhino horn, gaharu, or mahogany is another story. Large amounts of money are involved, the perpetrators are professionals, often armed and politically connected, and they are willing to assume high risks for high gain. Park enforcement capacity is rarely up to the task of combating gangs of professional criminals, so action at the national or international level is required. Elephant poaching, for example, was not controlled until the international community banned the sale and export of ivory. In such situations, international pressure can offer the only viable solution.

Political Instability

At any given time, approximately a quarter of all the world's developing countries suffer from political instability, meaning civil war, the presence of rebellious minority groups or insurrectionist bands in the hinterlands, and so forth. Parks are often overrun by armed rebels who help themselves to the available resources, whether precious minerals, fine hardwoods, or animal products.

The reflexive reaction of international organizations to such emergencies is to abandon the scene. But experience shows that in many instances parks and the resources they contain can be at least partially protected by dedicated local staff, even in the complete absence of any national authority. When personnel continue to receive moral, financial, and logistical support from the outside, they can often persevere in the face of adversity. Moral support is particularly important. If park personnel are going to put their lives on the line to save trees and animals, they need to know that the risks they are taking are understood and appreciated.

Internationalization

Where local institutions fail to provide the necessary institutional support to make parks work, various kinds of international assistance may be necessary to fill the gap. Assistance may range from simple financial support of local institutions, to the sponsoring of expatriate personnel, to the stationing of "naturekeeping" forces in the worst cases.

People in Parks

It is widely acknowledged that about 70 percent of tropical parks have people living within them, either legally or illegally. The issue of people in parks is thus nearly ubiquitous in developing countries and therefore unavoidable as a matter of the highest concern. The issue is often dismissed on the grounds that "the people have been there for centuries and have not severely damaged the environment." But such statements are backward-looking and blind to the fact that human impact, be it high or low at the moment, will inevitably grow in time through the combined effects of continuing population growth and the acquisition of modern technology.

The question of how to reduce the impacts of humans resident within parks leads to an admittedly complex and sensitive set of issues. But human impacts must be reduced or, better, eliminated completely, if parks are not to suffer progressive degradation. For a variety of reasons, the most common response of managers is to do nothing, a policy that is attractive because it represents the path of least resistance. Even if the immediate consequences of a do-nothing policy are negligible, the long-term consequences seldom are. And of course every delay increases the cost and difficulty of the action eventually taken.

Active relocation (buyout) programs represent the most direct and immediate of a spectrum of options open to managers but can be controversial if not handled generously and equitably. Active relocation carries the disadvantage that it requires a large upfront investment. "Push–pull" systems of disincentives and incentives can encourage people to relocate voluntarily, and are cost effective, but require patience and may not always work as intended. Proffering of family planning services is cost effective and beneficial but does not solve the problem.

The relevant circumstances will vary with each individual case and so will the available financial resources. There is thus no best policy to apply to the people-in-parks problem. But there is a worst policy and that is to look the other way and do nothing.

Alternative Management Models

A great diversity of models for protected-area management is being tested around the world, especially in countries or parks where the traditional public-sector management model has failed to achieve satisfactory results. A simple step is to recruit or accept volunteers to supplement a corps of public-sector guards. Use of external funds to supplement the public-sector budget can be more problematical because of legal restrictions that apply to public-sector agencies in many countries. In-kind donations of equipment can sometimes serve in lieu of direct financial assistance.

Increasingly, in countries all over the world, nongovernmental organizations (NGOs) and for-profit organizations are being contracted to assume partial or full responsibility for management of protected areas. Contracting or privatizing management entails both pros and cons. Among the pros are that the private sector can offer higher salaries to attract better-qualified personnel, can often maintain better morale, and can be more flexible in responding to emergencies or other unforeseen circumstances. Private organizations can also solicit financial support from the public or international sources, an option closed to most public agencies.

Offsetting these advantages are some notable disadvantages. Legal restrictions can bar the management agency from carrying out law enforcement, thereby leaving it dependent on the good will of local police for a crucial function. Whereas good salaries are one of the most compelling advantages of the private model, they can elicit jealousy and ill will among the less-well-paid public-sector officials who hold ultimate authority over parks. How such advantages and disadvantages balance out will depend on the particular legal and administrative structures of the country in question. There is no formulaic solution. Much creative thinking will be needed to discover optimal ways for the private sector to contribute to strengthening park management.

Financing

The financial landscape of international conservation is changing rapidly as new models and sources of funds appear on the scene. "Trust Funds for Nature" have already been established for more than thirty countries. These financial instruments are essentially endowments established for the purpose of providing stable revenue streams for the management of protected areas. Difficult issues arise over how to manage and disburse the funds. The details vary from country to country and have to be resolved through a process of negotiation. How well trust funds will serve over the long run remains to be seen, but the early signs are encouraging.

Partly in response to criticisms of the ICDP model, the World Bank, along with some of its financial partners, has launched a "Critical Ecosystem Partnership Fund," a new program being administered through Conservation International, a private organization. Most of the funds will be channeled through developing-country NGOs, greatly increasing their capacity to affect conservation on the ground.

Another highly promising development is the establishment of the Gordon and Betty Moore Foundation by one of the cofounders of the Intel Corporation. The foundation is poised to increase the funds available for international conservation by more than $250 million annually. To put this into perspective, the amount greatly exceeds the combined annual expenditure on international programs of all U.S. conservation organizations combined. A single foundation thus promises to revolutionize conservation finance on a global scale.

These developments signal a sea change in how conservation is financed and implemented all over the world. Decades ago, conservation was exclusively a public-sector responsibility. But increasingly, in a trend that has been gathering momentum for several decades, the private sector has been playing a larger role—in financing, in management, and even in land acquisition. Every indication is that these trends will continue to gather strength into the future. Where it will eventually lead we cannot say, but it is enormously encouraging that the private sector is taking the initiative where governments are lagging behind or defaulting on their responsibilities to the future.

Implementing Park Support Programs: Inside the Park
Analysis of Threats

Reduction of threats to parks requires a three-stage process: diagnosis of threats, formulation of a prescription for threat reduction, and implementation of the prescription on the ground. Since the vast majority of the world's protected areas do not benefit from the vigilance of any watchdog organization, there is currently no mechanism to identify and redress the problems of parks. On-site monitoring (a periodic audit) is required to identify threats and to evaluate priorities for responding to them. Conditions may vary enormously from one park to another within a given country, so an analysis must be made of the specific pressures and threats affecting each individual park, and of the deficiencies in the park's capacity to resist. Since threats can change rapidly, audits should be conducted at regular intervals.

In the absence of any systematic program to monitor the state of parks, it is impossible to know whether conservation efforts are being successful. Such a program is essential if the billions of dollars that are going into conservation worldwide are not to be squandered in failed programs. The results of monitoring can also serve to inform national governments of the success or failure of their own programs and to draw attention to problems wherever and whenever they occur. The organization conducting park audits should be strictly independent of organizations engaged in advocacy and park support programs so as to avoid conflicts of interest and to ensure the objectivity and credibility of the information.

If monitoring is to be more than a hollow exercise, it will be necessary to link monitoring to action. How such links can most effectively be structured remains an open question. Information can be made instantaneously available through the Internet and other channels, but the rapid translation of information into action is hampered by the slow bureaucratic processes that drive the large organizations which currently design and implement park support programs. Cutting response times and focusing action on current needs should be priorities in forging links between monitoring and action. In general, local NGOs should be better positioned to respond to changing needs than giant organizations based on another continent.

Reducing Threats

Short of a complete overhaul of a country's land tenure system, there are important steps that can be taken to reduce pressure on individual parks.

- Design conservation areas for ecological adequacy. The long-term integrity of any park depends on intrinsic features of design, such as size, defensibility of boundaries, and its ability to maintain ecological services and populations of rare and flagship species.
- A strong presence on the ground is essential. It provides the vigilance and enforcement capacity that is the single best indicator of successful parks.
- Make grants available for field projects, including Ph.D. research, for local and foreign students. Such field projects often create ties at many levels, from local to international, among people emotionally attached to "their" park.
- Assist local NGOs in securing land titles for both indigenous and nonindigenous populations living around park boundaries. A stable pattern of land ownership next to parks creates the best possible buffer against opportunistic encroachment by outsiders.
- Complete formal acquisition of park lands by buying out claimants and private inholders. Funds for the purchase of conservation lands are increasingly available from private sources in the industrialized world.
- Demarcate boundaries and post them clearly. Boundaries fronting on agricultural land, pasture, or plantation forests are inherently easier to patrol and tend to be more stable than those adjoining areas of shifting cultivation.
- Establish clear quid pro quo procedures for compensating local communities that have incurred significant opportunity costs through the creation of protected areas.
- Steer local people away from livelihoods based on extraction of natural resources and toward more intensive forms of land use in surrounding developed lands. The monitoring and regulation of extractive activities, because of their extensive nature, is very difficult.
- Promote ecotourism. A thriving tourism industry brings an important element of the business sector into alliance with conservation.

Developing country parks are increasingly being used by local citizens for recreation and as refuges from congested cities. Parks are thus acquiring national constituencies, a most encouraging trend that promises to reverse the resentment that built up when parks were viewed as the playgrounds of foreigners.

Implementing Park Support Programs: Outside the Park

Numerous ICDPs and many other park-protection initiatives have taught us several valuable lessons that go way beyond traditional park management:

- Success in conservation can often be attributed to the tireless efforts of unusually dedicated and charismatic individuals. Such individuals can appear in any country at any time and should receive the support of the greater conservation community whenever possible.
- Strengthen local NGOs. Fledgling institutions often lack expertise in such areas as fund raising, administration, project management, and public relations.
- Support the creation of NGOs that specialize in litigation and enforcement wherever such organizations can operate effectively. We realize, however, that legal solutions to conservation problems are only practical where the judicial system is shielded from political influence.
- Capacity building is vitally important to the success of conservation efforts everywhere. Thousands of people need to be trained worldwide, yet available fellowships meet only a tiny fraction of the need. The recently established Russell Train Education for Nature Fund administered by WWF-US is one program that provides such opportunities.
- Develop strong and diverse constituencies, including "friends-of-the-park" groups at both local and national levels. The media should be cultivated, as well as elements of the business community and local and national governments.
- Fight corruption. Newly published research has revealed that environmental sustainability is predicted remarkably well by the degree to which corruption is controlled, regardless of national income level.[2] The result corroborates our earlier failure to find any correlation between per capita income and the degree to which a country's parks were being degraded.[3] These observations underscore the importance of transparency and accountability as cultural values critical to successful conservation. Citizen activists can be a constructive force where

NGOs can challenge the government in court and where public opinion can apply pressure on politicians. One can hope that instantaneous global communication will bring about greater accountability, even where autocratic systems still persist.

• Lobby for the repeal of anticonservation legislation (e.g., subsidies on ranching, logging, etc.) and replace it with legislation that speeds up the transition from extensive (slash-and-burn) to intensive forms of land use (via appropriate subsidies and taxes).

• Lobby for greater institutional stature and independence of national park agencies. These agencies enjoy more prestige and political clout when they are not buried several layers deep in agriculture or forestry departments. Environment or natural resources ministries provide more congenial homes for parks departments.

• Lobby major donors to revise regulations that at present restrict disbursements to NGOs.

The Future of Tropical Conservation
The Next Decade

Many new models of park finance and management will be tested in the years to come. More parks will receive international support than ever before, a development that will be welcomed by both cash-strapped public-sector agencies and their governments. Generosity always carries the risk of establishing a culture of dependency, which is to be avoided. Governments need to acknowledge their fundamental responsibility for biodiversity preservation and conservation in general.

Support will increasingly be administered through public–private partnerships or fully private organizations. Mechanisms need to be found to overcome the critical weakness of private conservation, namely the lack of enforcement authority. Trust funds will help management agencies ride out political and economic ups and downs, but safeguards are needed to prevent the funds from being hijacked for nonconservation uses.

Park support will be less in the form of time-limited projects and more in the form of continuing partnerships, in which both sides are involved in setting priorities. A stronger presence on the ground, backed by local support groups in the cities, will not only promote the well-being of parks but also will serve to increase their public visibility and engage a national constituency for conservation. Gradually, nature will take its deserved place as an unquestioned cultural value in society after society around the globe.

Fifty Years Hence

In a more remote future, we predict that the pressures on parks will gradually subside as the human population stabilizes and urbanization relieves pressure on the land. Except in the poorest regions, slash-and-burn agriculture and rural economies based on the extraction of primary natural resources will become increasingly rare. Land use will intensify and stabilize, and the last settlement frontiers will close. The supremely destructive "frontier mentality" that is wreaking such havoc on the earth today will be but a footnote in the history books. Most countries will evolve toward a dichotomous landscape in which land will be dedicated to either supporting humans or supporting all the rest of creation.

Sustainable development will at last become a cultural value, taken seriously by citizens and politicians alike. The need to convert from non-sustainable to sustainable production processes will drive another technological revolution just now beginning with recycling, wind-power generation, and gas–electric "hybrid" autos. Most economic activity will be land-intensive or not directly dependent on the land.

Parks almost everywhere will attract greater numbers of visitors than today. Public use will soar in response to prosperity, urbanization, and greater ease of access. Ecotourism will become even more prominent than it is today as a major global industry and as an important source of employment for local residents. Larger, more prosperous constituencies will demand better public services, and parks will benefit by becoming stronger and better managed.

A picture of the future something like that described above will be the fate of nations that build democracy, stabilize their populations, and care for the renewable resources and environmental services that undergird prosperity. Unfortunately, not all nations will follow the same path. Some will falter—by failing to rid themselves of kleptocratic governments, by failing to defuse the population bomb, or simply by exhausting their natural resources and lapsing into unredeemable poverty. Nature cannot survive a century of greed or poverty with the market forces and technology that exist today. Conservation is therefore everybody's business, or should be. Maybe some day it will be.

Whether parks and the plants and animals they protect will survive to a more halcyon future of stability and prosperity depends on how well we deal with the pressures on them during the next few decades. Some parks will certainly be lost, but many can be saved. Saving them will require intelligence, resourcefulness, and perseverance. It won't be easy, but it will be worth the effort.

Notes

1. A. G. Bruner, R. E. Gullison, R. E. Rice, and G. A. B. da Fonseca, "Effectiveness of Parks in Protecting Tropical Biodiversity," *Science* 291 (2001): 125–128.

2. *The Economist* (27 January 2001): 74–75.

3. C. P. van Schaik, J. Terborgh, and B. Dugelby, "The Silent Crisis: The State of Rain Forest Nature Preserves," in *Last Stand: Protected Areas and the Defense of Tropical Biodiversity*, ed. R. Kramer, C. van Schaik, and J. Johnson (Oxford: Oxford University Press, 1997), 64–89.

CONTRIBUTORS

Dr. Benjamin Andriamihaja
National Director
ICTE/MICET Madagascar
III L102 Tsimbazaza
101 Antananarivo
B.P 3715
D73 III L
Madagascar
Phone: 261 20 22 35185
Email: micet@dts.mg

Dr. Mario A. Boza
Wildlife Conservation Society
Central America
Apartado Postal 246-2050
San Pedro
Costa Rica
Phone: (506) 224-9215
Fax: (506) 225-7516
Email: ecoamericas@amnet.co.cr

Dr. Katrina Brandon
Senior Research Fellow
Center for Applied Biodiversity
  Science
Conservation International
1919 M Street, N.W., Suite 600
Washington, D.C. 20036
USA
Phone: (202) 912-1369
Email: kbrandon@conservation.org

Dr. Warren Y. Brockelman
Foreign Lecturer
Faculty of Science, Biology
Mahidol University
Salaya Buddhamonthon
Nakhon Pathom
Thailand
Phone: 662-441-9003 x 1137
Email: scwbk@mahidol.ac.th

Bob Carlson
Director
Monteverde Cloud Forest Preserve
PO Box 55-5655
Monteverde Puntarenas
Costa Rica
Phone: (506) 645-5122
Fax: (506)645-5034
Email: monteverde@expresso.co.cr

Lisa Davenport
Research Associate
Center for Tropical Conservation
Duke University
Box 90381
Durham, North Carolina 27708
USA
Phone: (919) 490-9081
Fax: (919) 493-3695
Email: lisa.davenport@duke.edu

Dr. Marc J. Dourojeanni
Principal Environmental Advisor
Inter-American Development Bank
SEN Quadra 802 Conjunto F Lote 39
CEP 70800-400
Brasília, DF
Brazil
Phone: 55-61-317-4232
Fax: 55-61-321-3112
Email: Marcd@iadb.org

Peter A. Frykholm
Senior Editor
Peak Editing
P.O. Box 1308
Leadville, Colorado 80461
USA
Phone: (719) 486-3298
Email: peter@peakediting.com

Dr. Michael Griffiths
Co-Director
Leuser Management Unit-LDP
Jalan Dr. Mansyur No. 68
Medan Sumatra
20154 Indonesia
Phone: 62-61-821-6800
or 62-811-644251
Fax: 62-61-821-6808
Email: mgriff@indosat.net.id

Dr. Terese Hart
Senior Conservation Biologist
Wildlife Conservation Society
The Bronx Zoo
185th St. and Southern Blvd.
Bronx, New York 10460-1099
USA
Phone: (315)942-6935
Fax: 315-942-6936
Email: teresehart@aol.com

Dr. K. Ullas Karanth
Director–India Program
Wildlife Conservation Society
403, Seebo Apartments
26/2, Aga Abbas Ali Road
Bangalore 560 042
India
Phone: 91-80-559-1747
Fax: 91-80-559-1990
Email: ukaranth@vsnl.com

Dr. Randall Kramer
Professor of Resource and Environ-
    mental Economics
Nicholas School of the Environment
Duke University
Box 90328
Durham, North Carolina 27708
USA
Phone: (919) 613-8072
Fax: (919) 684-8741
Email: Kramer@duke.edu

Dr. Jeff Langholz
Assistant Professor
Monterey Institute of International
    Studies
425 Van Buren St.
Monterey, California 93940
USA
Phone: (831) 747-6519
Email: jeff.langholz@miis.edu

M. D. Madhusudan
Wildlife Ecologist
NCF Centre for Ecological Research
    and Conservation
3076/5, IV Cross, Gokulam Park
Mysore 570 002
India
Phone: +91-821-515 601
Fax: +91-821-510 852
Email: mdm@ncf-india.org

Richard Margoluis
2801 Adams Mill Road, Suite 210
Washington, D.C.   20009
USA
Phone: 312-917-0304
Fax: (312) 917-0334
Email: richard@FOSonline.org

Dr. John F. Oates
Department of Anthropology
Hunter College
695 Park Avenue
New York, New York 10021
USA
Phone: (212) 772-5473
Fax: (212) 772-5423
Email: joates@hejira.Hunter.cuny.edu

Suzanne Palminteri
Biodiversity Conservation Specialist
Monteverde Cloud Forest Preserve
PO Box 56-5655
Monteverde Puntarenas
Costa Rica
Phone: (506) 645-5122
Fax: (506)645-5034
Email: spalminteri@earthlink.net

Dr. Carlos A. Peres
Lecturer
School of Environmental Sciences
University of East Anglia
Norwich NR47TJ
UK
Phone: +44-1603-592549
Email: C.Peres@uea.ac.uk

Dr. George V. N. Powell
WWF Senior Conservation Specialist
Monteverde Cloud Forest Preserve
PO Box 56-5655
Monteverde Puntarenas
Costa Rica
Phone: (506) 645-5024
Fax: (506) 645-5034
Email: gpowell@sol.racsa.co.cr

Dr. Madhu Rao
Associate Conservation Ecologist
Wildlife Conservation Society
The Bronx Zoo
185th St. and Southern Blvd.
Bronx, New York 10460-1099
USA
Phone: (718) 220-5261
Fax: (718) 364-4275
Email: mrao@wcs.org

Dr. Herman D. Rijksen
Director
Institute for Nature Management
Postbus 23
6700 AA Wageningen
The Netherlands
Phone: +31 317 47 78 61
Fax: +31 317 424988
Email: H.D.RIJKSEN@ibn.dlo.nl

Fernando B. Rubio del Valle
Asesor Projecto
Conservando Castanhales
Apartado Postal No. 96
Puerto Maldonado
Peru
Email: rioamigos@terra.com.pe

Karl Ruf
Director
Gilman International Conservation
    Epulu Project
c/o White Oak Conservation Center
3823 Owens Road
Yulee, Florida 32097
USA
Email: karlr@wogilman.com

Rosie Ruf
Gilman International Conservation
    Epulu Project
c/o White Oak Conservation Center
3823 Owens Road
Yulee, Florida 32097
USA

Dr. Nick Salafsky
Foundations of Success
4109 Maryland Avenue
Bethesda, Maryland 20816
USA
Phone: 312-917-0304
Fax: (312) 917-0334
Email: Nick@FOSonline.org

Barry Spergel
Director and Legal Advisor for
    Conservation Finance
World Wildlife Fund
1250 24th St. NW
Washington, D.C. 20037-1175
USA
Phone: (202) 778-9655
Fax: (202) 861-8324
Email: barry.spergel@wwfus.org

Dr. Sompoad Srikosamatara
Associate Professor
Faculty of Science, Biology
Mahidol University
Rama VI Road
Bangkok 10400
73170 Thailand
Phone: [66] (2) 246-0063
Fax: [66] (2) 247-7051

Dr. Thomas T. Struhsaker
Research Scientist
Department of Biological
    Anthropology
Duke University
Box 90383
Durham, North Carolina 27708
USA
Phone: (919) 490-5352
Fax: (919) 493-3695
Email: TomStruh@duke.edu

Dr. John Terborgh
Co-Director
Center for Tropical Conservation
Duke University
Box 90381
Durham, North Carolina 27708
USA
Phone: (919) 490-9081
Fax: (919)493-3695
Email: manu@duke.edu

Dr. Caroline E. G. Tutin
Centre International de Recherches
    Medicales de Franceville
Station d'Etudes des Gorillas et
    Chimpanzees
BP 7847
Libreville
Gabon
Phone: 871 761 373 062
Fax: 871 761 373 064
Email: tutin@cirmfrv.fr

Dr. Carel van Schaik
Co-Director
Center for Tropical Conservation
Duke University
Box 90383
Durham, North Carolina 27708
USA
Phone: (919) 660-7390
Fax: (919) 660-7348
Email: Vschaik@acpub.duke.edu

Dr. Patricia C. Wright
Professor of Anthropology
Department of Anthropology
State University of New York
Stony Brook, New York 11794
USA
Phone: 516-632-7425/7656
Fax: (516) 632-9165
Email: PatCWright@aol.com

INDEX